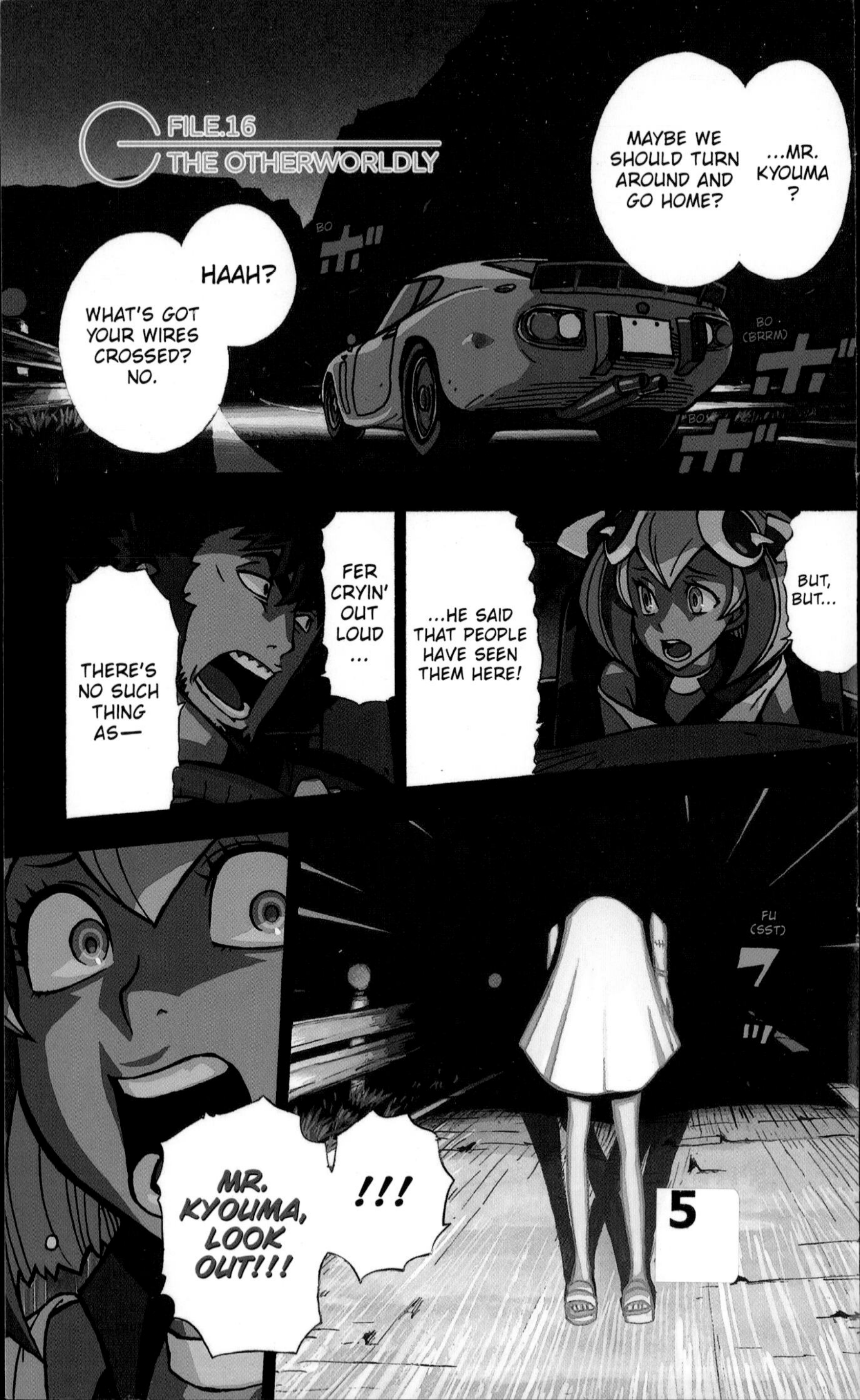
FILE.16
THE OTHERWORLDLY
...MR. KYOUMA ?
MAYBE WE SHOULD TURN AROUND AND GO HOME?
BO (BRRM)
BO
BO
HAAH?
WHAT'S GOT YOUR WIRES CROSSED? NO.
BUT, BUT...
...HE SAID THAT PEOPLE HAVE SEEN THEM HERE!
FER CRYIN' OUT LOUD ...
THERE'S NO SUCH THING AS—
FU (SST)
!!!
MR. KYOUMA, LOOK OUT!!!

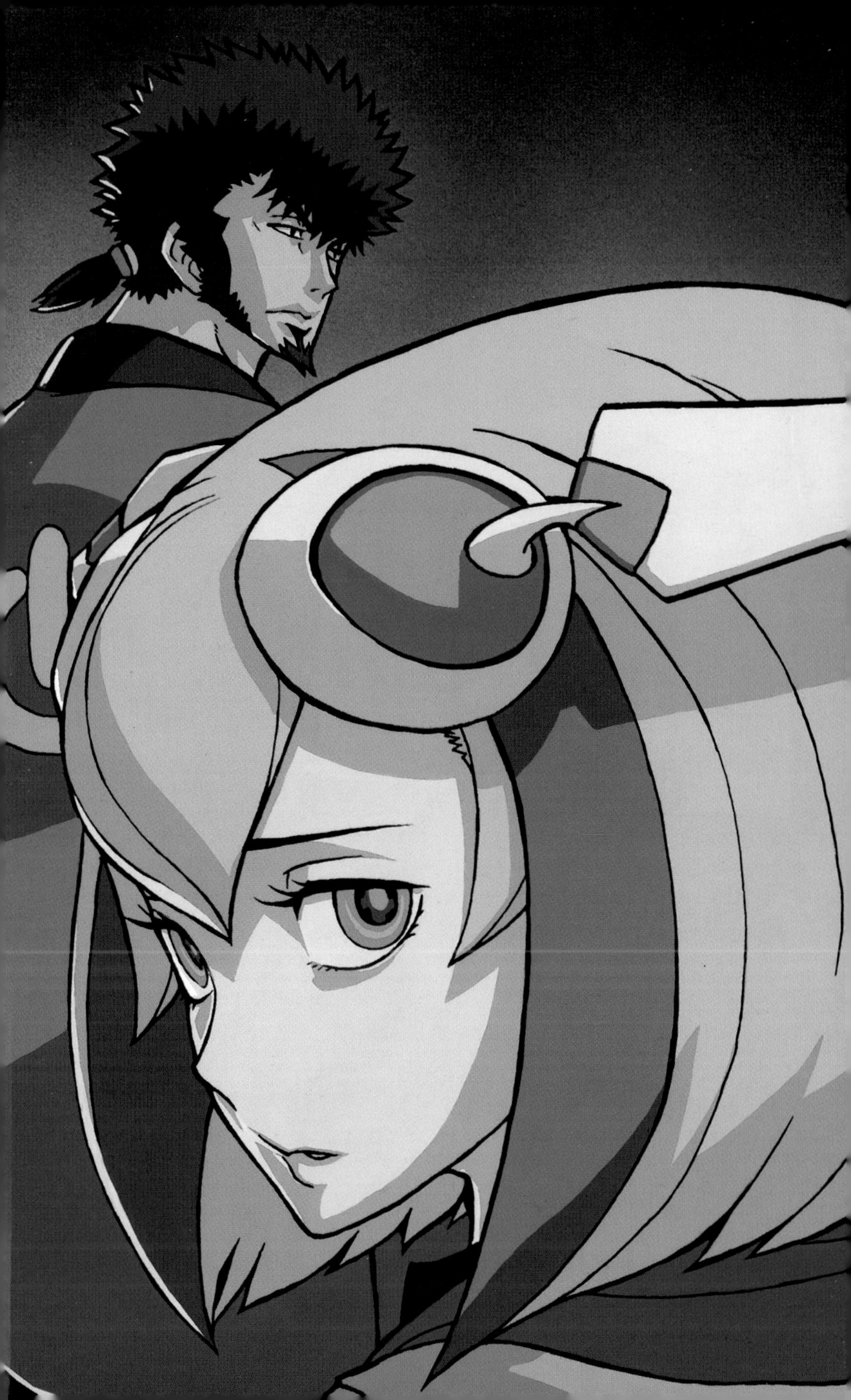

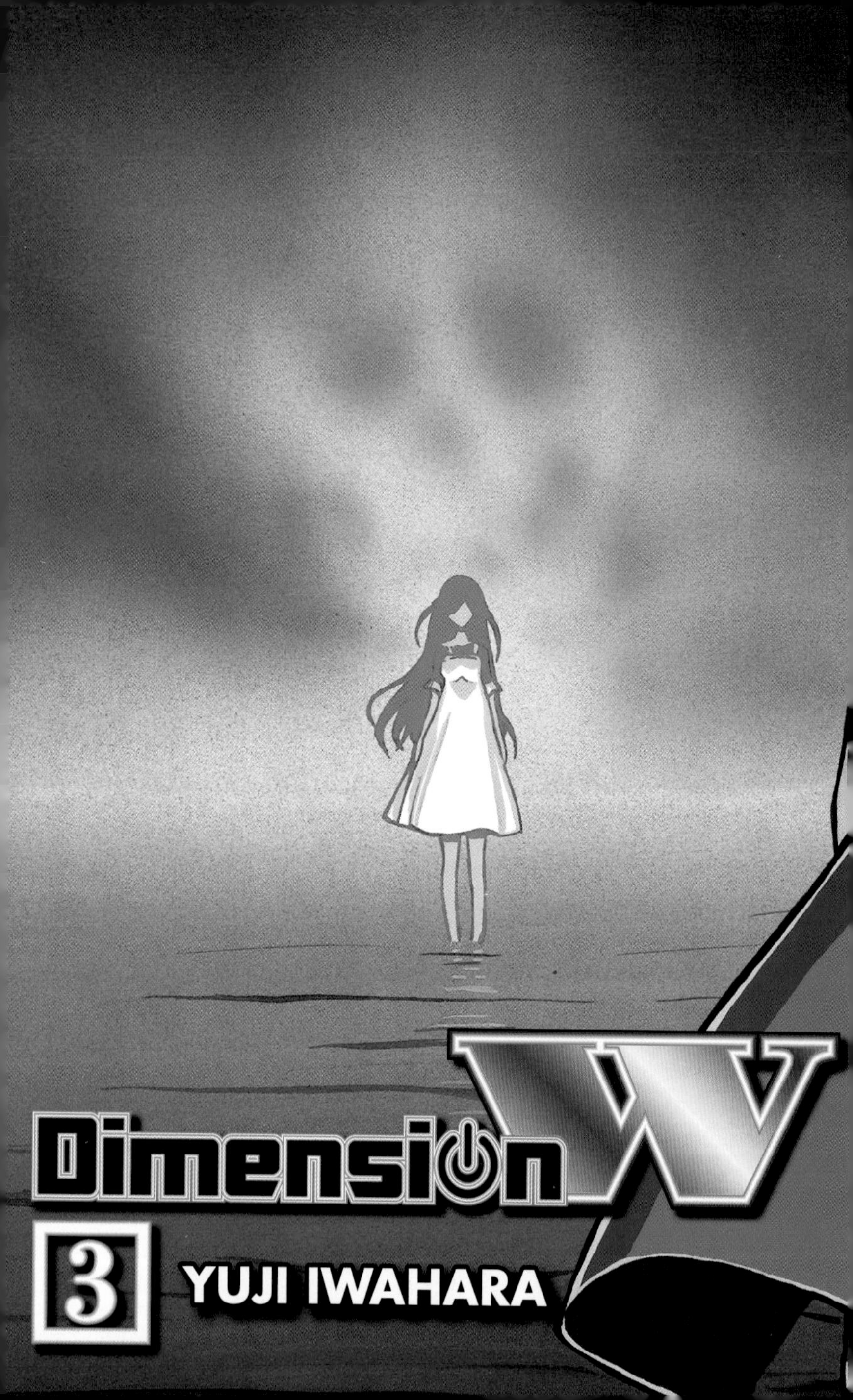
Dimension W
3
YUJI IWAHARA

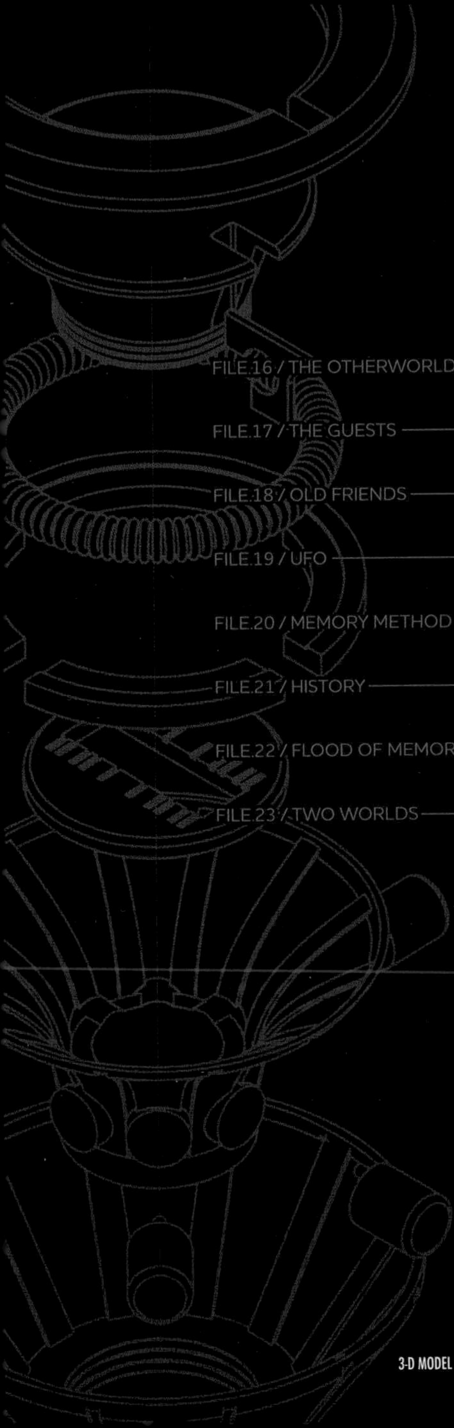

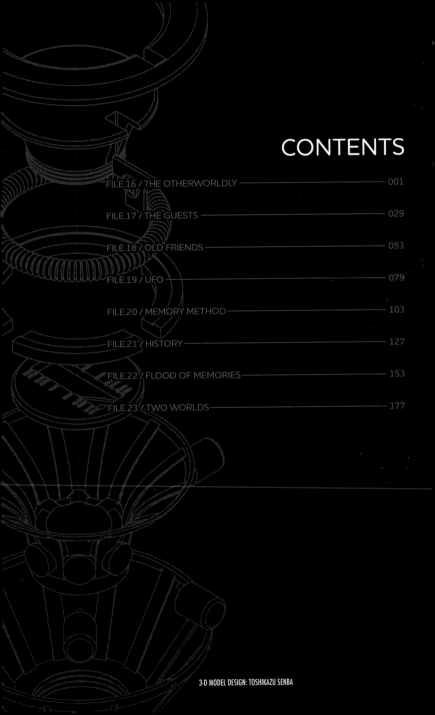

CONTENTS

3-D MODEL DESIGN: TOSHIKAZU SENBA

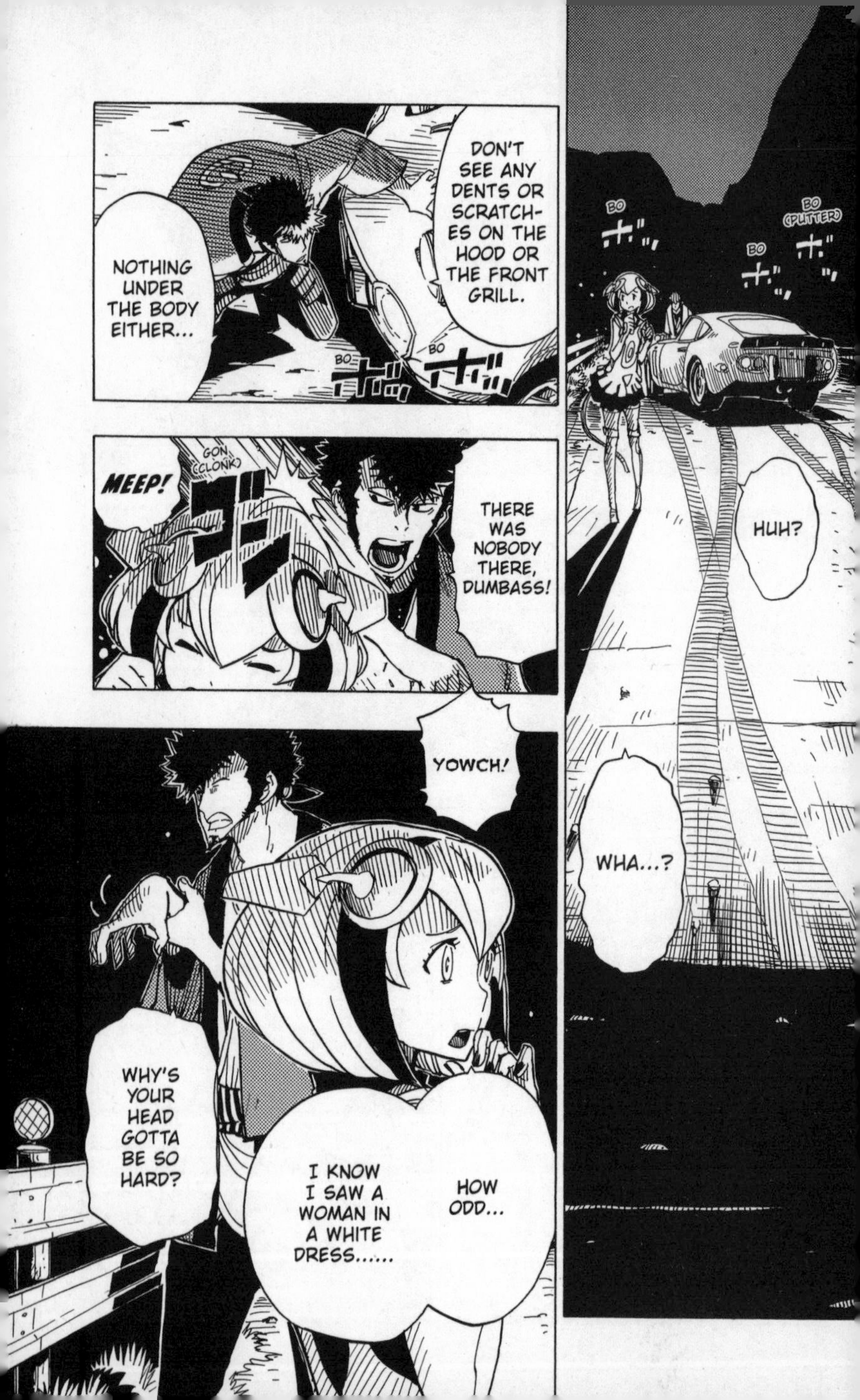
BO (PUTTER)
BO
BO
HUH?
WHA...?
DON'T SEE ANY DENTS OR SCRATCH-ES ON THE HOOD OR THE FRONT GRILL.
NOTHING UNDER THE BODY EITHER...
BO
BO
GON (CLONK)
THERE WAS NOBODY THERE, DUMBASS!
MEEP!
YOWCH!
HOW ODD...
I KNOW I SAW A WOMAN IN A WHITE DRESS......
WHY'S YOUR HEAD GOTTA BE SO HARD?

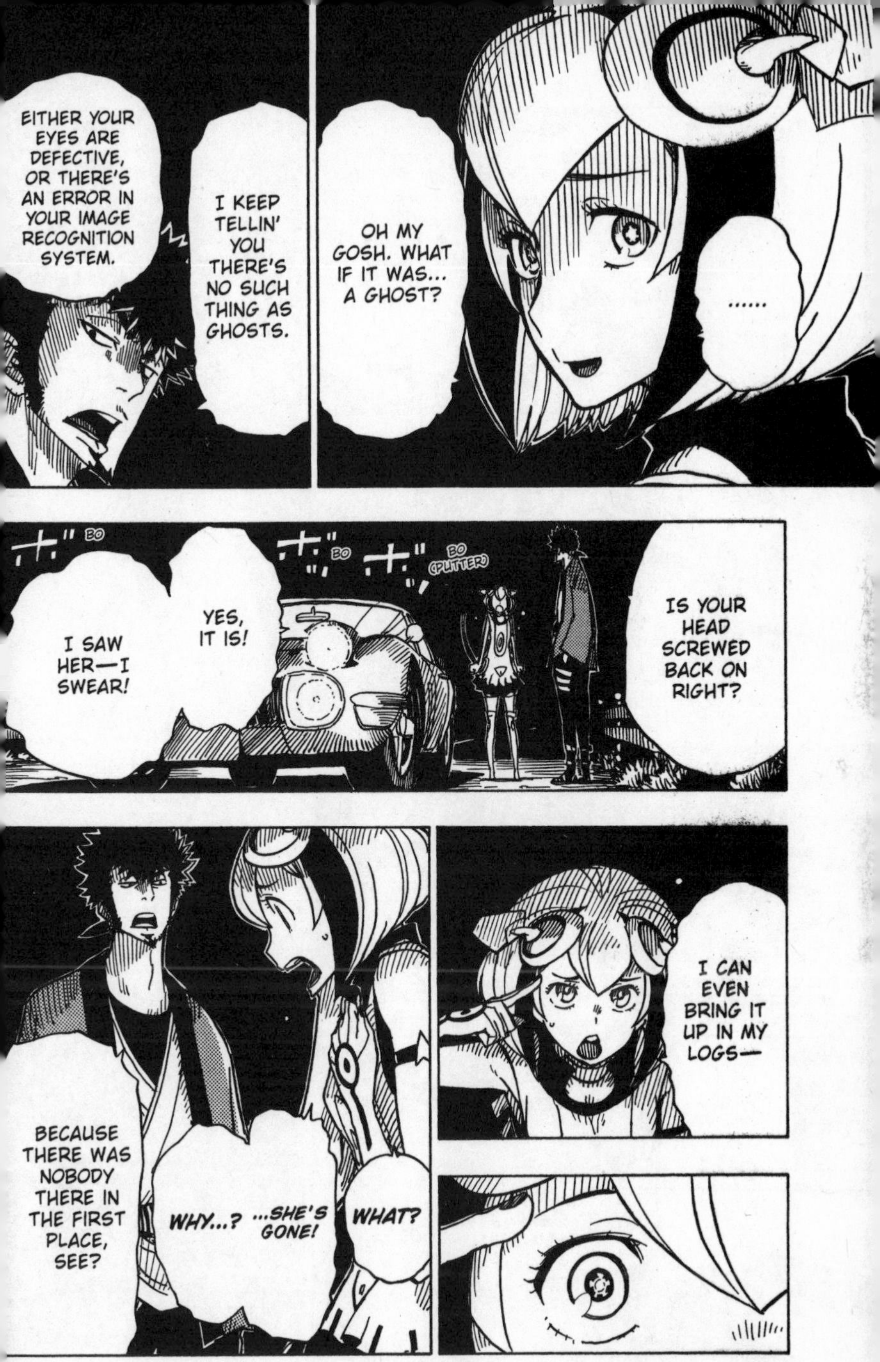
......
OH MY GOSH. WHAT IF IT WAS... A GHOST?
I KEEP TELLIN' YOU THERE'S NO SUCH THING AS GHOSTS.
EITHER YOUR EYES ARE DEFECTIVE, OR THERE'S AN ERROR IN YOUR IMAGE RECOGNITION SYSTEM.
IS YOUR HEAD SCREWED BACK ON RIGHT?
BO (PUTTER)
BO
BO
YES, IT IS!
I SAW HER—I SWEAR!
I CAN EVEN BRING IT UP IN MY LOGS—
WHAT?
...SHE'S GONE!
WHY...?
BECAUSE THERE WAS NOBODY THERE IN THE FIRST PLACE, SEE?

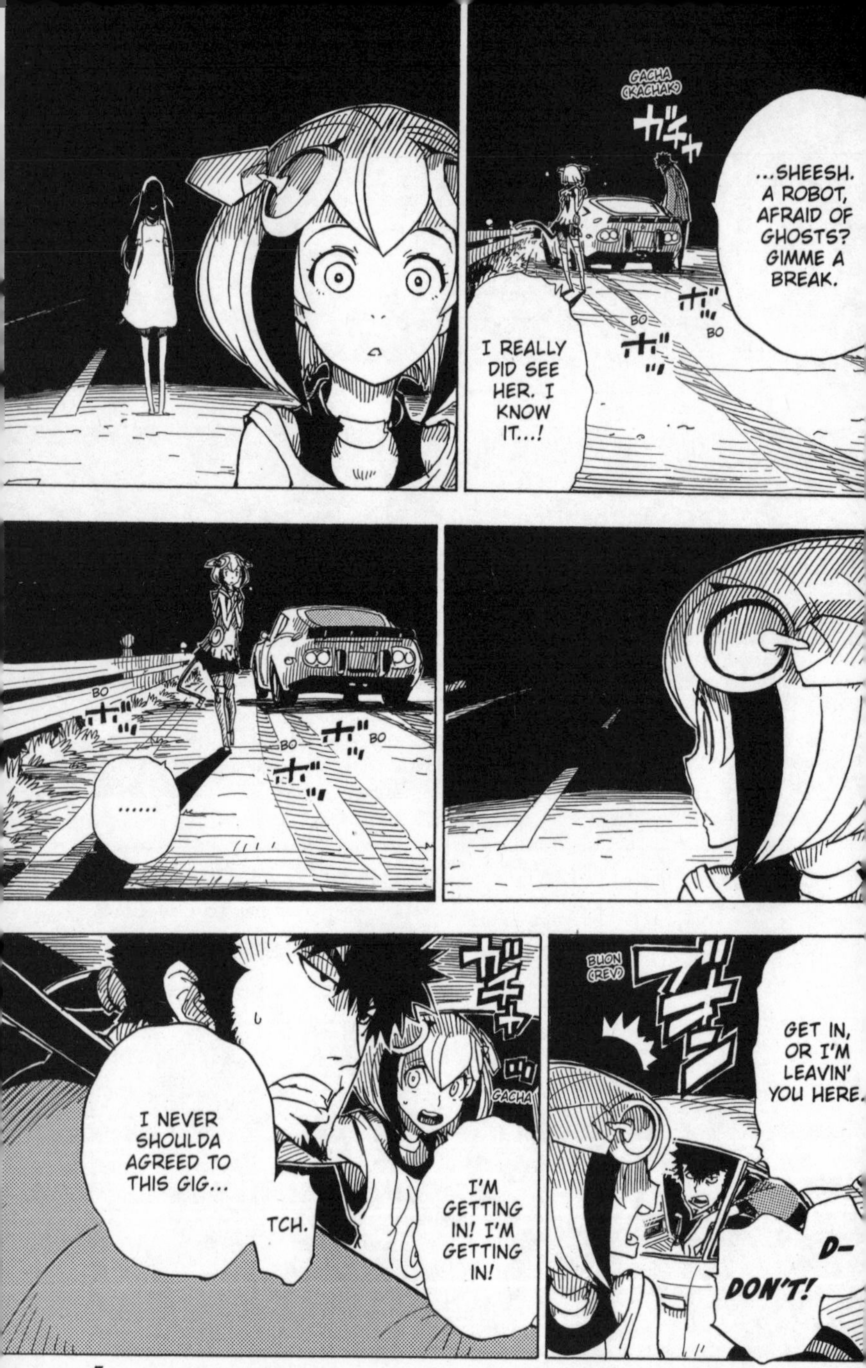
GACHA (KACHAK)
...SHEESH. A ROBOT, AFRAID OF GHOSTS? GIMME A BREAK.
BO
BO
I REALLY DID SEE HER. I KNOW IT...!
BO
BO
BO
......
BUON (REV)
GET IN, OR I'M LEAVIN' YOU HERE.
D- DON'T!
GACHA
I NEVER SHOULDA AGREED TO THIS GIG...
TCH.
I'M GETTING IN! I'M GETTING IN!

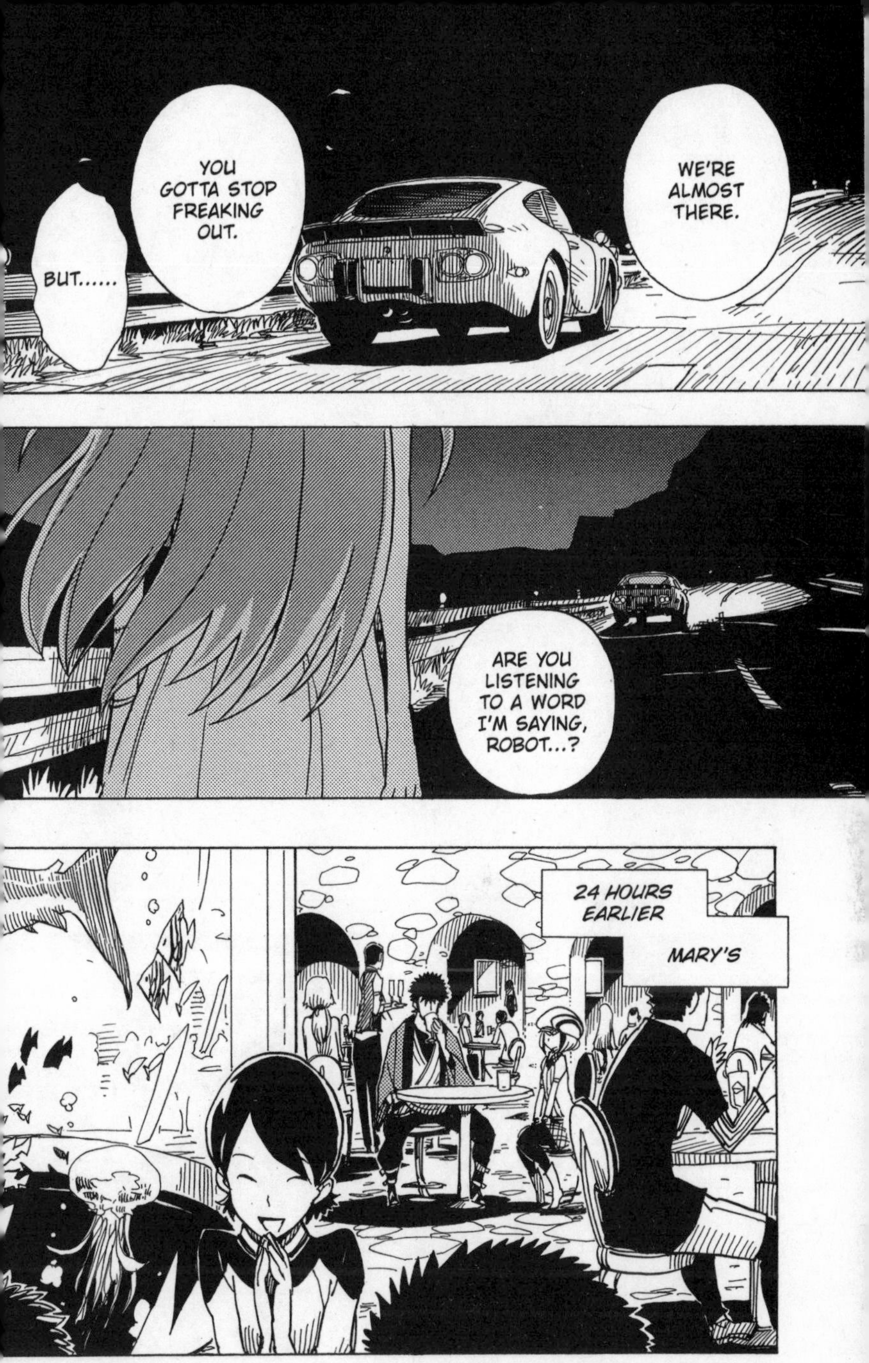
WE'RE ALMOST THERE.
YOU GOTTA STOP FREAKING OUT.
BUT......
ARE YOU LISTENING TO A WORD I'M SAYING, ROBOT...?
24 HOURS EARLIER
MARY'S

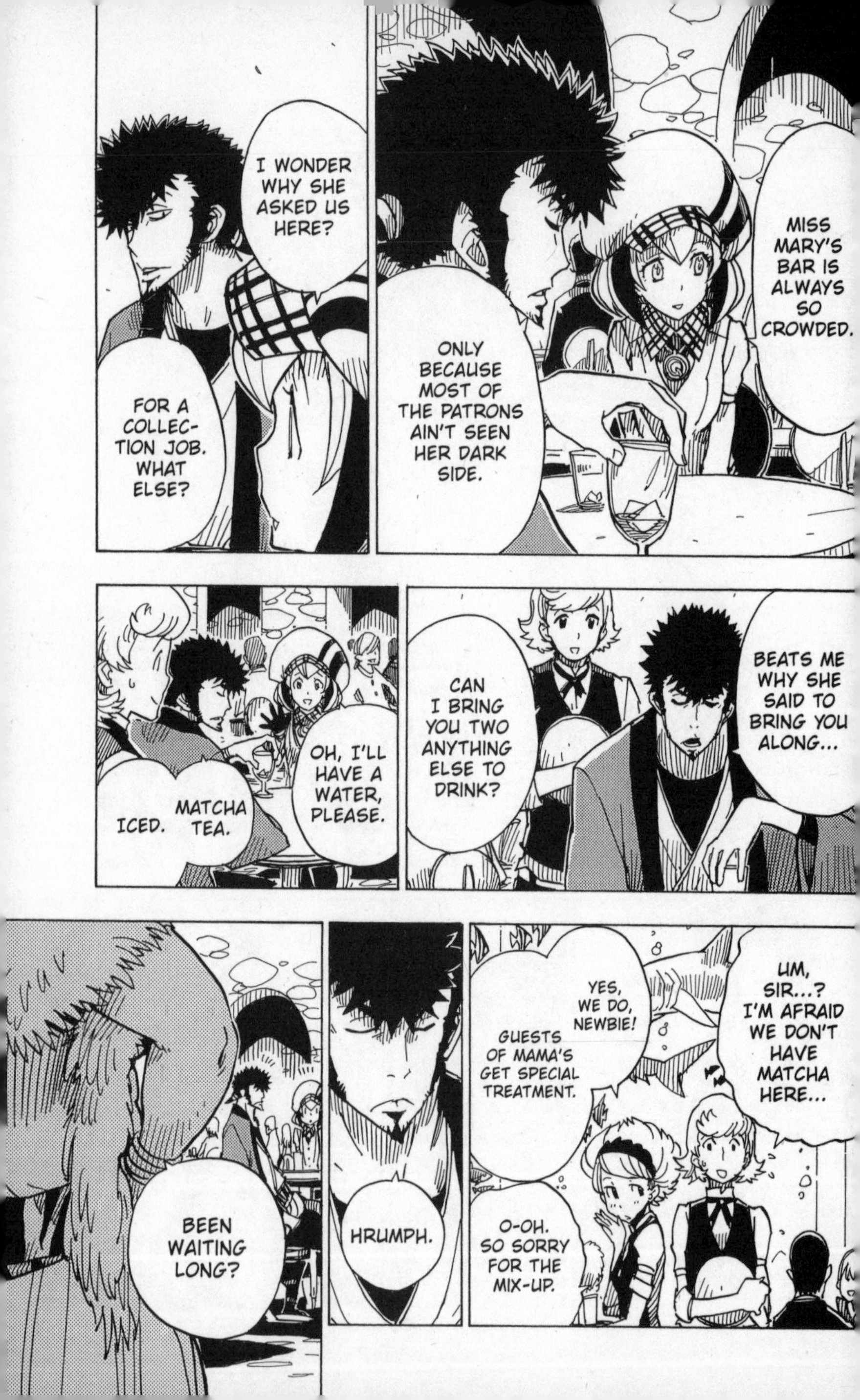
MISS MARY'S BAR IS ALWAYS SO CROWDED.
ONLY BECAUSE MOST OF THE PATRONS AIN'T SEEN HER DARK SIDE.
I WONDER WHY SHE ASKED US HERE?
FOR A COLLECTION JOB. WHAT ELSE?
BEATS ME WHY SHE SAID TO BRING YOU ALONG...
CAN I BRING YOU TWO ANYTHING ELSE TO DRINK?
OH, I'LL HAVE A WATER, PLEASE.
MATCHA TEA.
ICED.
UM, SIR...? I'M AFRAID WE DON'T HAVE MATCHA HERE...
YES, WE DO, NEWBIE!
GUESTS OF MAMA'S GET SPECIAL TREATMENT.
O-OH. SO SORRY FOR THE MIX-UP.
HRUMPH.
BEEN WAITING LONG?

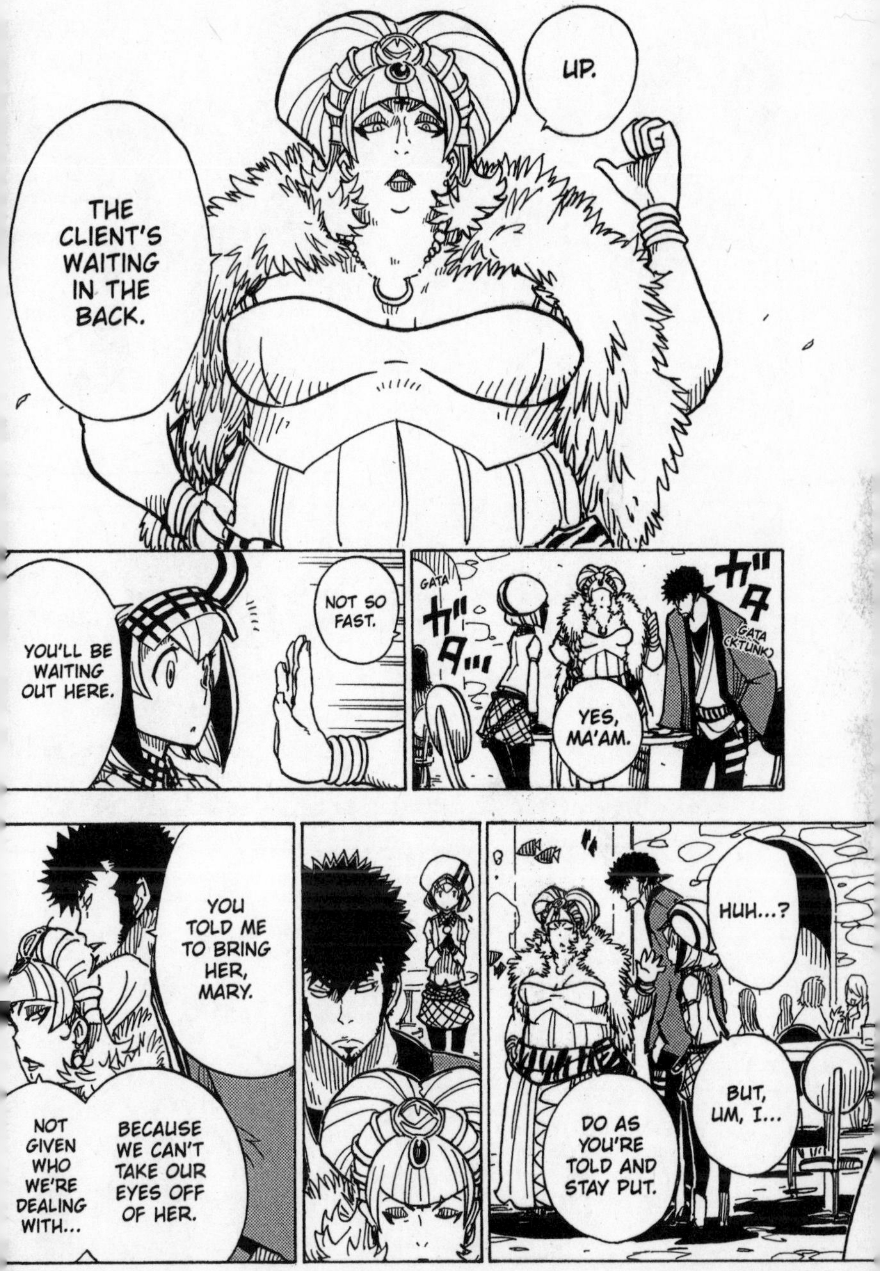
UP.
THE CLIENT'S WAITING IN THE BACK.
GATA (K-TUNK)
GATA
YES, MA'AM.
NOT SO FAST.
YOU'LL BE WAITING OUT HERE.
HUH...?
BUT, UM, I...
DO AS YOU'RE TOLD AND STAY PUT.
YOU TOLD ME TO BRING HER, MARY.
BECAUSE WE CAN'T TAKE OUR EYES OFF OF HER.
NOT GIVEN WHO WE'RE DEALING WITH...

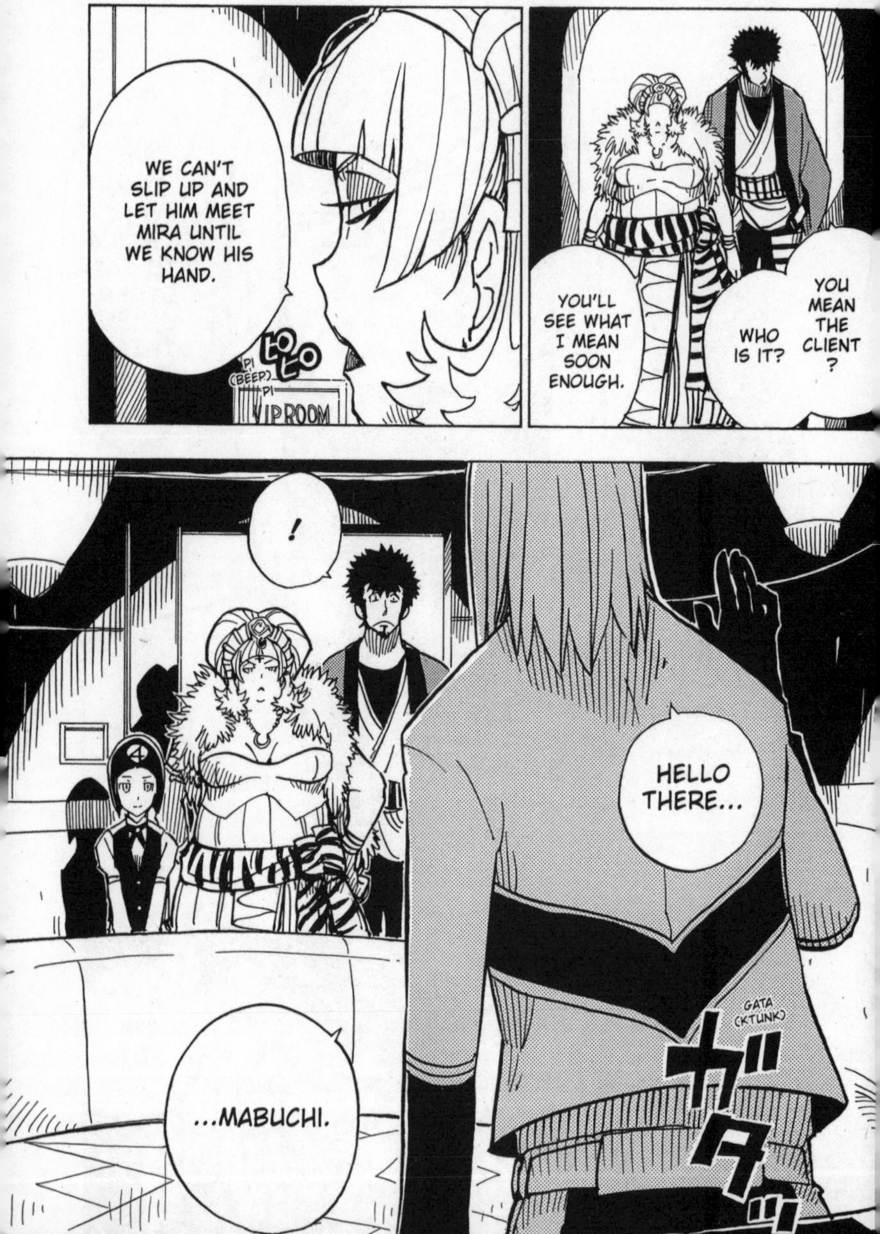
YOU MEAN THE CLIENT?
WHO IS IT?
YOU'LL SEE WHAT I MEAN SOON ENOUGH.
WE CAN'T SLIP UP AND LET HIM MEET MIRA UNTIL WE KNOW HIS HAND.
PI (BEEP) PI
VIP ROOM
!
HELLO THERE...
GATA (K-TUNK)
...MABUCHI.

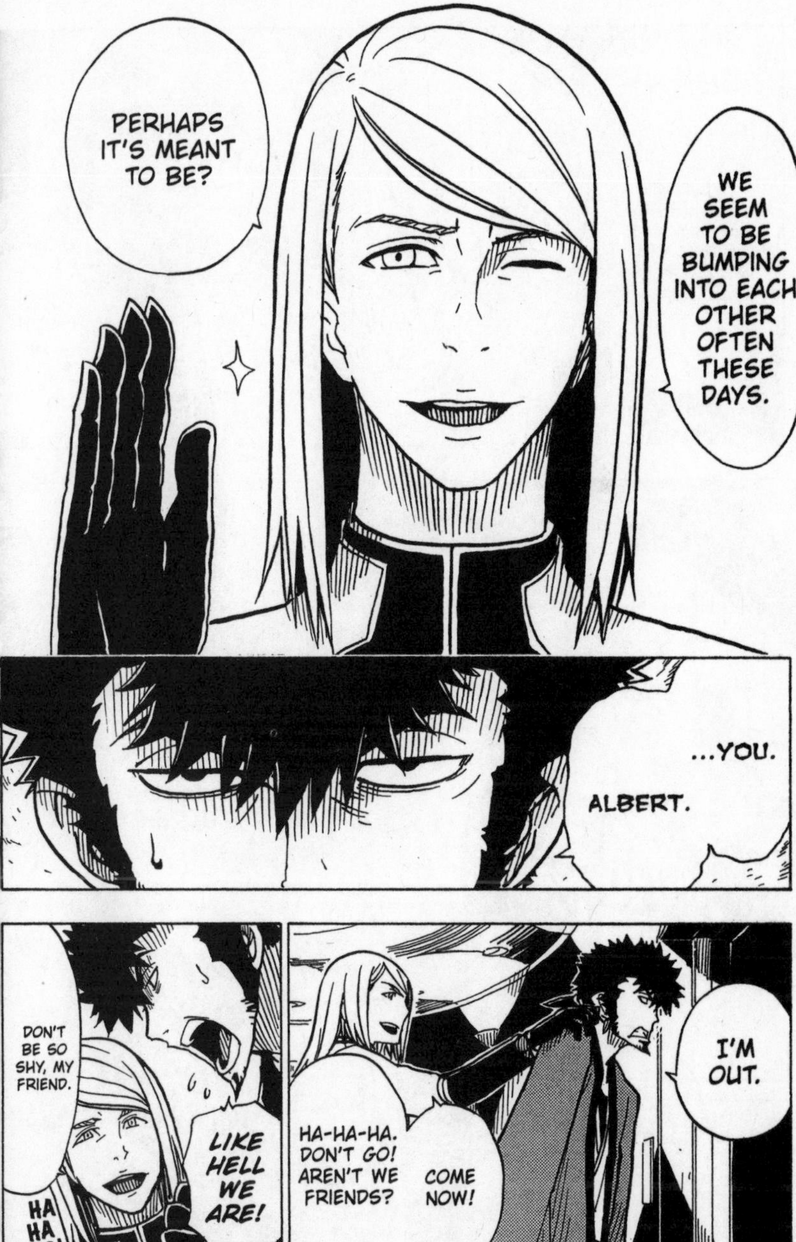
WE SEEM TO BE BUMPING INTO EACH OTHER OFTEN THESE DAYS.
PERHAPS IT'S MEANT TO BE?
...YOU.
ALBERT.
I'M OUT.
COME NOW!
HA-HA-HA. DON'T GO! AREN'T WE FRIENDS?
LIKE HELL WE ARE!
DON'T BE SO SHY, MY FRIEND.
HA HA HA!

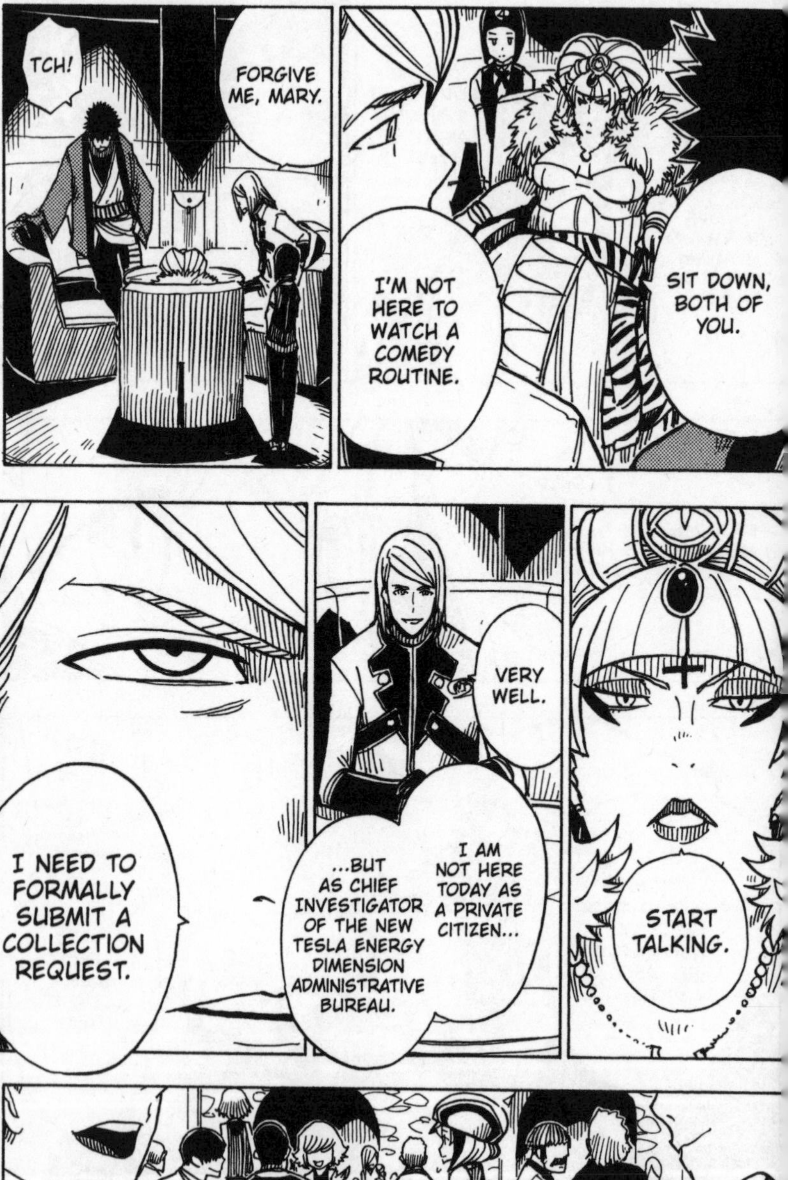
SIT DOWN, BOTH OF YOU.
I'M NOT HERE TO WATCH A COMEDY ROUTINE.
FORGIVE ME, MARY.
TCH!
START TALKING.
VERY WELL.
I AM NOT HERE TODAY AS A PRIVATE CITIZEN...
...BUT AS CHIEF INVESTIGATOR OF THE NEW TESLA ENERGY DIMENSION ADMINISTRATIVE BUREAU.
I NEED TO FORMALLY SUBMIT A COLLECTION REQUEST.

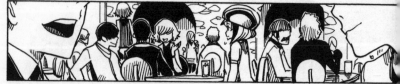

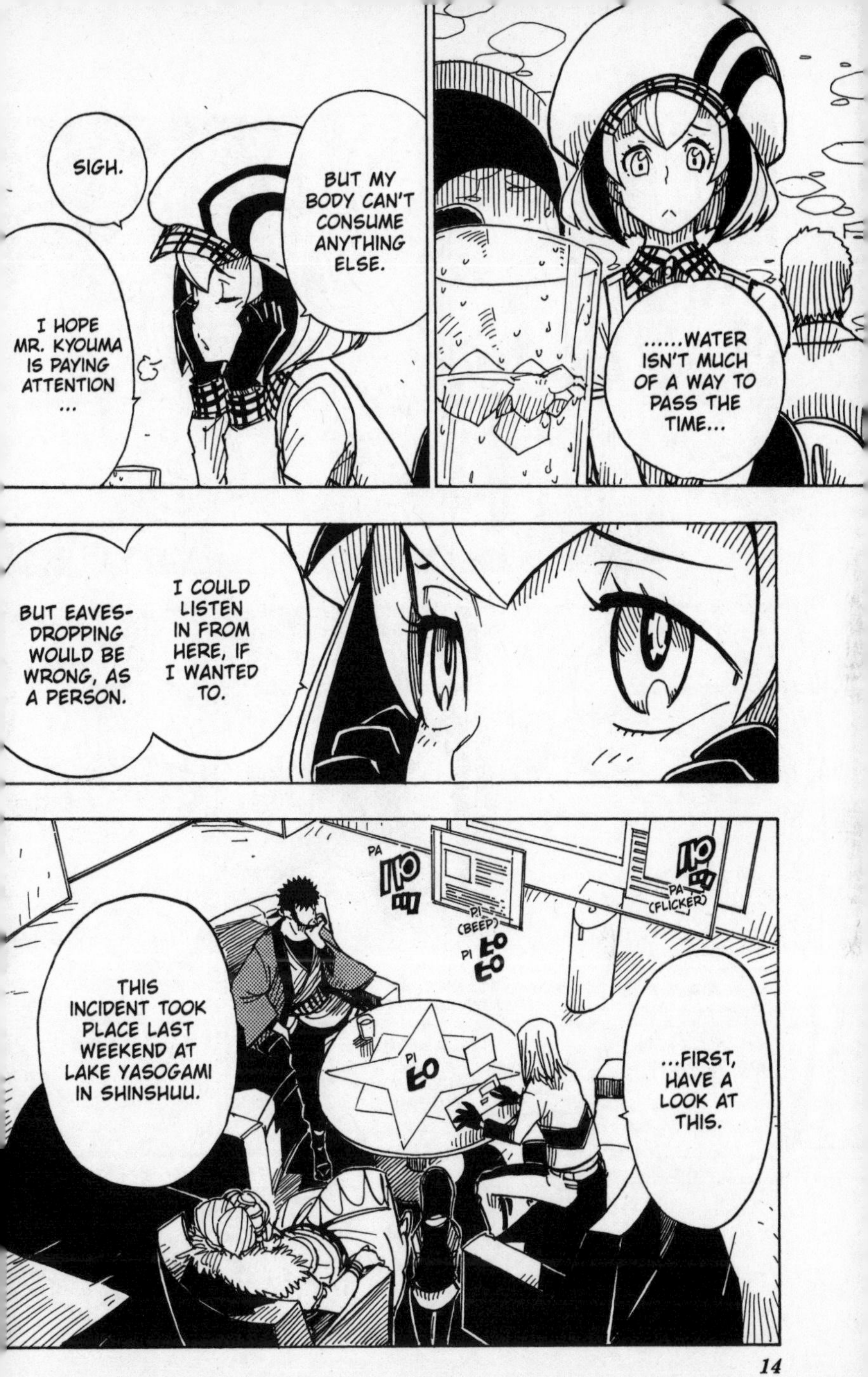
......WATER ISN'T MUCH OF A WAY TO PASS THE TIME...
BUT MY BODY CAN'T CONSUME ANYTHING ELSE.
SIGH.
I HOPE MR. KYOUMA IS PAYING ATTENTION ...
I COULD LISTEN IN FROM HERE, IF I WANTED TO.
BUT EAVES-DROPPING WOULD BE WRONG, AS A PERSON.
PA (FLICKER)
PA
PI (BEEP)
PI
PI
...FIRST, HAVE A LOOK AT THIS.
THIS INCIDENT TOOK PLACE LAST WEEKEND AT LAKE YASOGAMI IN SHINSHUU.

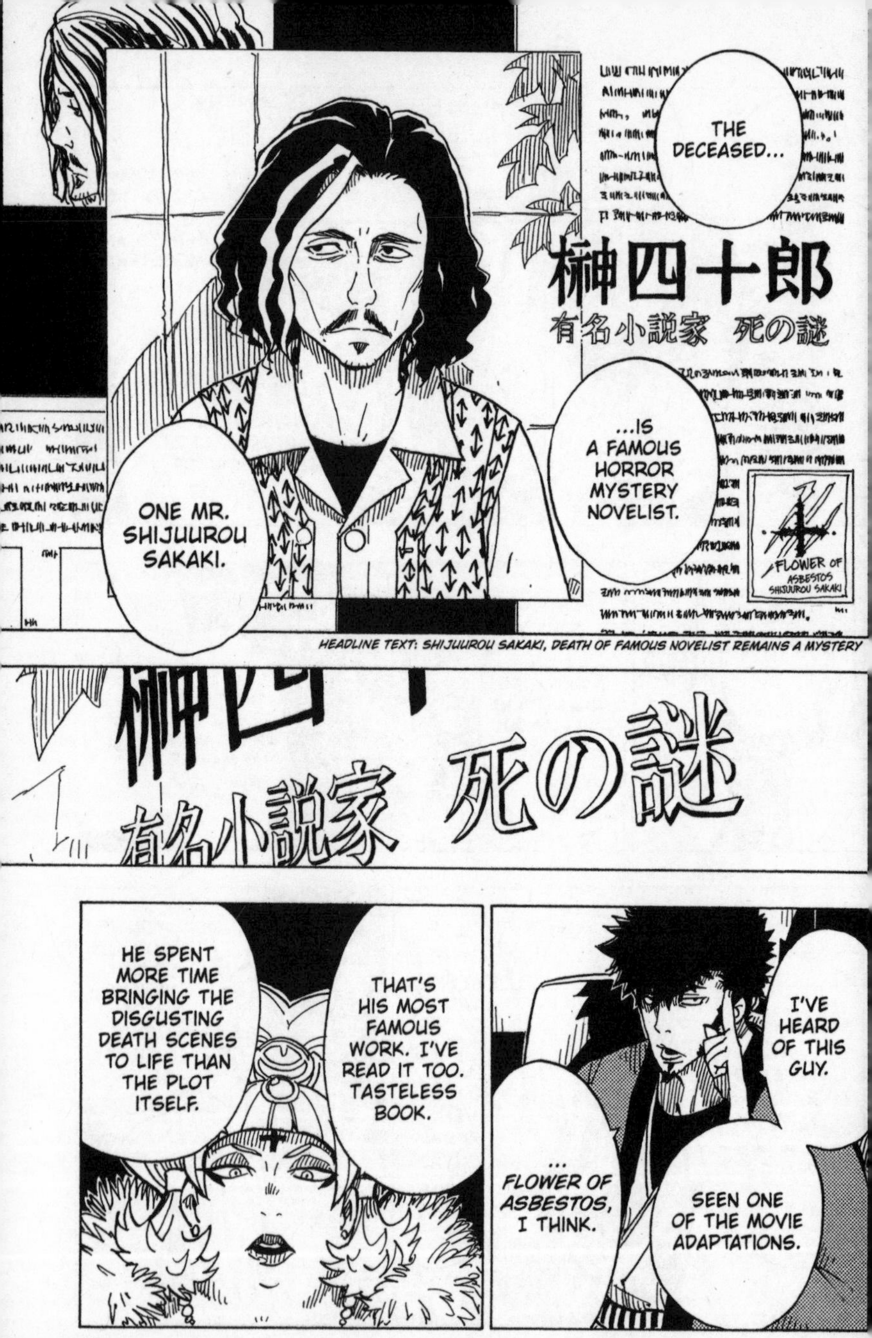
THE DECEASED...
榊四十郎
有名小説家　死の謎
...IS A FAMOUS HORROR MYSTERY NOVELIST.
FLOWER OF ASBESTOS SHIJUUROU SAKAKI
ONE MR. SHIJUUROU SAKAKI.
HEADLINE TEXT: SHIJUUROU SAKAKI, DEATH OF FAMOUS NOVELIST REMAINS A MYSTERY
有名小説家　死の謎
I'VE HEARD OF THIS GUY.
SEEN ONE OF THE MOVIE ADAPTATIONS.
...FLOWER OF ASBESTOS, I THINK.
THAT'S HIS MOST FAMOUS WORK. I'VE READ IT TOO. TASTELESS BOOK.
HE SPENT MORE TIME BRINGING THE DISGUSTING DEATH SCENES TO LIFE THAN THE PLOT ITSELF.

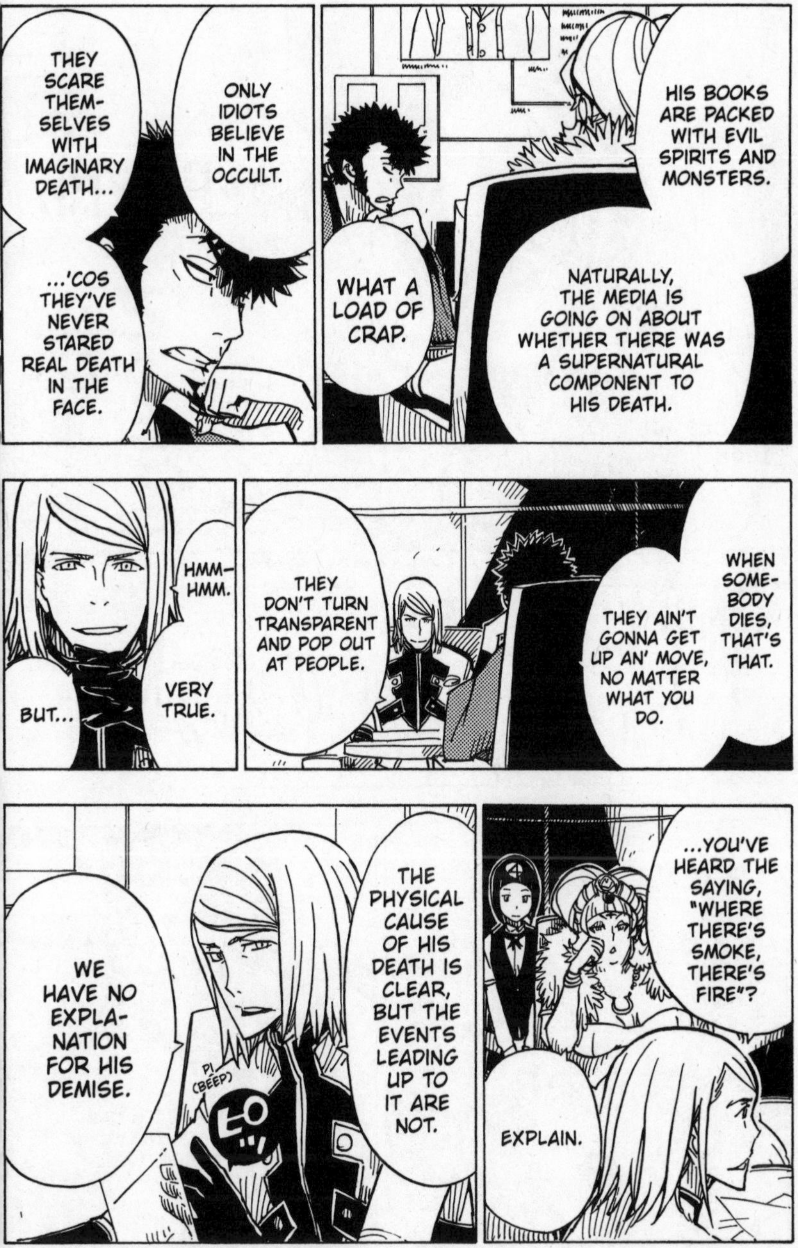
HIS BOOKS ARE PACKED WITH EVIL SPIRITS AND MONSTERS.
NATURALLY, THE MEDIA IS GOING ON ABOUT WHETHER THERE WAS A SUPERNATURAL COMPONENT TO HIS DEATH.
WHAT A LOAD OF CRAP.
ONLY IDIOTS BELIEVE IN THE OCCULT.
THEY SCARE THEM-SELVES WITH IMAGINARY DEATH...
...'COS THEY'VE NEVER STARED REAL DEATH IN THE FACE.
WHEN SOME-BODY DIES, THAT'S THAT.
THEY AIN'T GONNA GET UP AN' MOVE, NO MATTER WHAT YOU DO.
THEY DON'T TURN TRANSPARENT AND POP OUT AT PEOPLE.
HMM-HMM.
VERY TRUE.
BUT...
...YOU'VE HEARD THE SAYING, "WHERE THERE'S SMOKE, THERE'S FIRE"?
EXPLAIN.
THE PHYSICAL CAUSE OF HIS DEATH IS CLEAR, BUT THE EVENTS LEADING UP TO IT ARE NOT.
PI (BEEP)
WE HAVE NO EXPLA-NATION FOR HIS DEMISE.

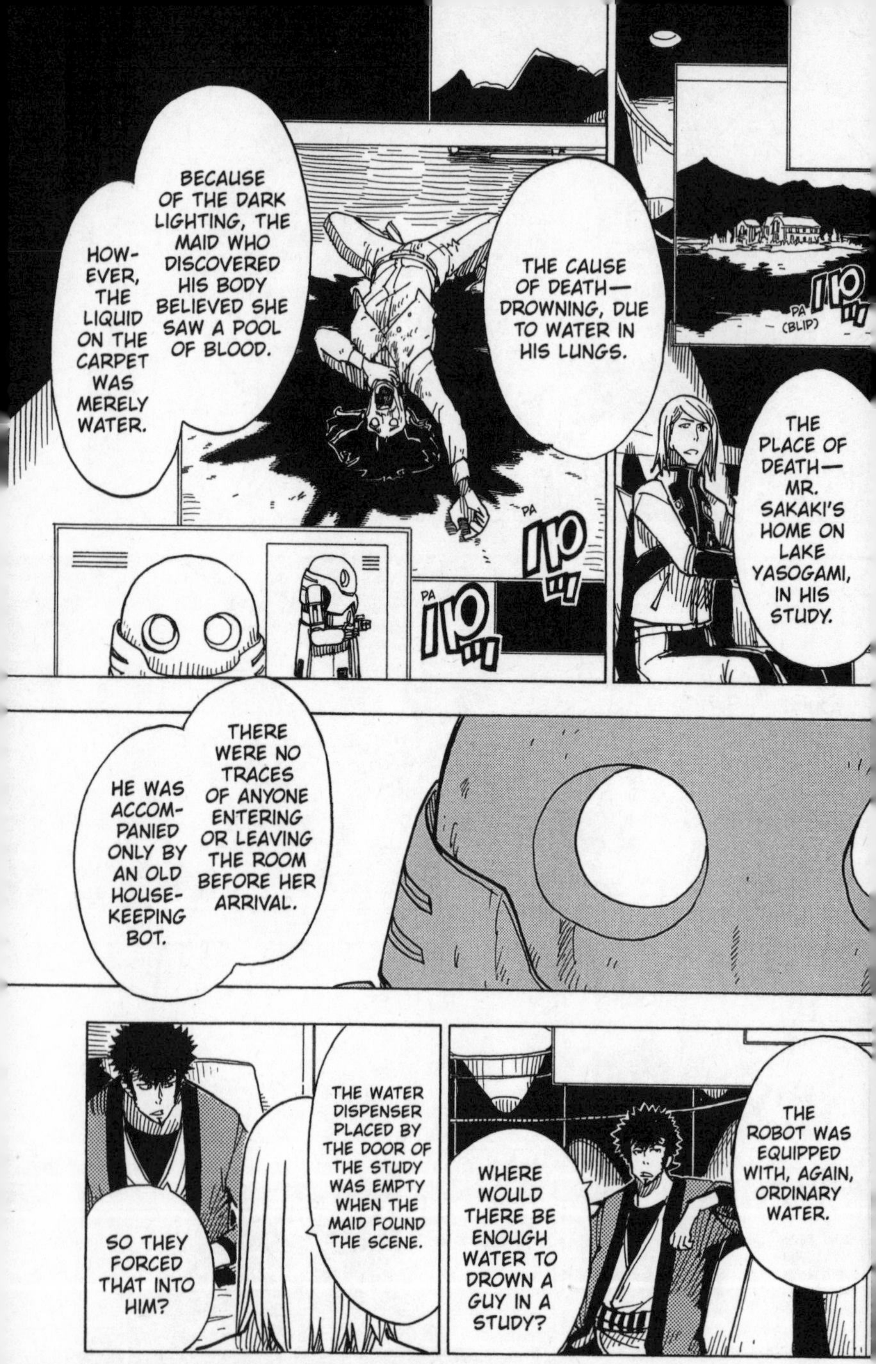
PA
(BLIP)
THE PLACE OF DEATH—MR. SAKAKI'S HOME ON LAKE YASOGAMI, IN HIS STUDY.
THE CAUSE OF DEATH—DROWNING, DUE TO WATER IN HIS LUNGS.
PA
BECAUSE OF THE DARK LIGHTING, THE MAID WHO DISCOVERED HIS BODY BELIEVED SHE SAW A POOL OF BLOOD.
HOW-EVER, THE LIQUID ON THE CARPET WAS MERELY WATER.
PA
THERE WERE NO TRACES OF ANYONE ENTERING OR LEAVING THE ROOM BEFORE HER ARRIVAL.
HE WAS ACCOM-PANIED ONLY BY AN OLD HOUSE-KEEPING BOT.
THE ROBOT WAS EQUIPPED WITH, AGAIN, ORDINARY WATER.
WHERE WOULD THERE BE ENOUGH WATER TO DROWN A GUY IN A STUDY?
THE WATER DISPENSER PLACED BY THE DOOR OF THE STUDY WAS EMPTY WHEN THE MAID FOUND THE SCENE.
SO THEY FORCED THAT INTO HIM?

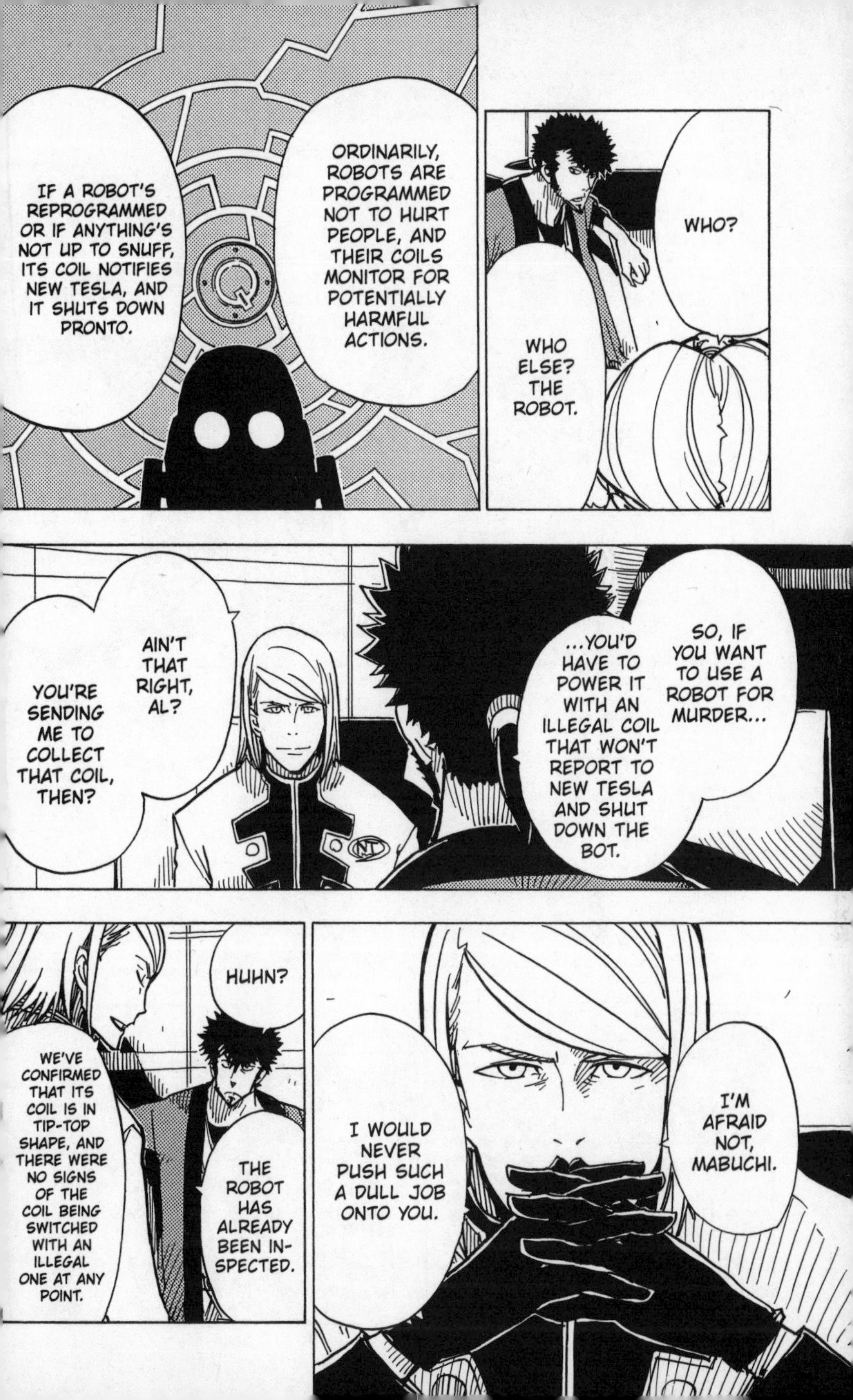
WHO?
WHO ELSE? THE ROBOT.
ORDINARILY, ROBOTS ARE PROGRAMMED NOT TO HURT PEOPLE, AND THEIR COILS MONITOR FOR POTENTIALLY HARMFUL ACTIONS.
IF A ROBOT'S REPROGRAMMED OR IF ANYTHING'S NOT UP TO SNUFF, ITS COIL NOTIFIES NEW TESLA, AND IT SHUTS DOWN PRONTO.
SO, IF YOU WANT TO USE A ROBOT FOR MURDER...
...YOU'D HAVE TO POWER IT WITH AN ILLEGAL COIL THAT WON'T REPORT TO NEW TESLA AND SHUT DOWN THE BOT.
AIN'T THAT RIGHT, AL?
YOU'RE SENDING ME TO COLLECT THAT COIL, THEN?
I'M AFRAID NOT, MABUCHI.
I WOULD NEVER PUSH SUCH A DULL JOB ONTO YOU.
HUHN?
THE ROBOT HAS ALREADY BEEN IN-SPECTED.
WE'VE CONFIRMED THAT ITS COIL IS IN TIP-TOP SHAPE, AND THERE WERE NO SIGNS OF THE COIL BEING SWITCHED WITH AN ILLEGAL ONE AT ANY POINT.

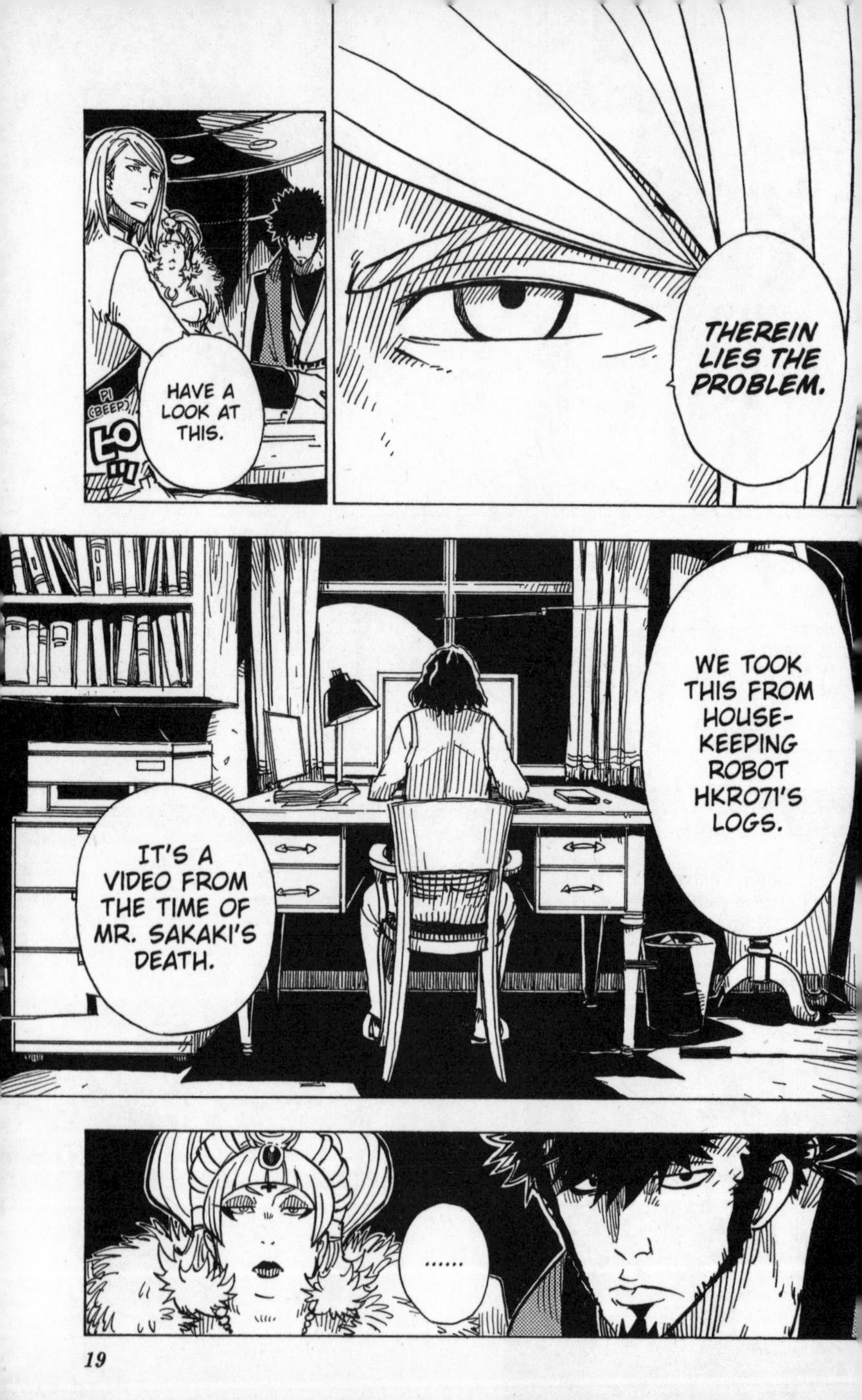
THEREIN LIES THE PROBLEM.
PI (BEEP)
HAVE A LOOK AT THIS.
WE TOOK THIS FROM HOUSE-KEEPING ROBOT HKR071'S LOGS.
IT'S A VIDEO FROM THE TIME OF MR. SAKAKI'S DEATH.
......

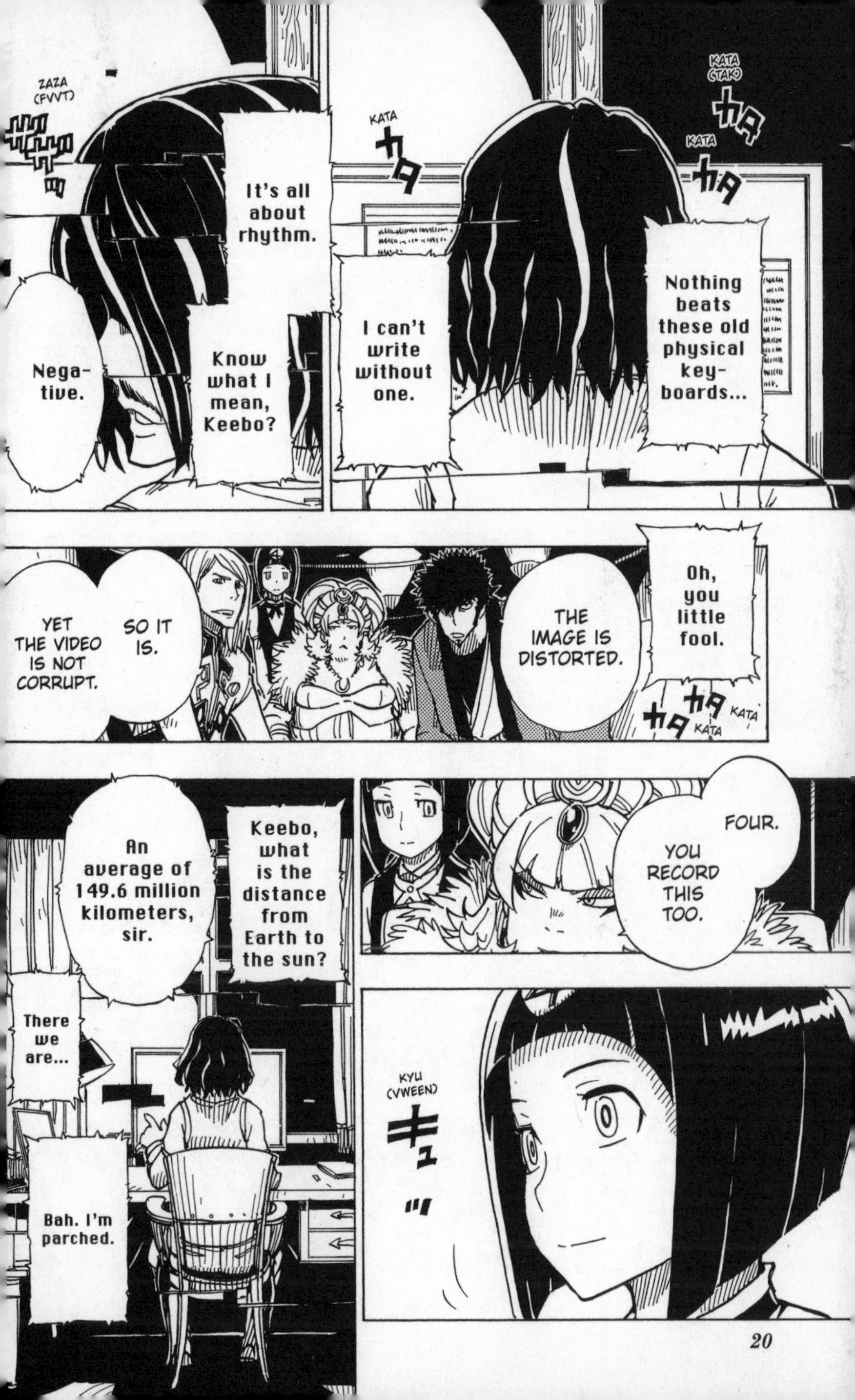
KATA (TAK)
カタ
KATA
カタ
Nothing beats these old physical key-boards...
KATA
カタ
I can't write without one.
It's all about rhythm.
Know what I mean, Keebo?
Nega-tive.
ZAZA (FVVT)
Oh, you little fool.
カタ KATA
カタ KATA
THE IMAGE IS DISTORTED.
SO IT IS.
YET THE VIDEO IS NOT CORRUPT.
FOUR.
YOU RECORD THIS TOO.
KYU (VWEEN)
キュ
Keebo, what is the distance from Earth to the sun?
An average of 149.6 million kilometers, sir.
There we are...
Bah. I'm parched.

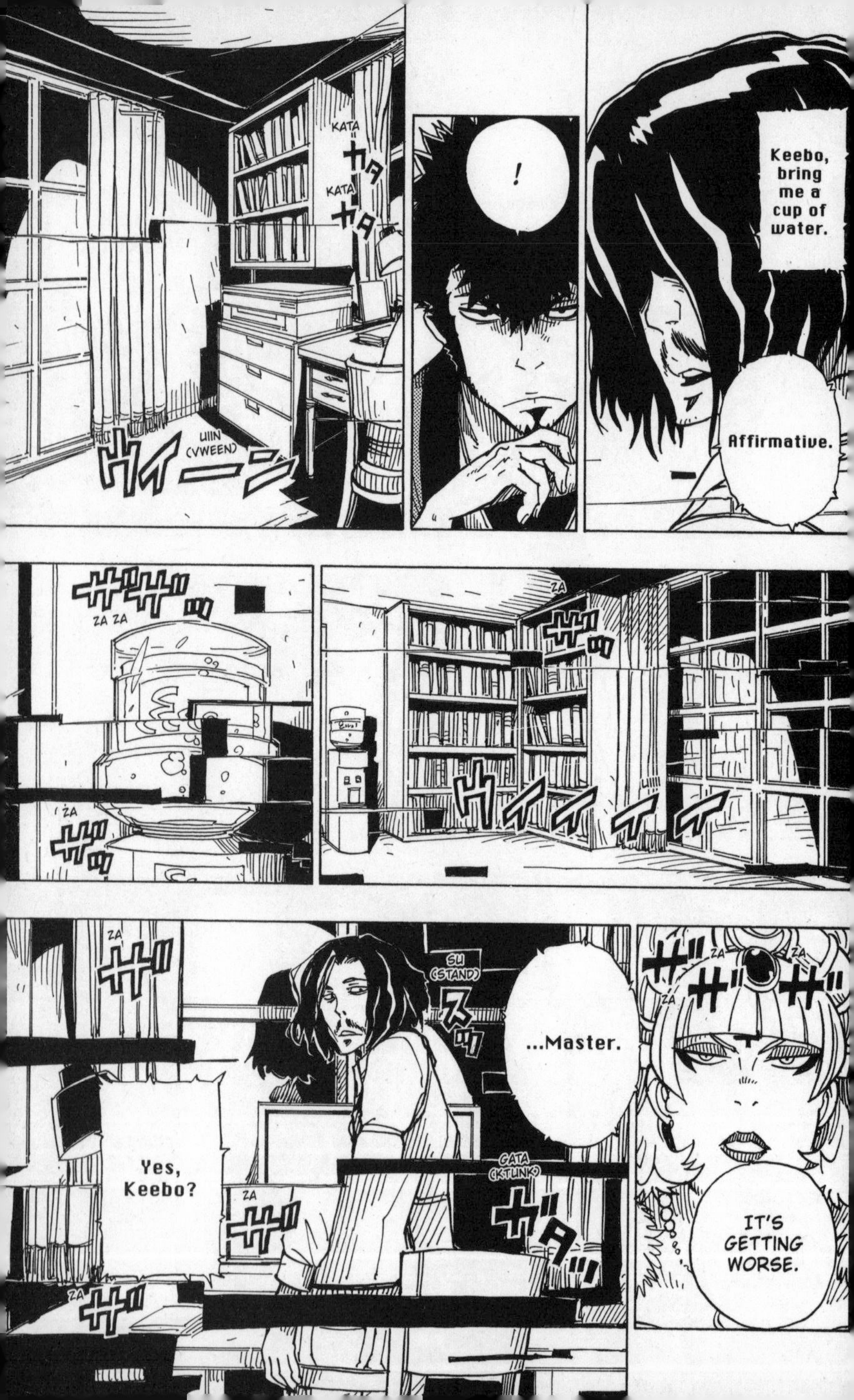
Keebo, bring me a cup of water.
Affirmative.
!
KATA
カタ
KATA
カタ
UIIN (VWEEN)
ウィーン
ZA
ザッ
ウィイイイイ
ZA ZA
ザザッ
ZA
ザッ
ZA ZA ZA
ザ ザ ザ
IT'S GETTING WORSE.
...Master.
SU (STAND)
スッ
GATA (KTUNK)
ガタッ
ZA
ザッ
Yes, Keebo?
ZA
ザッ
ZA
ザッ

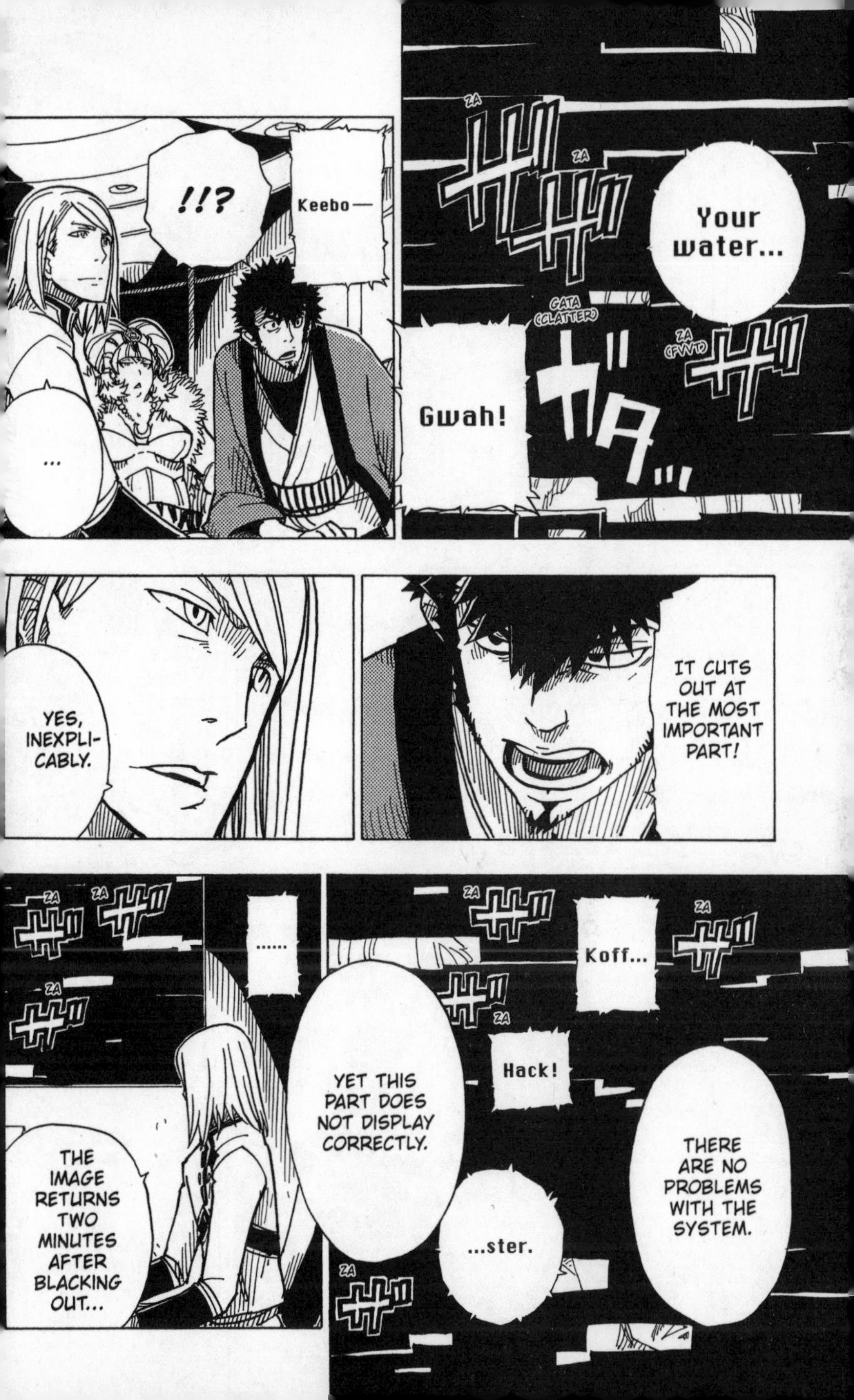
ZA
ZA
Your water...
GATA (CLATTER)
ZA (FVVT)
Gwah!
Keebo—
!!?
...
IT CUTS OUT AT THE MOST IMPORTANT PART!
YES, INEXPLICABLY.
ZA
Koff...
ZA
ZA
Hack!
THERE ARE NO PROBLEMS WITH THE SYSTEM.
...ster.
ZA
ZA
ZA
ZA
......
THE IMAGE RETURNS TWO MINUTES AFTER BLACKING OUT...
YET THIS PART DOES NOT DISPLAY CORRECTLY.

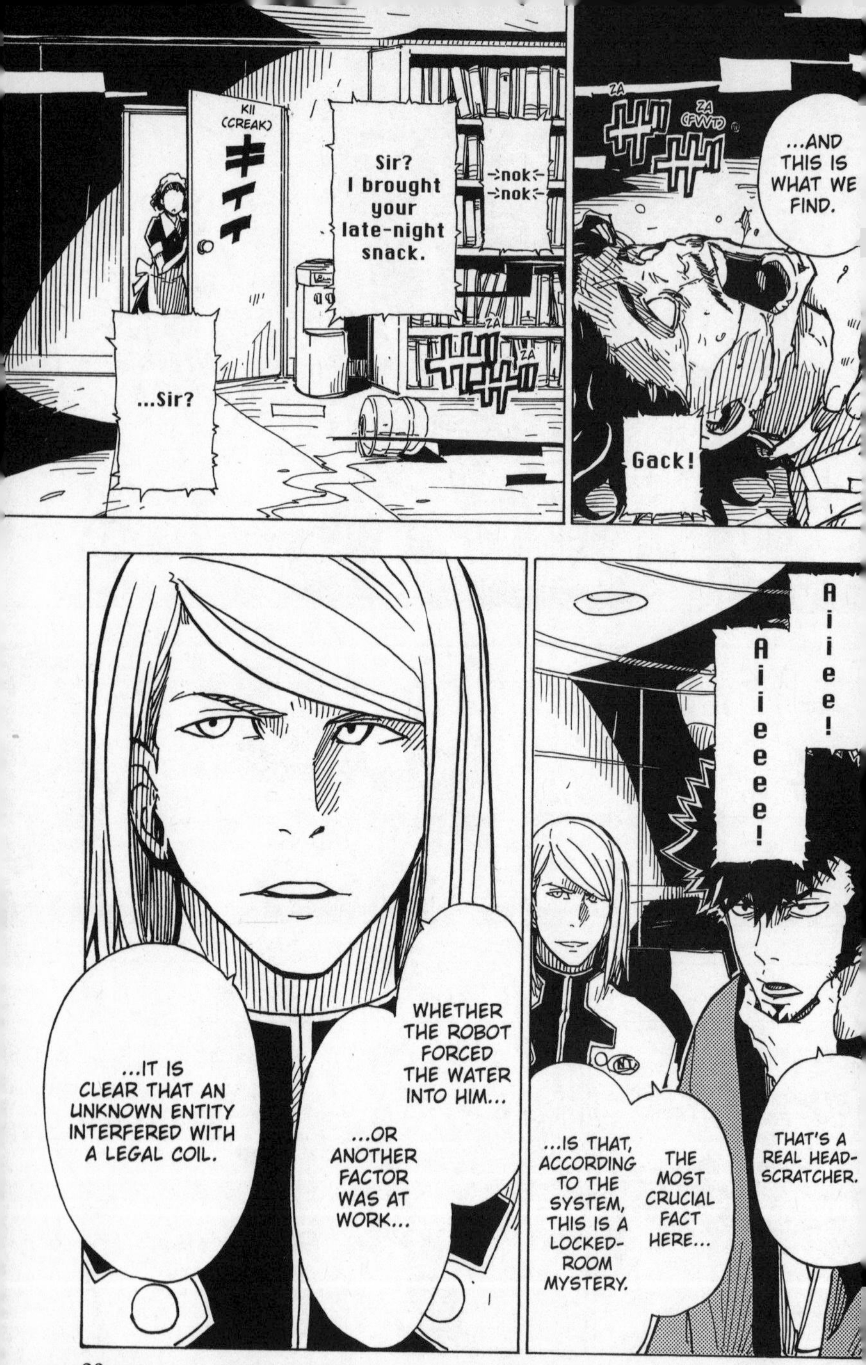
ZA
ZA (FVVT)
...AND THIS IS WHAT WE FIND.
Gack!
nok nok
Sir? I brought your late-night snack.
KII (CREAK)
ZA ZA
...Sir?
Aiiee!
Aiieeee!
THAT'S A REAL HEAD-SCRATCHER.
THE MOST CRUCIAL FACT HERE...
...IS THAT, ACCORDING TO THE SYSTEM, THIS IS A LOCKED-ROOM MYSTERY.
WHETHER THE ROBOT FORCED THE WATER INTO HIM...
...OR ANOTHER FACTOR WAS AT WORK...
...IT IS CLEAR THAT AN UNKNOWN ENTITY INTERFERED WITH A LEGAL COIL.

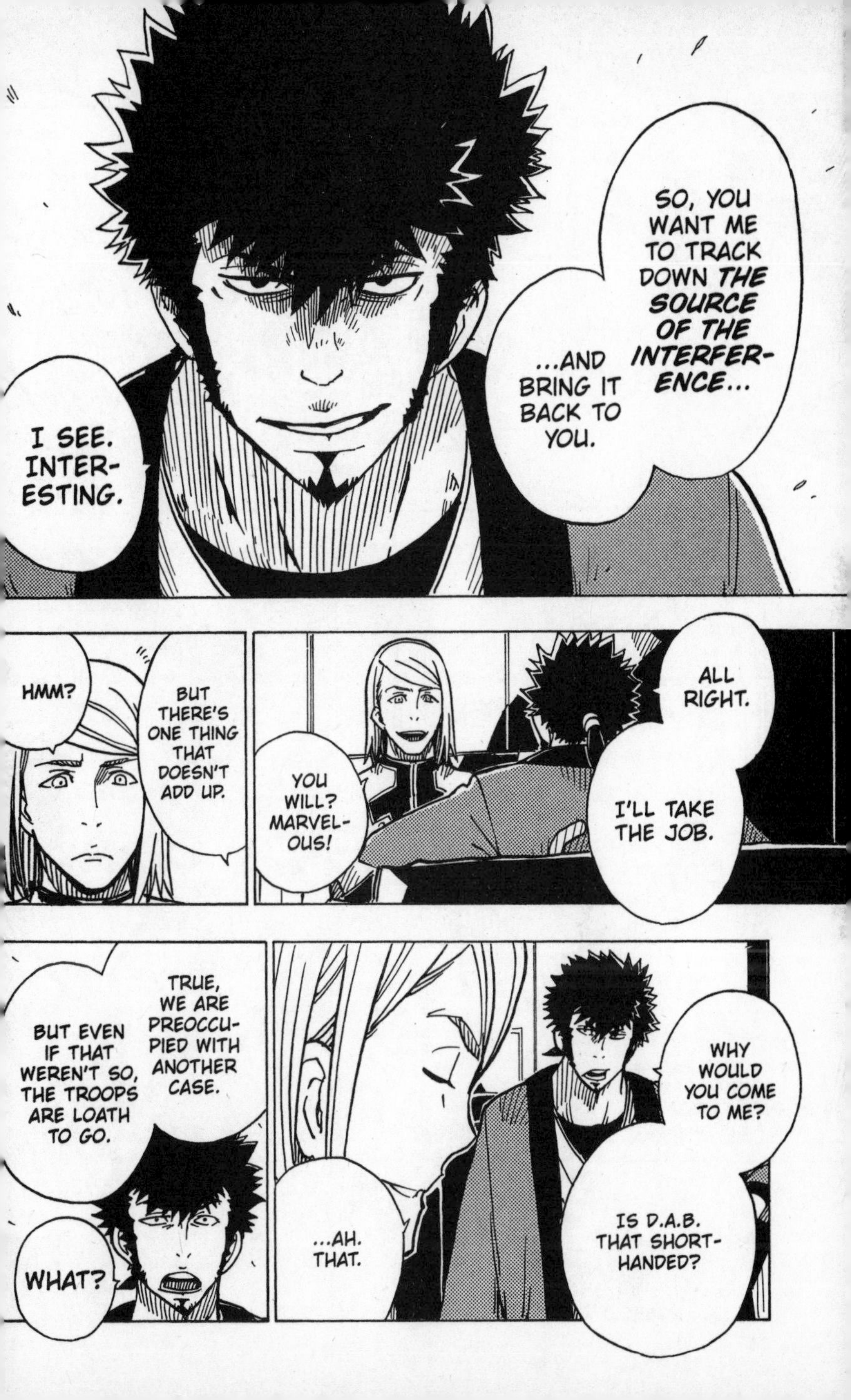
SO, YOU WANT ME TO TRACK DOWN THE SOURCE OF THE INTERFERENCE...
...AND BRING IT BACK TO YOU.
I SEE. INTERESTING.
ALL RIGHT.
I'LL TAKE THE JOB.
YOU WILL? MARVELOUS!
BUT THERE'S ONE THING THAT DOESN'T ADD UP.
HMM?
WHY WOULD YOU COME TO ME?
IS D.A.B. THAT SHORT-HANDED?
...AH. THAT.
TRUE, WE ARE PREOCCUPIED WITH ANOTHER CASE.
BUT EVEN IF THAT WEREN'T SO, THE TROOPS ARE LOATH TO GO.
WHAT?

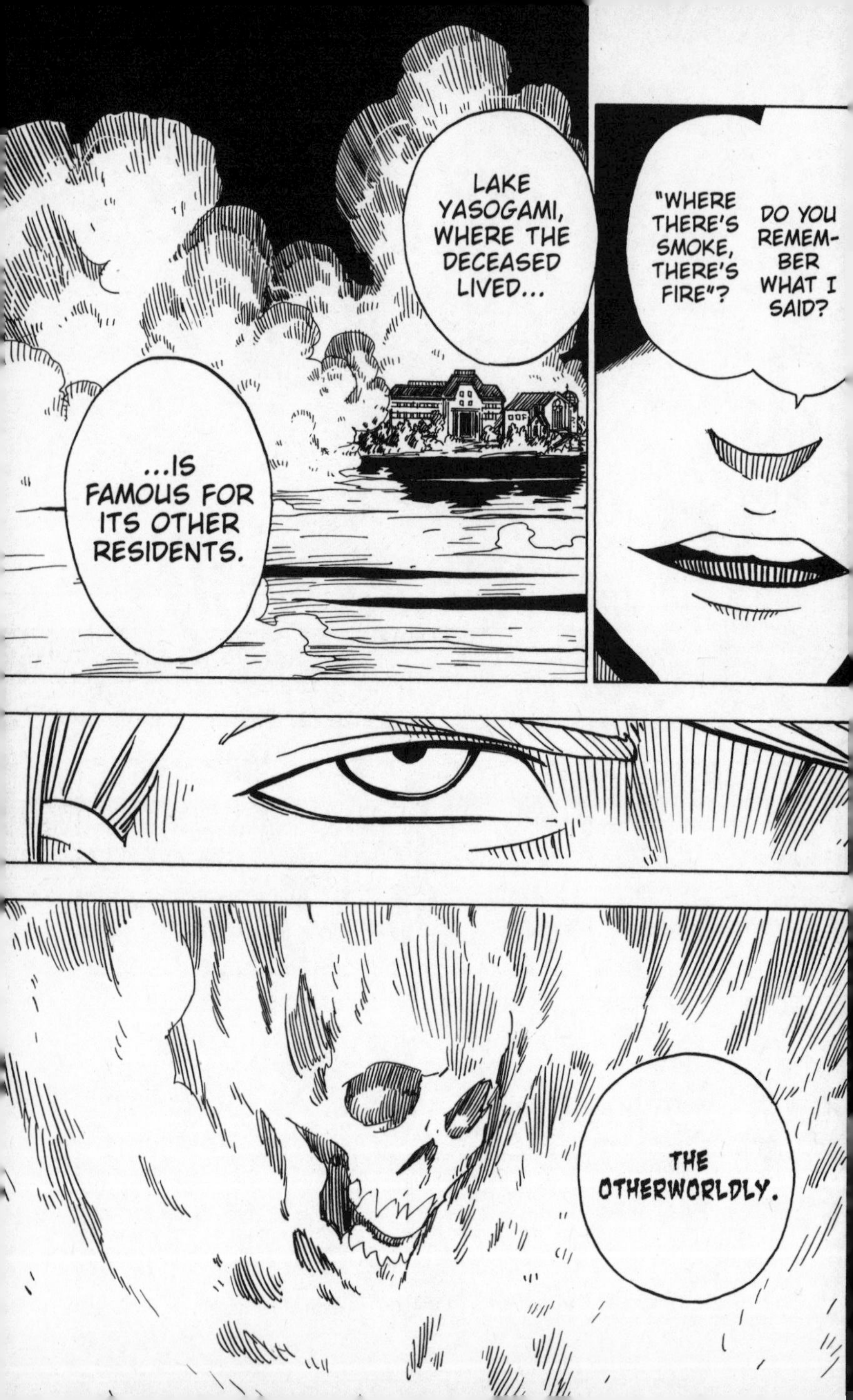
DO YOU REMEMBER WHAT I SAID?
"WHERE THERE'S SMOKE, THERE'S FIRE"?
LAKE YASOGAMI, WHERE THE DECEASED LIVED...
...IS FAMOUS FOR ITS OTHER RESIDENTS.
THE OTHERWORLDLY.

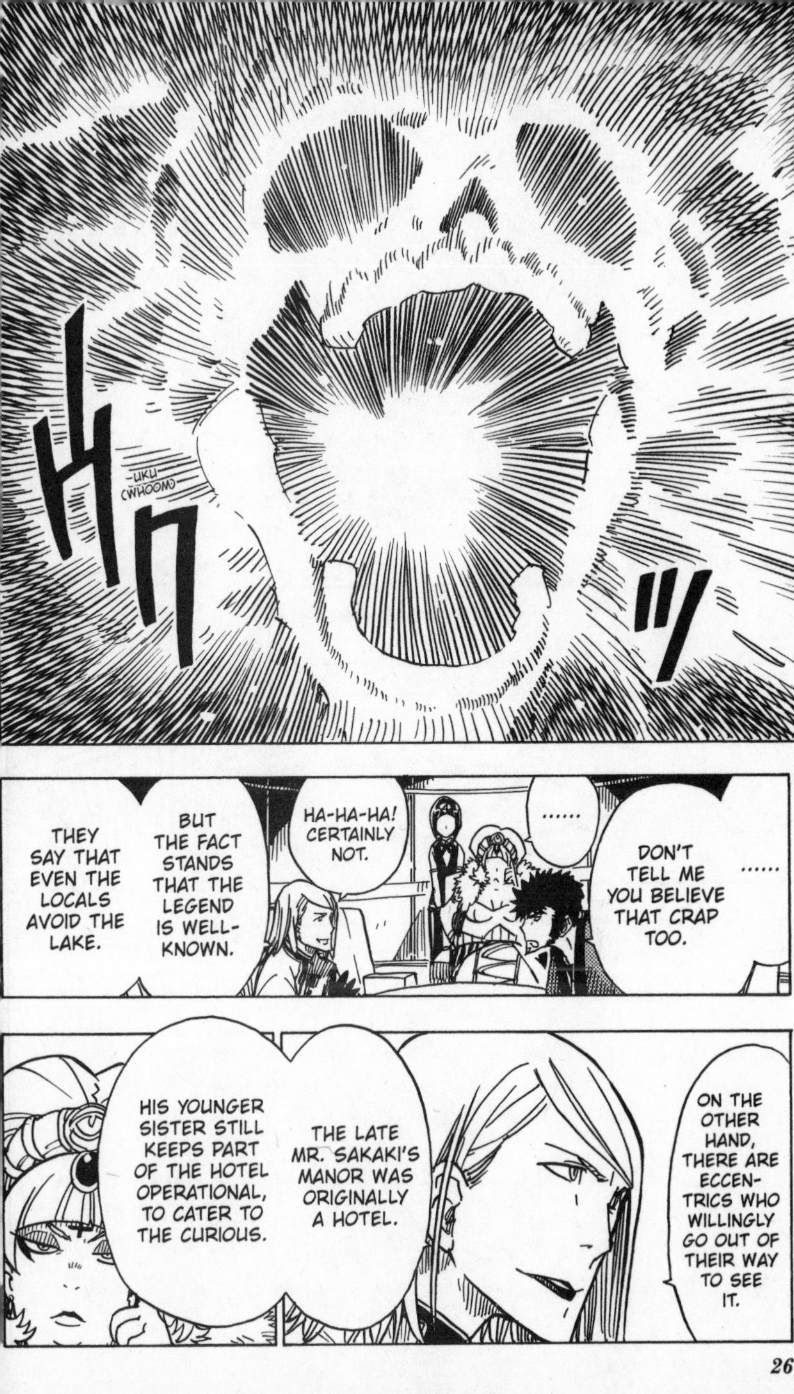
-UKU (WHOOM)
......
DON'T TELL ME YOU BELIEVE THAT CRAP TOO.
......
HA-HA-HA! CERTAINLY NOT.
BUT THE FACT STANDS THAT THE LEGEND IS WELL-KNOWN.
THEY SAY THAT EVEN THE LOCALS AVOID THE LAKE.
ON THE OTHER HAND, THERE ARE ECCEN-TRICS WHO WILLINGLY GO OUT OF THEIR WAY TO SEE IT.
THE LATE MR. SAKAKI'S MANOR WAS ORIGINALLY A HOTEL.
HIS YOUNGER SISTER STILL KEEPS PART OF THE HOTEL OPERATIONAL, TO CATER TO THE CURIOUS.

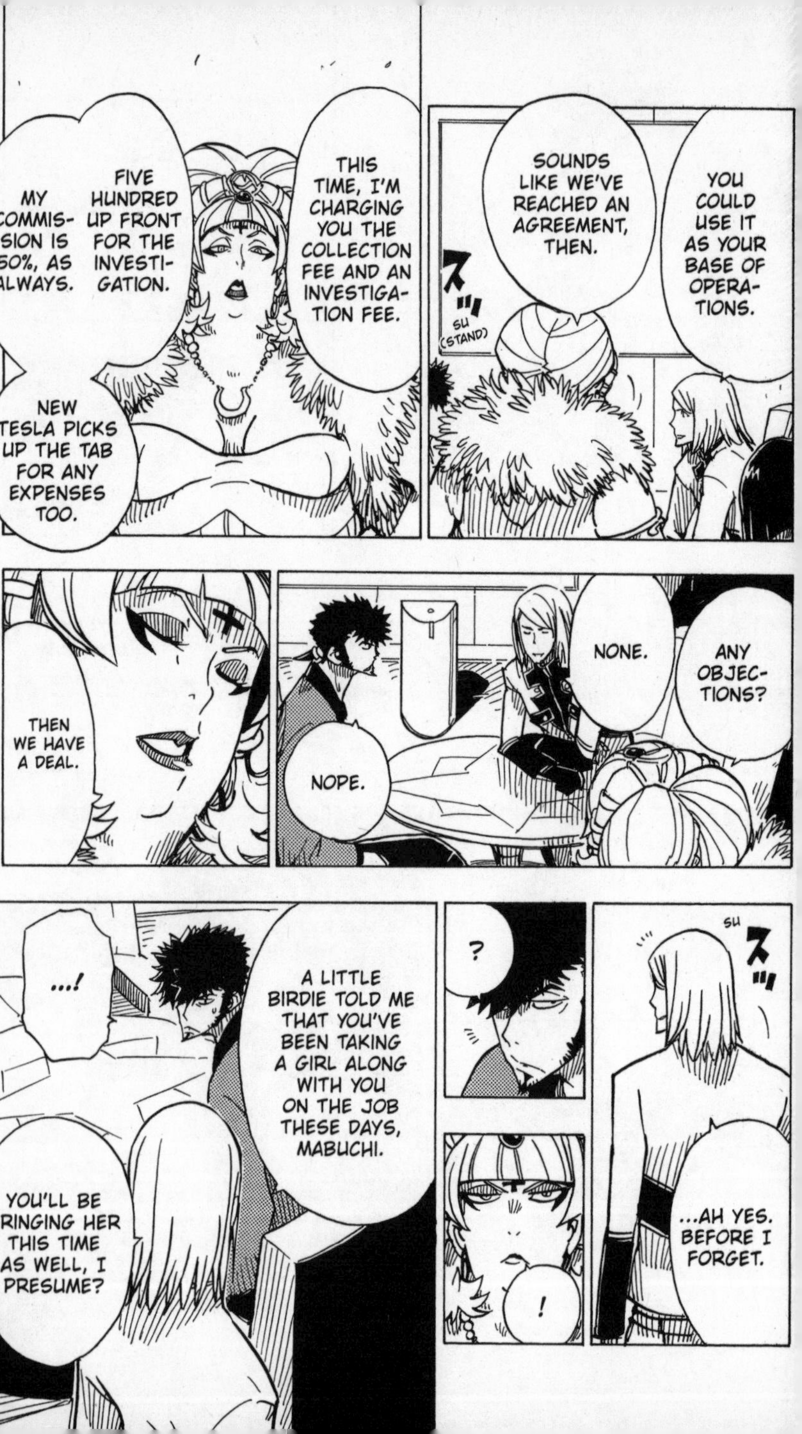
YOU COULD USE IT AS YOUR BASE OF OPERATIONS.
SOUNDS LIKE WE'VE REACHED AN AGREEMENT, THEN.
SU (STAND)
THIS TIME, I'M CHARGING YOU THE COLLECTION FEE AND AN INVESTIGATION FEE.
FIVE HUNDRED UP FRONT FOR THE INVESTIGATION.
MY COMMISSION IS 50%, AS ALWAYS.
NEW TESLA PICKS UP THE TAB FOR ANY EXPENSES TOO.
ANY OBJECTIONS?
NONE.
NOPE.
THEN WE HAVE A DEAL.
SU
...AH YES. BEFORE I FORGET.
?
!
A LITTLE BIRDIE TOLD ME THAT YOU'VE BEEN TAKING A GIRL ALONG WITH YOU ON THE JOB THESE DAYS, MABUCHI.
YOU'LL BE BRINGING HER THIS TIME AS WELL, I PRESUME?
...!

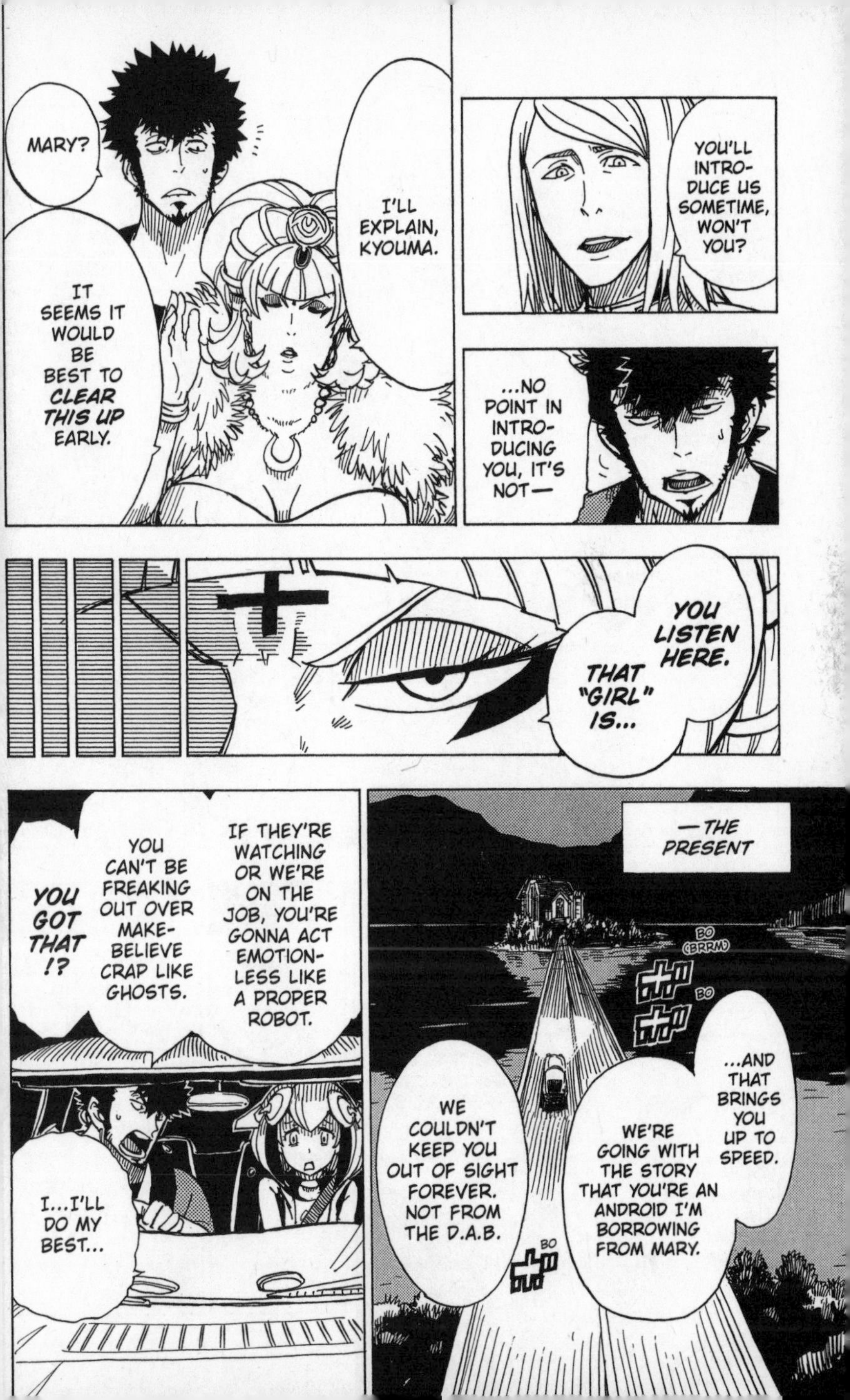
YOU'LL INTRODUCE US SOMETIME, WON'T YOU?
...NO POINT IN INTRODUCING YOU, IT'S NOT—
I'LL EXPLAIN, KYOUMA.
MARY?
IT SEEMS IT WOULD BE BEST TO CLEAR THIS UP EARLY.
YOU LISTEN HERE. THAT "GIRL" IS...
—THE PRESENT
BO (BRRM)
BO
...AND THAT BRINGS YOU UP TO SPEED.
WE'RE GOING WITH THE STORY THAT YOU'RE AN ANDROID I'M BORROWING FROM MARY.
WE COULDN'T KEEP YOU OUT OF SIGHT FOREVER. NOT FROM THE D.A.B.
BO
IF THEY'RE WATCHING OR WE'RE ON THE JOB, YOU'RE GONNA ACT EMOTIONLESS LIKE A PROPER ROBOT.
YOU CAN'T BE FREAKING OUT OVER MAKE-BELIEVE CRAP LIKE GHOSTS.
YOU GOT THAT!?
I...I'LL DO MY BEST...

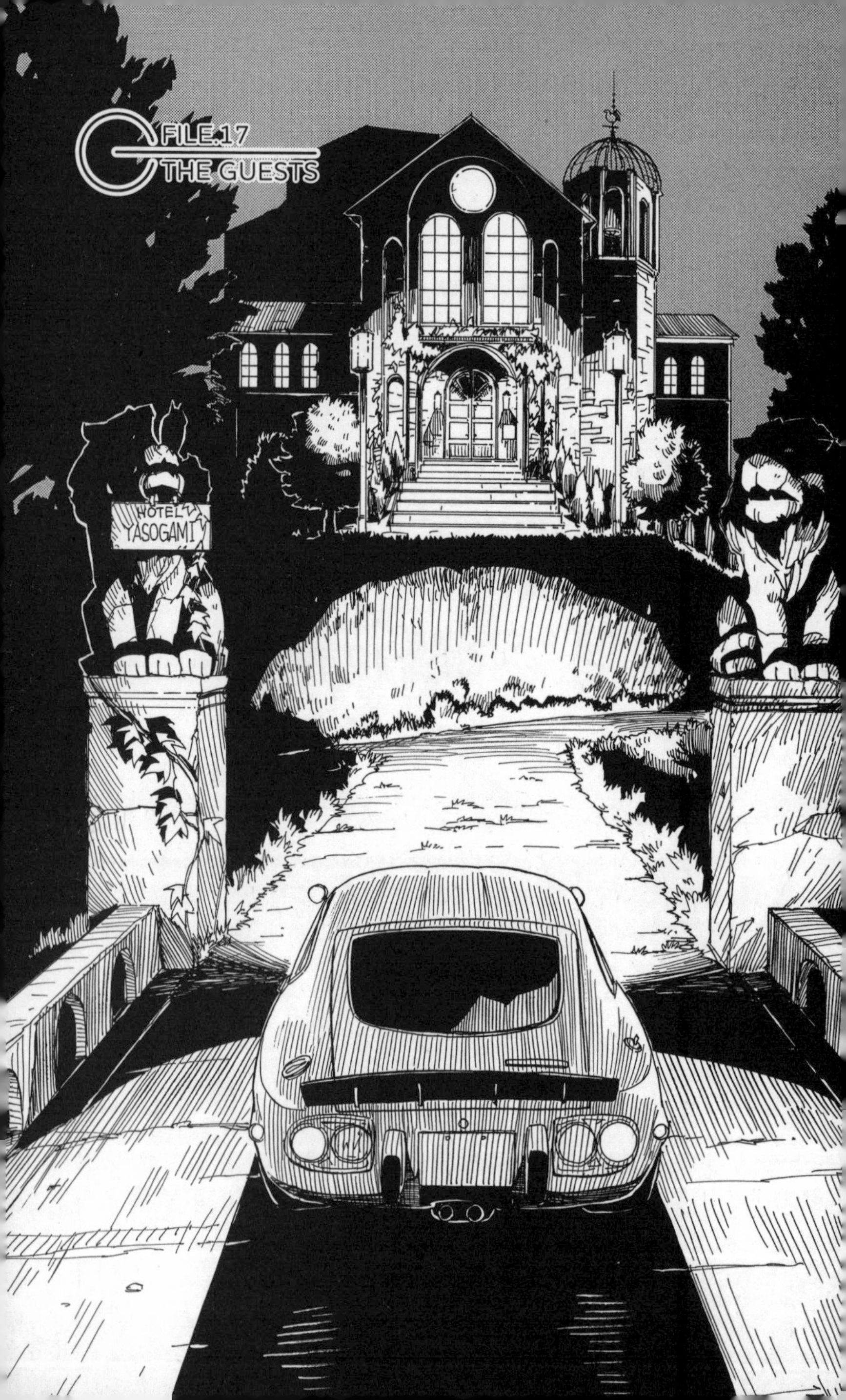
FILE.17
THE GUESTS
HOTEL
YASOGAMI

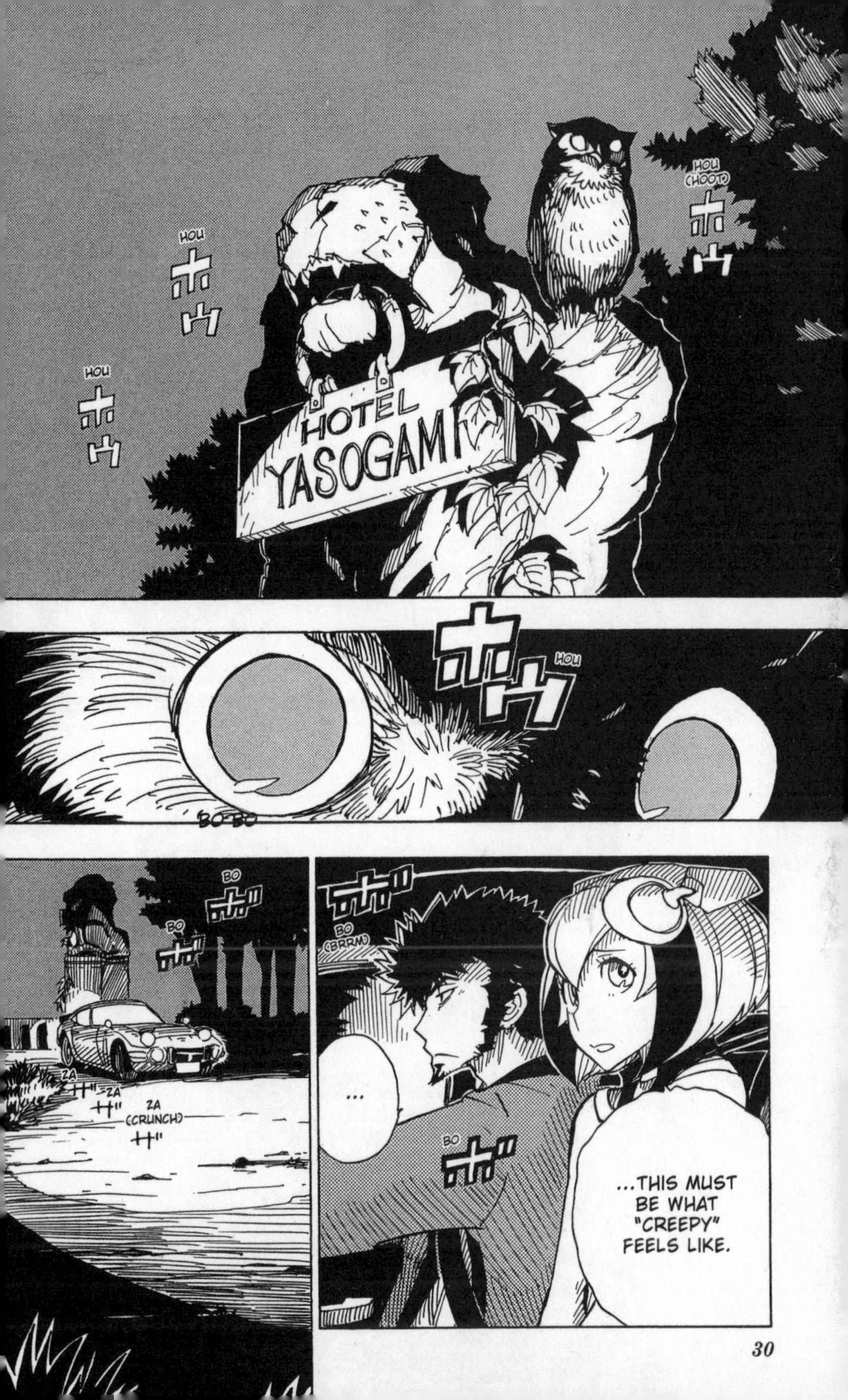
HOU (HOOT)
ホウ
HOU
ホウ
HOU
ホウ
HOTEL YASOGAMI
ホウ
HOU
BO BO
ボボ
BO (BRRM)
...
BO
ボ
...THIS MUST BE WHAT "CREEPY" FEELS LIKE.
BO
ボ
BO
ボ
ZA
ザ
ZA
ザ
ZA (CRUNCH)
ザ

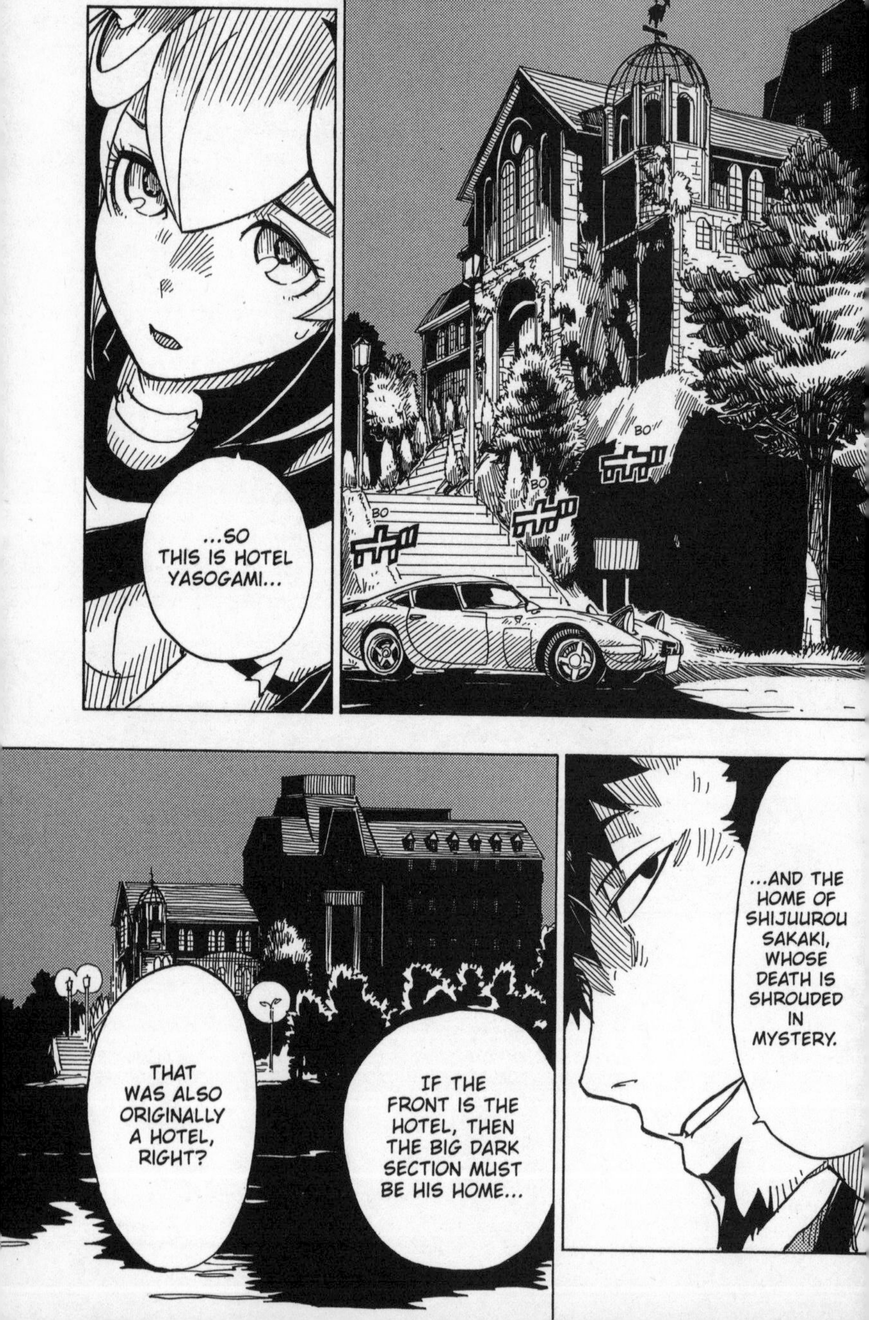
BO
BO
BO
...SO THIS IS HOTEL YASOGAMI...
...AND THE HOME OF SHIJUUROU SAKAKI, WHOSE DEATH IS SHROUDED IN MYSTERY.
IF THE FRONT IS THE HOTEL, THEN THE BIG DARK SECTION MUST BE HIS HOME...
THAT WAS ALSO ORIGINALLY A HOTEL, RIGHT?

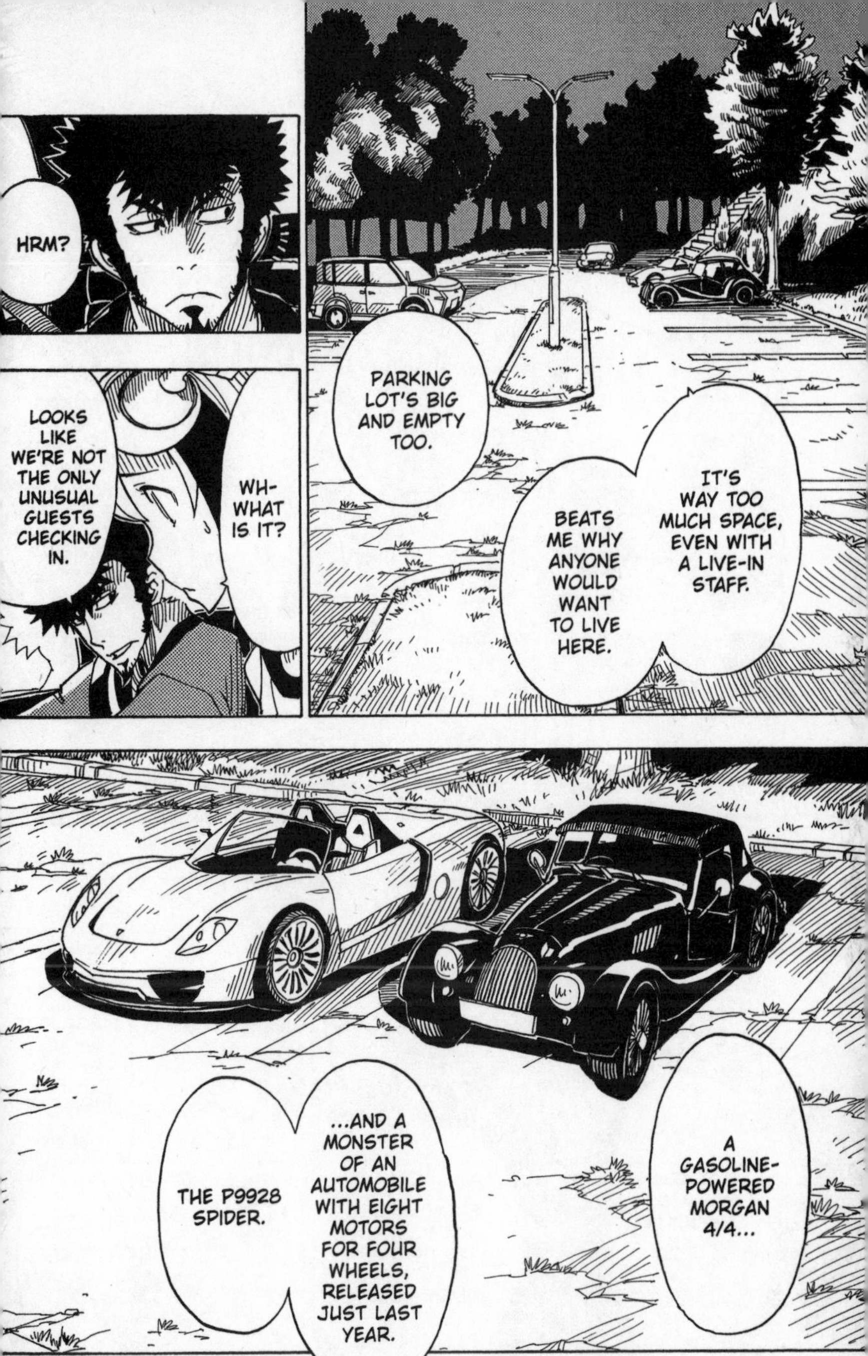
PARKING LOT'S BIG AND EMPTY TOO.
IT'S WAY TOO MUCH SPACE, EVEN WITH A LIVE-IN STAFF.
BEATS ME WHY ANYONE WOULD WANT TO LIVE HERE.
HRM?
WH-WHAT IS IT?
LOOKS LIKE WE'RE NOT THE ONLY UNUSUAL GUESTS CHECKING IN.
A GASOLINE-POWERED MORGAN 4/4...
...AND A MONSTER OF AN AUTOMOBILE WITH EIGHT MOTORS FOR FOUR WHEELS, RELEASED JUST LAST YEAR.
THE P9928 SPIDER.

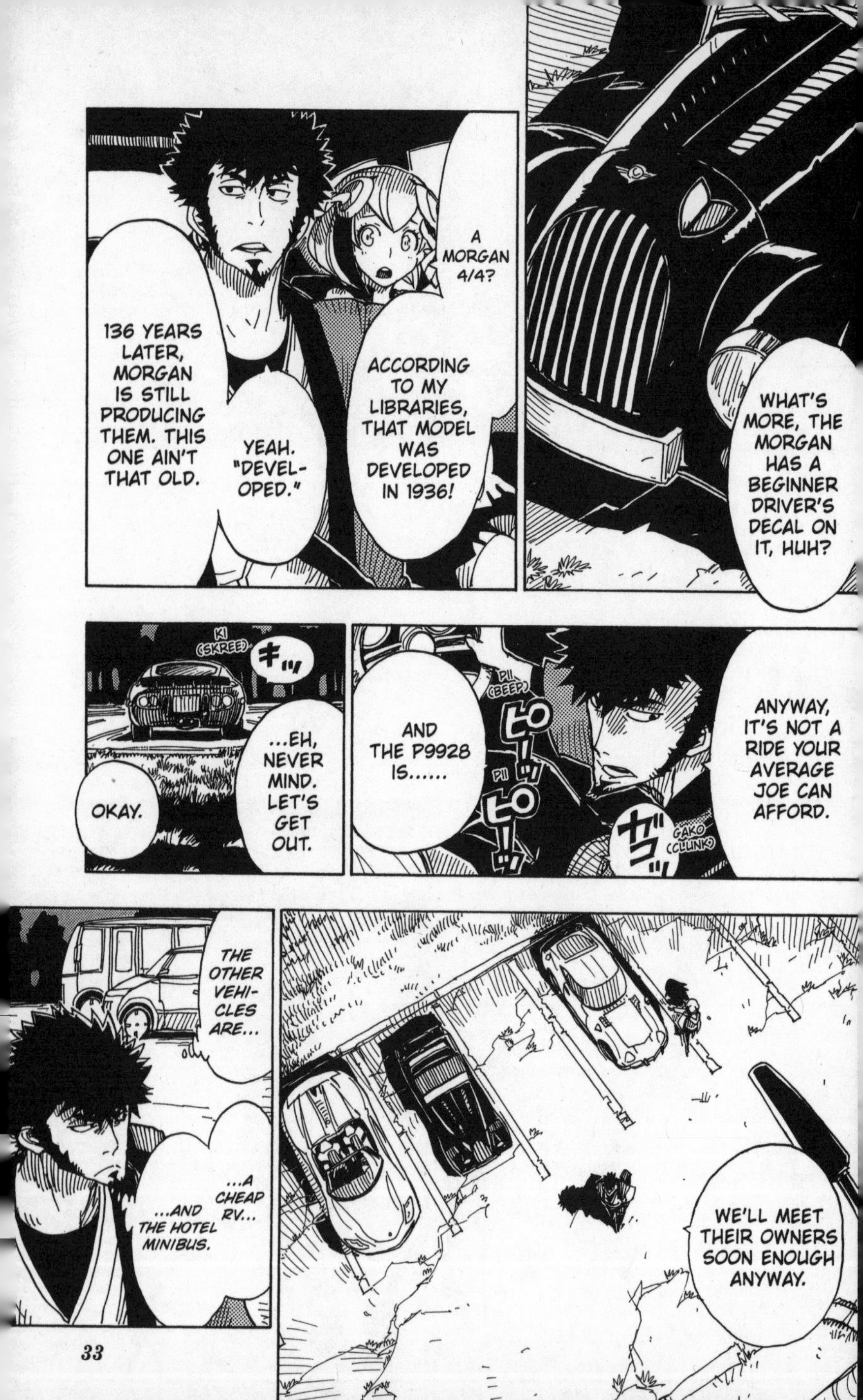
WHAT'S MORE, THE MORGAN HAS A BEGINNER DRIVER'S DECAL ON IT, HUH?
A MORGAN 4/4?
ACCORDING TO MY LIBRARIES, THAT MODEL WAS DEVELOPED IN 1936!
YEAH. "DEVEL-OPED."
136 YEARS LATER, MORGAN IS STILL PRODUCING THEM. THIS ONE AIN'T THAT OLD.
ANYWAY, IT'S NOT A RIDE YOUR AVERAGE JOE CAN AFFORD.
GAKO (CLUNK)
PII (BEEP)
PII
AND THE P9928 IS......
KI (SKREE)
...EH, NEVER MIND. LET'S GET OUT.
OKAY.
WE'LL MEET THEIR OWNERS SOON ENOUGH ANYWAY.
THE OTHER VEHI-CLES ARE...
...A CHEAP RV...
...AND THE HOTEL MINIBUS.

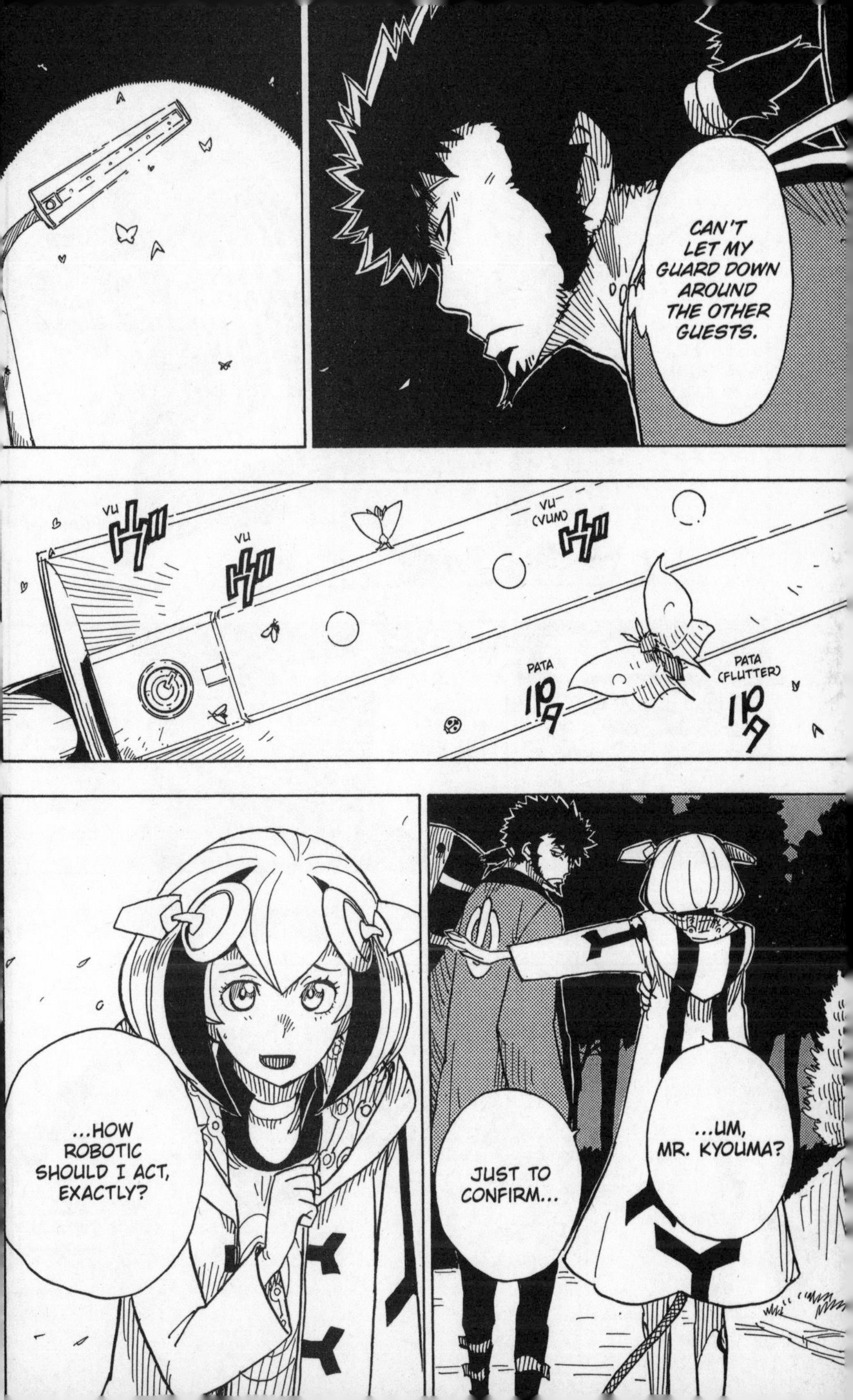
CAN'T LET MY GUARD DOWN AROUND THE OTHER GUESTS.
PATA (FLUTTER)
PATA
VU (VUM)
VU
VU
...UM, MR. KYOUMA?
JUST TO CONFIRM...
...HOW ROBOTIC SHOULD I ACT, EXACTLY?

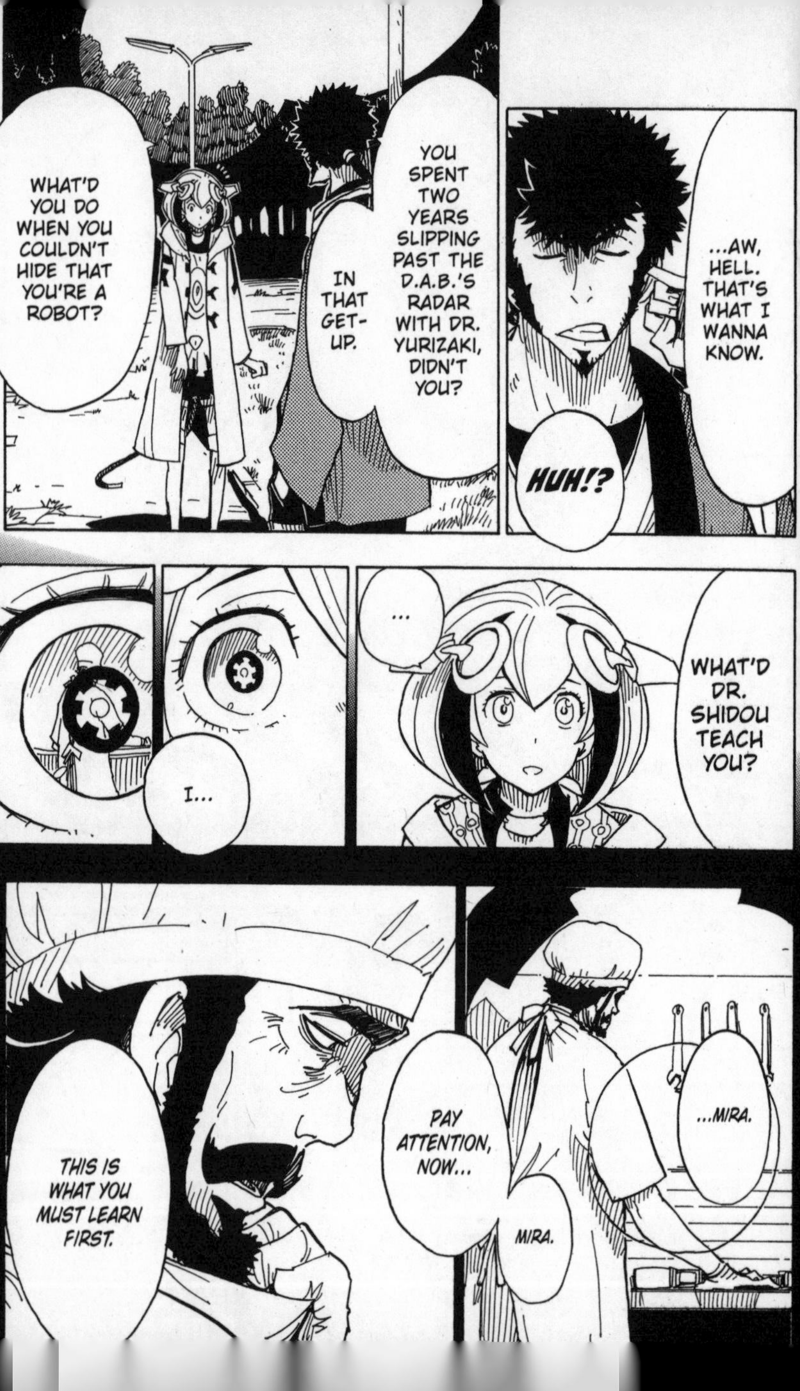
...AW, HELL. THAT'S WHAT I WANNA KNOW.
HUH!?
YOU SPENT TWO YEARS SLIPPING PAST THE D.A.B.'S RADAR WITH DR. YURIZAKI, DIDN'T YOU?
IN THAT GET-UP.
WHAT'D YOU DO WHEN YOU COULDN'T HIDE THAT YOU'RE A ROBOT?
WHAT'D DR. SHIDOU TEACH YOU?
...
I...
...MIRA.
MIRA.
PAY ATTENTION, NOW...
THIS IS WHAT YOU MUST LEARN FIRST.

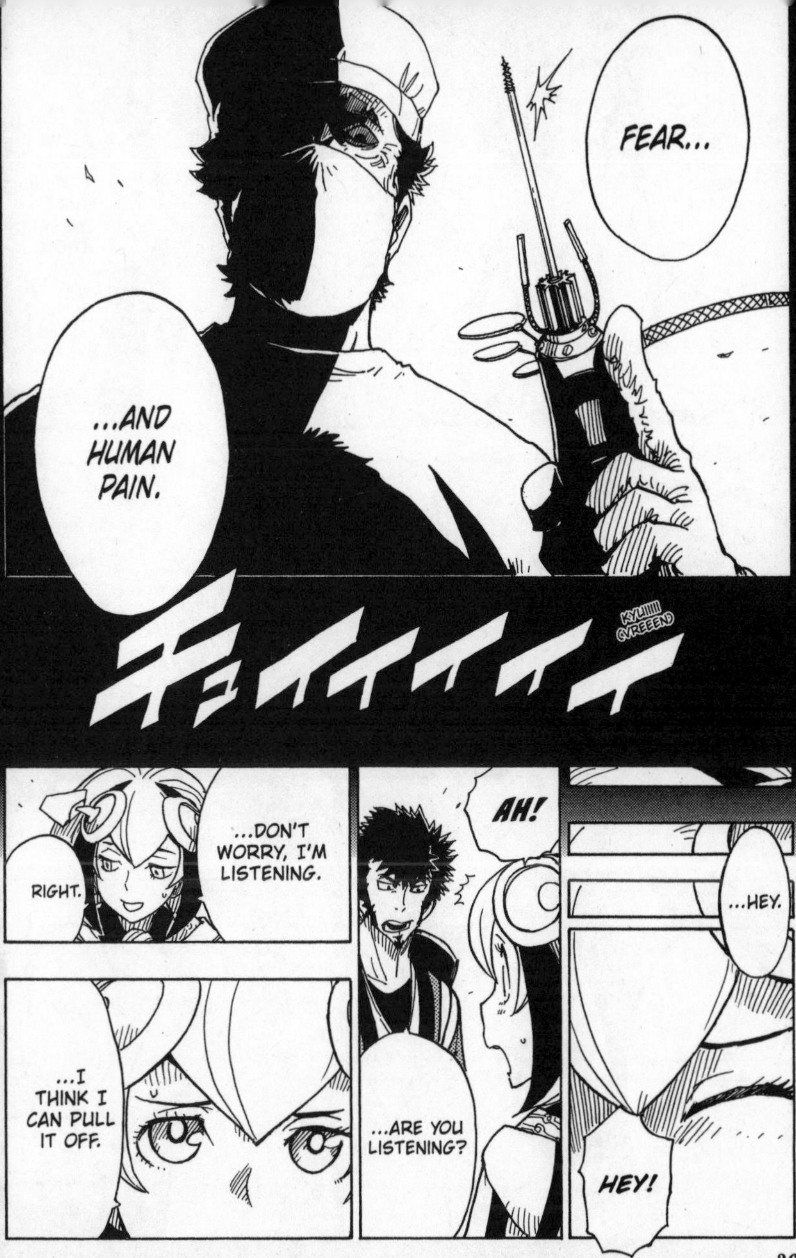
FEAR...
...AND HUMAN PAIN.
KYUIIIII (VREEEN)
...HEY.
HEY!
AH!
...ARE YOU LISTENING?
...DON'T WORRY, I'M LISTENING.
RIGHT.
...I THINK I CAN PULL IT OFF.

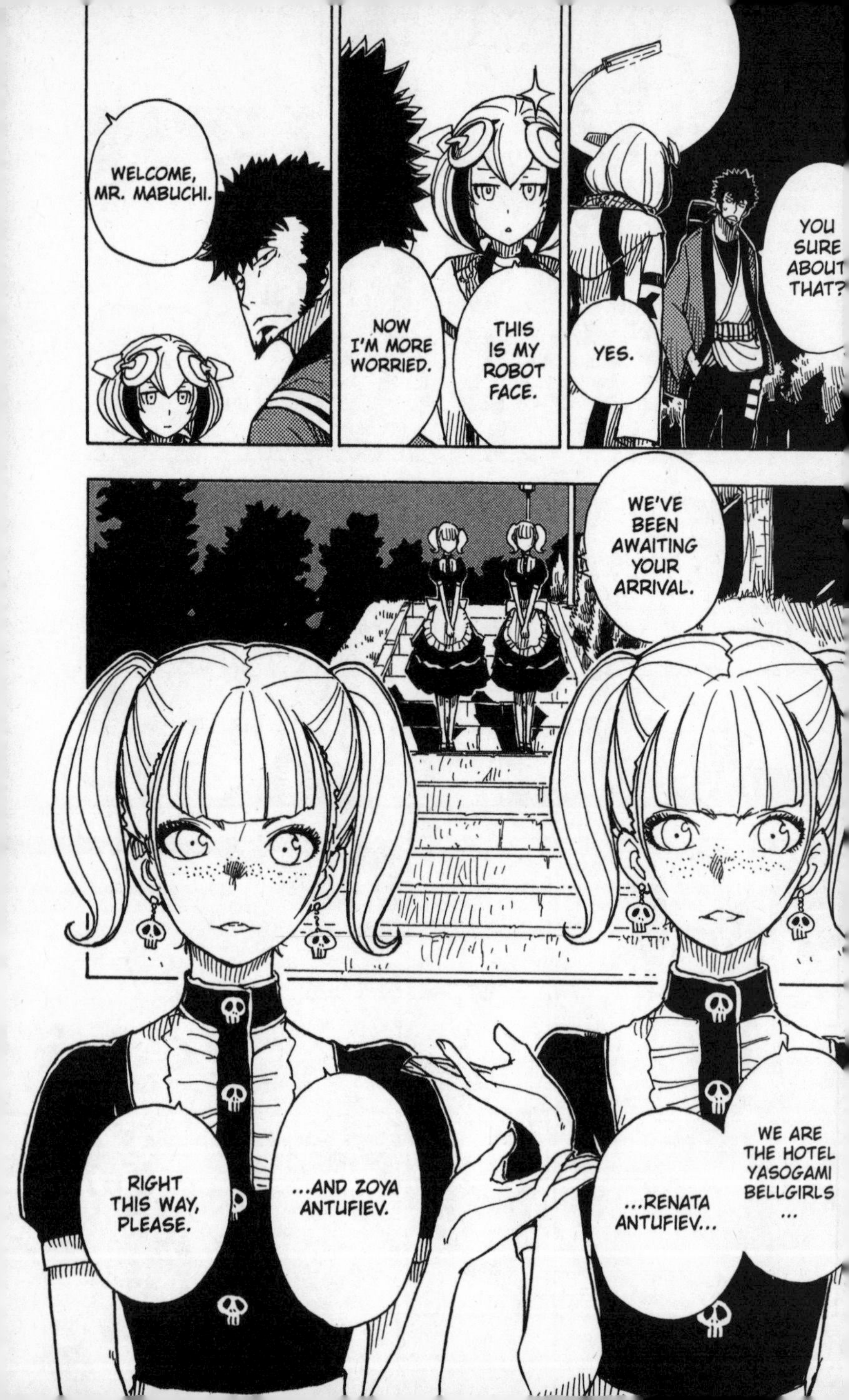
YOU SURE ABOUT THAT?
YES.
THIS IS MY ROBOT FACE.
NOW I'M MORE WORRIED.
WELCOME, MR. MABUCHI.
WE'VE BEEN AWAITING YOUR ARRIVAL.
WE ARE THE HOTEL YASOGAMI BELLGIRLS ...
...RENATA ANTUFIEV...
...AND ZOYA ANTUFIEV.
RIGHT THIS WAY, PLEASE.

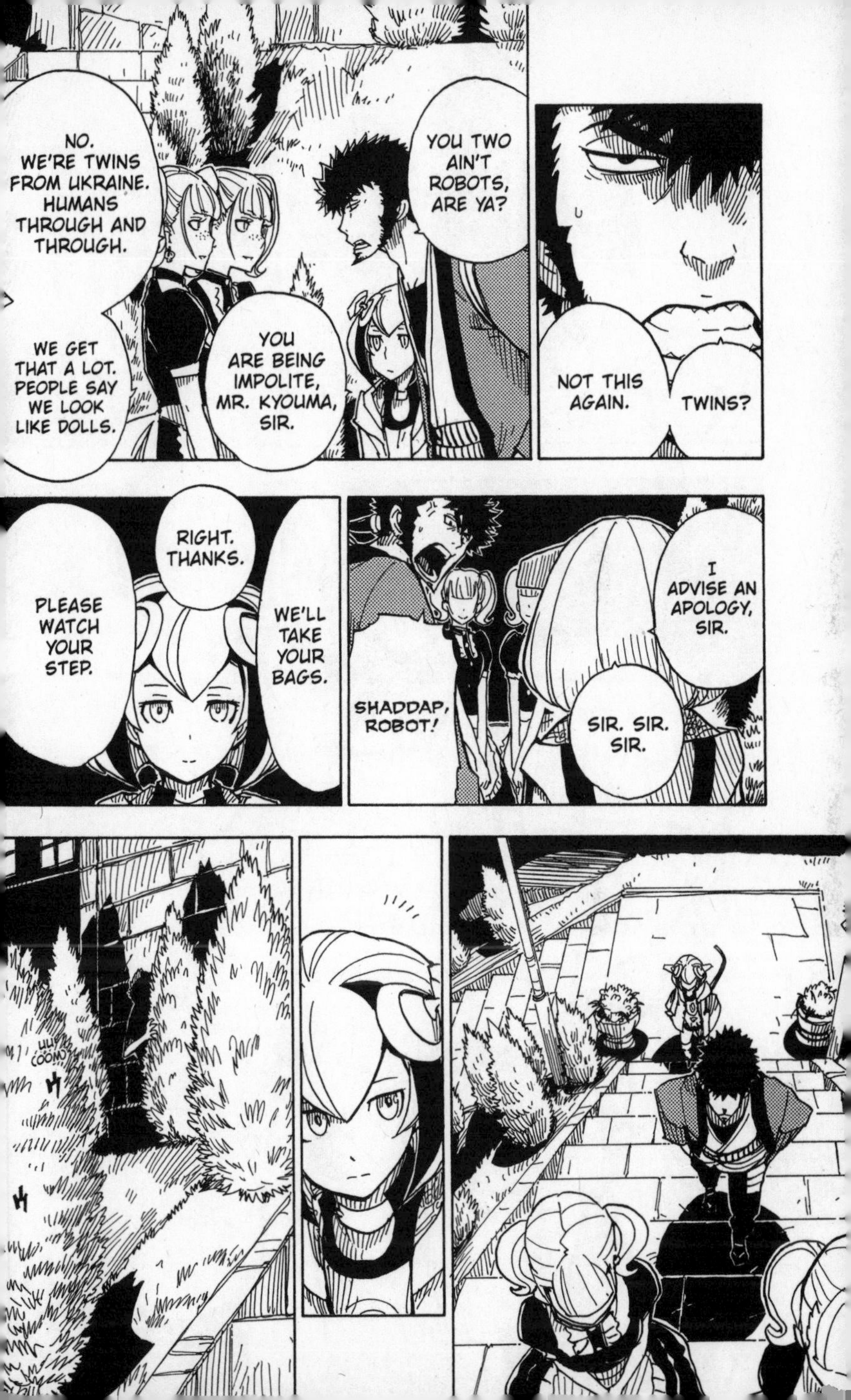
TWINS?
NOT THIS AGAIN.
YOU TWO AIN'T ROBOTS, ARE YA?
NO. WE'RE TWINS FROM UKRAINE. HUMANS THROUGH AND THROUGH.
YOU ARE BEING IMPOLITE, MR. KYOUMA, SIR.
WE GET THAT A LOT. PEOPLE SAY WE LOOK LIKE DOLLS.
I ADVISE AN APOLOGY, SIR.
SIR. SIR. SIR.
SHADDAP, ROBOT!
WE'LL TAKE YOUR BAGS.
RIGHT. THANKS.
PLEASE WATCH YOUR STEP.

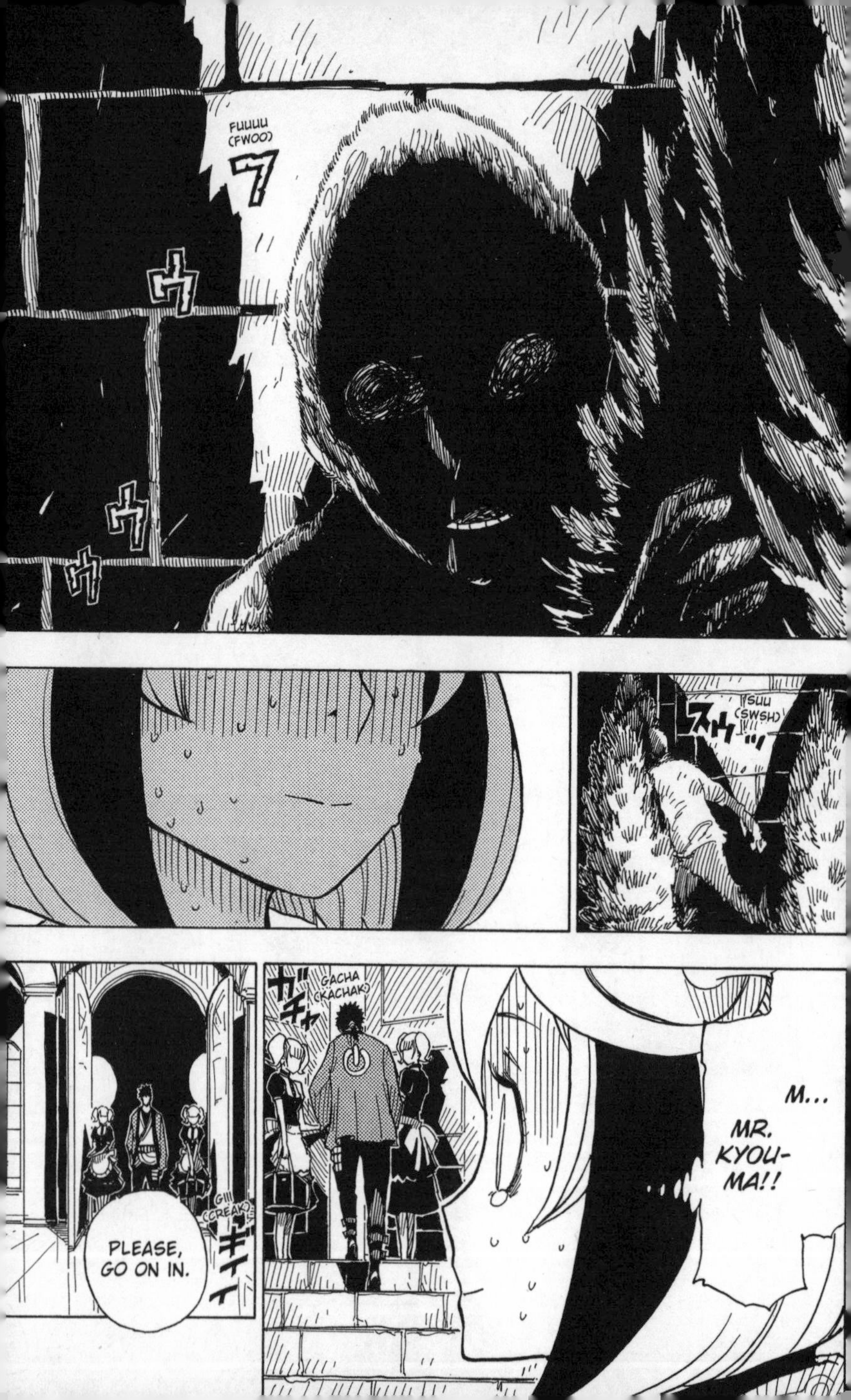
FUUUU (FWOO)
SUU (SWSH)
GACHA (KACHAK)
M...
MR. KYOU-MA!!
GIII (CREAK)
PLEASE, GO ON IN.

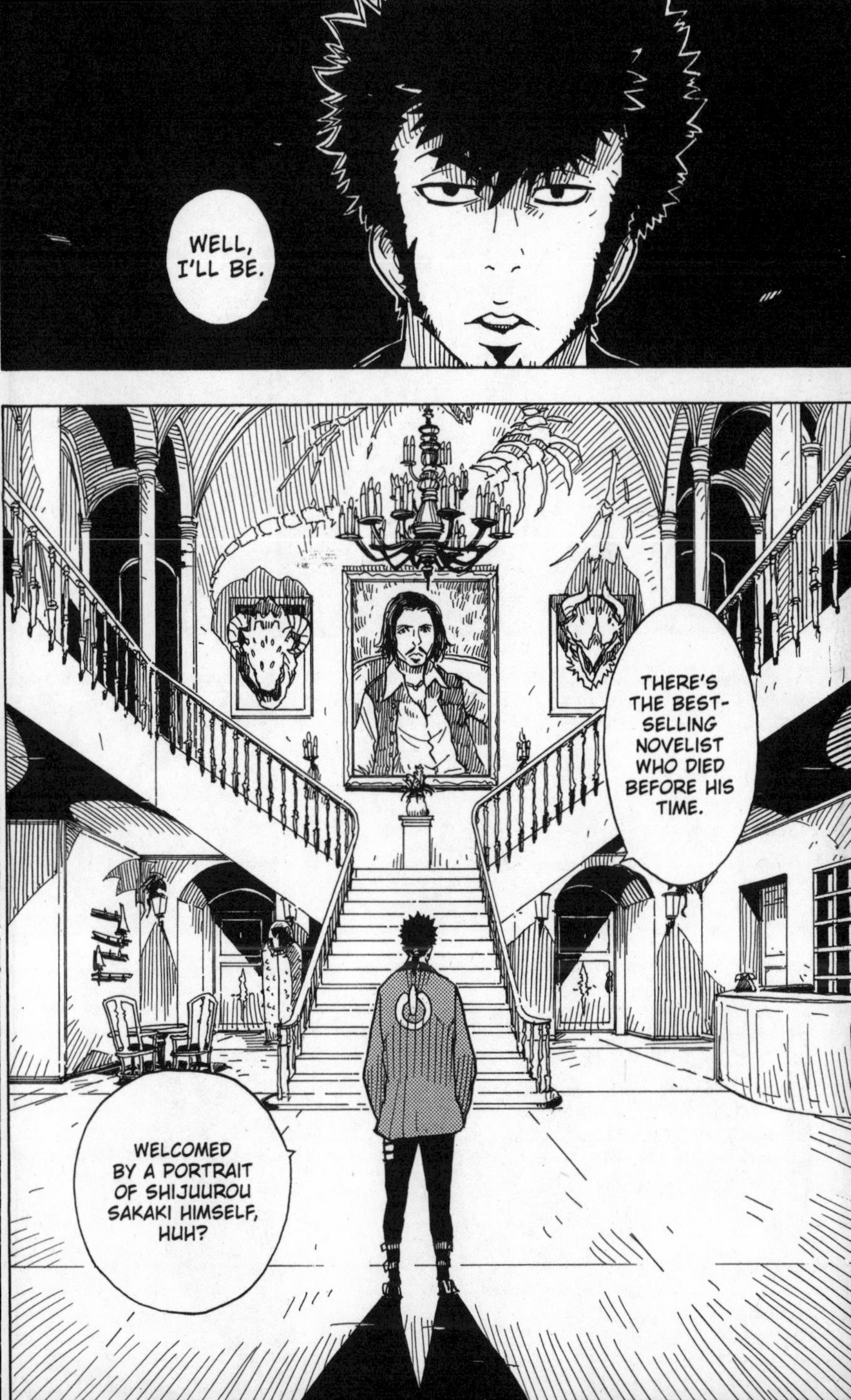
WELL, I'LL BE.
THERE'S THE BEST-SELLING NOVELIST WHO DIED BEFORE HIS TIME.
WELCOMED BY A PORTRAIT OF SHIJUUROU SAKAKI HIMSELF, HUH?

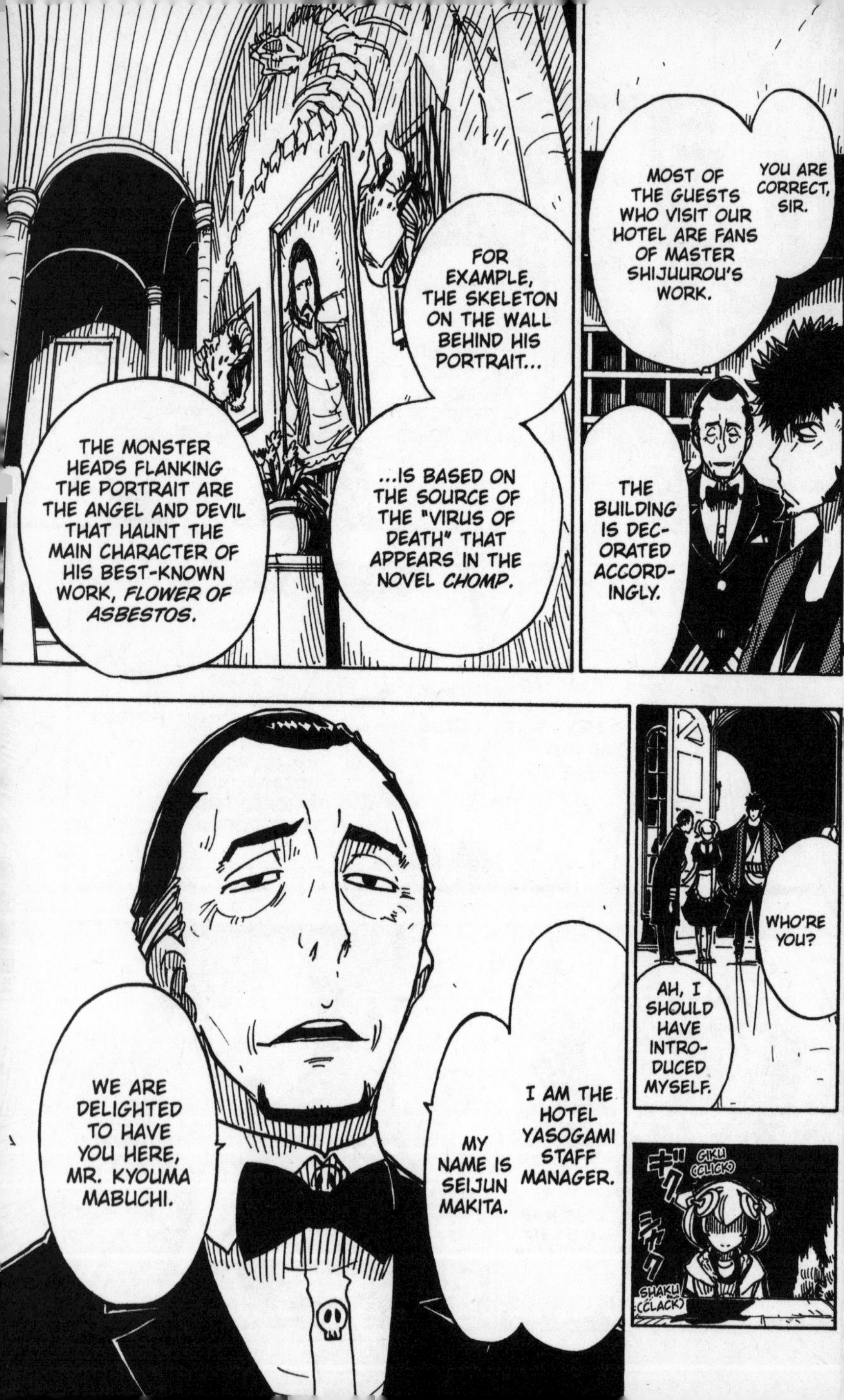
YOU ARE CORRECT, SIR.
MOST OF THE GUESTS WHO VISIT OUR HOTEL ARE FANS OF MASTER SHIJUUROU'S WORK.
THE BUILDING IS DEC-ORATED ACCORD-INGLY.
FOR EXAMPLE, THE SKELETON ON THE WALL BEHIND HIS PORTRAIT...
...IS BASED ON THE SOURCE OF THE "VIRUS OF DEATH" THAT APPEARS IN THE NOVEL *CHOMP*.
THE MONSTER HEADS FLANKING THE PORTRAIT ARE THE ANGEL AND DEVIL THAT HAUNT THE MAIN CHARACTER OF HIS BEST-KNOWN WORK, *FLOWER OF ASBESTOS*.
WHO'RE YOU?
AH, I SHOULD HAVE INTRO-DUCED MYSELF.
ギク
GIKU (CLICK)
シャク
SHAKU (CLACK)
I AM THE HOTEL YASOGAMI STAFF MANAGER.
MY NAME IS SEIJUN MAKITA.
WE ARE DELIGHTED TO HAVE YOU HERE, MR. KYOUMA MABUCHI.

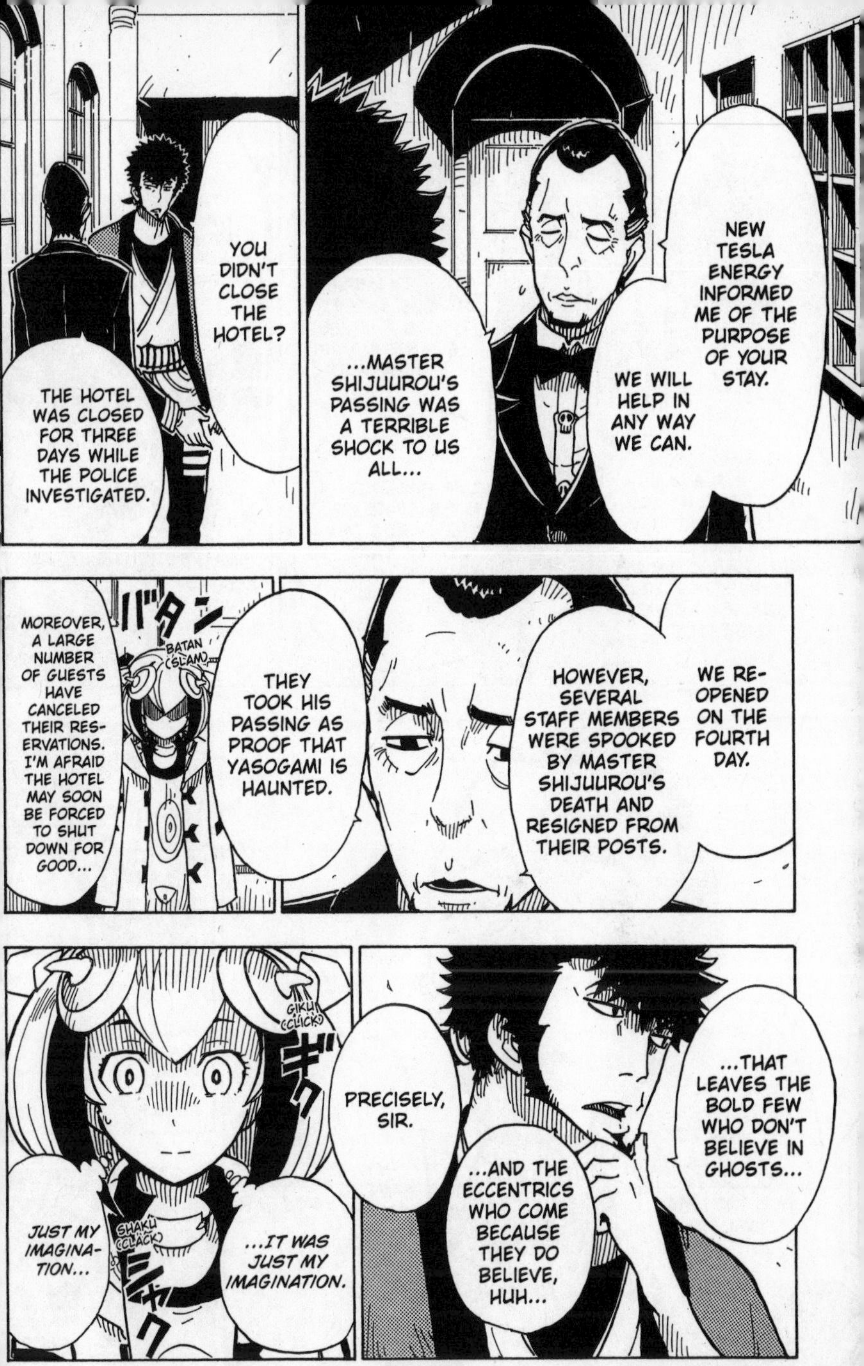
NEW TESLA ENERGY INFORMED ME OF THE PURPOSE OF YOUR STAY.
WE WILL HELP IN ANY WAY WE CAN.
...MASTER SHIJUUROU'S PASSING WAS A TERRIBLE SHOCK TO US ALL...
YOU DIDN'T CLOSE THE HOTEL?
THE HOTEL WAS CLOSED FOR THREE DAYS WHILE THE POLICE INVESTIGATED.
WE RE-OPENED ON THE FOURTH DAY.
HOWEVER, SEVERAL STAFF MEMBERS WERE SPOOKED BY MASTER SHIJUUROU'S DEATH AND RESIGNED FROM THEIR POSTS.
THEY TOOK HIS PASSING AS PROOF THAT YASOGAMI IS HAUNTED.
バタン
BATAN (SLAM)
MOREOVER, A LARGE NUMBER OF GUESTS HAVE CANCELED THEIR RES-ERVATIONS. I'M AFRAID THE HOTEL MAY SOON BE FORCED TO SHUT DOWN FOR GOOD...
...THAT LEAVES THE BOLD FEW WHO DON'T BELIEVE IN GHOSTS...
...AND THE ECCENTRICS WHO COME BECAUSE THEY DO BELIEVE, HUH...
PRECISELY, SIR.
GIKU (CLICK)
ギク
...IT WAS JUST MY IMAGINATION.
SHAKU (CLACK)
シャク
JUST MY IMAGINA-TION...

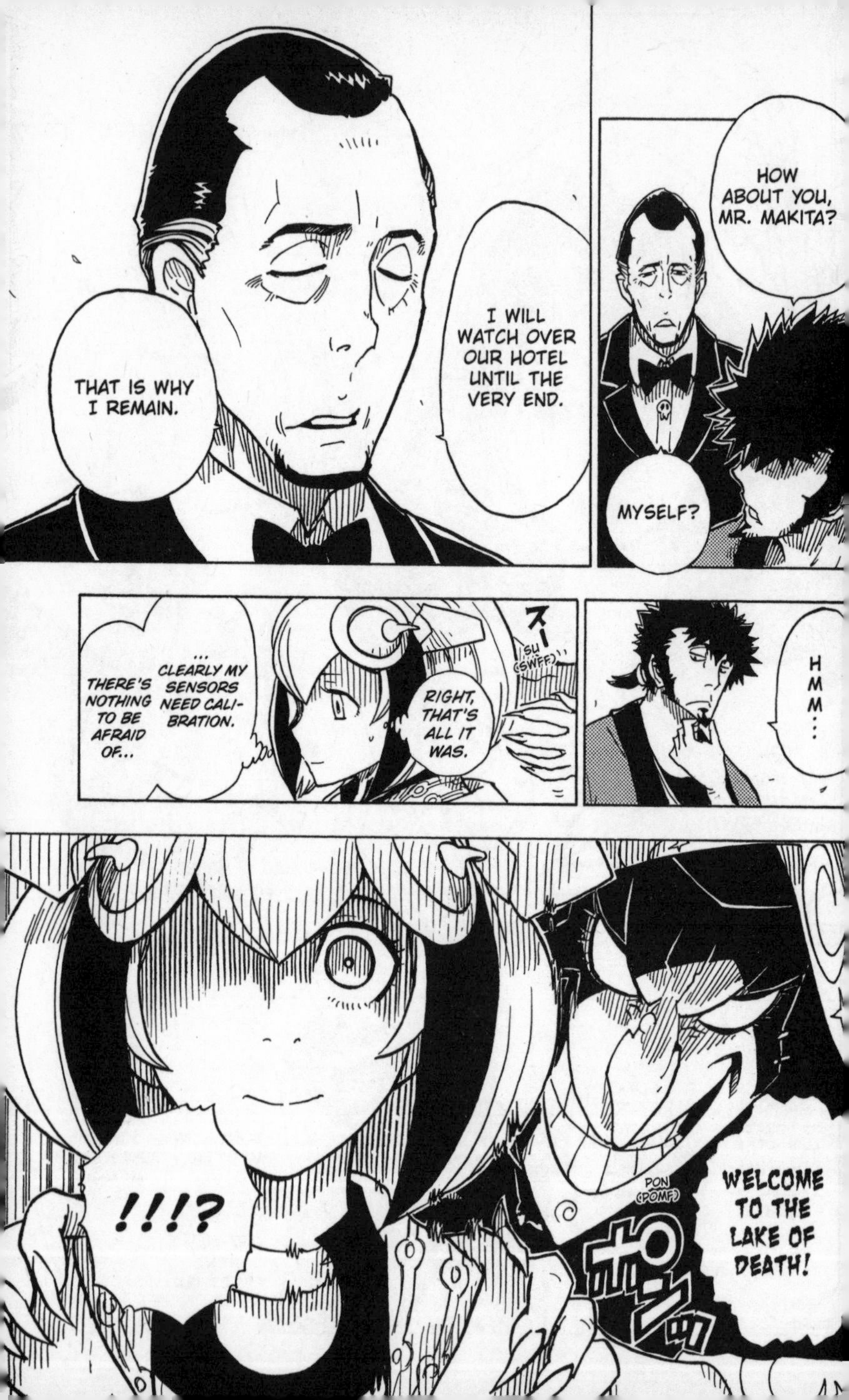
HOW ABOUT YOU, MR. MAKITA?
MYSELF?
I WILL WATCH OVER OUR HOTEL UNTIL THE VERY END.
THAT IS WHY I REMAIN.
HMM...
スー SU (SWFF)
RIGHT, THAT'S ALL IT WAS.
...CLEARLY MY SENSORS NEED CALIBRATION.
THERE'S NOTHING TO BE AFRAID OF...
WELCOME TO THE LAKE OF DEATH!
PON (POMF)
!!!?

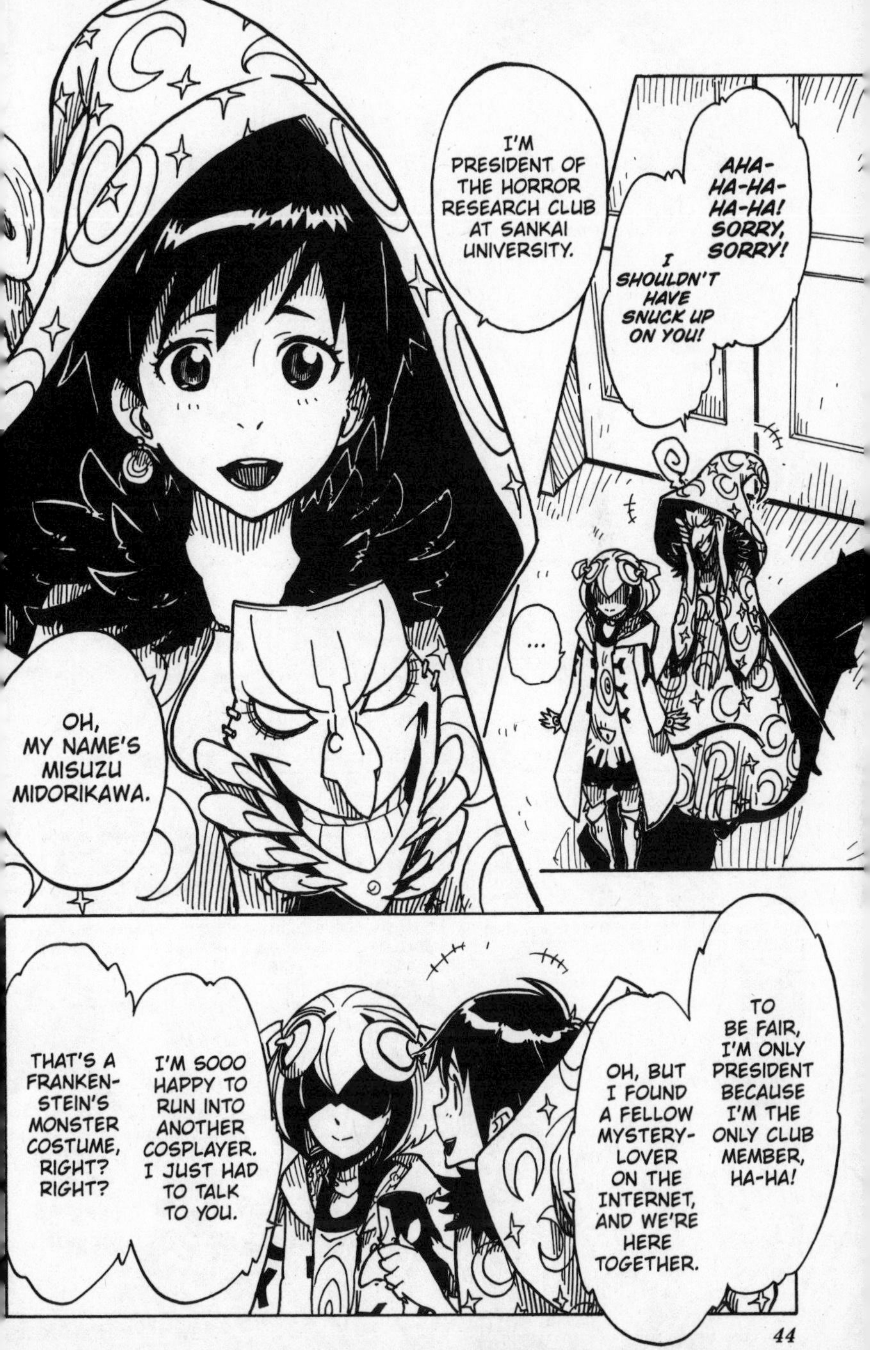
AHA-HA-HA-HA-HA! SORRY, SORRY!
I SHOULDN'T HAVE SNUCK UP ON YOU!
...
I'M PRESIDENT OF THE HORROR RESEARCH CLUB AT SANKAI UNIVERSITY.
OH, MY NAME'S MISUZU MIDORIKAWA.
TO BE FAIR, I'M ONLY PRESIDENT BECAUSE I'M THE ONLY CLUB MEMBER, HA-HA!
OH, BUT I FOUND A FELLOW MYSTERY-LOVER ON THE INTERNET, AND WE'RE HERE TOGETHER.
I'M SOOO HAPPY TO RUN INTO ANOTHER COSPLAYER. I JUST HAD TO TALK TO YOU.
THAT'S A FRANKEN-STEIN'S MONSTER COSTUME, RIGHT? RIGHT?

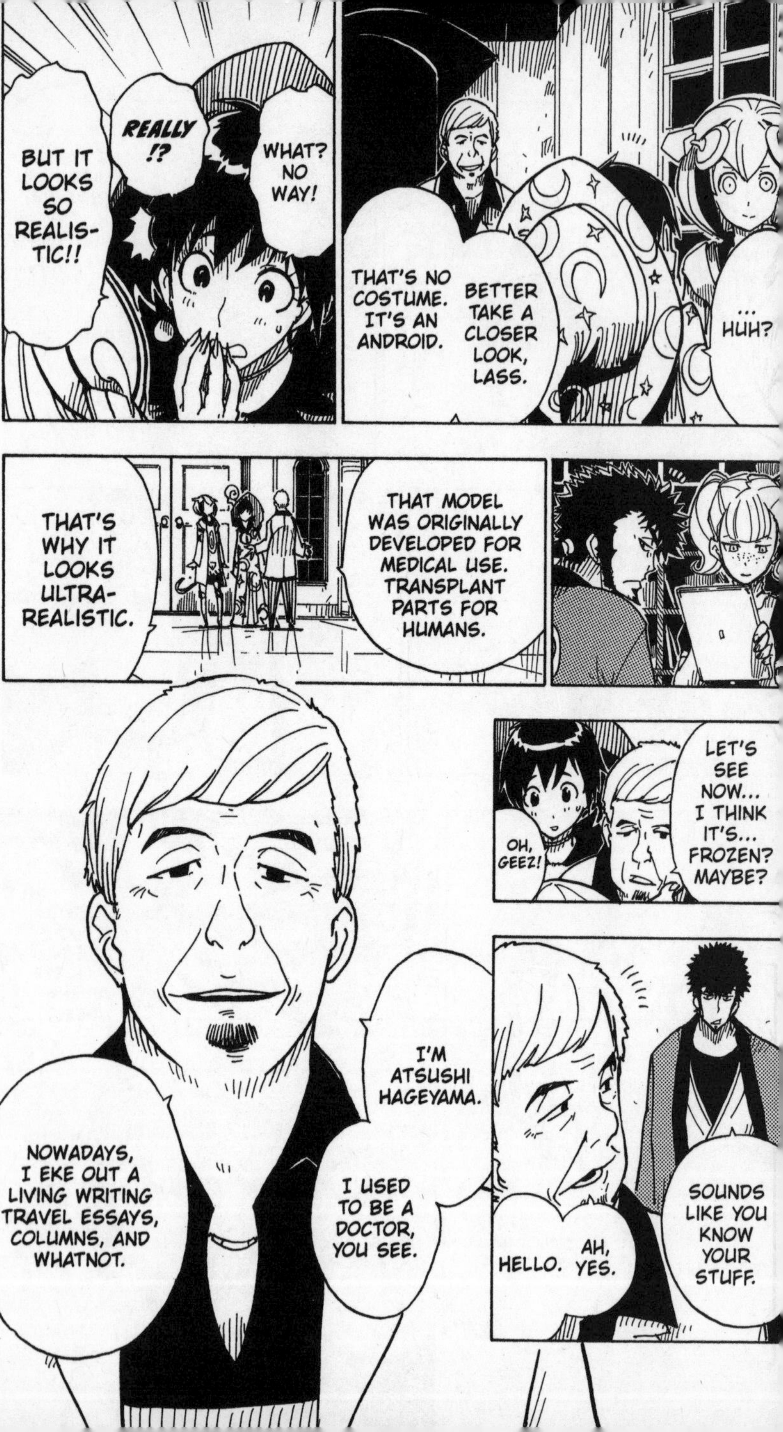
...HUH?
BETTER TAKE A CLOSER LOOK, LASS.
THAT'S NO COSTUME. IT'S AN ANDROID.
WHAT? NO WAY!
REALLY!?
BUT IT LOOKS SO REALISTIC!!
THAT MODEL WAS ORIGINALLY DEVELOPED FOR MEDICAL USE. TRANSPLANT PARTS FOR HUMANS.
THAT'S WHY IT LOOKS ULTRA-REALISTIC.
LET'S SEE NOW... I THINK IT'S... FROZEN? MAYBE?
OH, GEEZ!
SOUNDS LIKE YOU KNOW YOUR STUFF.
AH, YES.
HELLO.
I'M ATSUSHI HAGEYAMA.
I USED TO BE A DOCTOR, YOU SEE.
NOWADAYS, I EKE OUT A LIVING WRITING TRAVEL ESSAYS, COLUMNS, AND WHATNOT.

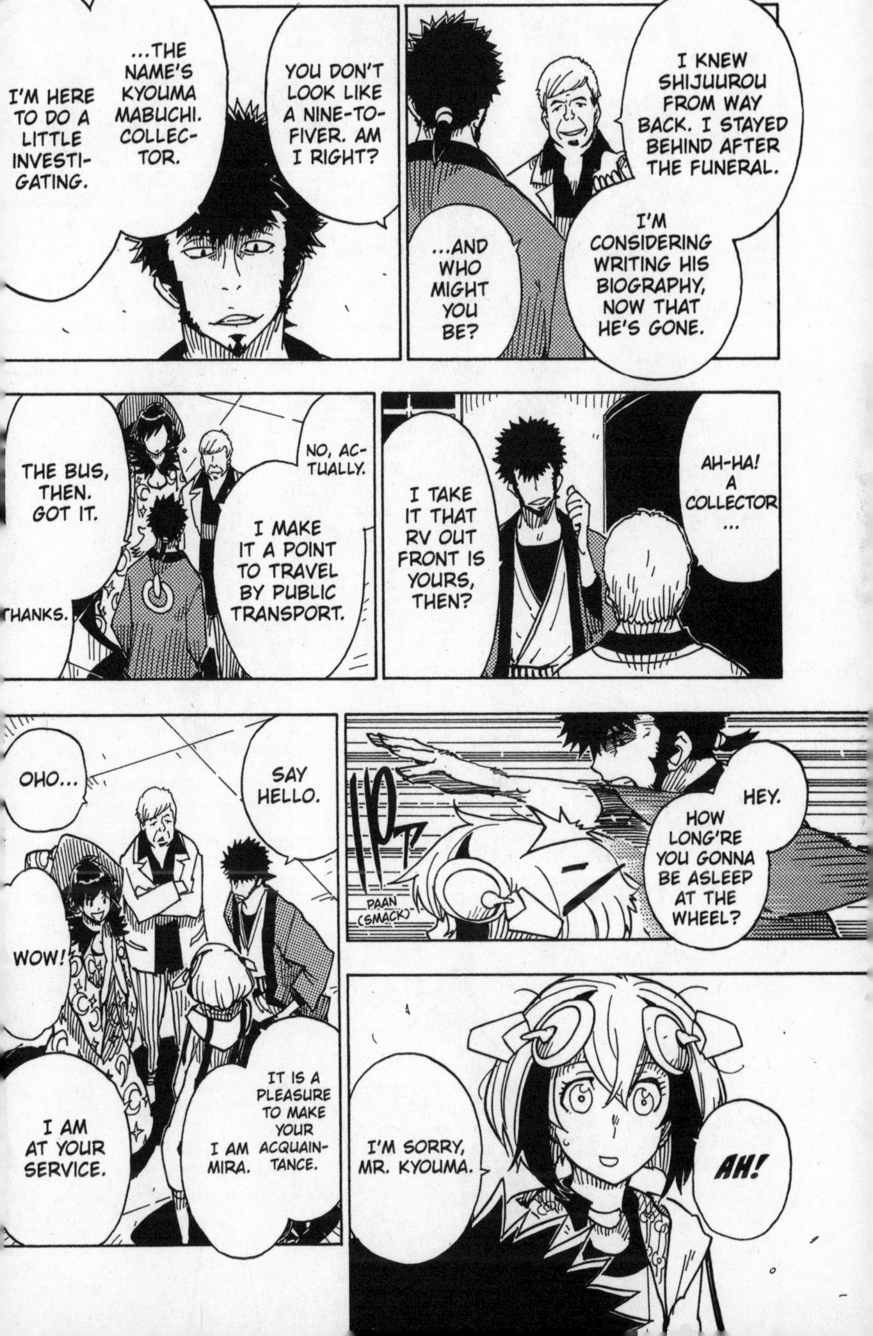
I KNEW SHIJUUROU FROM WAY BACK. I STAYED BEHIND AFTER THE FUNERAL.
I'M CONSIDERING WRITING HIS BIOGRAPHY, NOW THAT HE'S GONE.
...AND WHO MIGHT YOU BE?
YOU DON'T LOOK LIKE A NINE-TO-FIVER. AM I RIGHT?
...THE NAME'S KYOUMA MABUCHI. COLLECTOR.
I'M HERE TO DO A LITTLE INVESTIGATING.
AH-HA! A COLLECTOR...
I TAKE IT THAT RV OUT FRONT IS YOURS, THEN?
NO, ACTUALLY.
I MAKE IT A POINT TO TRAVEL BY PUBLIC TRANSPORT.
THE BUS, THEN. GOT IT.
THANKS.
HEY. HOW LONG'RE YOU GONNA BE ASLEEP AT THE WHEEL?
PAAN (SMACK)
AH!
I'M SORRY, MR. KYOUMA.
SAY HELLO.
OHO...
WOW!
IT IS A PLEASURE TO MAKE YOUR ACQUAINTANCE.
I AM MIRA.
I AM AT YOUR SERVICE.

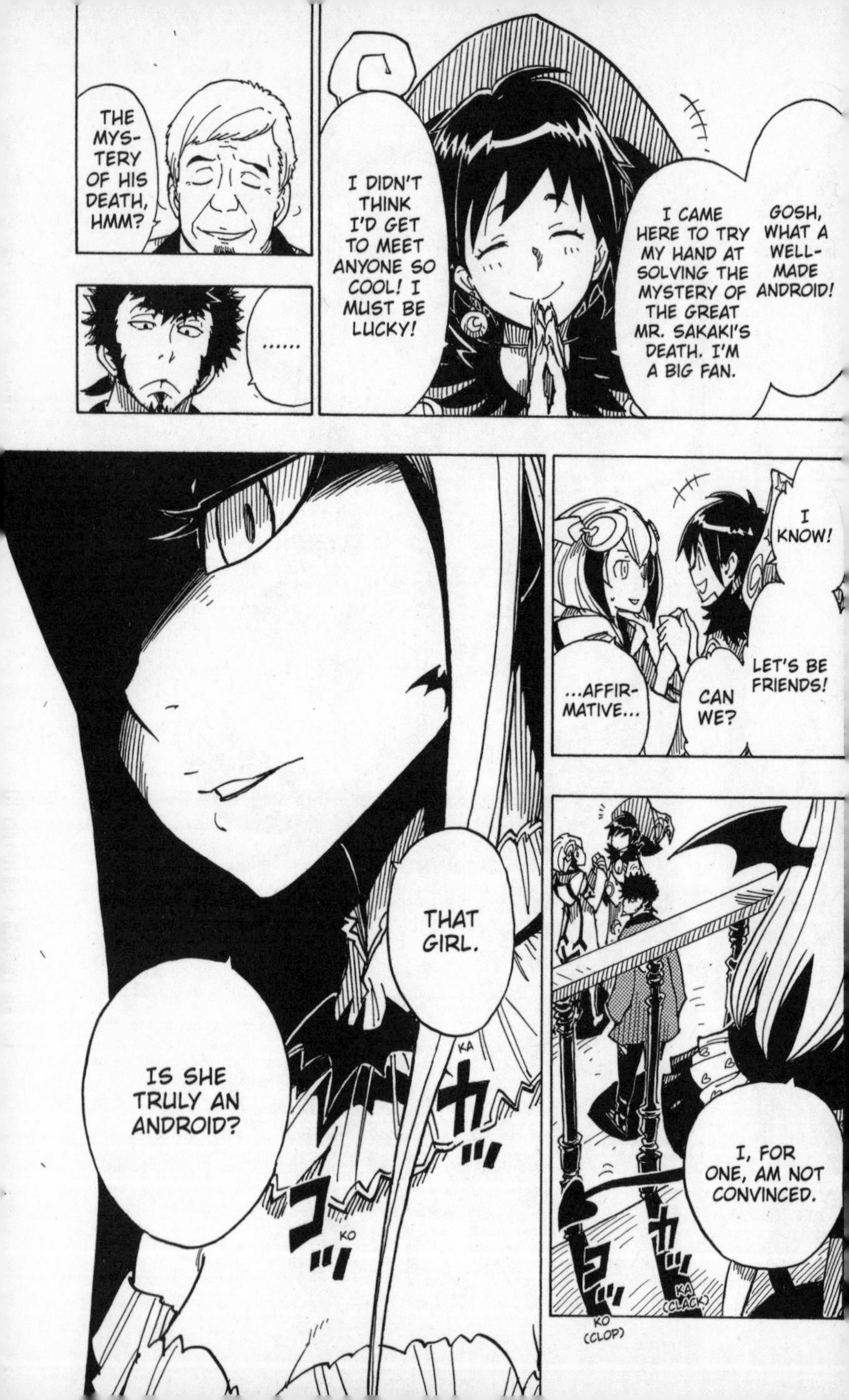
GOSH, WHAT A WELL-MADE ANDROID!
I CAME HERE TO TRY MY HAND AT SOLVING THE MYSTERY OF THE GREAT MR. SAKAKI'S DEATH. I'M A BIG FAN.
I DIDN'T THINK I'D GET TO MEET ANYONE SO COOL! I MUST BE LUCKY!
THE MYS-TERY OF HIS DEATH, HMM?
......
I KNOW!
LET'S BE FRIENDS!
CAN WE?
...AFFIR-MATIVE...
I, FOR ONE, AM NOT CONVINCED.
KA (CLACK)
KO (CLOP)
THAT GIRL.
IS SHE TRULY AN ANDROID?
KA
KO

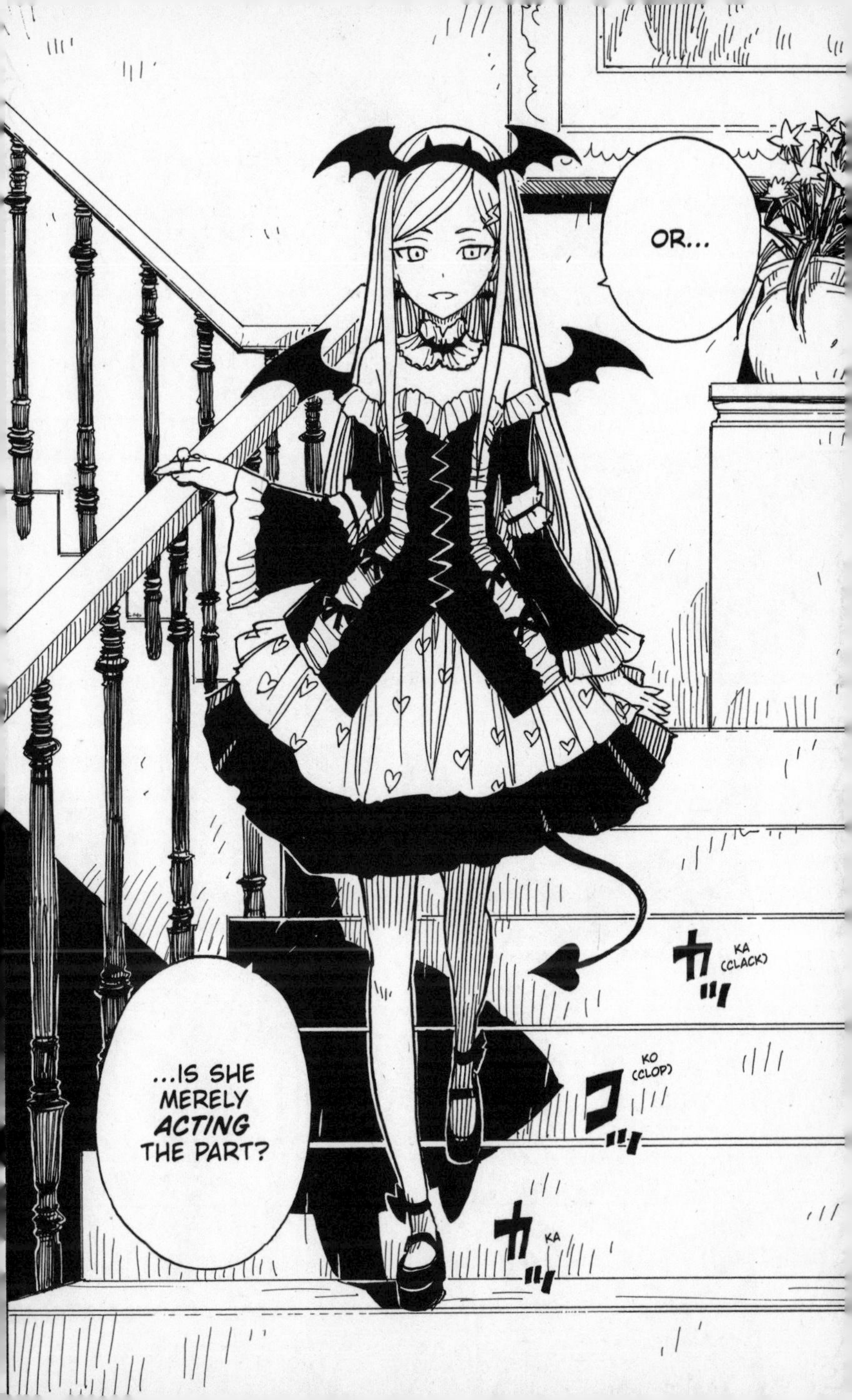
OR...
カッ KA (CLACK)
コッ KO (CLOP)
カッ KA
...IS SHE MERELY *ACTING* THE PART?

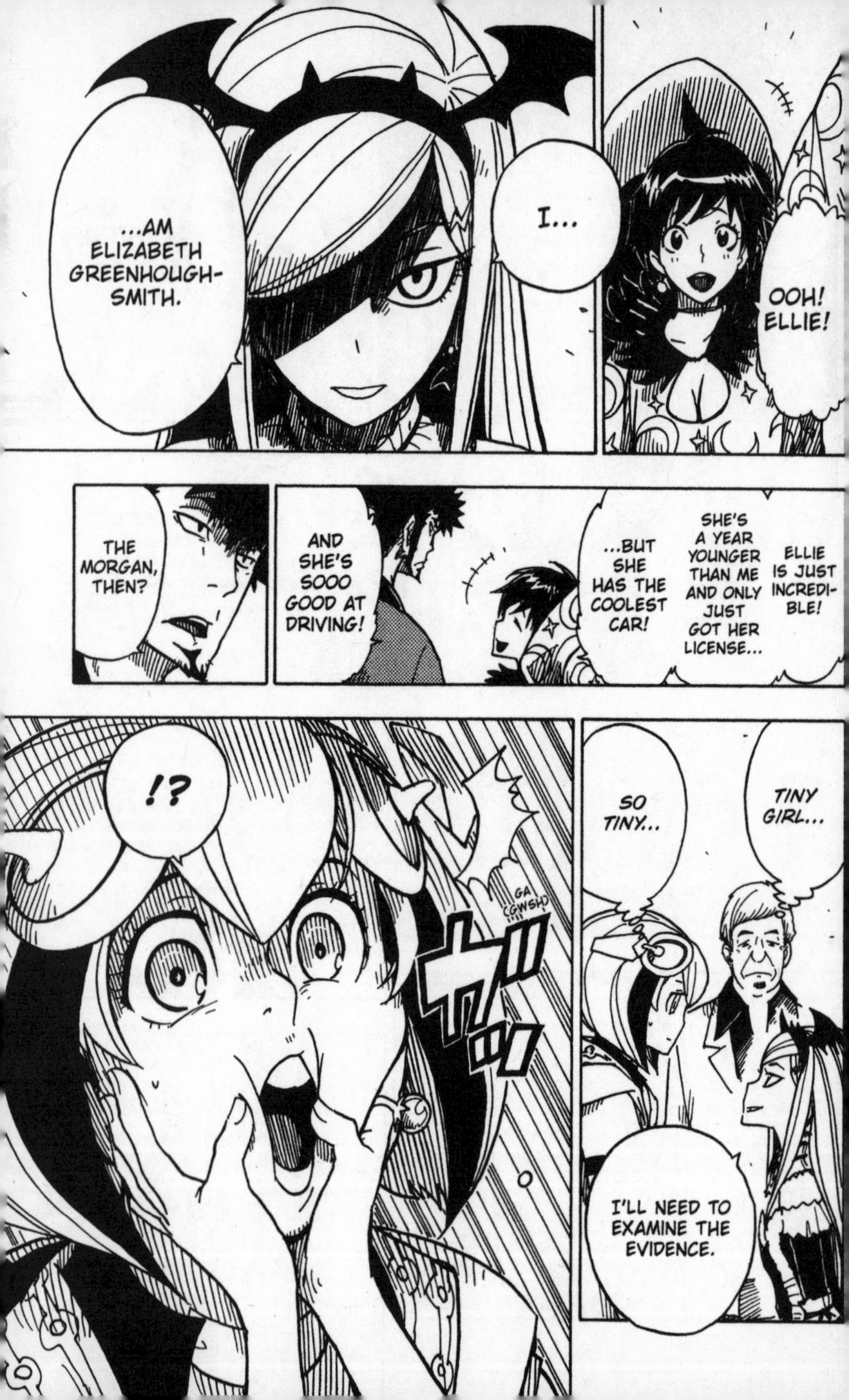
OOH! ELLIE!
I...
...AM ELIZABETH GREENHOUGH-SMITH.
ELLIE IS JUST INCREDIBLE!
SHE'S A YEAR YOUNGER THAN ME AND ONLY JUST GOT HER LICENSE...
...BUT SHE HAS THE COOLEST CAR!
AND SHE'S SOOO GOOD AT DRIVING!
THE MORGAN, THEN?
TINY GIRL...
SO TINY...
I'LL NEED TO EXAMINE THE EVIDENCE.
!?
GA (GWSH)

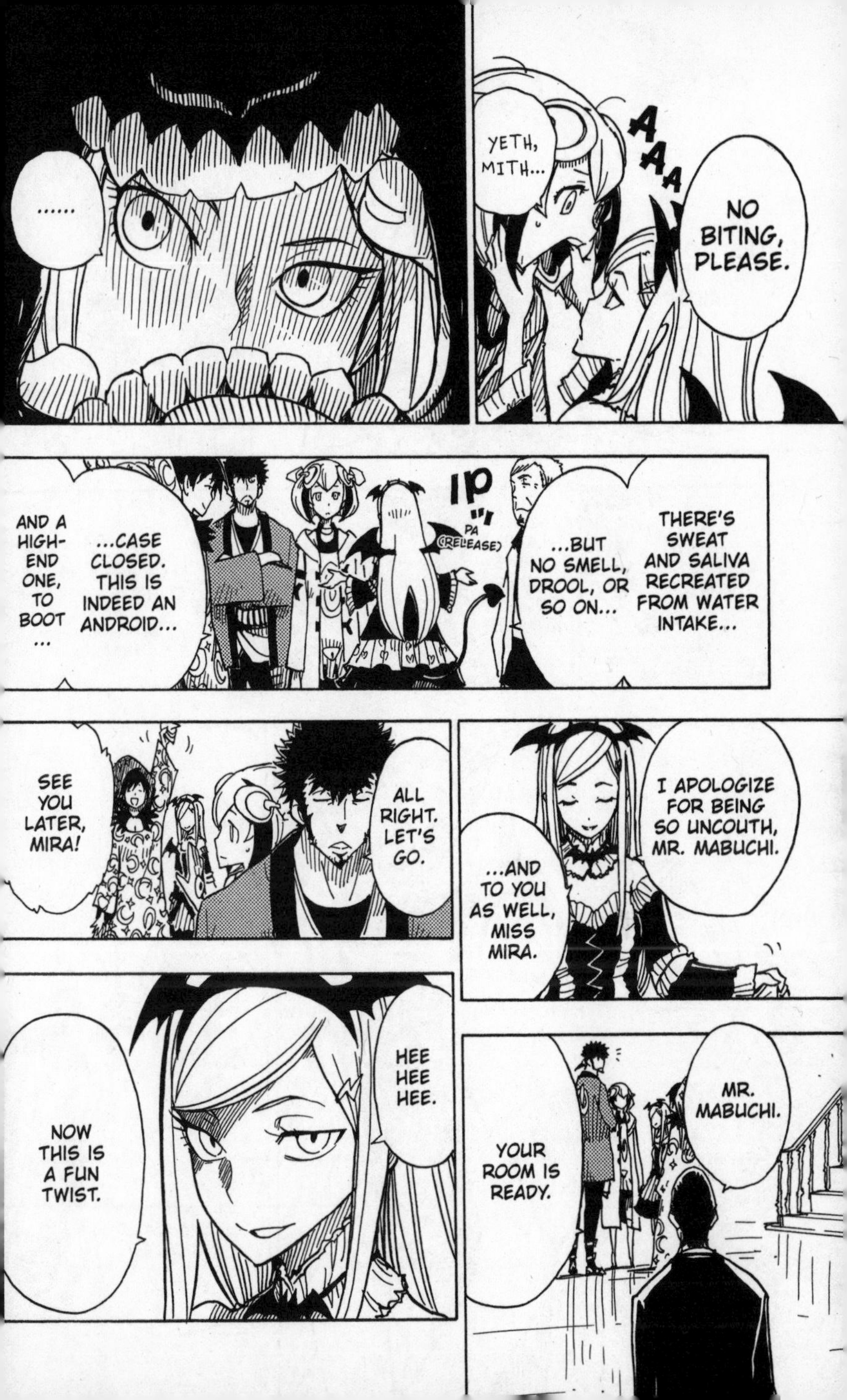
NO BITING, PLEASE.
AAA
YETH, MITH...
......
THERE'S SWEAT AND SALIVA RECREATED FROM WATER INTAKE...
...BUT NO SMELL, DROOL, OR SO ON...
PA (RELEASE)
...CASE CLOSED. THIS IS INDEED AN ANDROID...
AND A HIGH-END ONE, TO BOOT ...
I APOLOGIZE FOR BEING SO UNCOUTH, MR. MABUCHI.
...AND TO YOU AS WELL, MISS MIRA.
ALL RIGHT. LET'S GO.
SEE YOU LATER, MIRA!
MR. MABUCHI.
YOUR ROOM IS READY.
HEE HEE HEE.
NOW THIS IS A FUN TWIST.

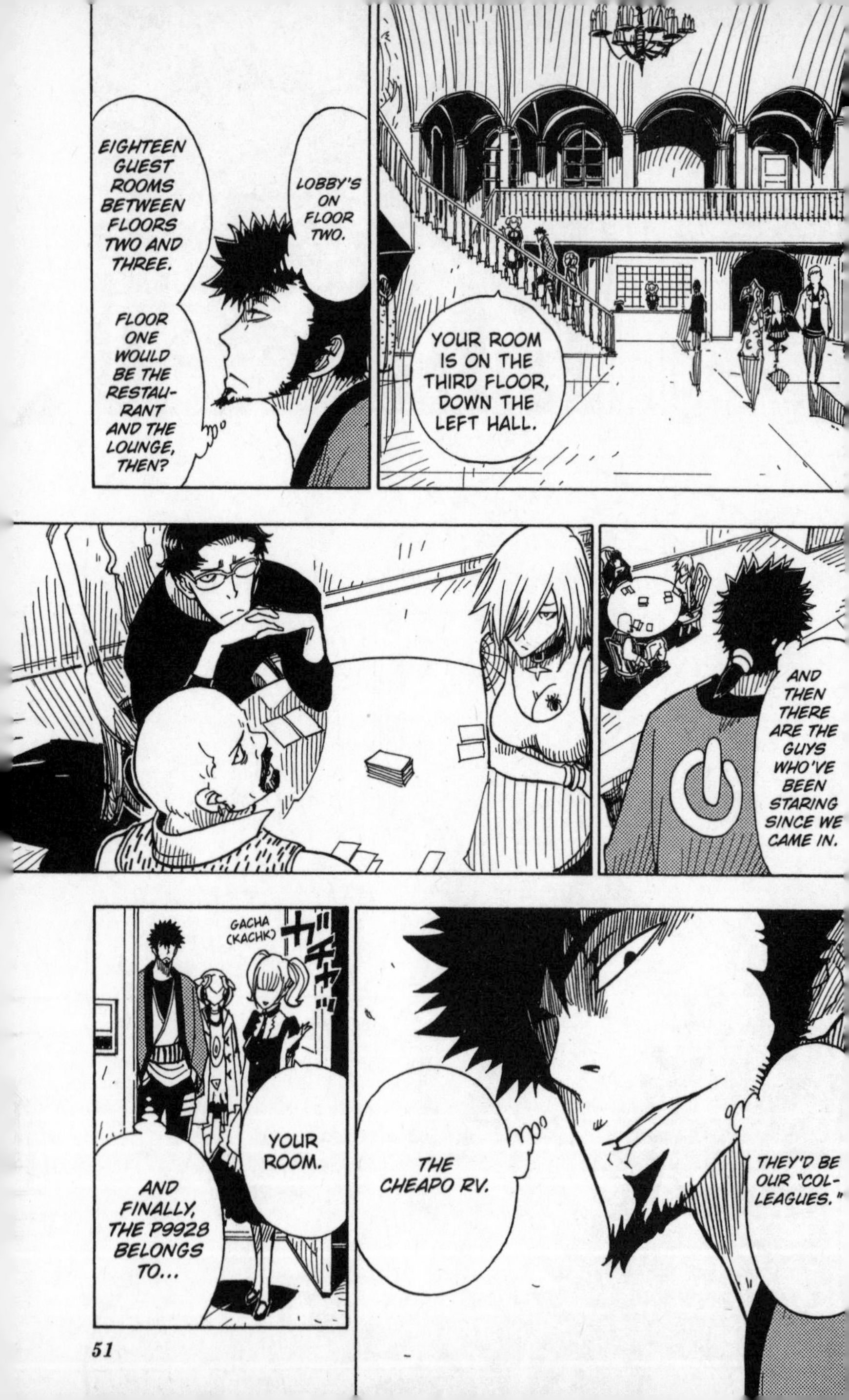
YOUR ROOM IS ON THE THIRD FLOOR, DOWN THE LEFT HALL.
LOBBY'S ON FLOOR TWO.
EIGHTEEN GUEST ROOMS BETWEEN FLOORS TWO AND THREE.
FLOOR ONE WOULD BE THE RESTAURANT AND THE LOUNGE, THEN?
AND THEN THERE ARE THE GUYS WHO'VE BEEN STARING SINCE WE CAME IN.
THEY'D BE OUR "COLLEAGUES."
THE CHEAPO RV.
GACHA (KACHK)
YOUR ROOM.
AND FINALLY, THE P9928 BELONGS TO...

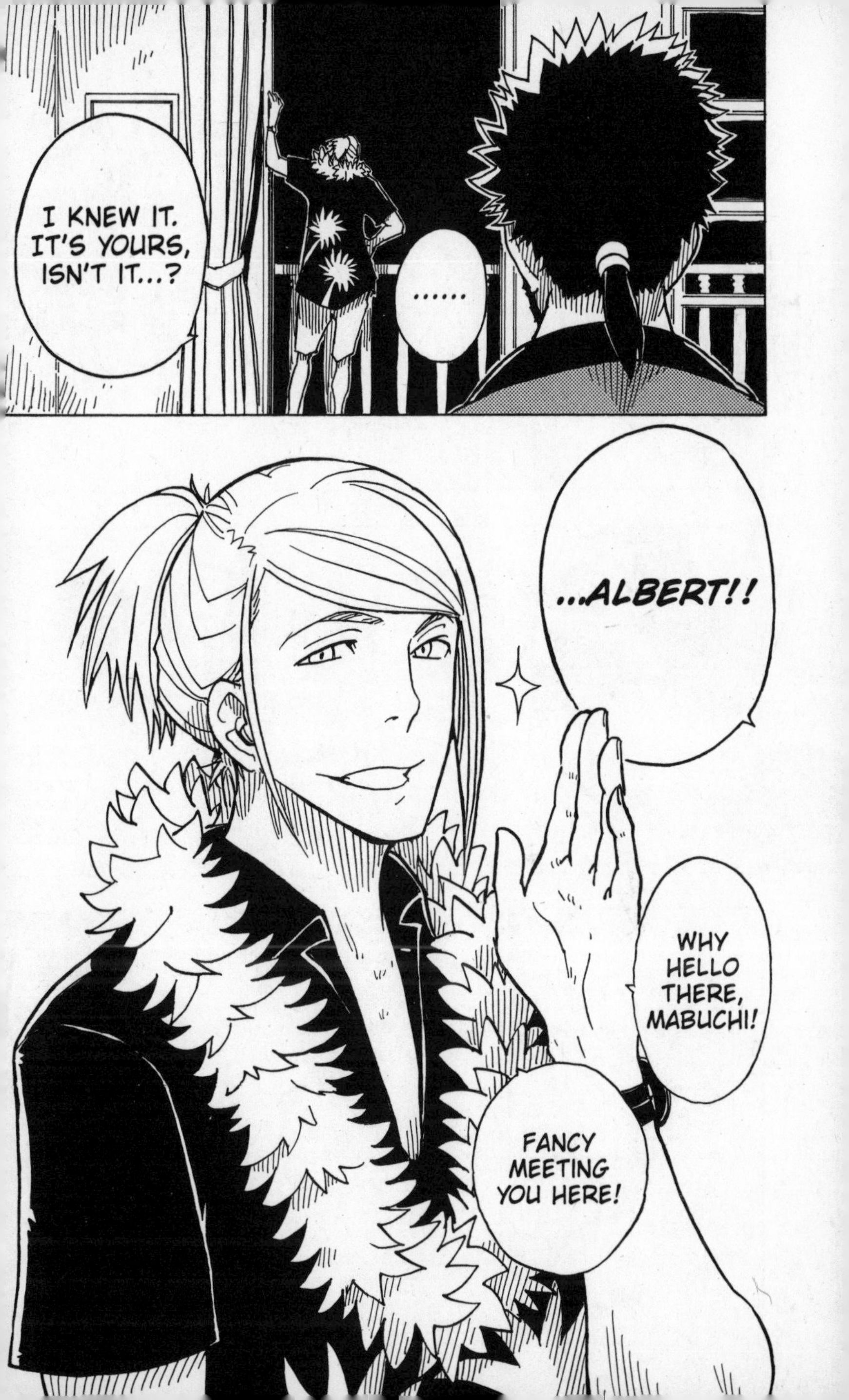
......
I KNEW IT. IT'S YOURS, ISN'T IT...?
...ALBERT!!
WHY HELLO THERE, MABUCHI!
FANCY MEETING YOU HERE!

FILE.18
OLD FRIENDS

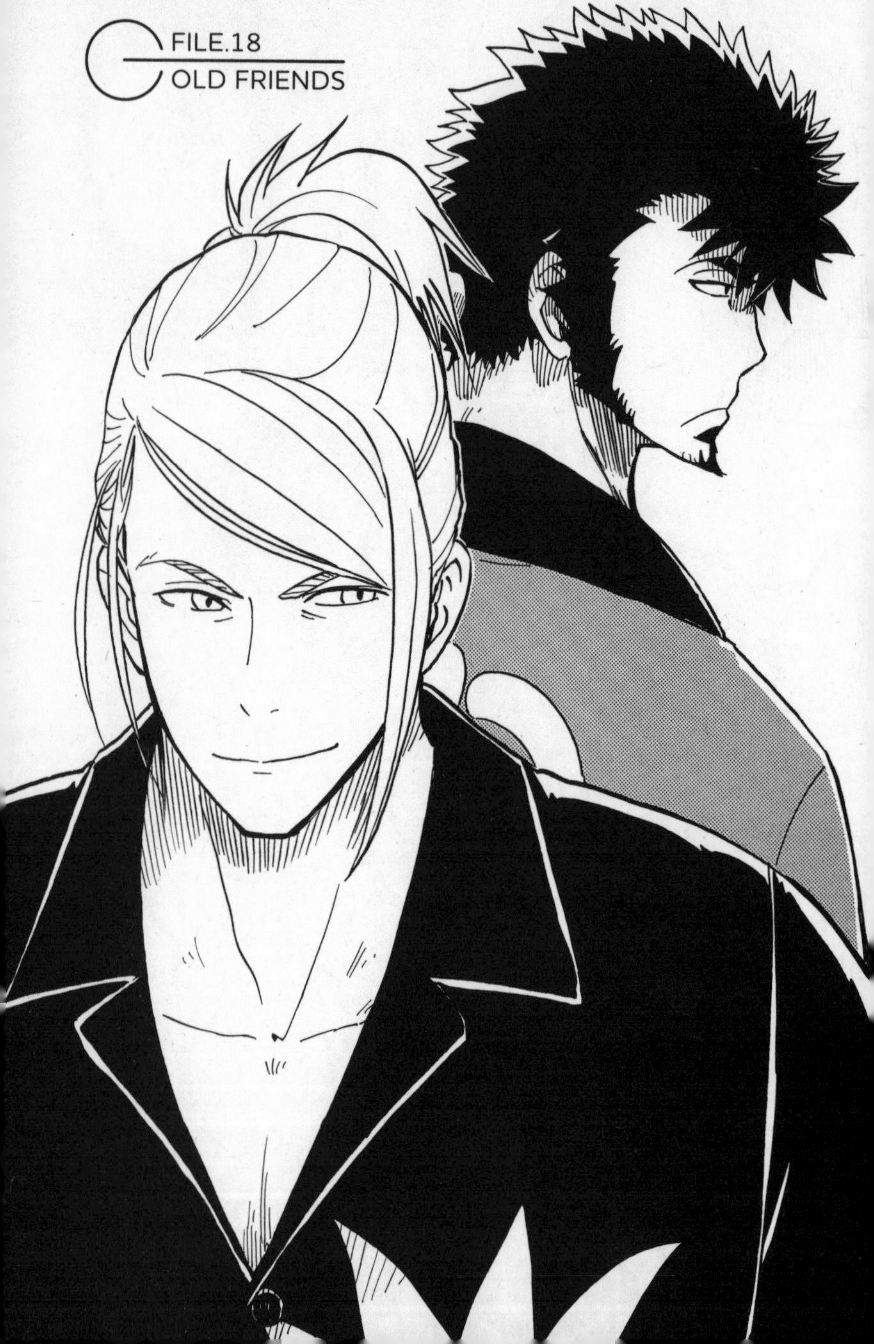

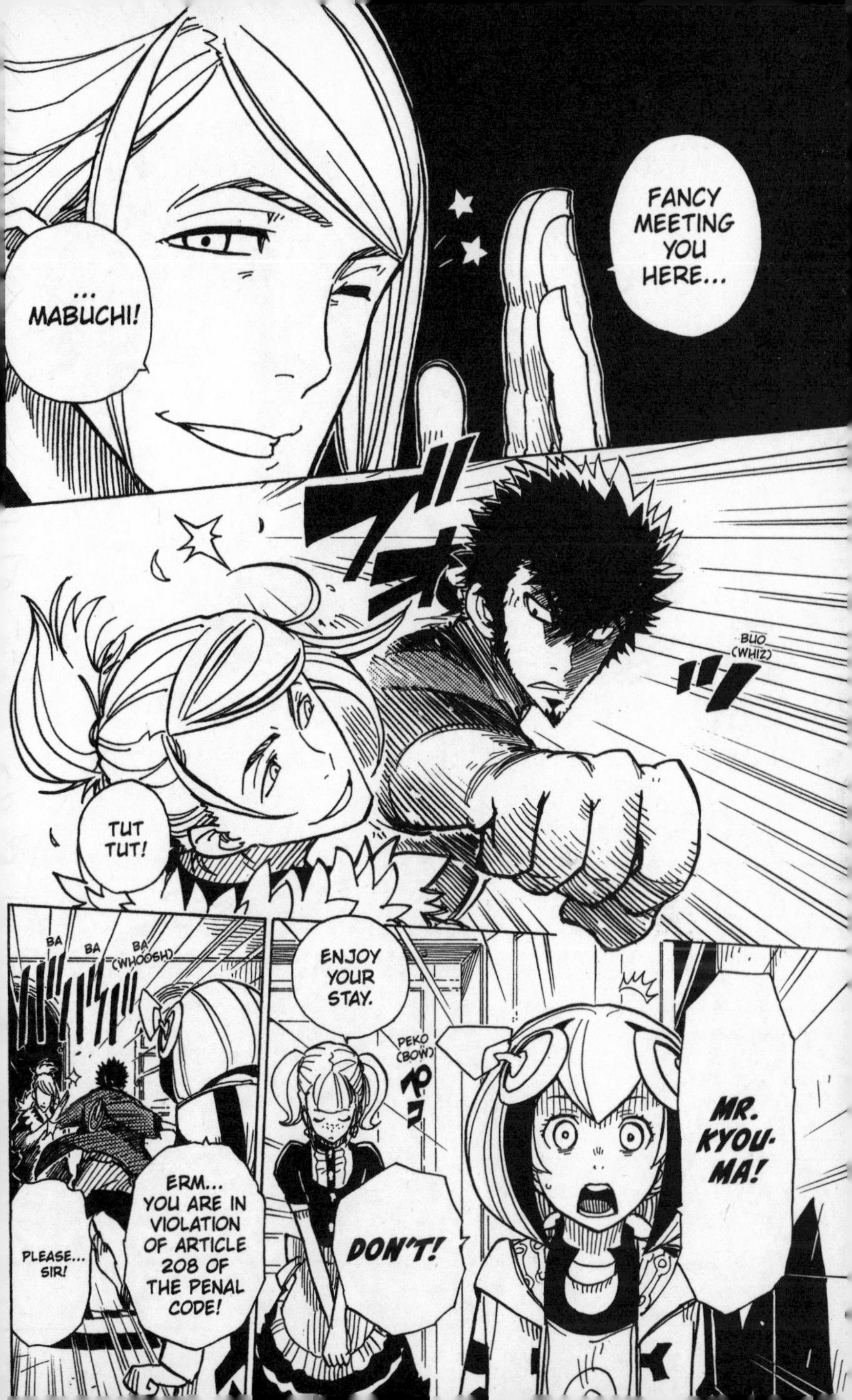
FANCY MEETING YOU HERE...
...MABUCHI!
BUO (WHIZ)
TUT TUT!
MR. KYOU-MA!
DON'T!
ENJOY YOUR STAY.
PEKO (BOW)
BA BA BA (WHOOSH)
ERM... YOU ARE IN VIOLATION OF ARTICLE 208 OF THE PENAL CODE!
PLEASE... SIR!

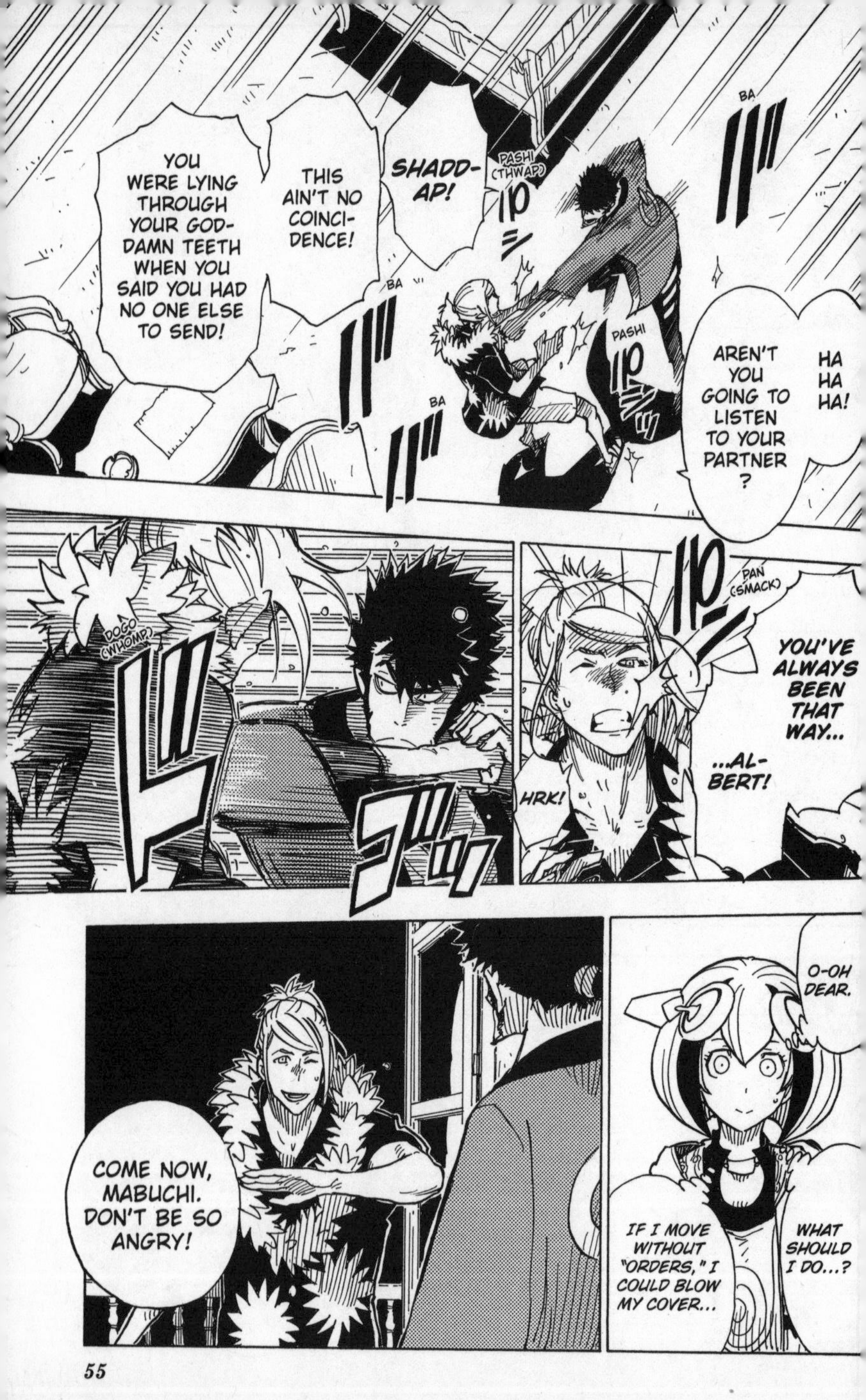
HA HA HA!
AREN'T YOU GOING TO LISTEN TO YOUR PARTNER?
BA
PASHI (THWAP)
SHADD-AP!
THIS AIN'T NO COINCIDENCE!
YOU WERE LYING THROUGH YOUR GOD-DAMN TEETH WHEN YOU SAID YOU HAD NO ONE ELSE TO SEND!
PASHI
BA
BA
PAN (SMACK)
YOU'VE ALWAYS BEEN THAT WAY...
...AL-BERT!
HRK!
DOGO (WHOMP)
O-OH DEAR.
WHAT SHOULD I DO...?
IF I MOVE WITHOUT "ORDERS," I COULD BLOW MY COVER...
COME NOW, MABUCHI. DON'T BE SO ANGRY!

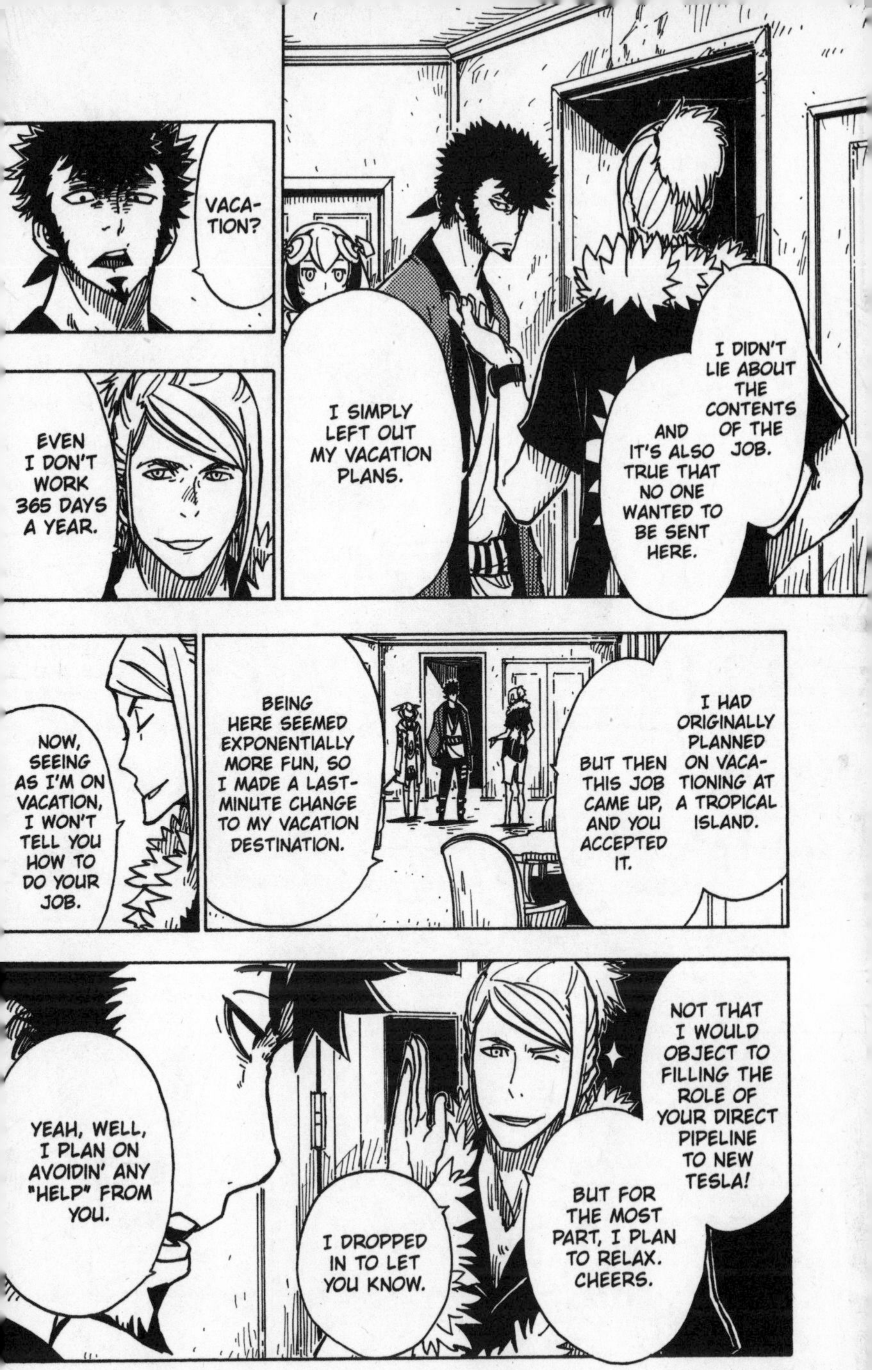

I DIDN'T LIE ABOUT THE CONTENTS OF THE JOB.
AND IT'S ALSO TRUE THAT NO ONE WANTED TO BE SENT HERE.
I SIMPLY LEFT OUT MY VACATION PLANS.
VACA-TION?
EVEN I DON'T WORK 365 DAYS A YEAR.
I HAD ORIGINALLY PLANNED ON VACA-TIONING AT A TROPICAL ISLAND.
BUT THEN THIS JOB CAME UP, AND YOU ACCEPTED IT.
BEING HERE SEEMED EXPONENTIALLY MORE FUN, SO I MADE A LAST-MINUTE CHANGE TO MY VACATION DESTINATION.
NOW, SEEING AS I'M ON VACATION, I WON'T TELL YOU HOW TO DO YOUR JOB.
NOT THAT I WOULD OBJECT TO FILLING THE ROLE OF YOUR DIRECT PIPELINE TO NEW TESLA!
BUT FOR THE MOST PART, I PLAN TO RELAX. CHEERS.
I DROPPED IN TO LET YOU KNOW.
YEAH, WELL, I PLAN ON AVOIDIN' ANY "HELP" FROM YOU.

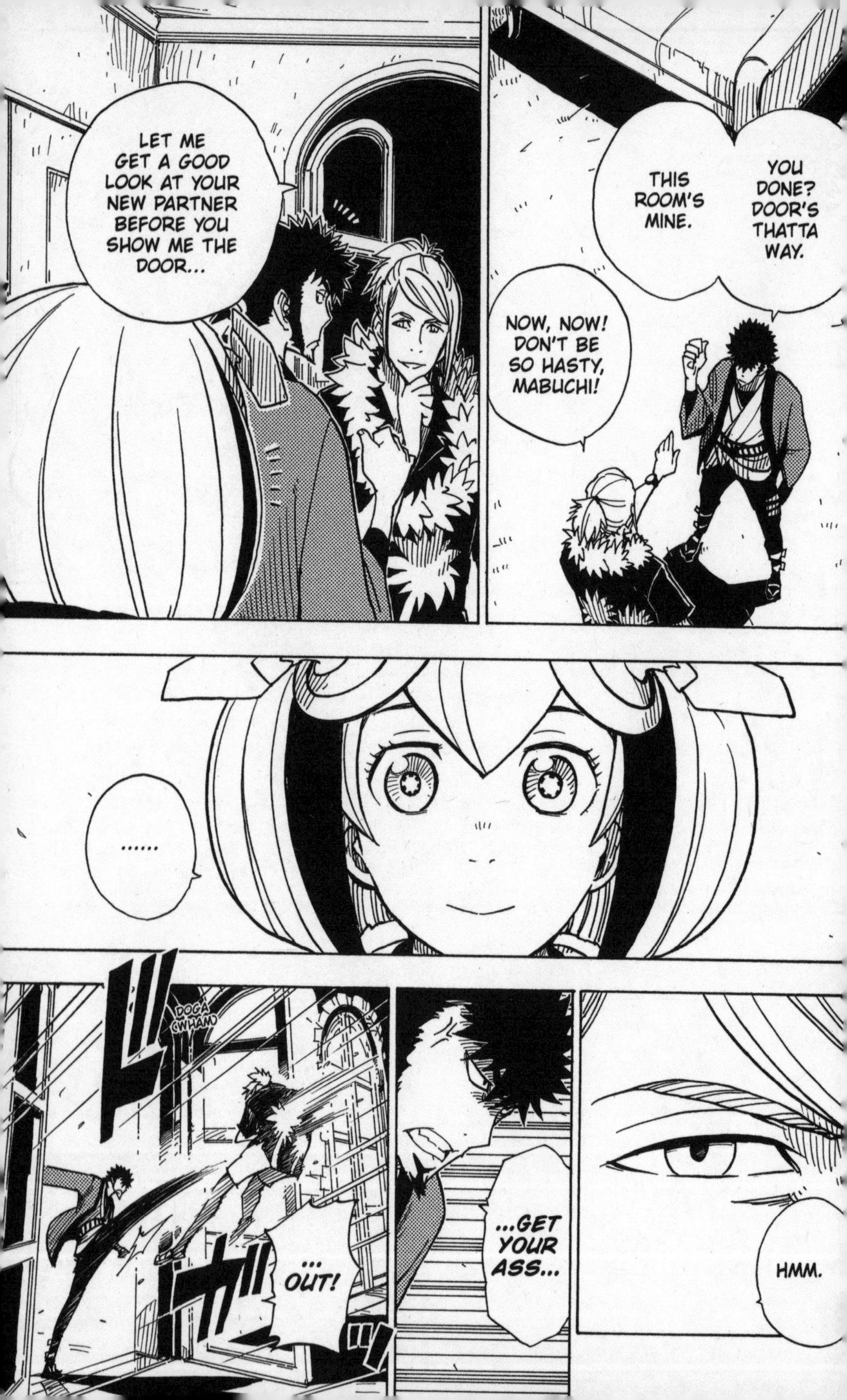
YOU DONE? DOOR'S THATTA WAY.
THIS ROOM'S MINE.
NOW, NOW! DON'T BE SO HASTY, MABUCHI!
LET ME GET A GOOD LOOK AT YOUR NEW PARTNER BEFORE YOU SHOW ME THE DOOR...
......
HMM.
...GET YOUR ASS...
...OUT!
DOGA (WHAM)

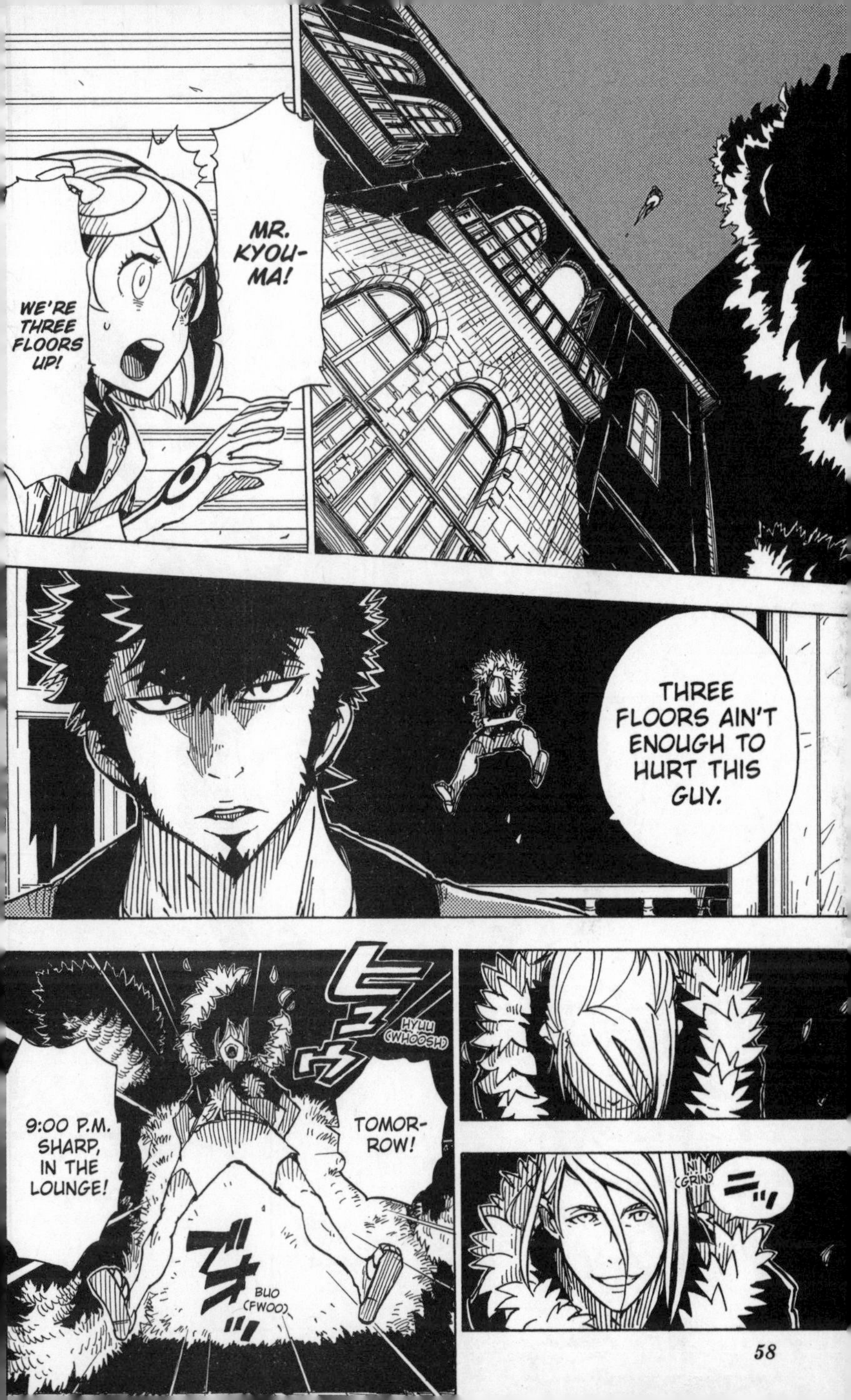
MR. KYOU-MA!
WE'RE THREE FLOORS UP!
THREE FLOORS AIN'T ENOUGH TO HURT THIS GUY.
NI (GRIN)
HYUU (WHOOSH)
TOMOR-ROW!
9:00 P.M. SHARP, IN THE LOUNGE!
BUO (FWOO)

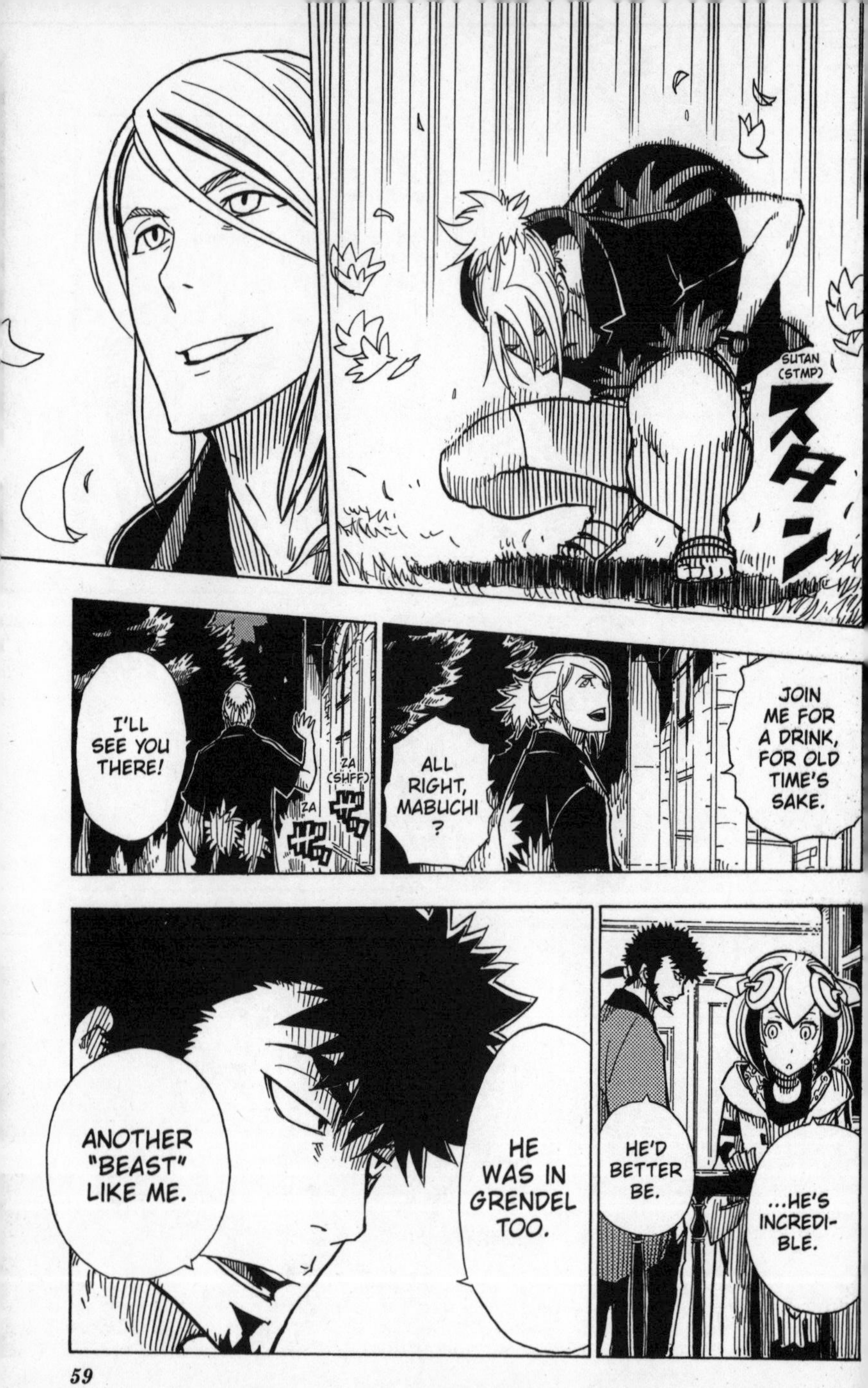
SUTAN (STMP)
スタン
JOIN ME FOR A DRINK, FOR OLD TIME'S SAKE.
ALL RIGHT, MABUCHI?
ZA (SHFF)
ZA
I'LL SEE YOU THERE!
...HE'S INCREDI-BLE.
HE'D BETTER BE.
HE WAS IN GRENDEL TOO.
ANOTHER "BEAST" LIKE ME.

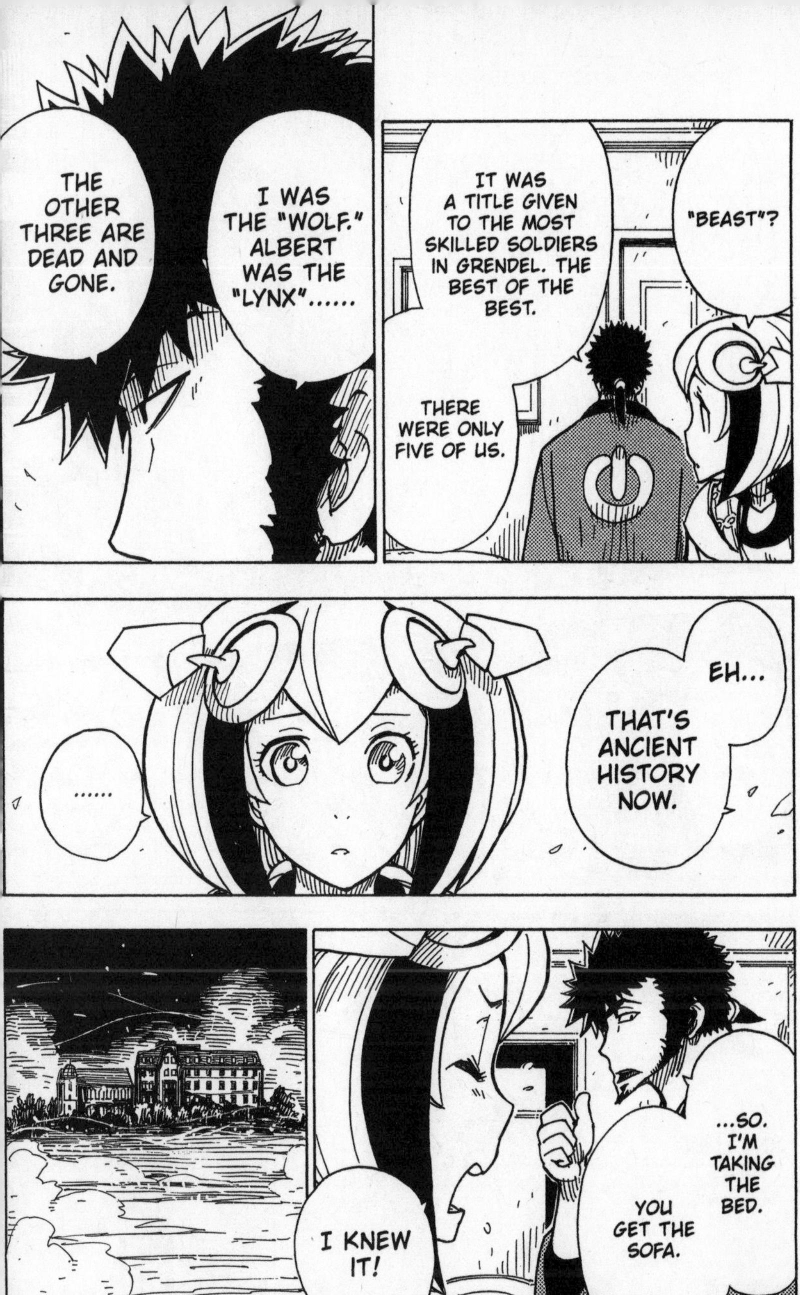
"BEAST"?
IT WAS A TITLE GIVEN TO THE MOST SKILLED SOLDIERS IN GRENDEL. THE BEST OF THE BEST.
THERE WERE ONLY FIVE OF US.
I WAS THE "WOLF." ALBERT WAS THE "LYNX"......
THE OTHER THREE ARE DEAD AND GONE.
EH...
THAT'S ANCIENT HISTORY NOW.
......
...SO. I'M TAKING THE BED.
YOU GET THE SOFA.
I KNEW IT!

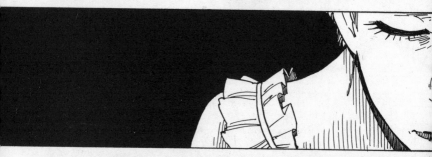

...BIG BROTHER...

I'M SORRY...

61

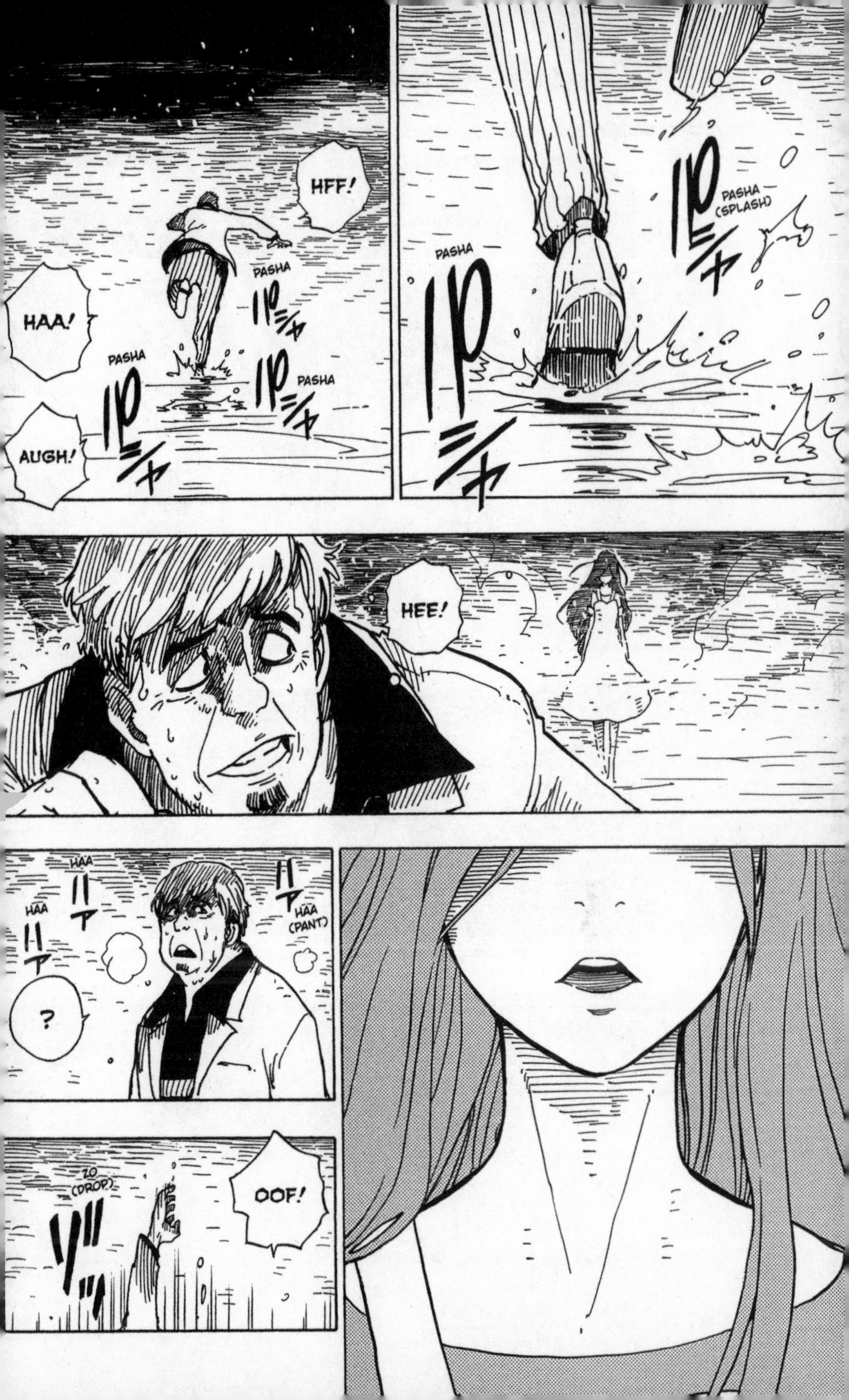
PASHA (SPLASH)
PASHA
HFF!
HAA!
PASHA
PASHA
PASHA
AUGH!
HEE!
HAA
HAA (PANT)
HAA
?
OOF!
ZO (DROP)

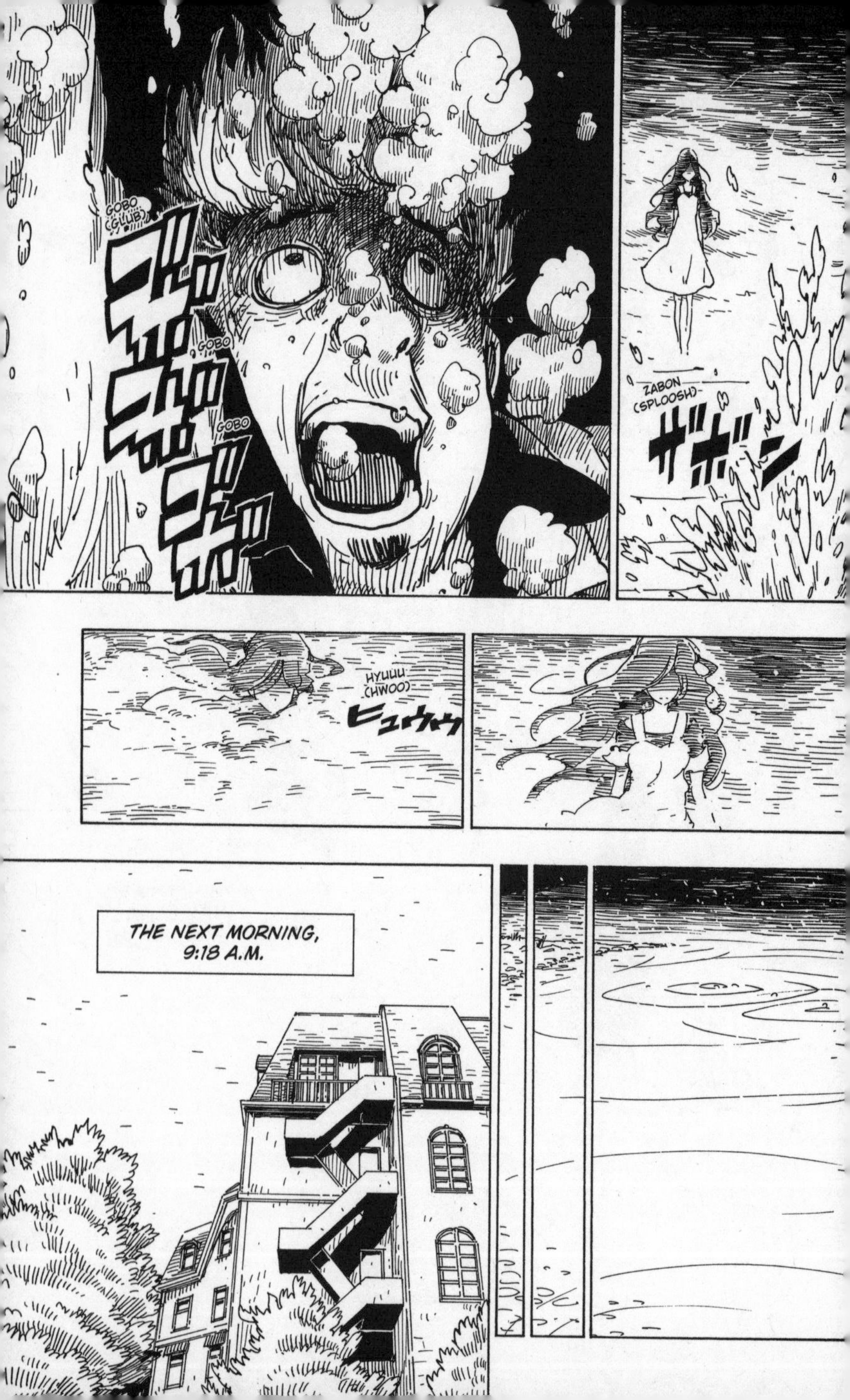
ZABON (SPLOOSH)
ザボン
GOBO... (GLUB)
GOBO
GOBO
HYUUU (HWOO)
ヒュウウウ
THE NEXT MORNING, 9:18 A.M.

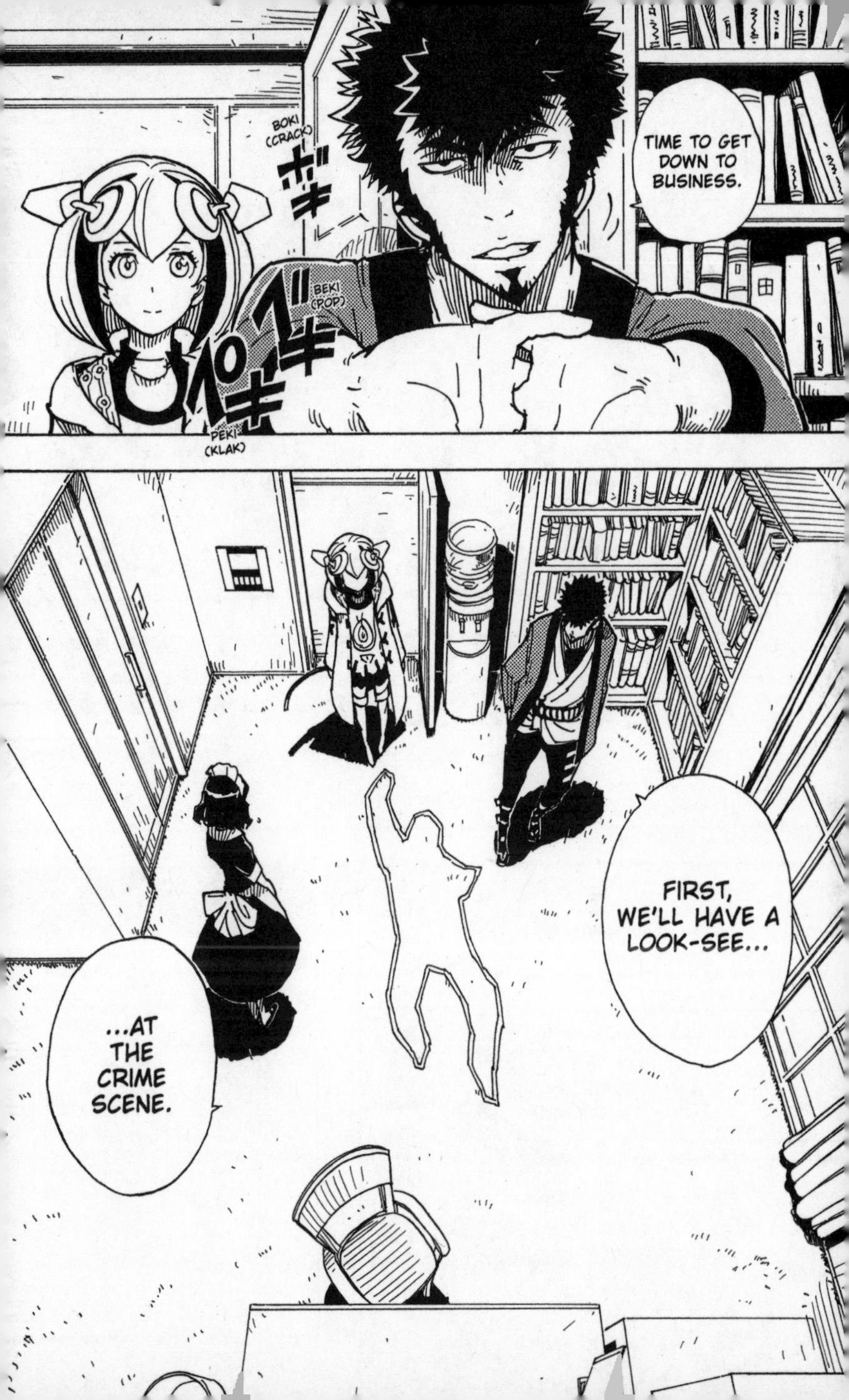
TIME TO GET DOWN TO BUSINESS.
BOKI (CRACK)
BEKI (POP)
PEKI (KLAK)
FIRST, WE'LL HAVE A LOOK-SEE...
...AT THE CRIME SCENE.

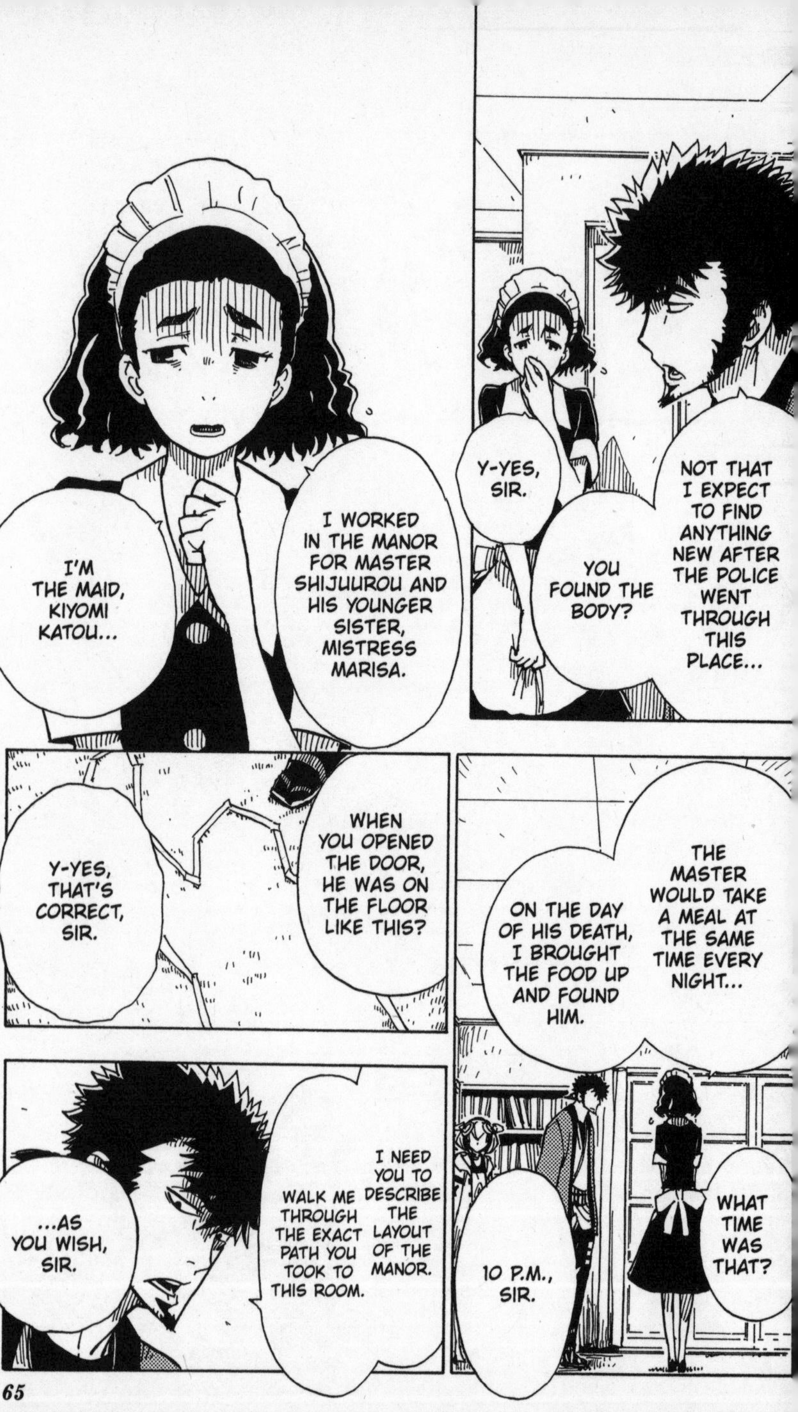
NOT THAT I EXPECT TO FIND ANYTHING NEW AFTER THE POLICE WENT THROUGH THIS PLACE...
YOU FOUND THE BODY?
Y-YES, SIR.
I WORKED IN THE MANOR FOR MASTER SHIJUUROU AND HIS YOUNGER SISTER, MISTRESS MARISA.
I'M THE MAID, KIYOMI KATOU...
THE MASTER WOULD TAKE A MEAL AT THE SAME TIME EVERY NIGHT...
ON THE DAY OF HIS DEATH, I BROUGHT THE FOOD UP AND FOUND HIM.
WHAT TIME WAS THAT?
10 P.M., SIR.
WHEN YOU OPENED THE DOOR, HE WAS ON THE FLOOR LIKE THIS?
Y-YES, THAT'S CORRECT, SIR.
I NEED YOU TO DESCRIBE THE LAYOUT OF THE MANOR.
WALK ME THROUGH THE EXACT PATH YOU TOOK TO THIS ROOM.
...AS YOU WISH, SIR.

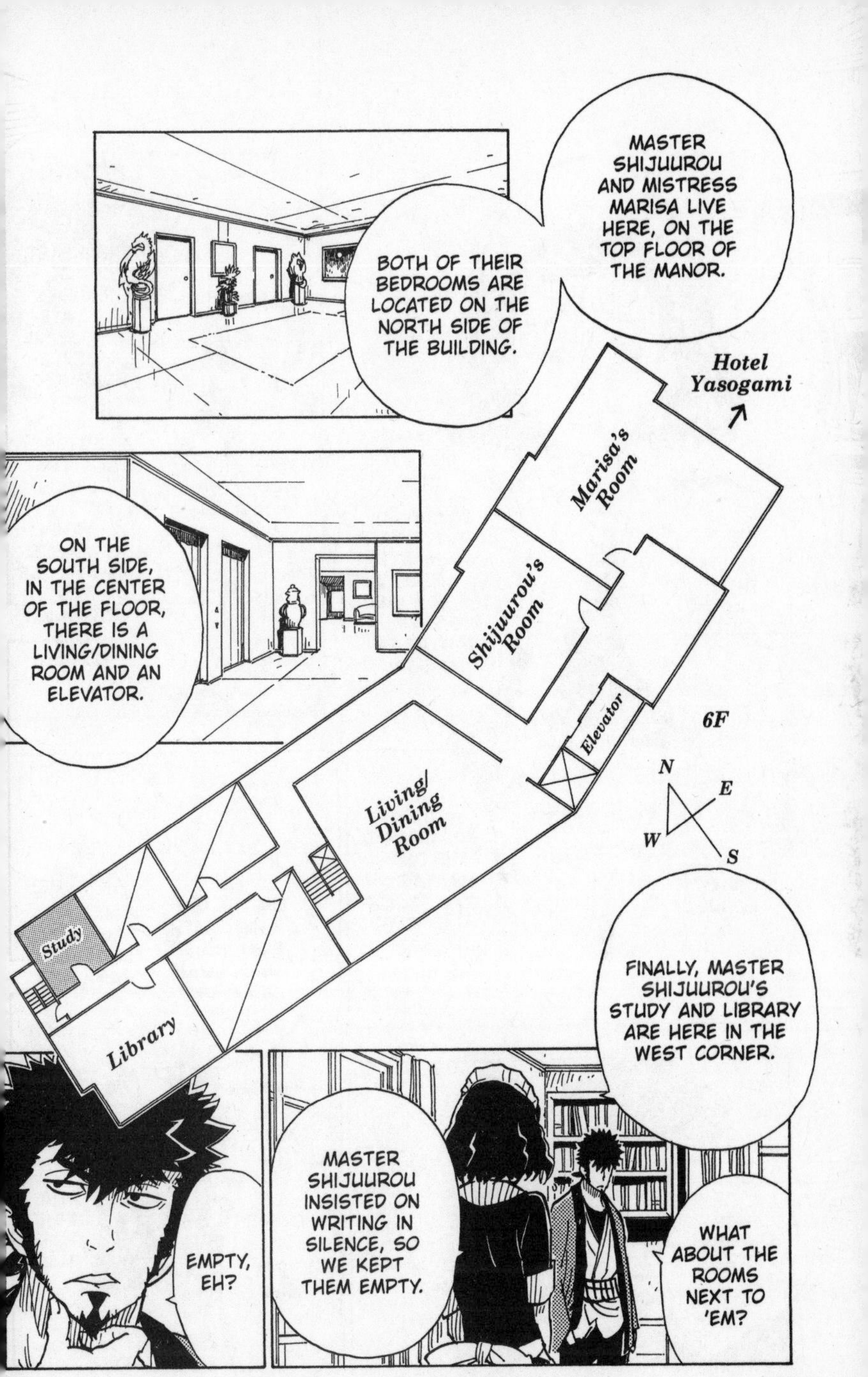
MASTER SHIJUUROU AND MISTRESS MARISA LIVE HERE, ON THE TOP FLOOR OF THE MANOR.
BOTH OF THEIR BEDROOMS ARE LOCATED ON THE NORTH SIDE OF THE BUILDING.
Hotel Yasogami
Marisa's Room
Shijuurou's Room
6F
Elevator
N
E
W
S
Living/ Dining Room
Study
Library
ON THE SOUTH SIDE, IN THE CENTER OF THE FLOOR, THERE IS A LIVING/DINING ROOM AND AN ELEVATOR.
FINALLY, MASTER SHIJUUROU'S STUDY AND LIBRARY ARE HERE IN THE WEST CORNER.
WHAT ABOUT THE ROOMS NEXT TO 'EM?
MASTER SHIJUUROU INSISTED ON WRITING IN SILENCE, SO WE KEPT THEM EMPTY.
EMPTY, EH?

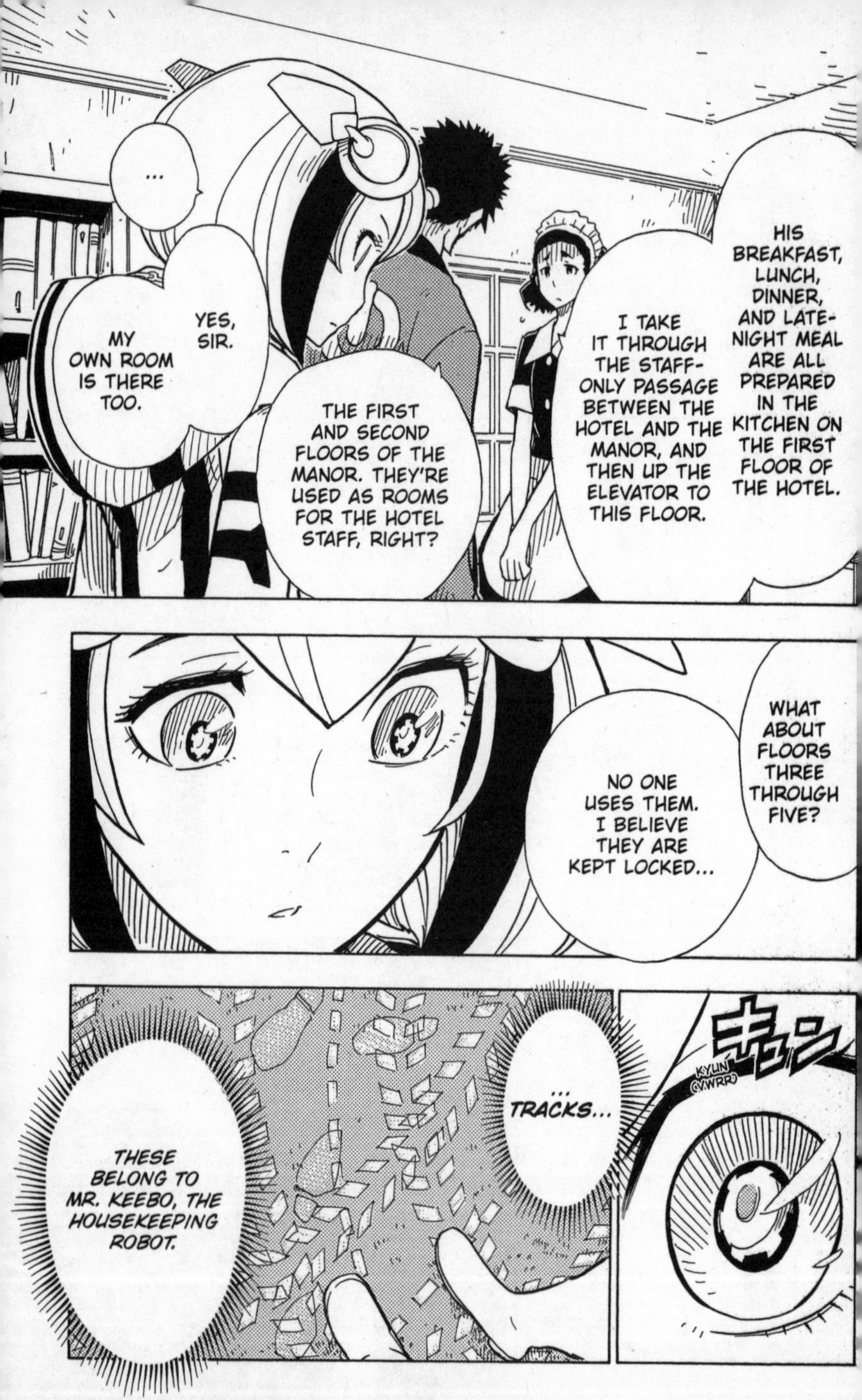
HIS BREAKFAST, LUNCH, DINNER, AND LATE-NIGHT MEAL ARE ALL PREPARED IN THE KITCHEN ON THE FIRST FLOOR OF THE HOTEL.
I TAKE IT THROUGH THE STAFF-ONLY PASSAGE BETWEEN THE HOTEL AND THE MANOR, AND THEN UP THE ELEVATOR TO THIS FLOOR.
THE FIRST AND SECOND FLOORS OF THE MANOR. THEY'RE USED AS ROOMS FOR THE HOTEL STAFF, RIGHT?
YES, SIR.
MY OWN ROOM IS THERE TOO.
...
WHAT ABOUT FLOORS THREE THROUGH FIVE?
NO ONE USES THEM. I BELIEVE THEY ARE KEPT LOCKED...
キュン
KYUN (V-WRR)
...TRACKS...
THESE BELONG TO MR. KEEBO, THE HOUSEKEEPING ROBOT.

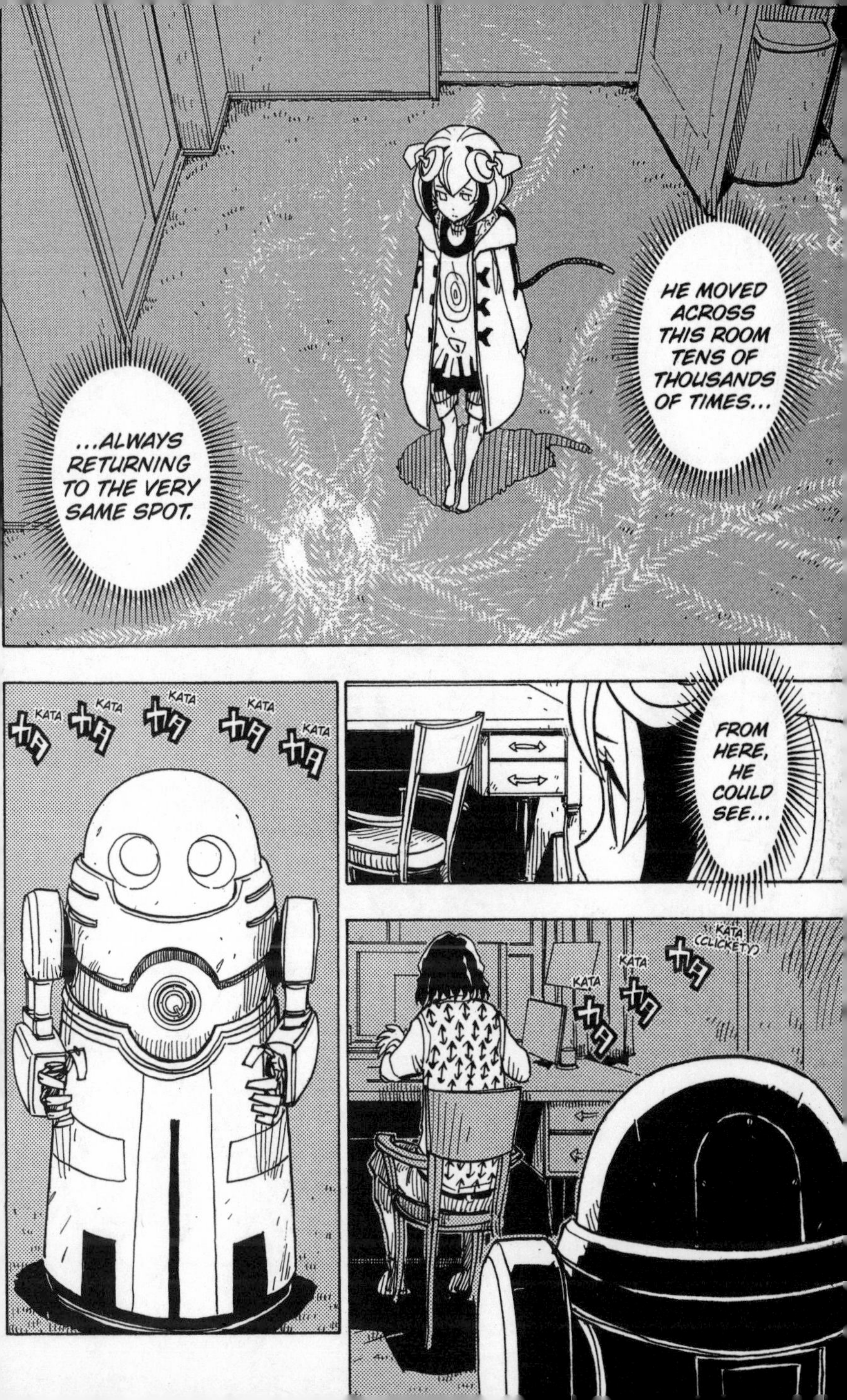
HE MOVED ACROSS THIS ROOM TENS OF THOUSANDS OF TIMES...
...ALWAYS RETURNING TO THE VERY SAME SPOT.
FROM HERE, HE COULD SEE...
カタ KATA (CLICKETY)
カタ KATA
カタ KATA
カタ KATA
カタ KATA
カタ KATA
カタ KATA
カタ KATA

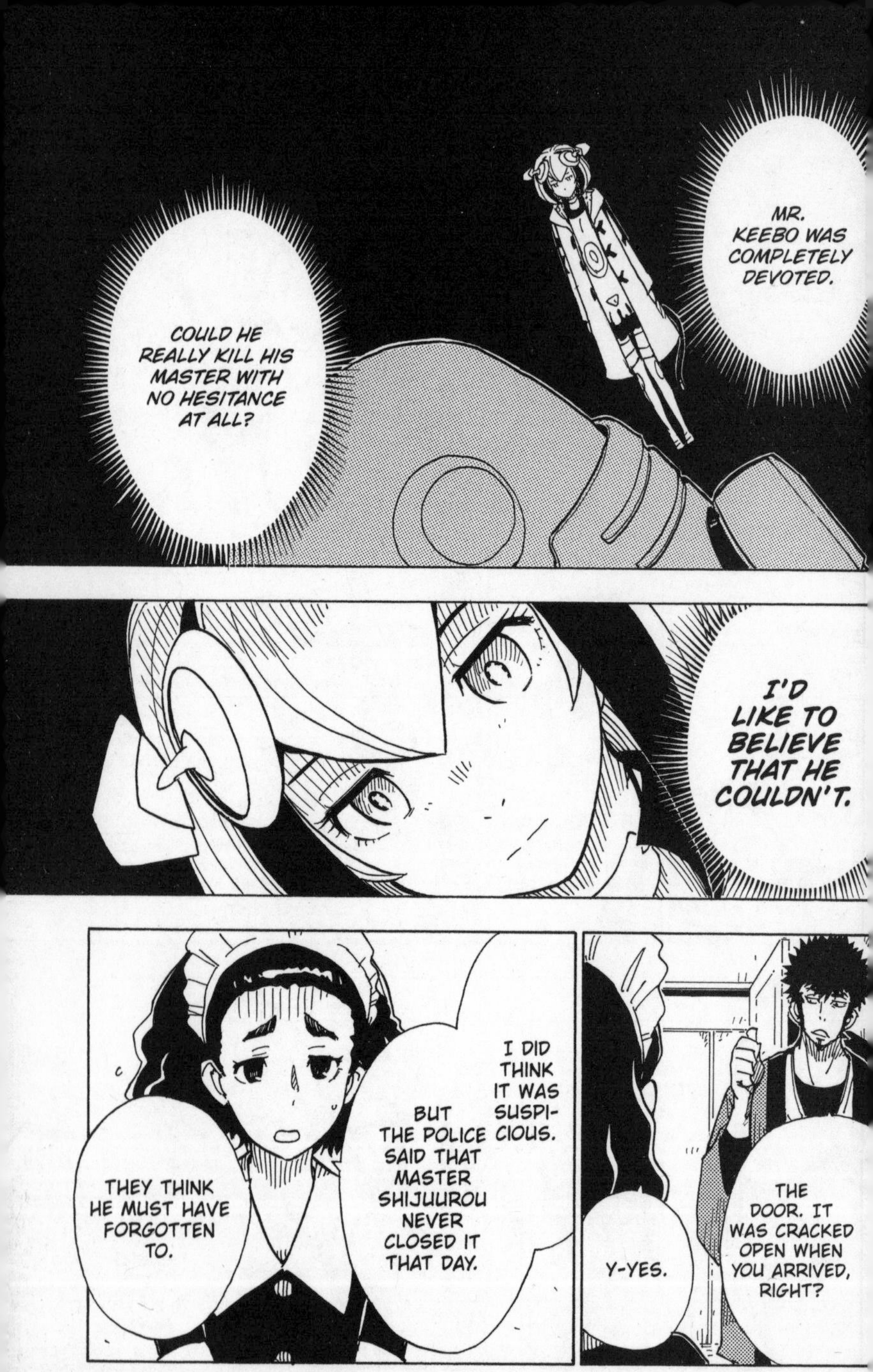
MR. KEEBO WAS COMPLETELY DEVOTED.
COULD HE REALLY KILL HIS MASTER WITH NO HESITANCE AT ALL?
I'D LIKE TO BELIEVE THAT HE COULDN'T.
THE DOOR. IT WAS CRACKED OPEN WHEN YOU ARRIVED, RIGHT?
Y-YES.
I DID THINK IT WAS SUSPICIOUS.
BUT THE POLICE SAID THAT MASTER SHIJUUROU NEVER CLOSED IT THAT DAY.
THEY THINK HE MUST HAVE FORGOTTEN TO.

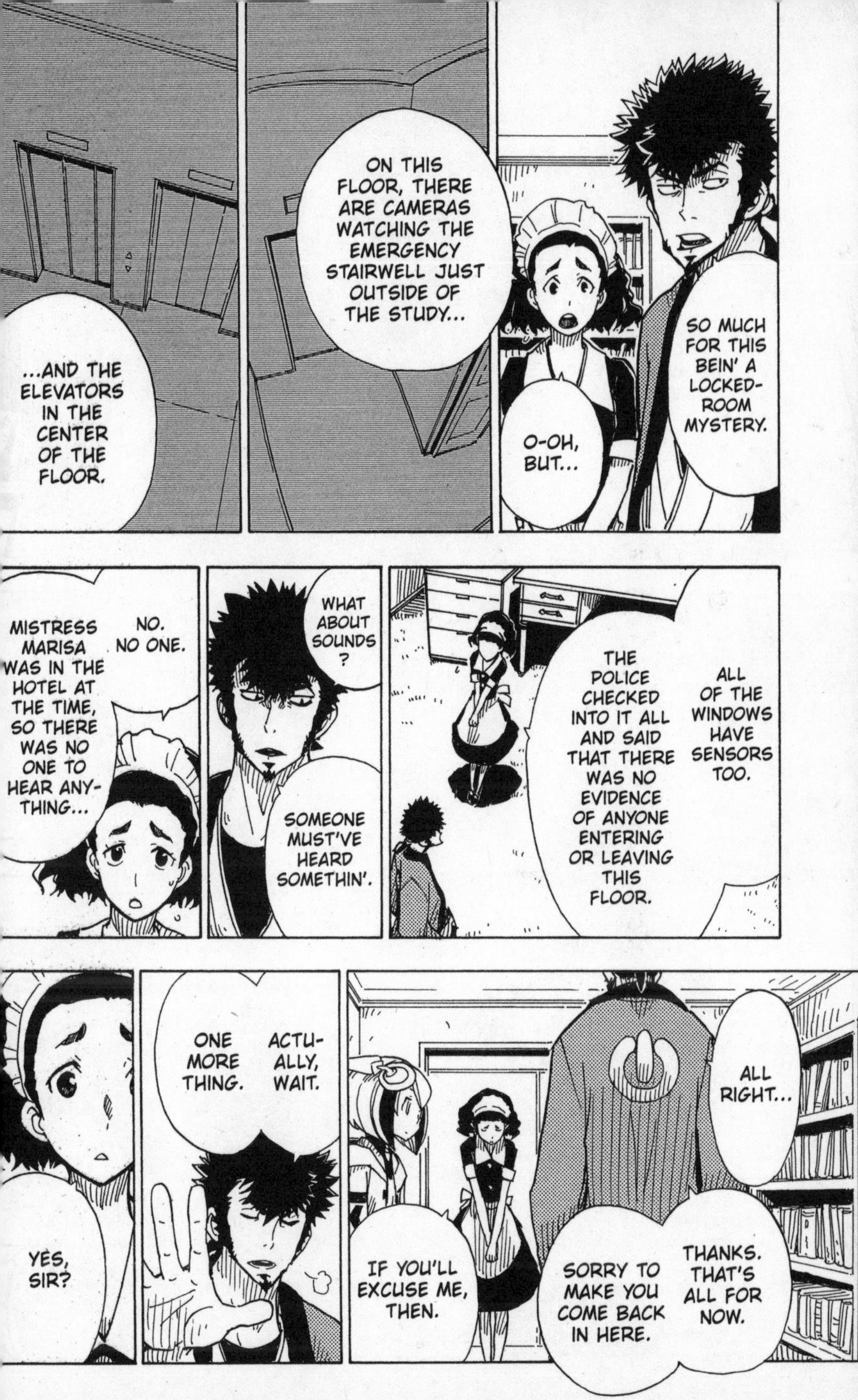
SO MUCH FOR THIS BEIN' A LOCKED-ROOM MYSTERY.
O-OH, BUT...
ON THIS FLOOR, THERE ARE CAMERAS WATCHING THE EMERGENCY STAIRWELL JUST OUTSIDE OF THE STUDY...
...AND THE ELEVATORS IN THE CENTER OF THE FLOOR.
ALL OF THE WINDOWS HAVE SENSORS TOO.
THE POLICE CHECKED INTO IT ALL AND SAID THAT THERE WAS NO EVIDENCE OF ANYONE ENTERING OR LEAVING THIS FLOOR.
WHAT ABOUT SOUNDS?
SOMEONE MUST'VE HEARD SOMETHIN'.
NO. NO ONE.
MISTRESS MARISA WAS IN THE HOTEL AT THE TIME, SO THERE WAS NO ONE TO HEAR ANYTHING...
ALL RIGHT...
THANKS. THAT'S ALL FOR NOW.
SORRY TO MAKE YOU COME BACK IN HERE.
IF YOU'LL EXCUSE ME, THEN.
ACTUALLY, WAIT.
ONE MORE THING.
YES, SIR?

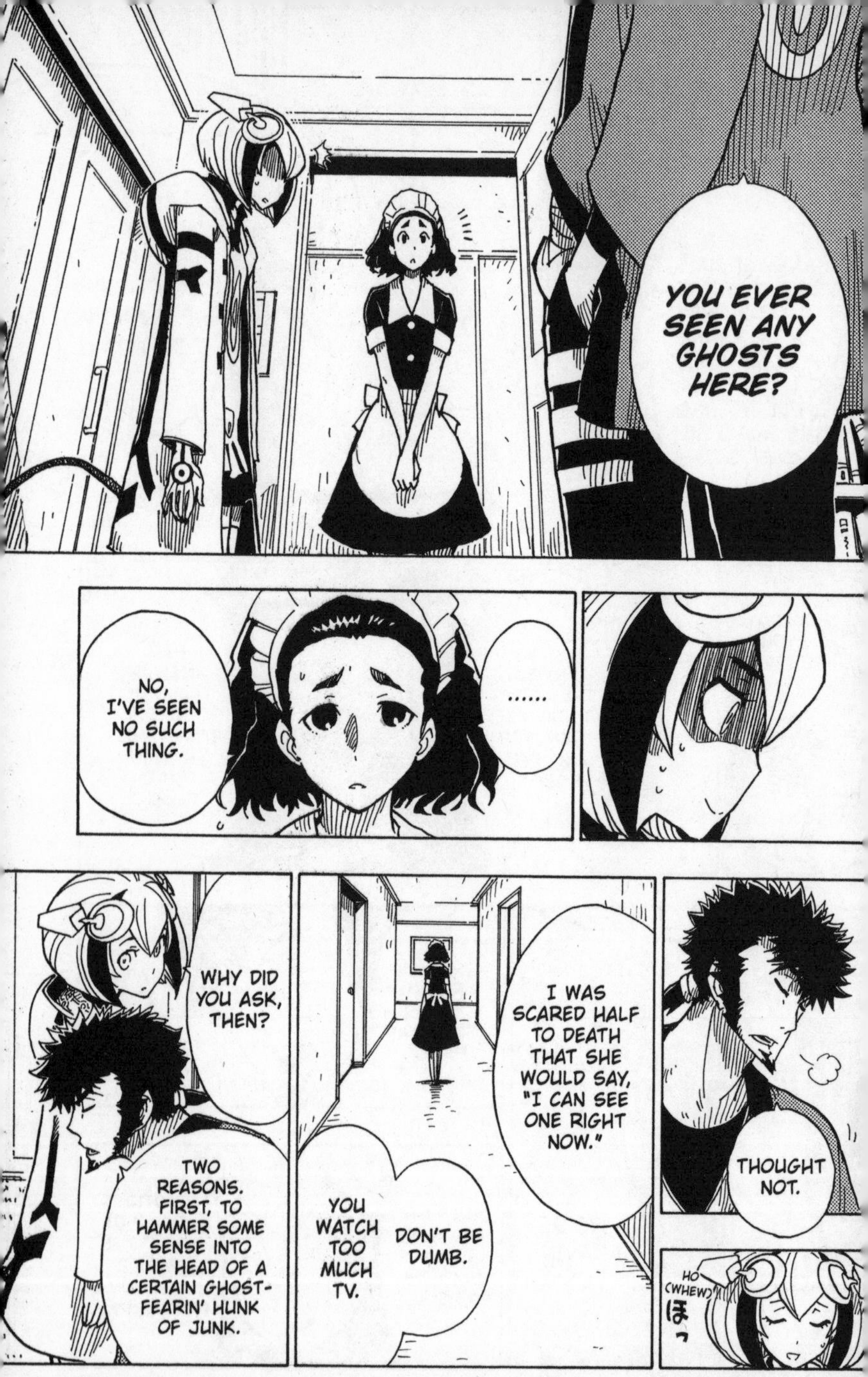
YOU EVER SEEN ANY GHOSTS HERE?
......
NO, I'VE SEEN NO SUCH THING.
THOUGHT NOT.
HO (WHEW)
ほっ
I WAS SCARED HALF TO DEATH THAT SHE WOULD SAY, "I CAN SEE ONE RIGHT NOW."
DON'T BE DUMB.
YOU WATCH TOO MUCH TV.
WHY DID YOU ASK, THEN?
TWO REASONS. FIRST, TO HAMMER SOME SENSE INTO THE HEAD OF A CERTAIN GHOST-FEARIN' HUNK OF JUNK.

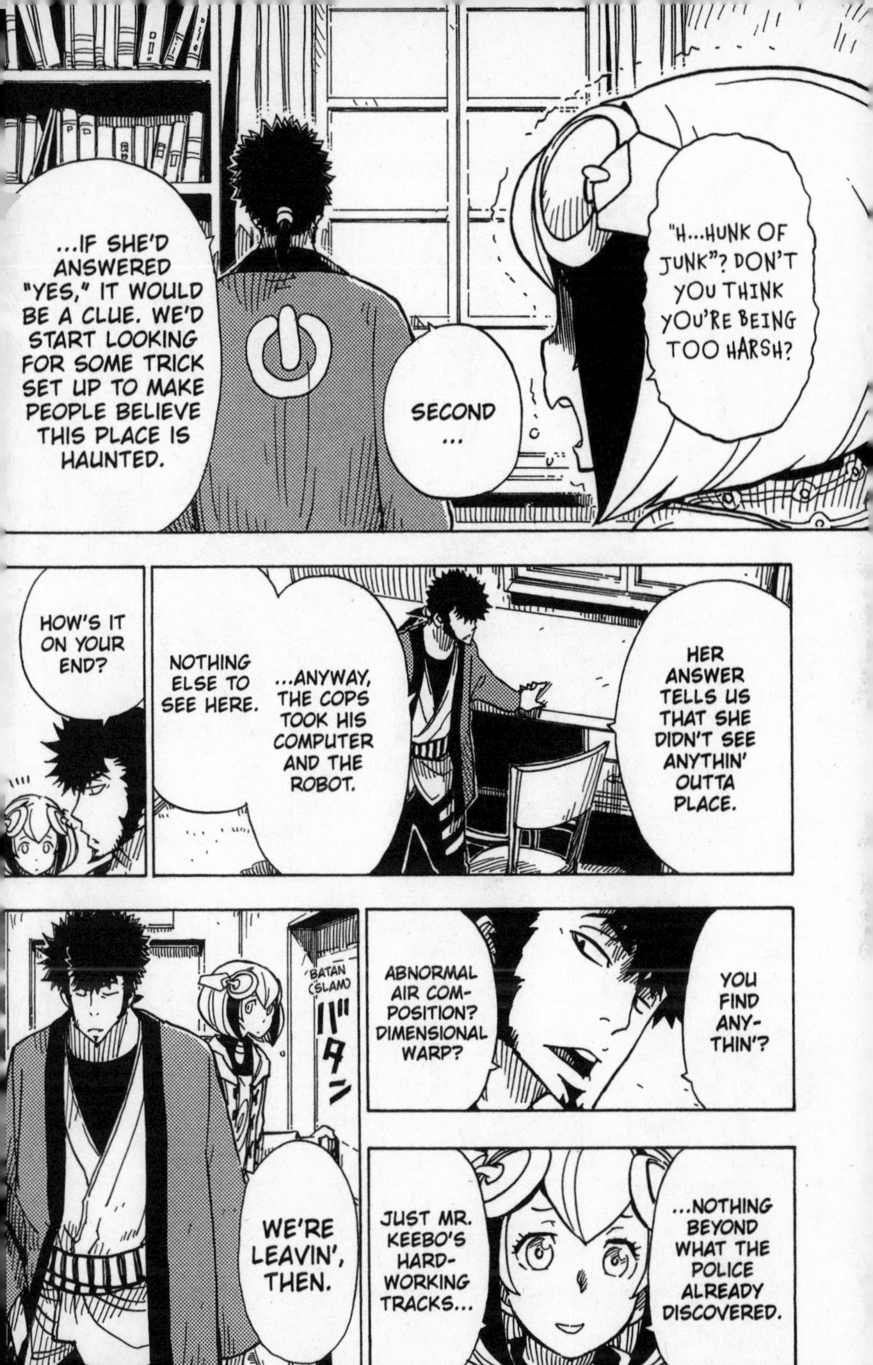
"H...HUNK OF JUNK"? DON'T YOU THINK YOU'RE BEING TOO HARSH?
SECOND ...
...IF SHE'D ANSWERED "YES," IT WOULD BE A CLUE. WE'D START LOOKING FOR SOME TRICK SET UP TO MAKE PEOPLE BELIEVE THIS PLACE IS HAUNTED.
HER ANSWER TELLS US THAT SHE DIDN'T SEE ANYTHIN' OUTTA PLACE.
...ANYWAY, THE COPS TOOK HIS COMPUTER AND THE ROBOT.
NOTHING ELSE TO SEE HERE.
HOW'S IT ON YOUR END?
YOU FIND ANY-THIN'?
ABNORMAL AIR COM-POSITION? DIMENSIONAL WARP?
...NOTHING BEYOND WHAT THE POLICE ALREADY DISCOVERED.
JUST MR. KEEBO'S HARD-WORKING TRACKS...
BATAN (SLAM)
バタン
WE'RE LEAVIN', THEN.

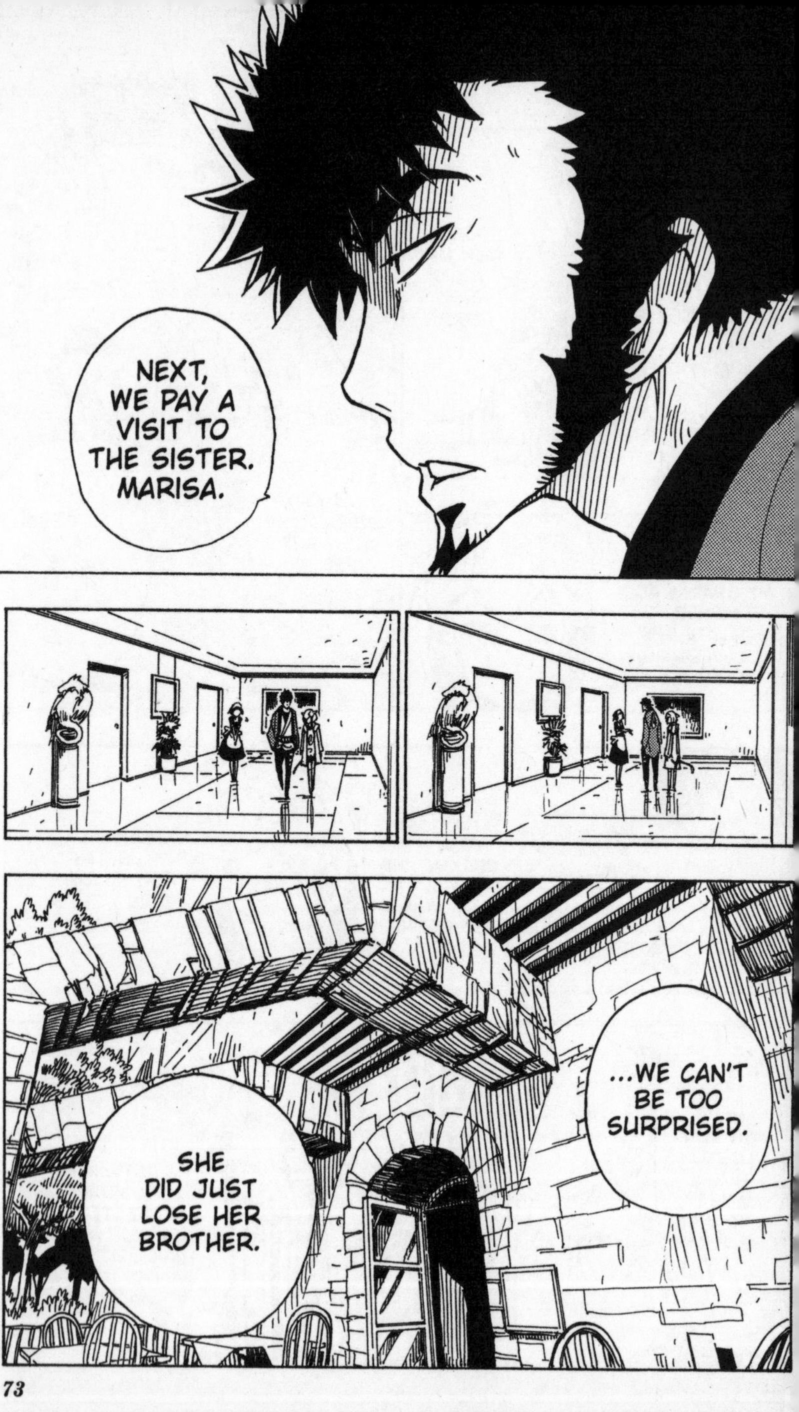
NEXT, WE PAY A VISIT TO THE SISTER. MARISA.
...WE CAN'T BE TOO SURPRISED.
SHE DID JUST LOSE HER BROTHER.

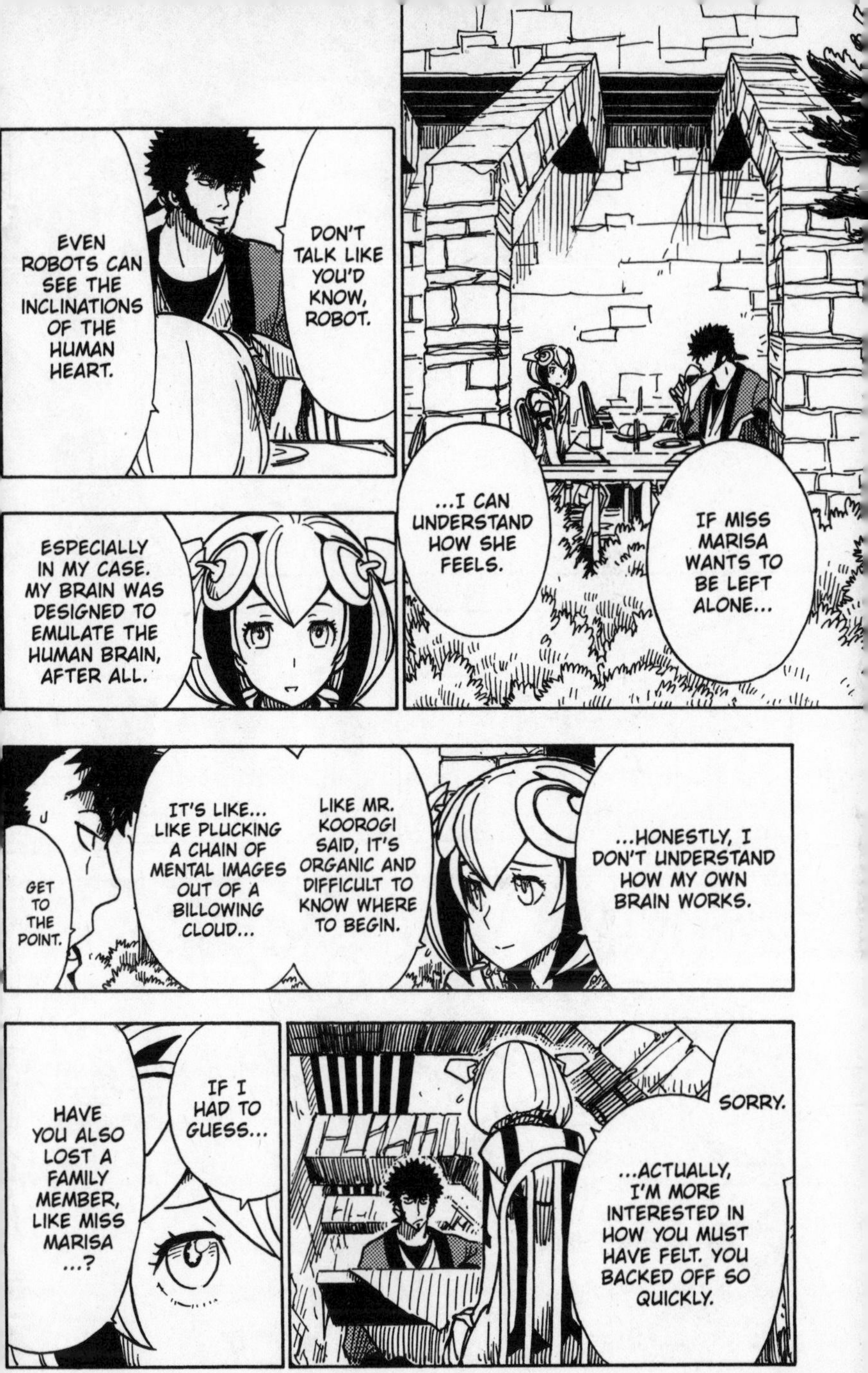
IF MISS MARISA WANTS TO BE LEFT ALONE...
...I CAN UNDERSTAND HOW SHE FEELS.
DON'T TALK LIKE YOU'D KNOW, ROBOT.
EVEN ROBOTS CAN SEE THE INCLINATIONS OF THE HUMAN HEART.
ESPECIALLY IN MY CASE. MY BRAIN WAS DESIGNED TO EMULATE THE HUMAN BRAIN, AFTER ALL.
...HONESTLY, I DON'T UNDERSTAND HOW MY OWN BRAIN WORKS.
LIKE MR. KOOROGI SAID, IT'S ORGANIC AND DIFFICULT TO KNOW WHERE TO BEGIN.
IT'S LIKE... LIKE PLUCKING A CHAIN OF MENTAL IMAGES OUT OF A BILLOWING CLOUD...
GET TO THE POINT.
SORRY.
...ACTUALLY, I'M MORE INTERESTED IN HOW YOU MUST HAVE FELT. YOU BACKED OFF SO QUICKLY.
IF I HAD TO GUESS...
HAVE YOU ALSO LOST A FAMILY MEMBER, LIKE MISS MARISA ...?

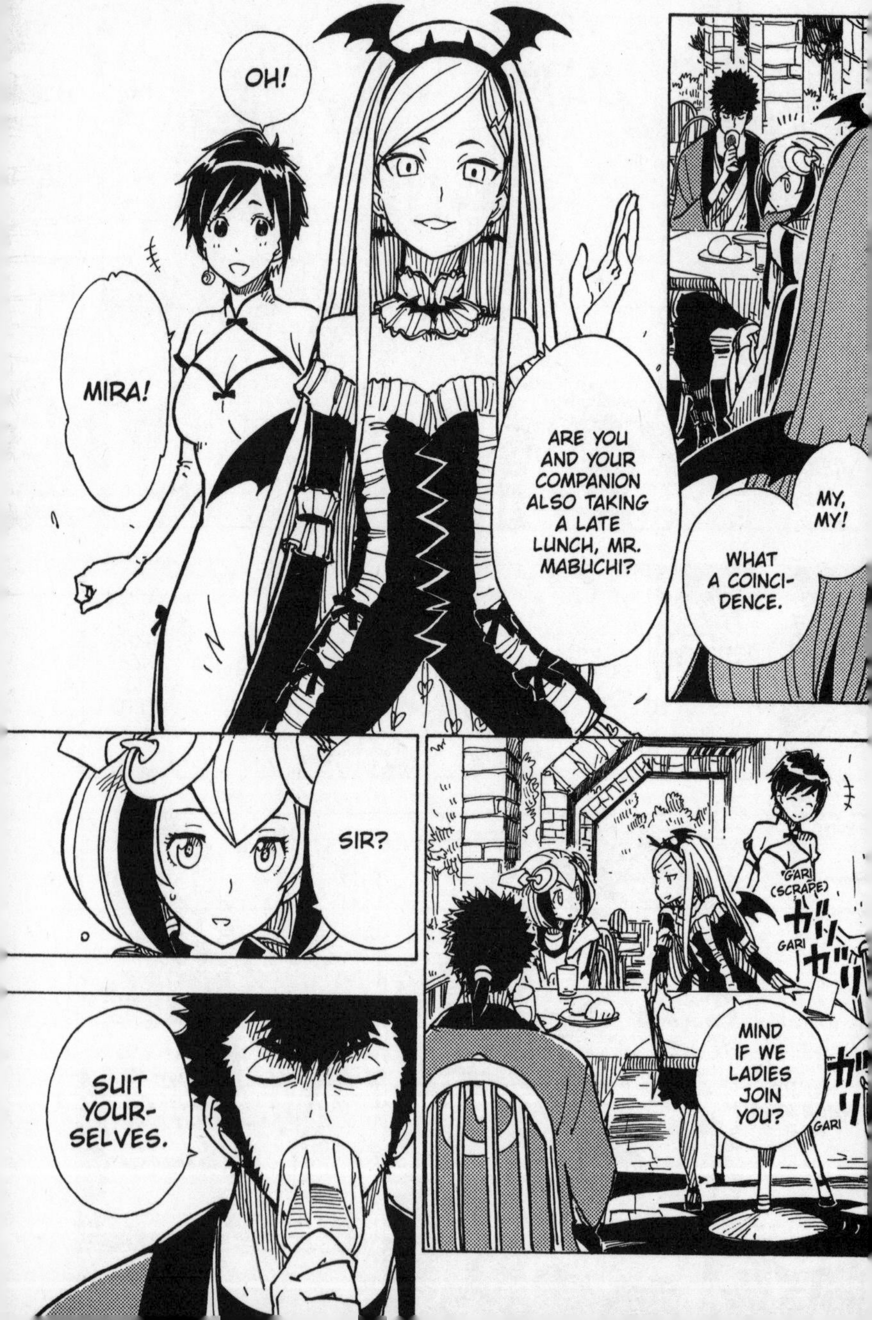
MY, MY!
WHAT A COINCIDENCE.
ARE YOU AND YOUR COMPANION ALSO TAKING A LATE LUNCH, MR. MABUCHI?
OH!
MIRA!
ガリ GARI (SCRAPE)
ガリ GARI
MIND IF WE LADIES JOIN YOU?
ガリ GARI
SIR?
SUIT YOURSELVES.

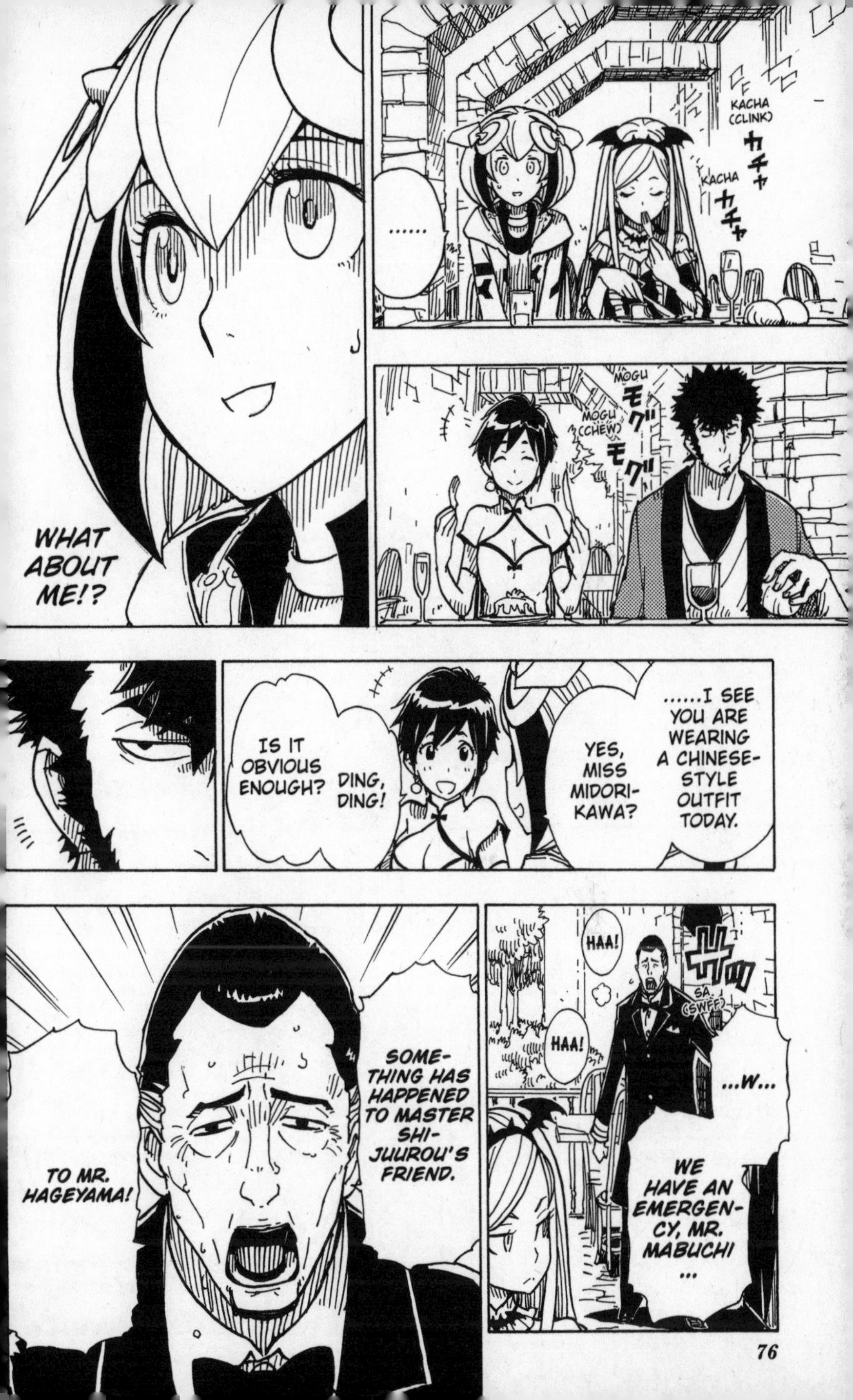
......
KACHA (CLINK)
カチャ
KACHA
カチャ
MOGU
モグ
MOGU (CHEW)
モグ
WHAT ABOUT ME!?
......I SEE YOU ARE WEARING A CHINESE-STYLE OUTFIT TODAY.
YES, MISS MIDORI-KAWA?
DING, DING!
IS IT OBVIOUS ENOUGH?
SA (SWFF)
HAA!
HAA!
...W...
WE HAVE AN EMERGEN-CY, MR. MABUCHI ...
SOME-THING HAS HAPPENED TO MASTER SHI-JUUROU'S FRIEND.
TO MR. HAGEYAMA!

Dimension W

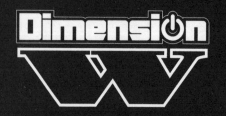

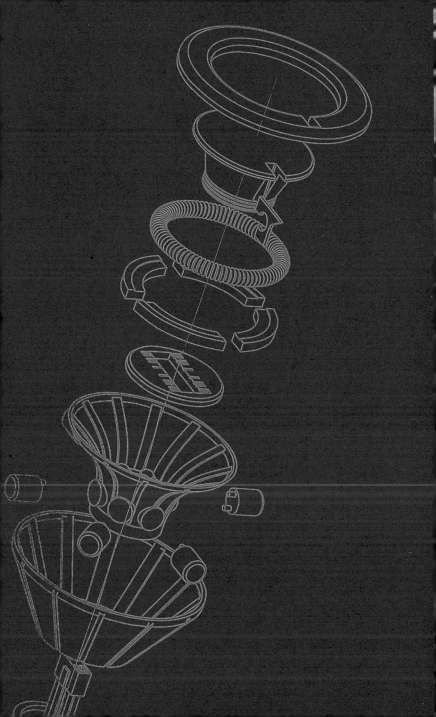

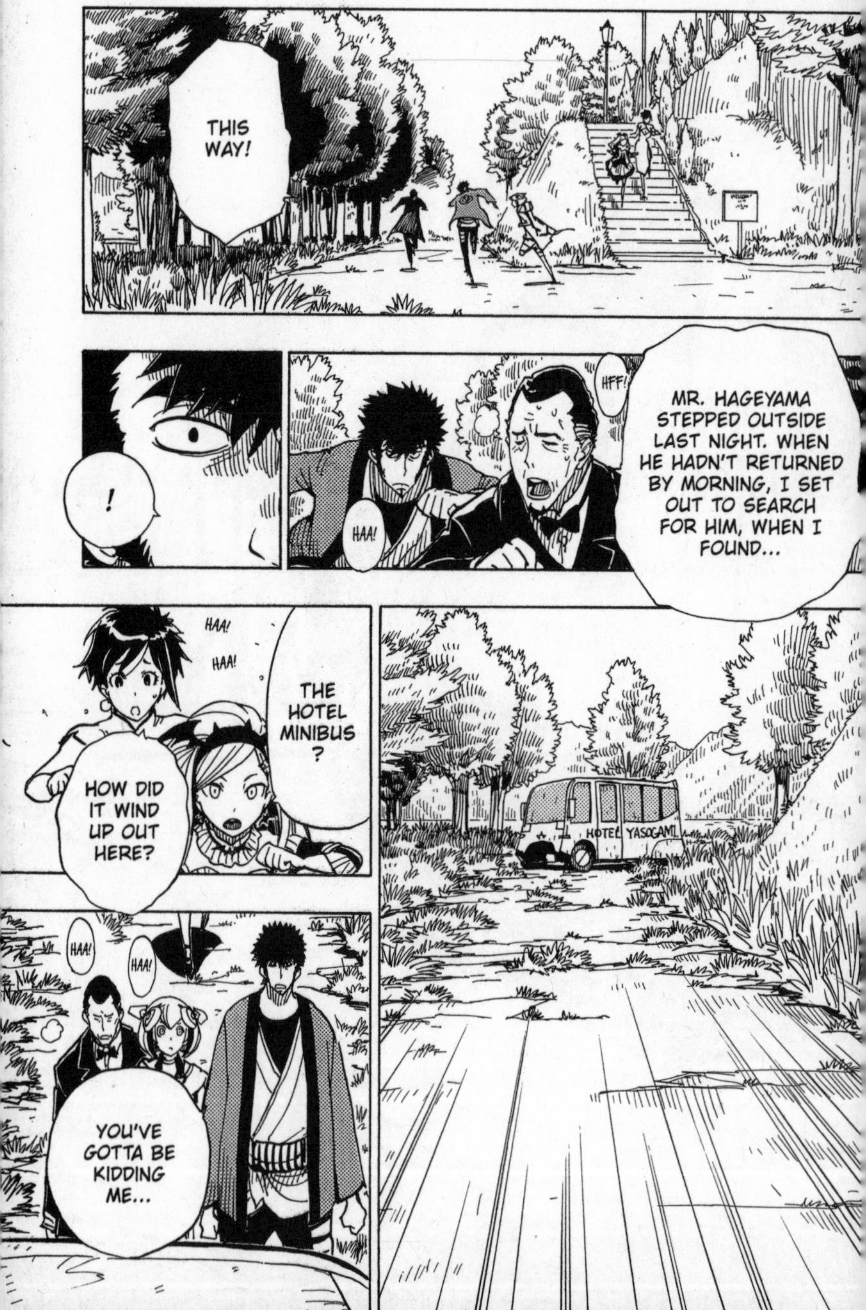
THIS WAY!
MR. HAGEYAMA STEPPED OUTSIDE LAST NIGHT. WHEN HE HADN'T RETURNED BY MORNING, I SET OUT TO SEARCH FOR HIM, WHEN I FOUND...
HFF!
HAA!
!
HOTEL YASOGAMI
THE HOTEL MINIBUS?
HAA!
HAA!
HOW DID IT WIND UP OUT HERE?
HAA!
HAA!
YOU'VE GOTTA BE KIDDING ME...

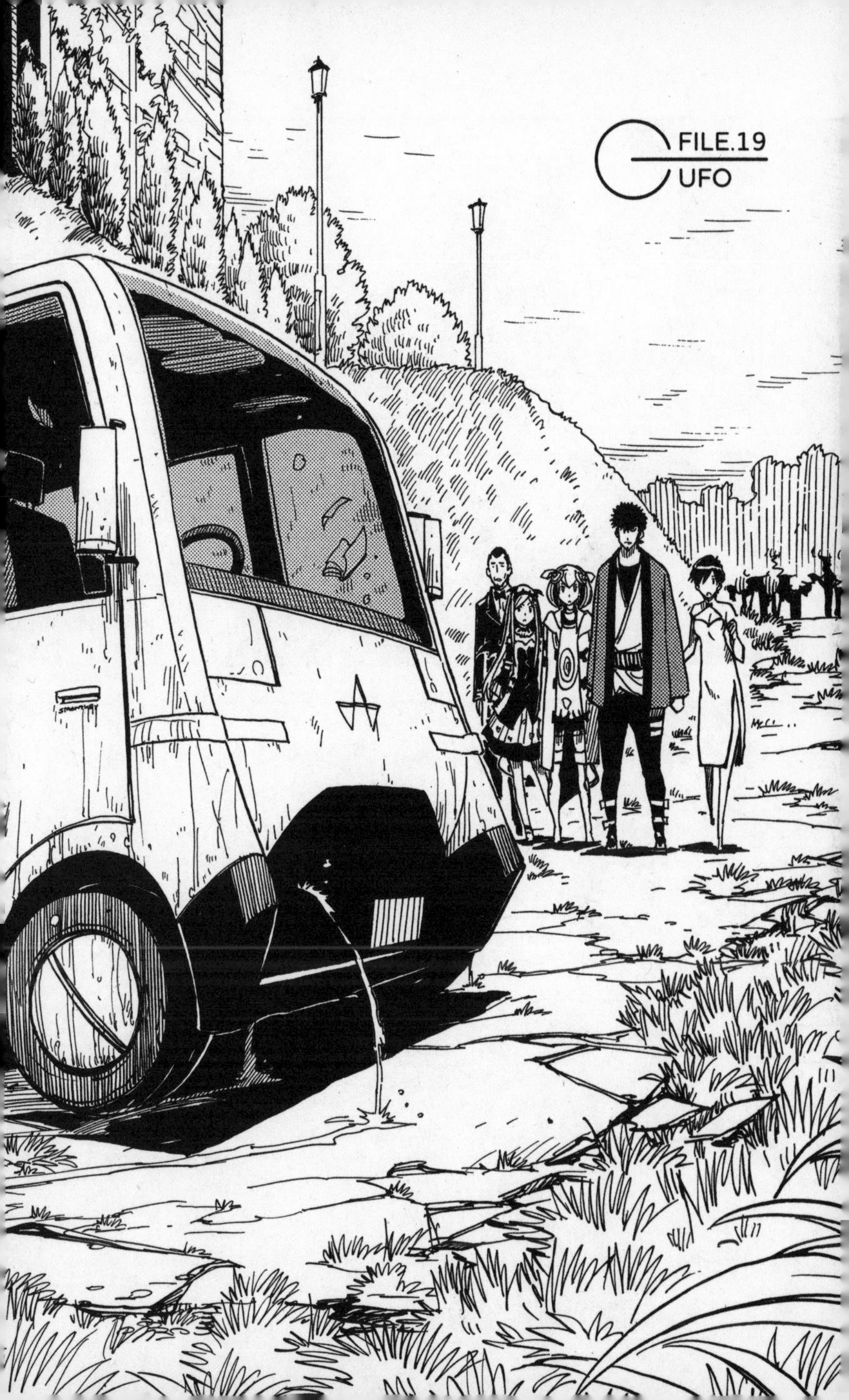
FILE.19
UFO

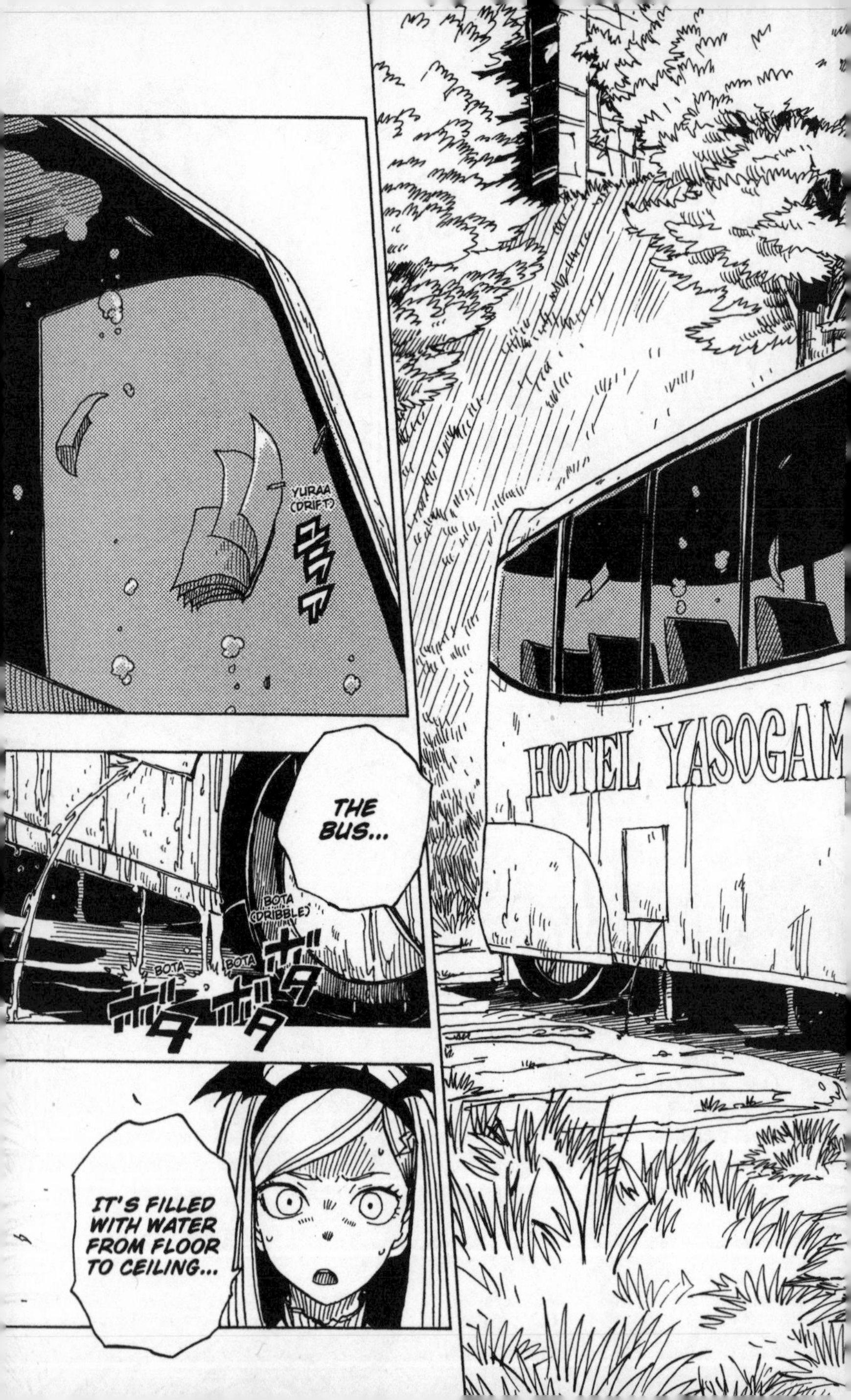
HOTEL YASOGAM
YURAA (DRIFT)
ユラァ
THE BUS...
BOTA (DRIBBLE)
ボタ
BOTA
ボタ
BOTA
ボタ
IT'S FILLED WITH WATER FROM FLOOR TO CEILING...

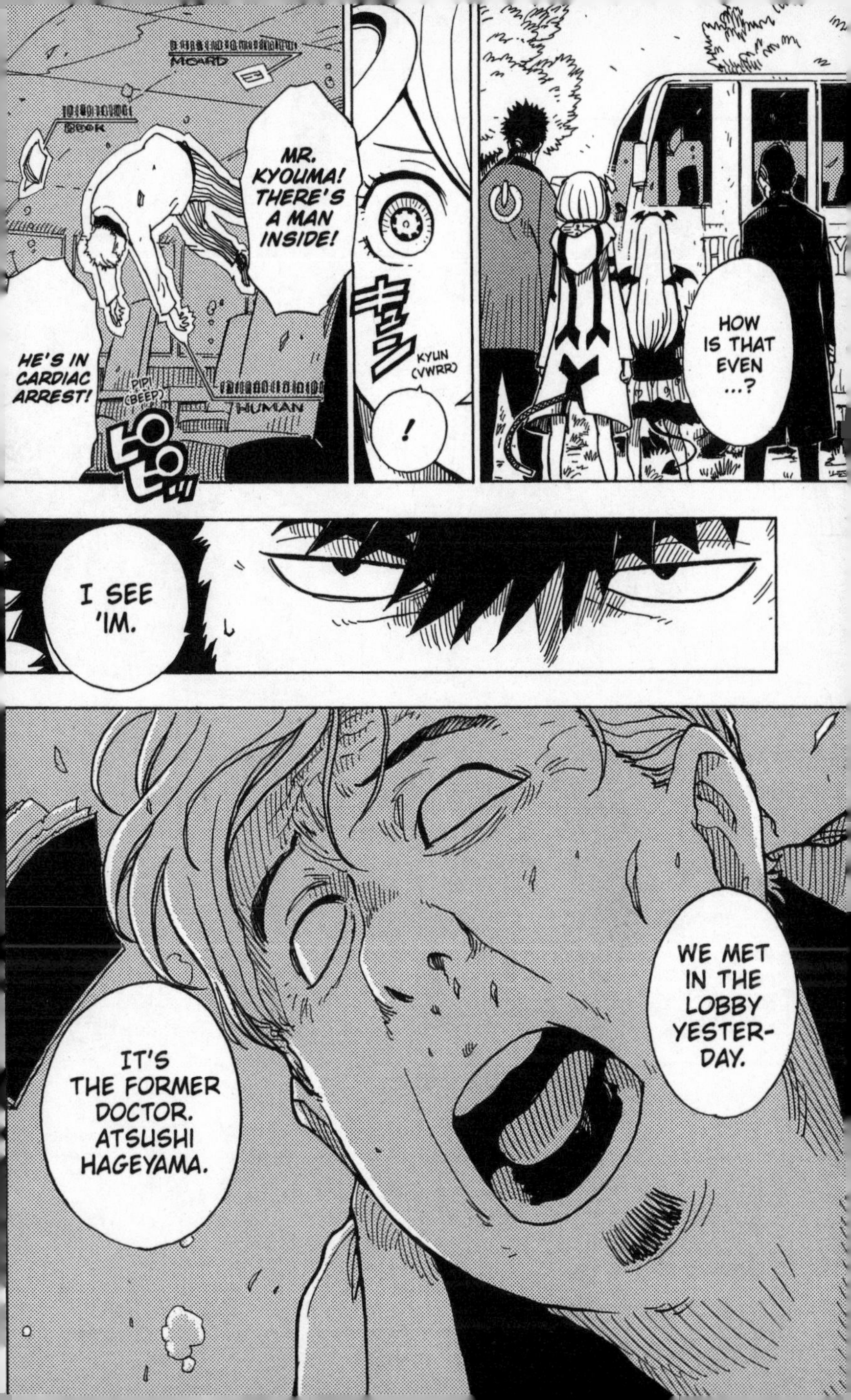
HOW IS THAT EVEN ...?
KYUN (VWRR)
!
MR. KYOUMA! THERE'S A MAN INSIDE!
BOOK
HUMAN
PIPI (BEEP)
HE'S IN CARDIAC ARREST!
I SEE 'IM.
WE MET IN THE LOBBY YESTER-DAY.
IT'S THE FORMER DOCTOR. ATSUSHI HAGEYAMA.

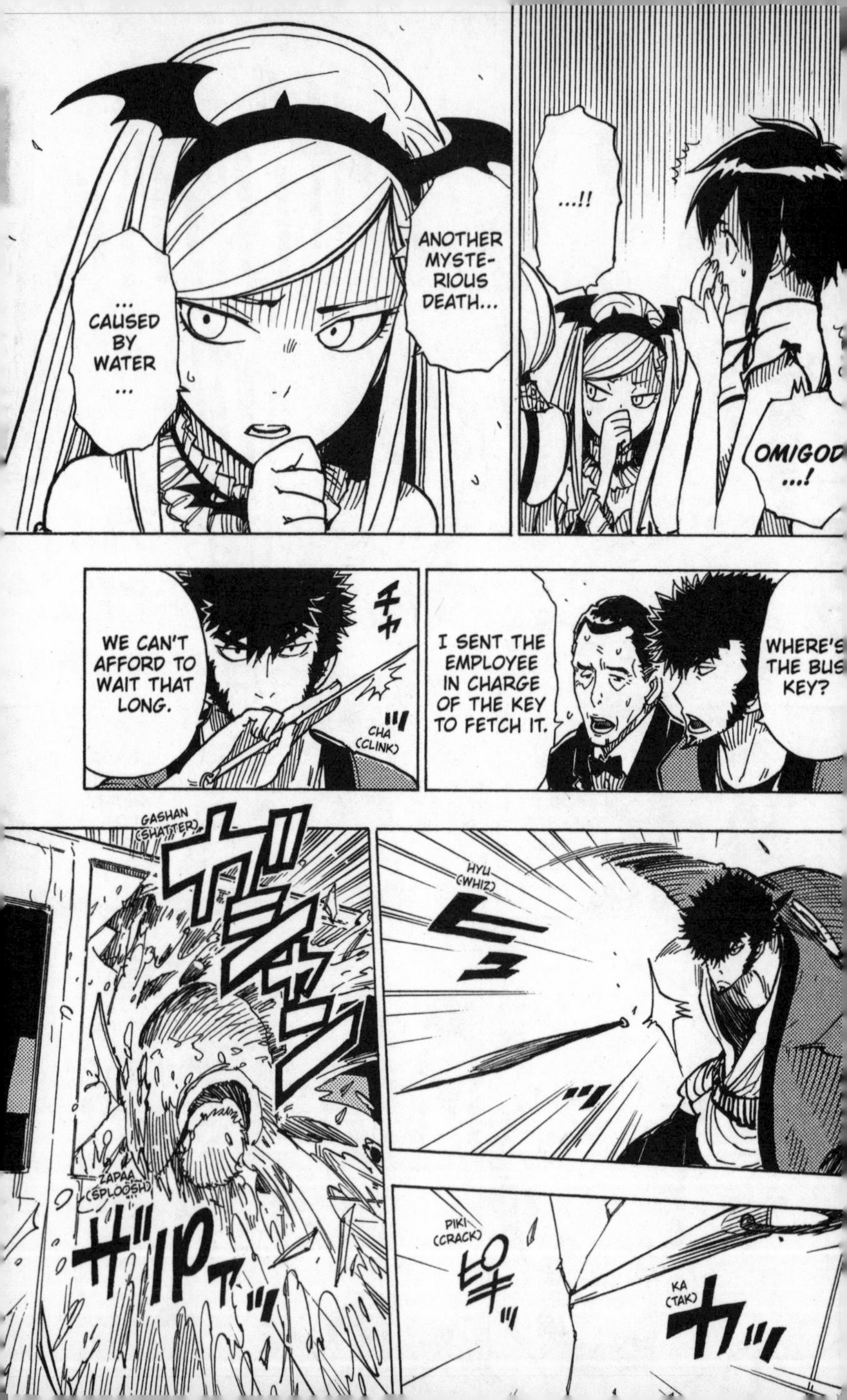
...!!
OMIGOD ...!
ANOTHER MYSTERIOUS DEATH...
... CAUSED BY WATER ...
WHERE'S THE BUS KEY?
I SENT THE EMPLOYEE IN CHARGE OF THE KEY TO FETCH IT.
WE CAN'T AFFORD TO WAIT THAT LONG.
CHA (CLINK)
HYU (WHIZ)
PIKI (CRACK)
KA (TAK)
GASHAN (SHATTER)
ZAPAA (SPLOOSH)

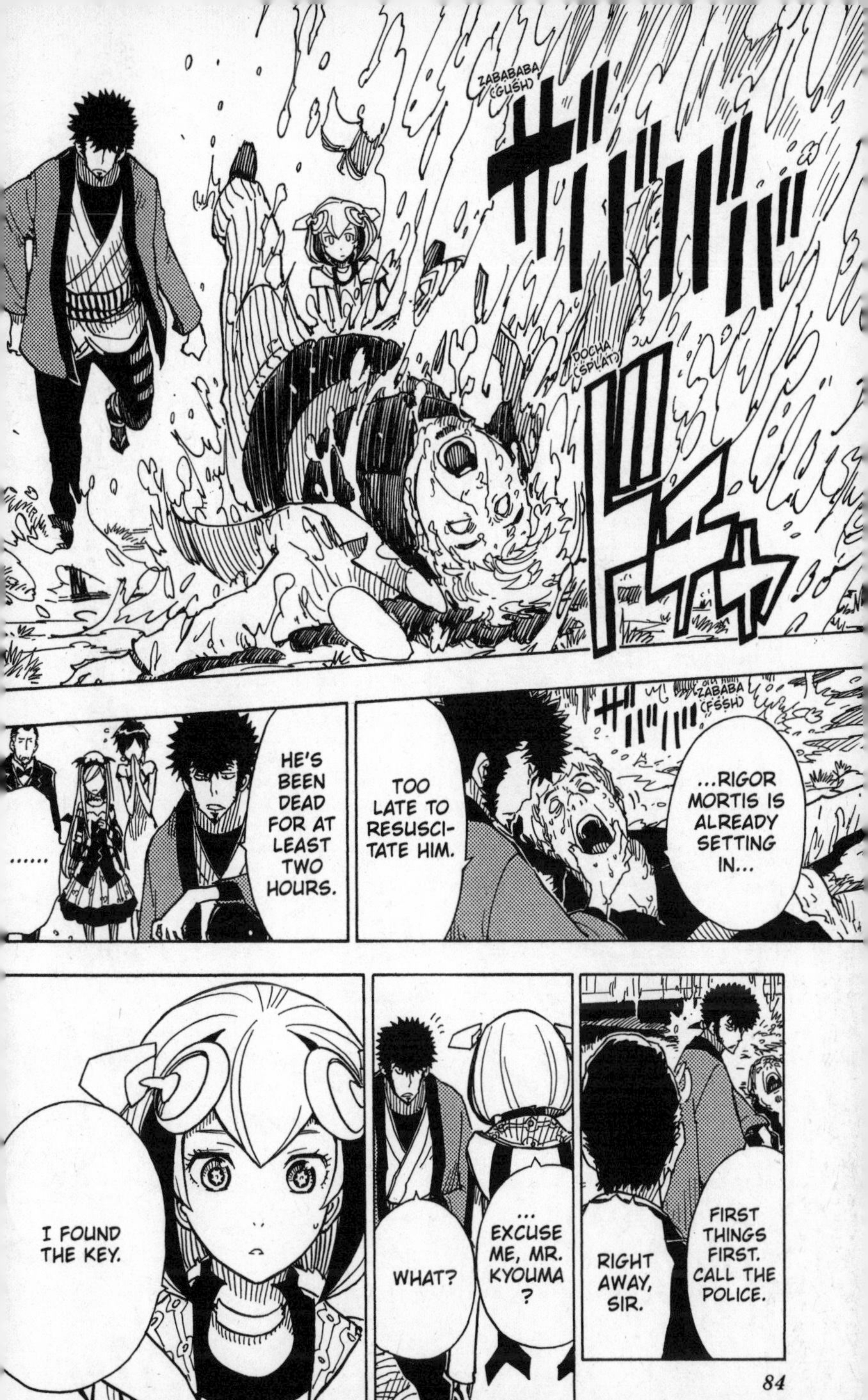

ZABABABA (GUSH)
DOCHA (SPLAT)
ZABABA (FSSH)
...RIGOR MORTIS IS ALREADY SETTING IN...
TOO LATE TO RESUSCI-TATE HIM.
HE'S BEEN DEAD FOR AT LEAST TWO HOURS.
......
FIRST THINGS FIRST. CALL THE POLICE.
RIGHT AWAY, SIR.
... EXCUSE ME, MR. KYOUMA ?
WHAT?
I FOUND THE KEY.

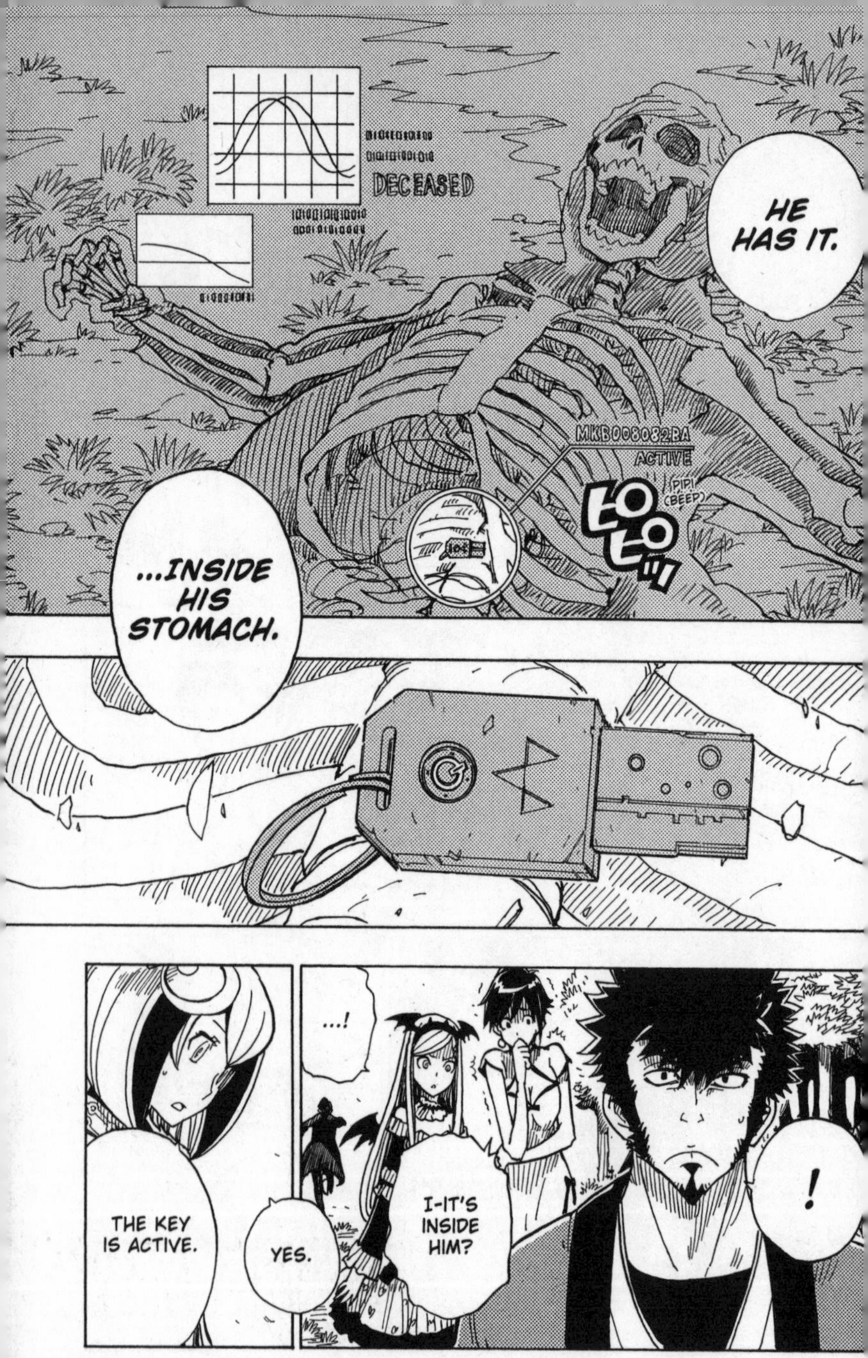
DECEASED
HE HAS IT.
MKB008082BA
ACTIVE
PIPI (BEEP)
...INSIDE HIS STOMACH.
!
...!
I-IT'S INSIDE HIM?
YES.
THE KEY IS ACTIVE.

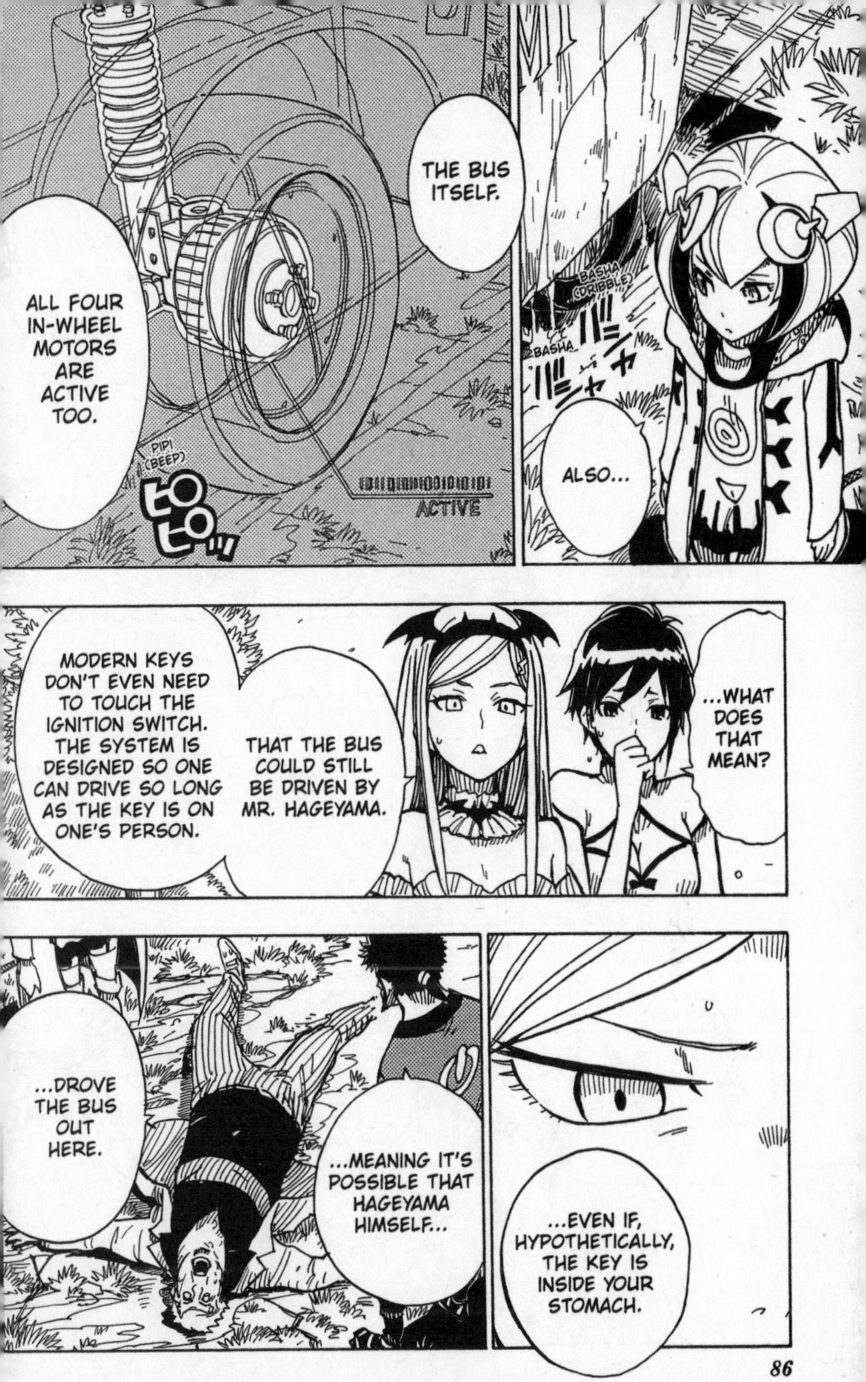
BASHA (DRIBBLE)
BASHA
ALSO...
THE BUS ITSELF.
ALL FOUR IN-WHEEL MOTORS ARE ACTIVE TOO.
PIPI (BEEP)
ACTIVE
...WHAT DOES THAT MEAN?
THAT THE BUS COULD STILL BE DRIVEN BY MR. HAGEYAMA.
MODERN KEYS DON'T EVEN NEED TO TOUCH THE IGNITION SWITCH. THE SYSTEM IS DESIGNED SO ONE CAN DRIVE SO LONG AS THE KEY IS ON ONE'S PERSON.
...EVEN IF, HYPOTHETICALLY, THE KEY IS INSIDE YOUR STOMACH.
...MEANING IT'S POSSIBLE THAT HAGEYAMA HIMSELF...
...DROVE THE BUS OUT HERE.

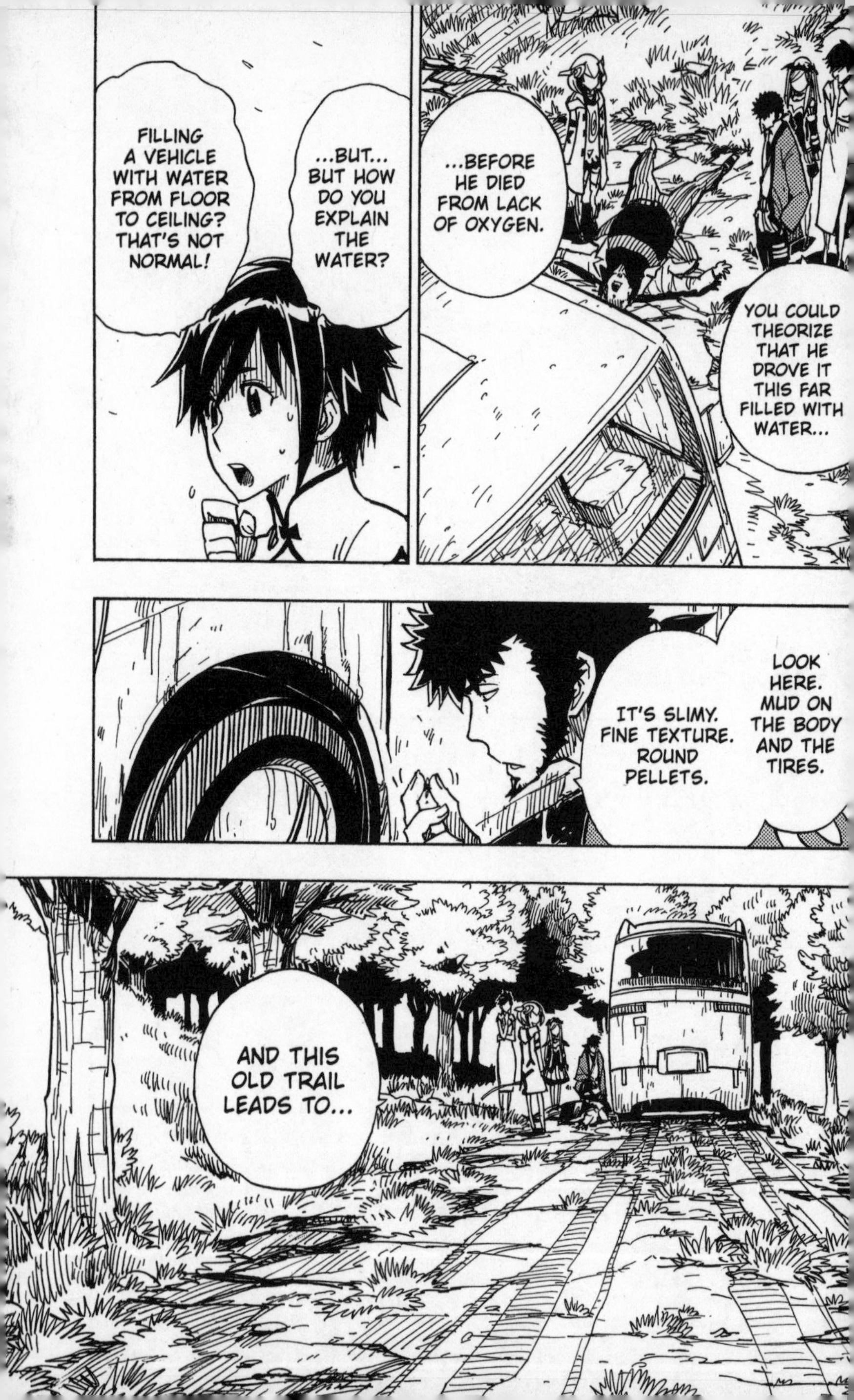
YOU COULD THEORIZE THAT HE DROVE IT THIS FAR FILLED WITH WATER...
...BEFORE HE DIED FROM LACK OF OXYGEN.
...BUT... BUT HOW DO YOU EXPLAIN THE WATER?
FILLING A VEHICLE WITH WATER FROM FLOOR TO CEILING? THAT'S NOT NORMAL!
LOOK HERE. MUD ON THE BODY AND THE TIRES.
IT'S SLIMY. FINE TEXTURE. ROUND PELLETS.
AND THIS OLD TRAIL LEADS TO...

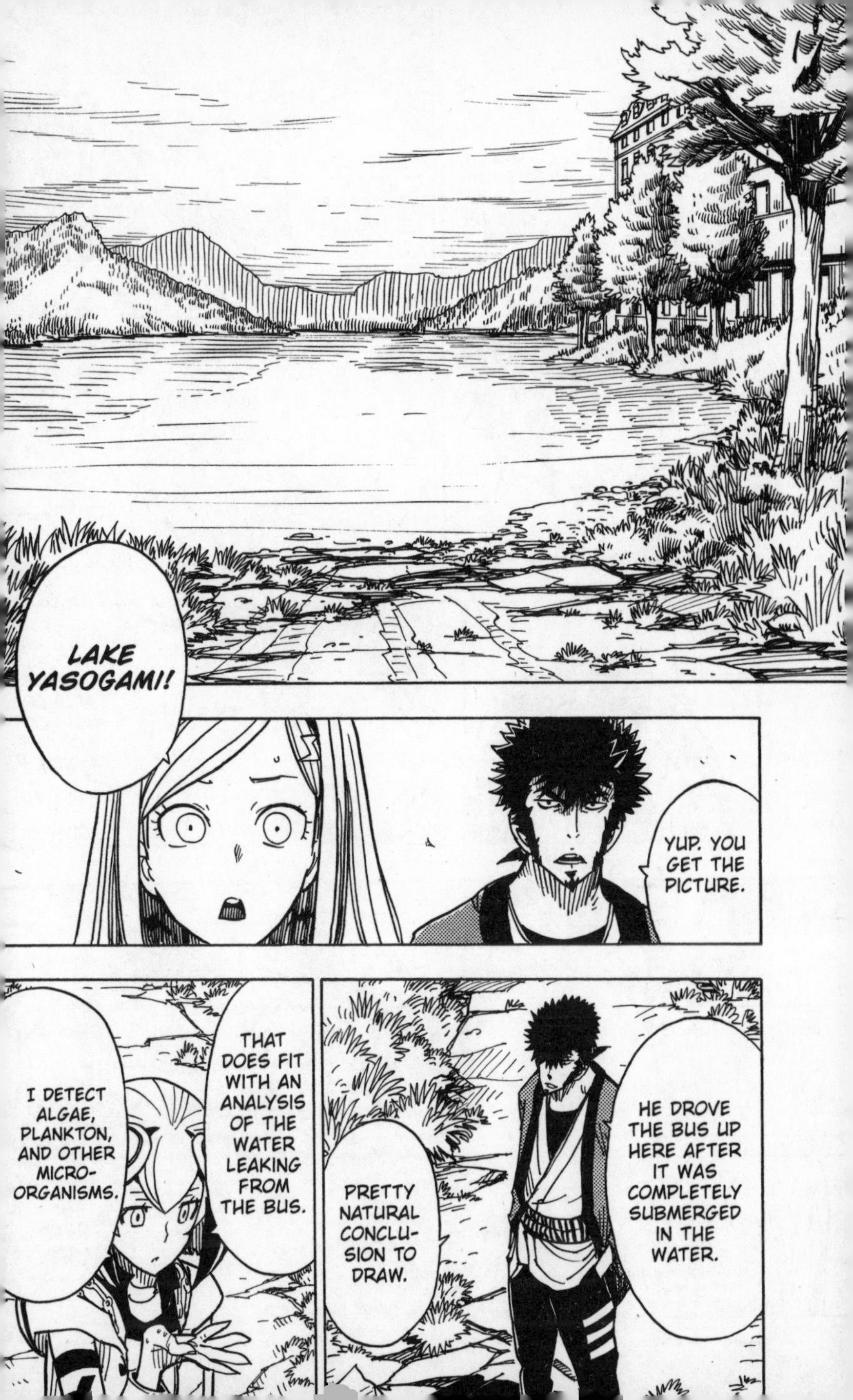

LAKE YASOGAMI!
YUP. YOU GET THE PICTURE.
HE DROVE THE BUS UP HERE AFTER IT WAS COMPLETELY SUBMERGED IN THE WATER.
PRETTY NATURAL CONCLUSION TO DRAW.
THAT DOES FIT WITH AN ANALYSIS OF THE WATER LEAKING FROM THE BUS.
I DETECT ALGAE, PLANKTON, AND OTHER MICRO-ORGANISMS.

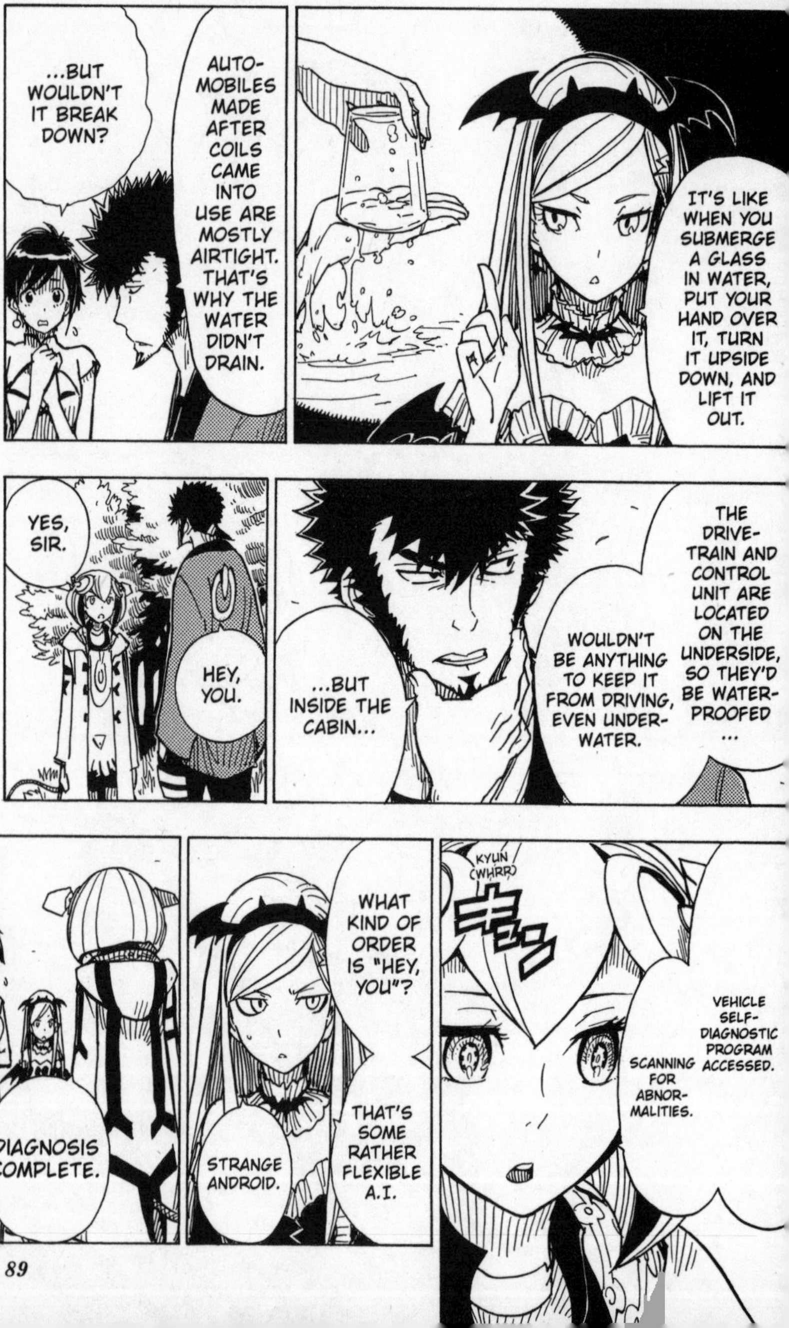

IT'S LIKE WHEN YOU SUBMERGE A GLASS IN WATER, PUT YOUR HAND OVER IT, TURN IT UPSIDE DOWN, AND LIFT IT OUT.
AUTO-MOBILES MADE AFTER COILS CAME INTO USE ARE MOSTLY AIRTIGHT. THAT'S WHY THE WATER DIDN'T DRAIN.
...BUT WOULDN'T IT BREAK DOWN?
THE DRIVE-TRAIN AND CONTROL UNIT ARE LOCATED ON THE UNDERSIDE, SO THEY'D BE WATER-PROOFED ...
WOULDN'T BE ANYTHING TO KEEP IT FROM DRIVING, EVEN UNDER-WATER.
...BUT INSIDE THE CABIN...
HEY, YOU.
YES, SIR.
KYUN (WHRR)
VEHICLE SELF-DIAGNOSTIC PROGRAM ACCESSED.
SCANNING FOR ABNOR-MALITIES.
WHAT KIND OF ORDER IS "HEY, YOU"?
THAT'S SOME RATHER FLEXIBLE A.I.
STRANGE ANDROID.
DIAGNOSIS COMPLETE.

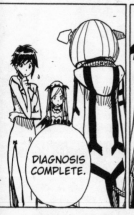

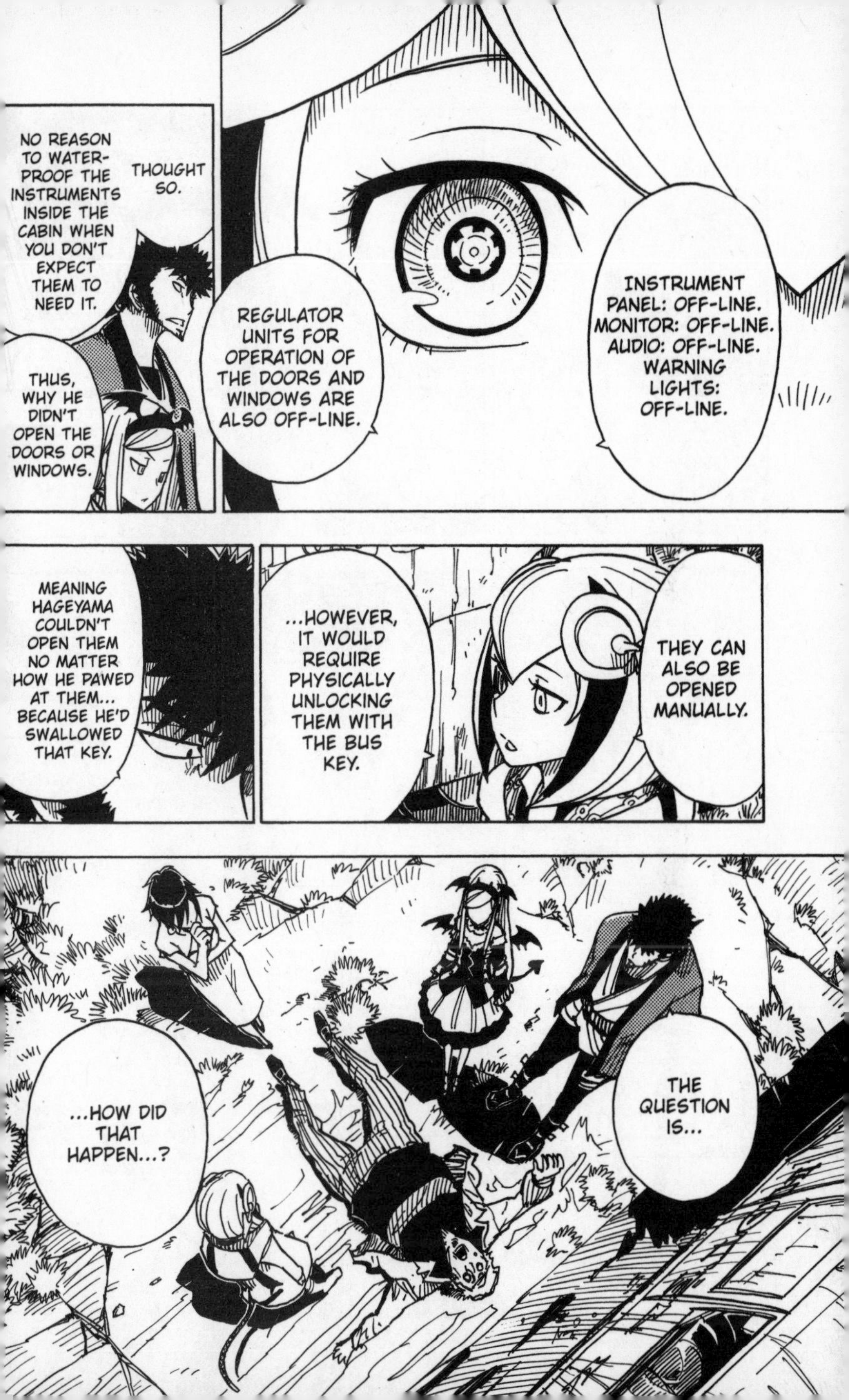
INSTRUMENT PANEL: OFF-LINE. MONITOR: OFF-LINE. AUDIO: OFF-LINE. WARNING LIGHTS: OFF-LINE.
REGULATOR UNITS FOR OPERATION OF THE DOORS AND WINDOWS ARE ALSO OFF-LINE.
THOUGHT SO.
NO REASON TO WATER-PROOF THE INSTRUMENTS INSIDE THE CABIN WHEN YOU DON'T EXPECT THEM TO NEED IT.
THUS, WHY HE DIDN'T OPEN THE DOORS OR WINDOWS.
THEY CAN ALSO BE OPENED MANUALLY.
...HOWEVER, IT WOULD REQUIRE PHYSICALLY UNLOCKING THEM WITH THE BUS KEY.
MEANING HAGEYAMA COULDN'T OPEN THEM NO MATTER HOW HE PAWED AT THEM... BECAUSE HE'D SWALLOWED THAT KEY.
THE QUESTION IS...
...HOW DID THAT HAPPEN...?

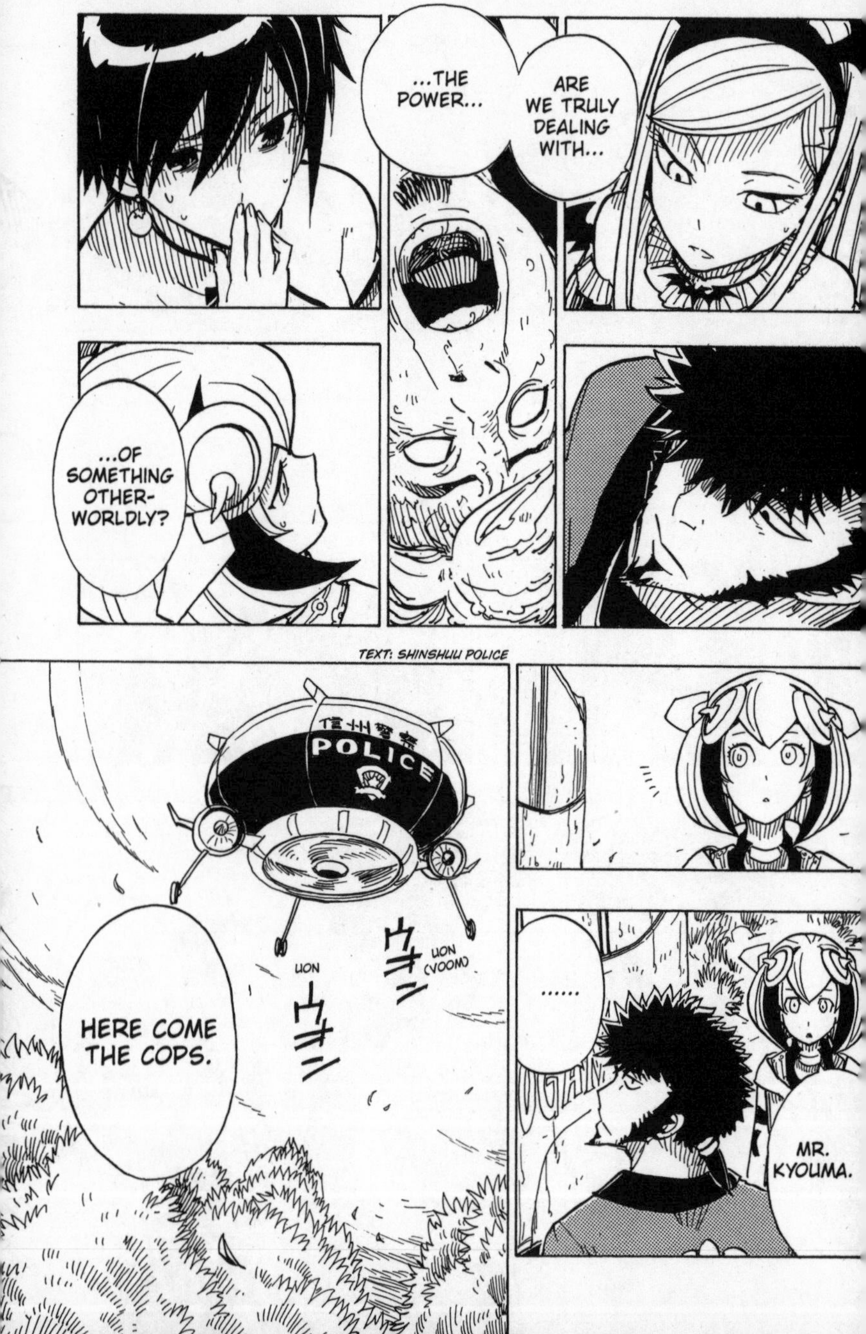
ARE WE TRULY DEALING WITH...
...THE POWER...
...OF SOMETHING OTHER-WORLDLY?
TEXT: SHINSHUU POLICE
......
MR. KYOUMA.
信州警察
POLICE
ウォン
UON (VOOM)
ウォン
UON
HERE COME THE COPS.

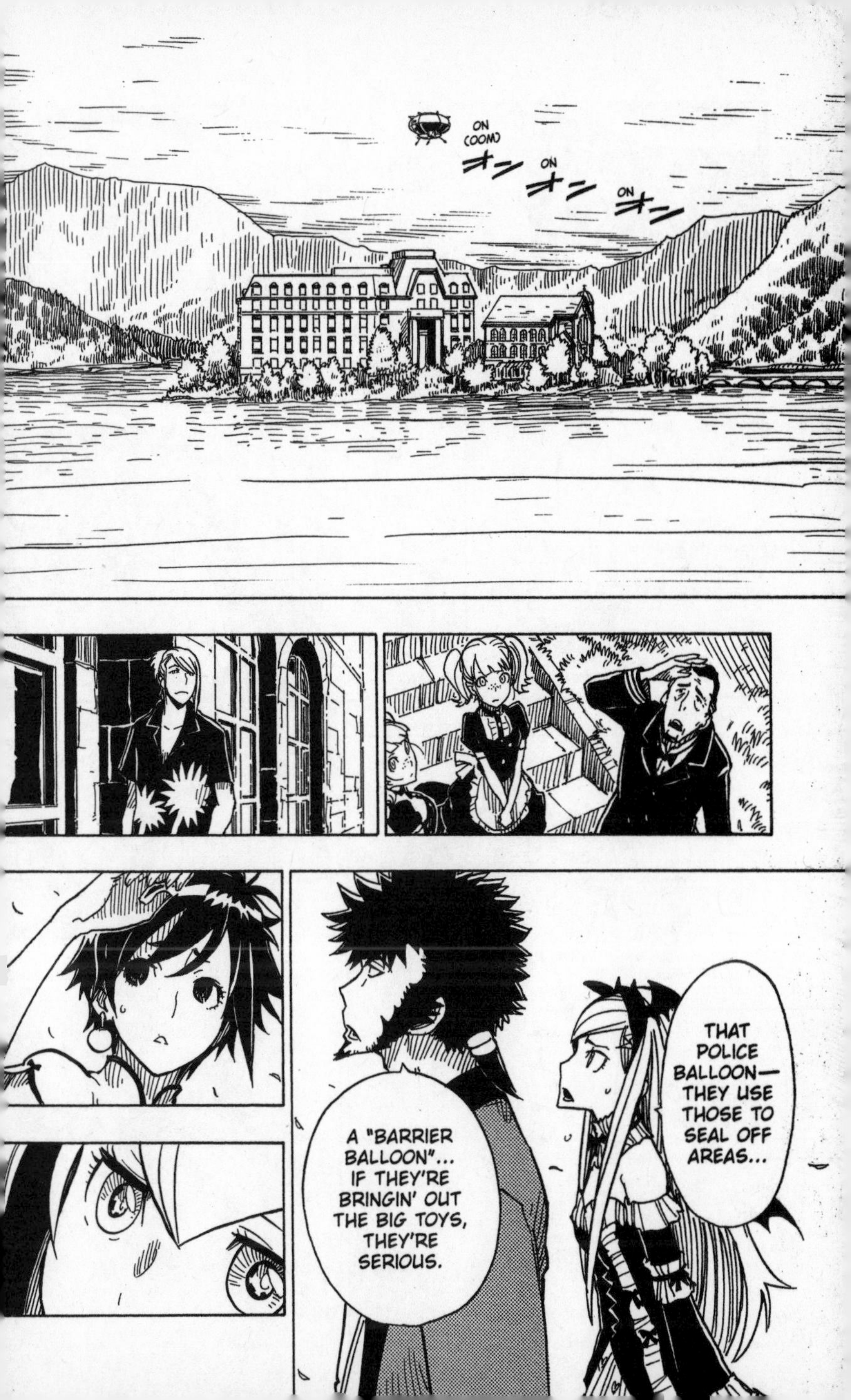
ON (OOM)
オン
ON
オン
ON
オン
THAT POLICE BALLOON—THEY USE THOSE TO SEAL OFF AREAS...
A "BARRIER BALLOON"... IF THEY'RE BRINGIN' OUT THE BIG TOYS, THEY'RE SERIOUS.

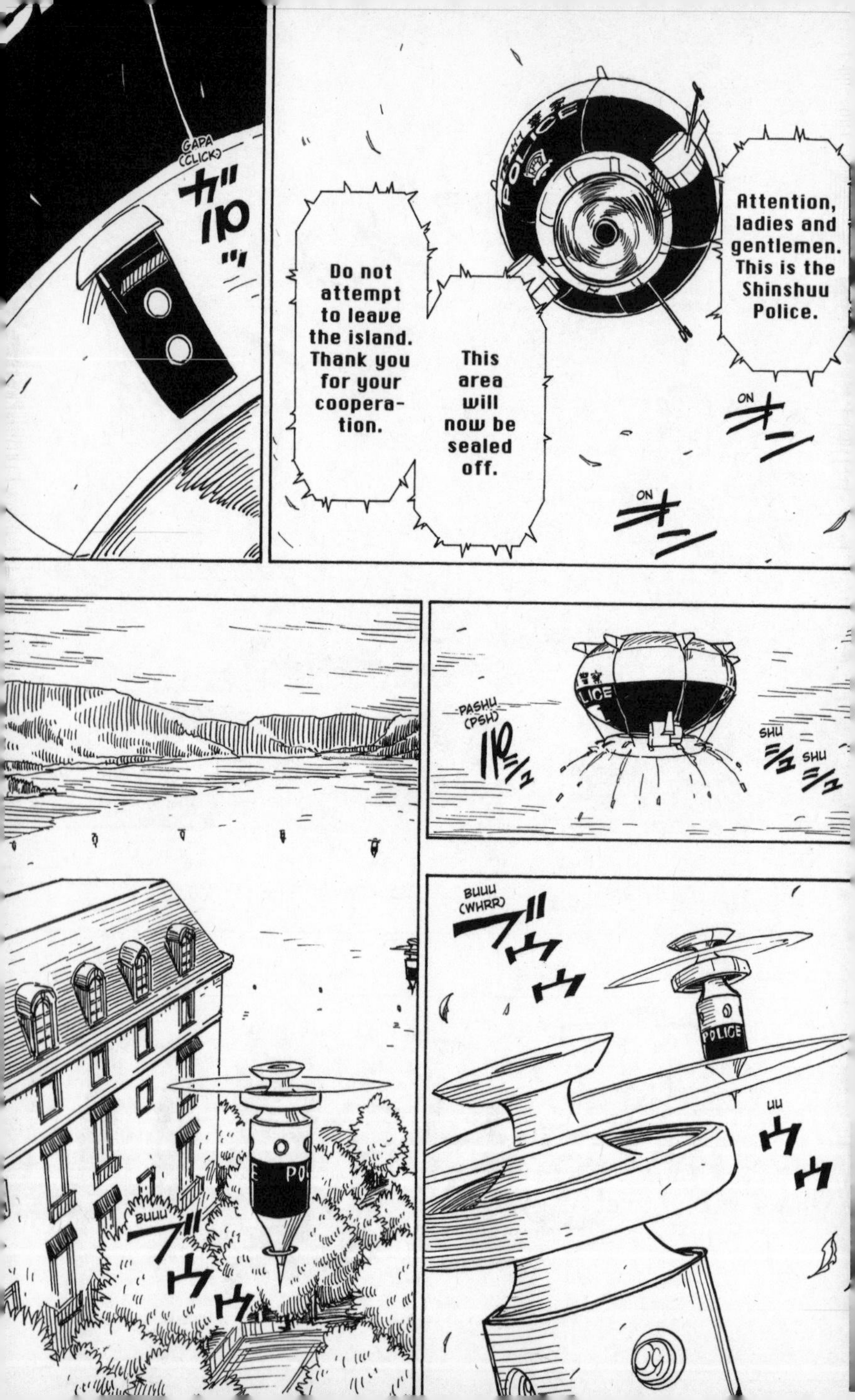
Attention, ladies and gentlemen. This is the Shinshuu Police.
This area will now be sealed off.
Do not attempt to leave the island. Thank you for your cooperation.
ON
オン
ON
オン
GAPA (CLICK)
ガパッ
SHU
シュ
SHU
シュ
PASHU (PSH)
パシュ
BUUU (WHRR)
ブゥゥ
UU
ウゥ
BUUU
ブゥゥ

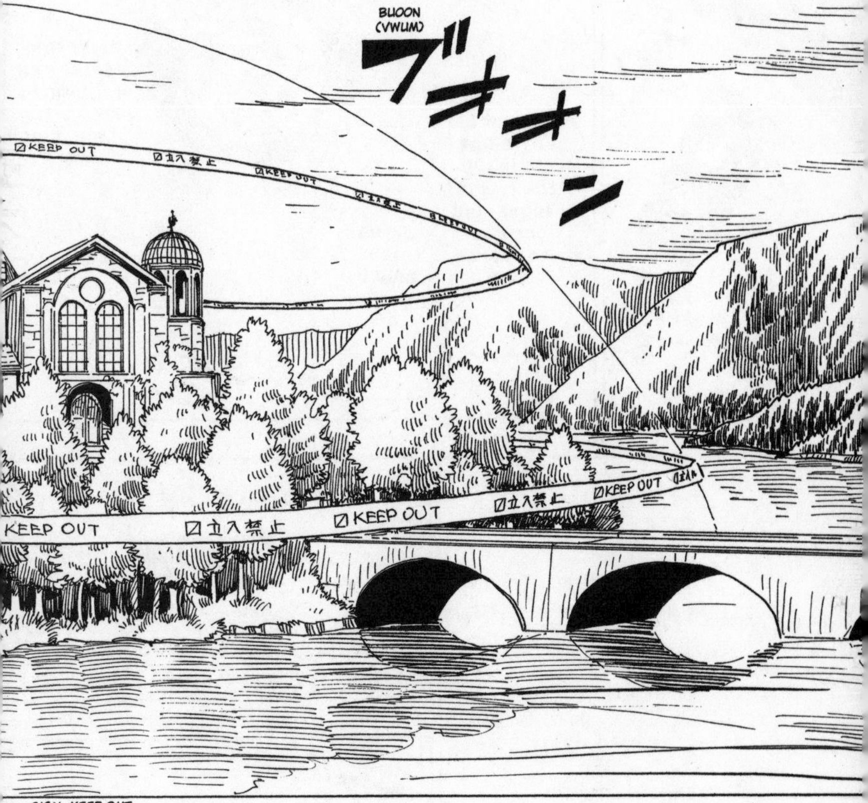
BUOON
(VWUM)
ブオォン
KEEP OUT
立入禁止
KEEP OUT
立入禁止
KEEP OUT
立入禁止
KEEP OUT
KEEP OUT
立入禁止

SIGN: KEEP OUT

SIGN: LOCKDOWN

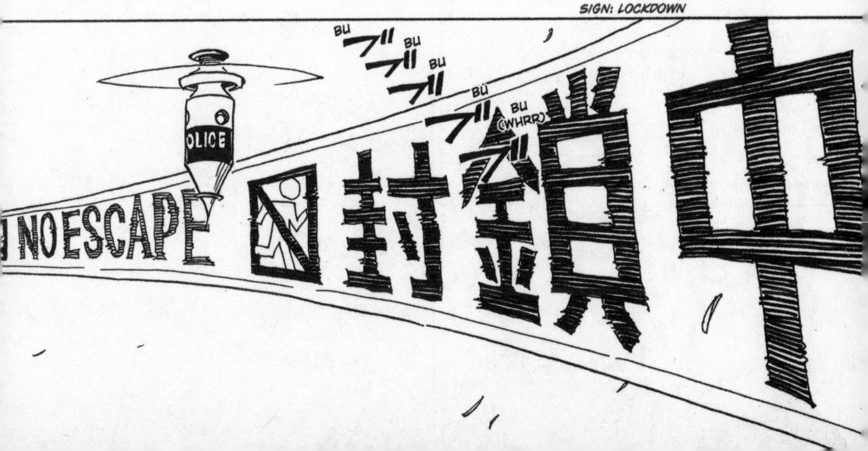
BU
ブ
BU
ブ
BU
ブ
BU
ブ
BU
(WHRR)
ヴ
OLICE
NOESCAPE
封鎖中

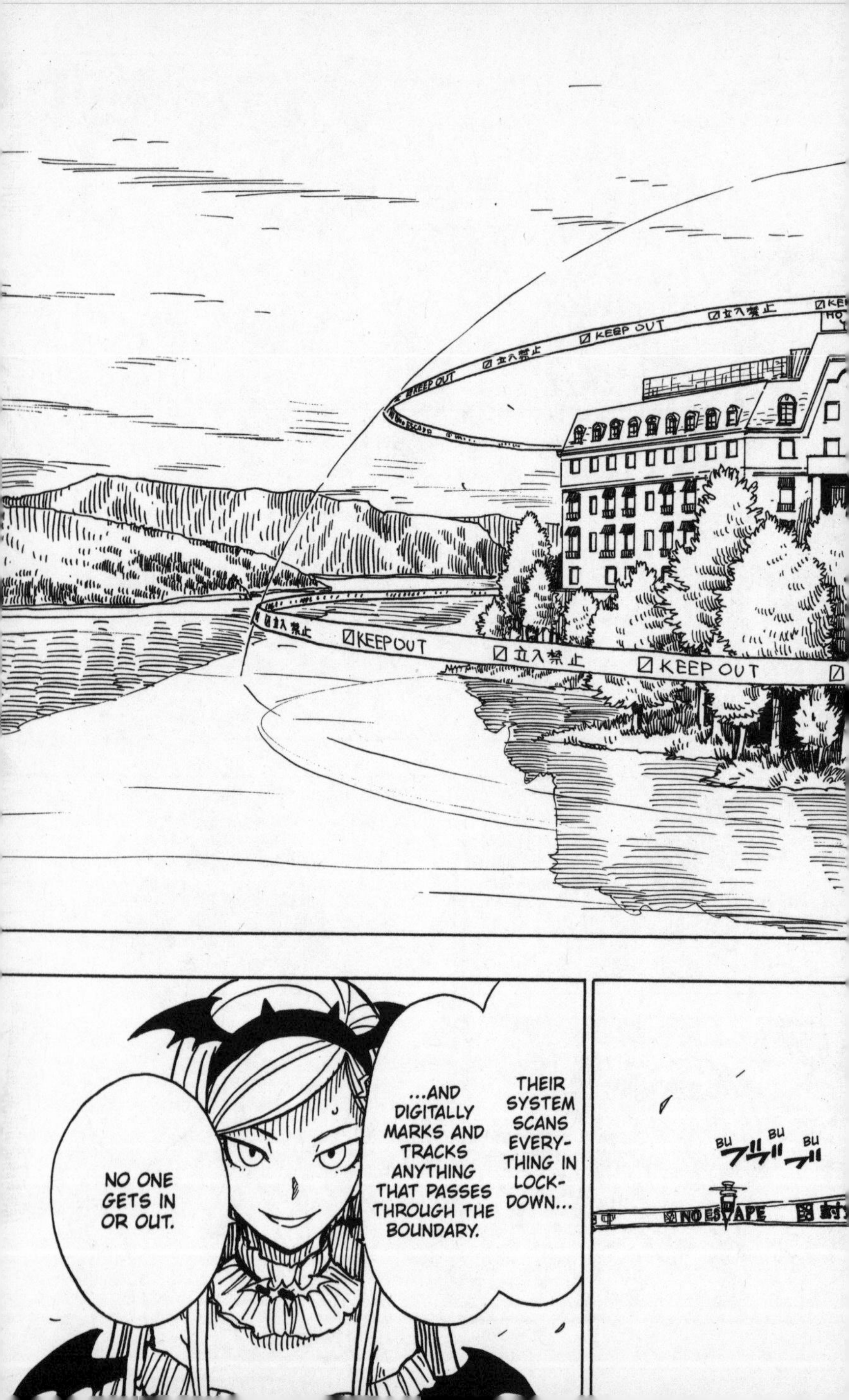
KEEP OUT
立入禁止
KEEP OUT
立入禁止
KEEP OUT
BU BU BU
THEIR SYSTEM SCANS EVERY-THING IN LOCK-DOWN...
...AND DIGITALLY MARKS AND TRACKS ANYTHING THAT PASSES THROUGH THE BOUNDARY.
NO ONE GETS IN OR OUT.

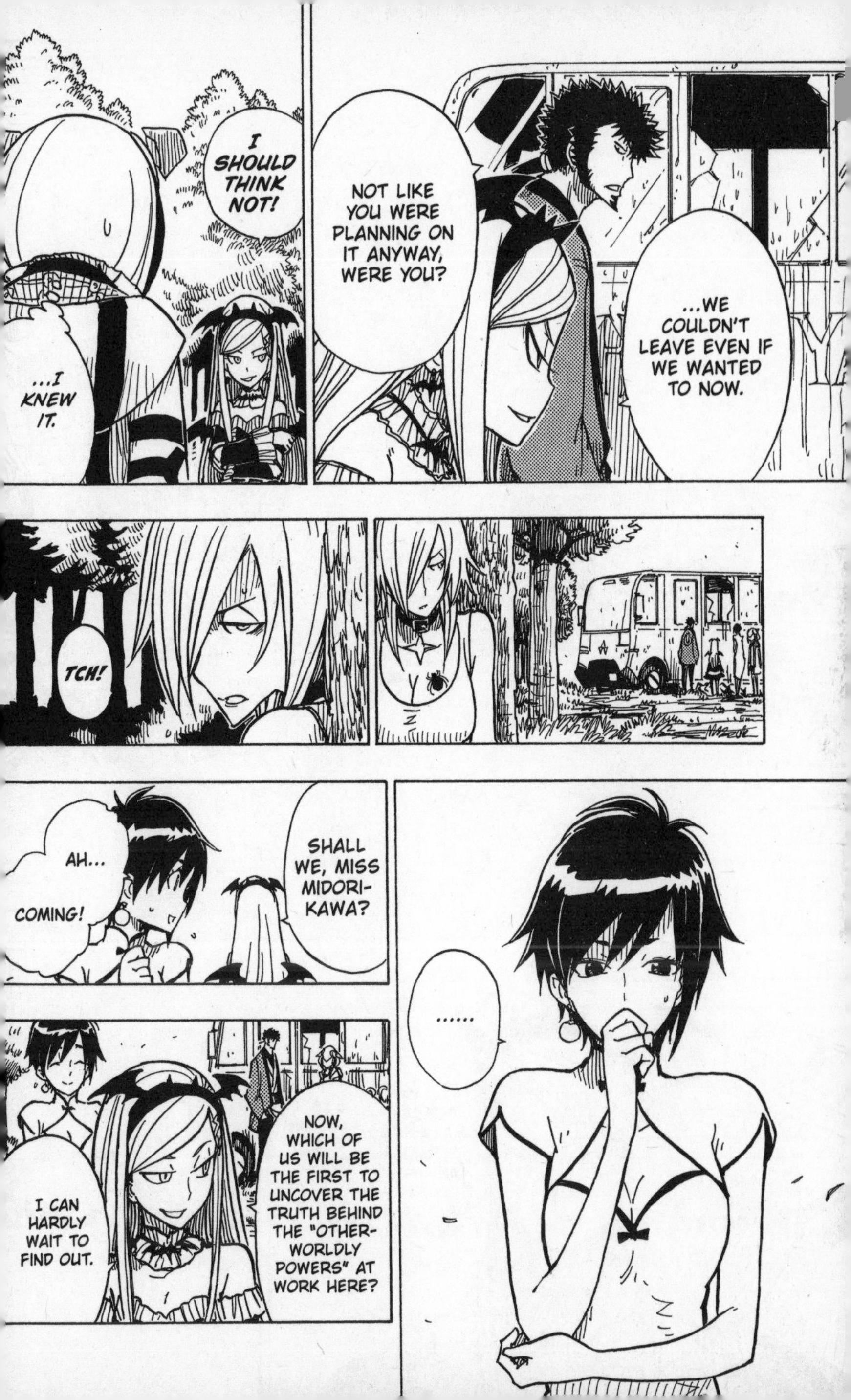
...WE COULDN'T LEAVE EVEN IF WE WANTED TO NOW.
NOT LIKE YOU WERE PLANNING ON IT ANYWAY, WERE YOU?
I SHOULD THINK NOT!
...I KNEW IT.
TCH!
......
SHALL WE, MISS MIDORI-KAWA?
AH...
COMING!
NOW, WHICH OF US WILL BE THE FIRST TO UNCOVER THE TRUTH BEHIND THE "OTHER-WORLDLY POWERS" AT WORK HERE?
I CAN HARDLY WAIT TO FIND OUT.

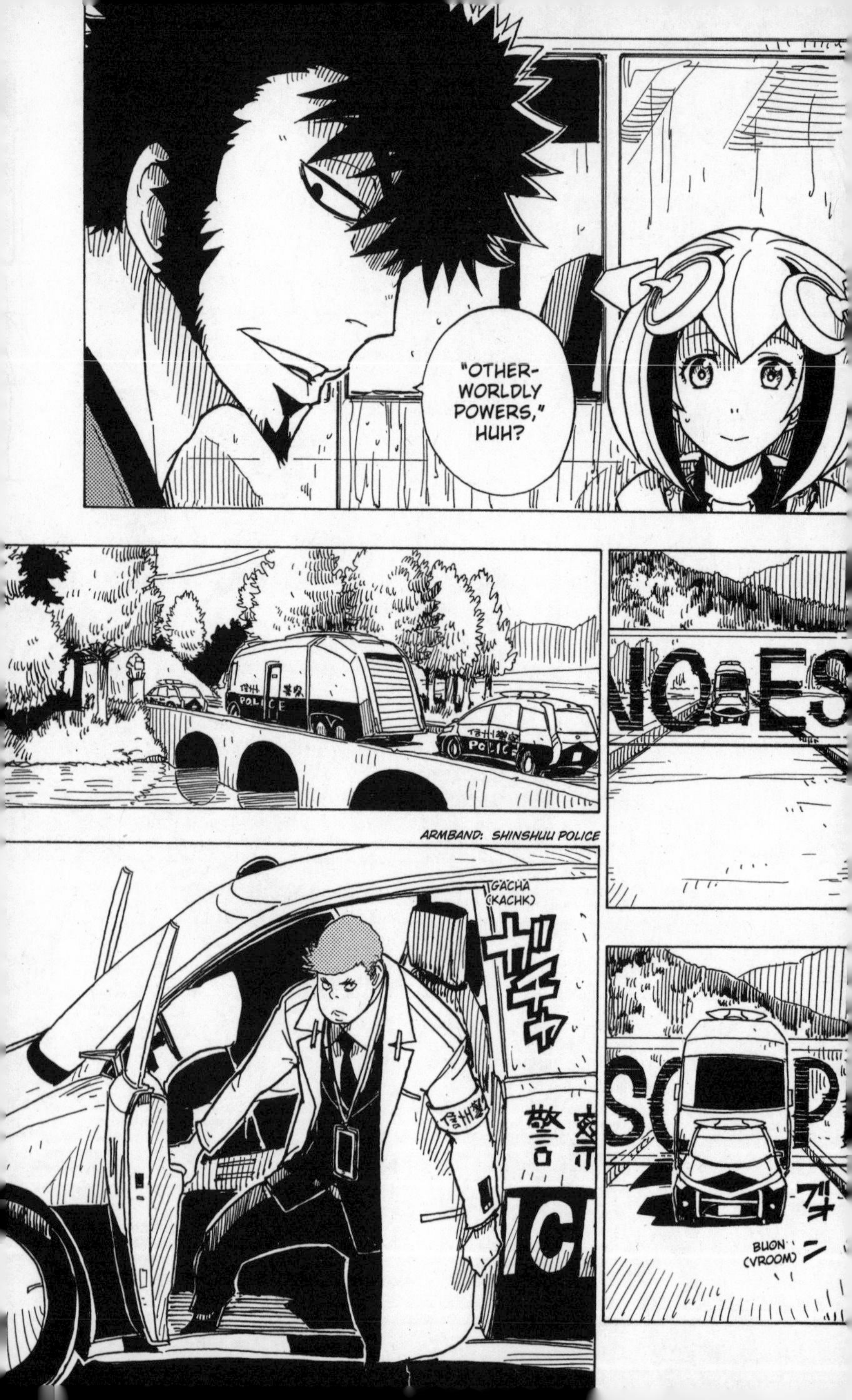
"OTHER-WORLDLY POWERS," HUH?
BUON (VROOM)
ARMBAND: SHINSHUU POLICE
GACHA (KACHK)

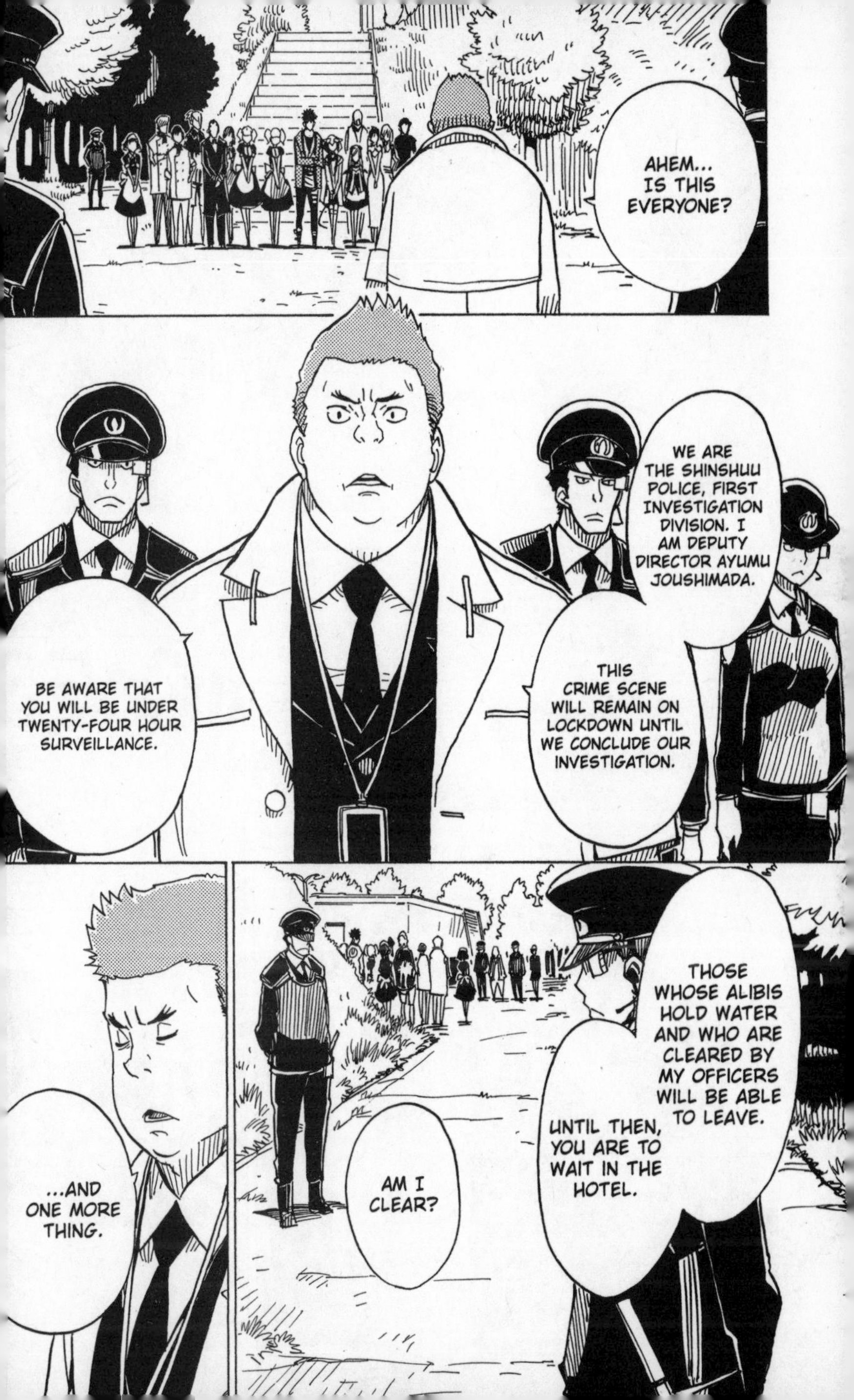
AHEM... IS THIS EVERYONE?
WE ARE THE SHINSHUU POLICE, FIRST INVESTIGATION DIVISION. I AM DEPUTY DIRECTOR AYUMU JOUSHIMADA.
THIS CRIME SCENE WILL REMAIN ON LOCKDOWN UNTIL WE CONCLUDE OUR INVESTIGATION.
BE AWARE THAT YOU WILL BE UNDER TWENTY-FOUR HOUR SURVEILLANCE.
THOSE WHOSE ALIBIS HOLD WATER AND WHO ARE CLEARED BY MY OFFICERS WILL BE ABLE TO LEAVE.
UNTIL THEN, YOU ARE TO WAIT IN THE HOTEL.
AM I CLEAR?
...AND ONE MORE THING.

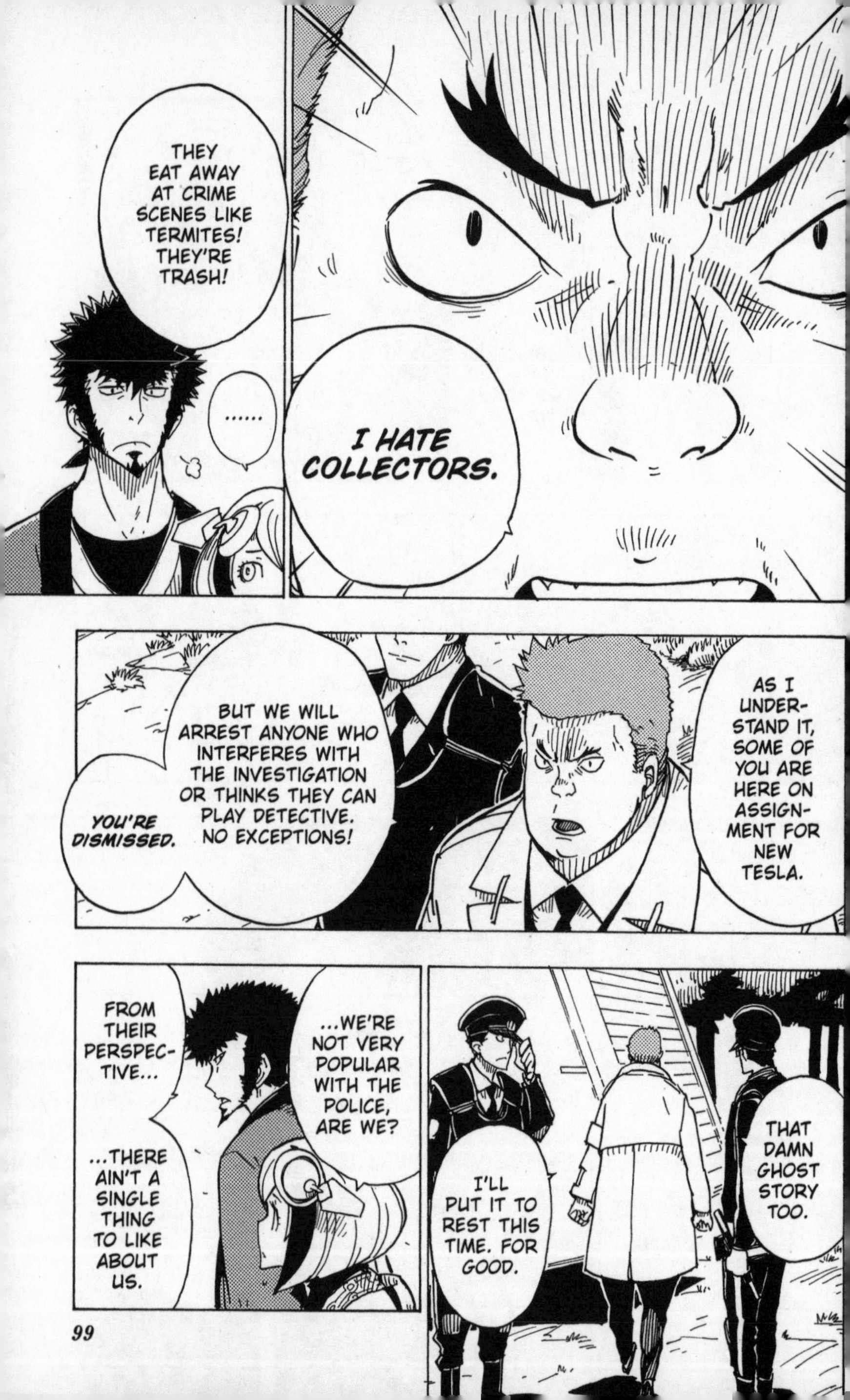
I HATE COLLECTORS.
THEY EAT AWAY AT CRIME SCENES LIKE TERMITES! THEY'RE TRASH!
......
AS I UNDER-STAND IT, SOME OF YOU ARE HERE ON ASSIGN-MENT FOR NEW TESLA.
BUT WE WILL ARREST ANYONE WHO INTERFERES WITH THE INVESTIGATION OR THINKS THEY CAN PLAY DETECTIVE. NO EXCEPTIONS!
YOU'RE DISMISSED.
THAT DAMN GHOST STORY TOO.
I'LL PUT IT TO REST THIS TIME. FOR GOOD.
...WE'RE NOT VERY POPULAR WITH THE POLICE, ARE WE?
FROM THEIR PERSPEC-TIVE...
...THERE AIN'T A SINGLE THING TO LIKE ABOUT US.

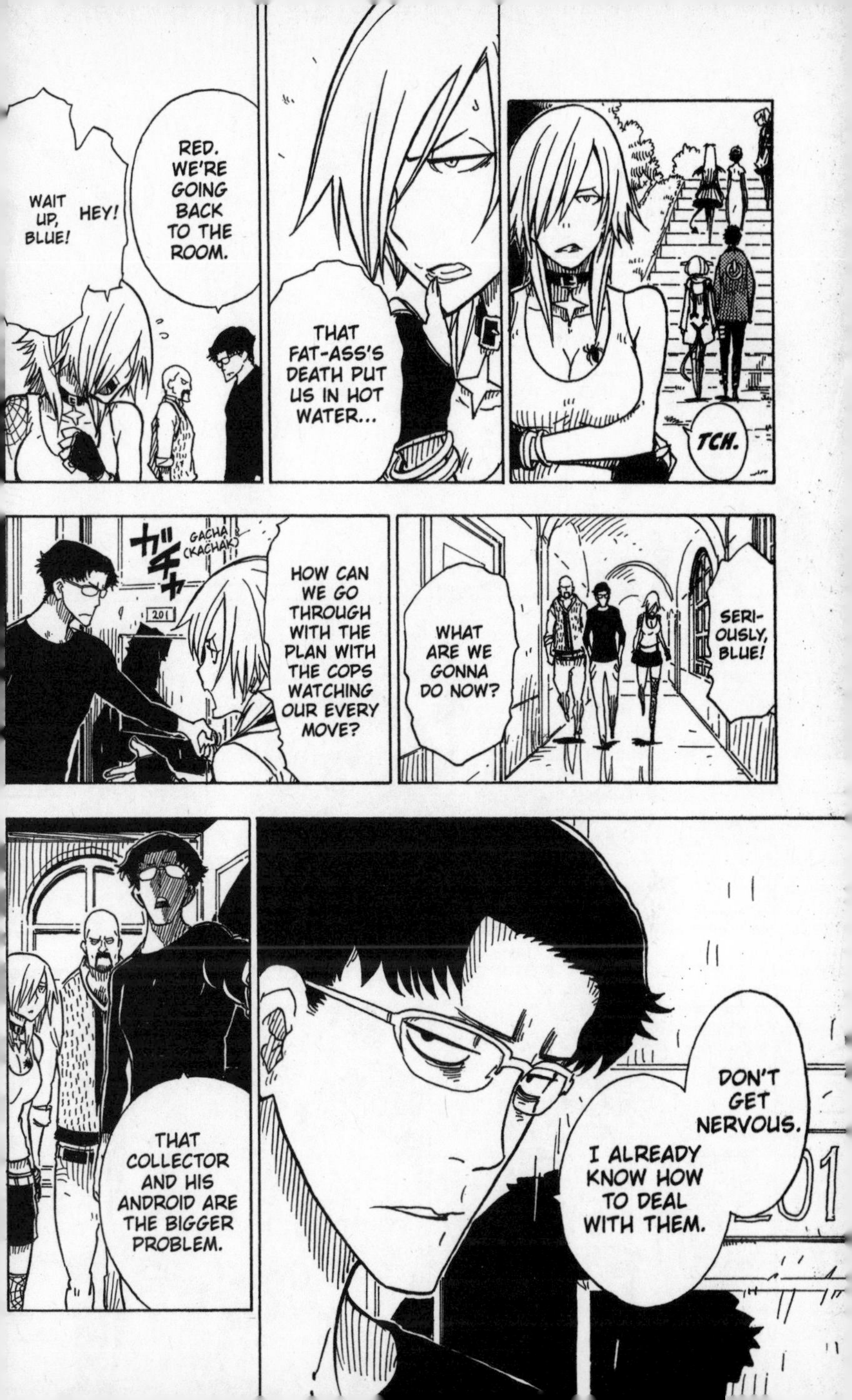
TCH.
THAT FAT-ASS'S DEATH PUT US IN HOT WATER...
RED. WE'RE GOING BACK TO THE ROOM.
HEY!
WAIT UP, BLUE!
SERI-OUSLY, BLUE!
WHAT ARE WE GONNA DO NOW?
HOW CAN WE GO THROUGH WITH THE PLAN WITH THE COPS WATCHING OUR EVERY MOVE?
ガチャ
GACHA (KACHAK)
DON'T GET NERVOUS.
I ALREADY KNOW HOW TO DEAL WITH THEM.
THAT COLLECTOR AND HIS ANDROID ARE THE BIGGER PROBLEM.

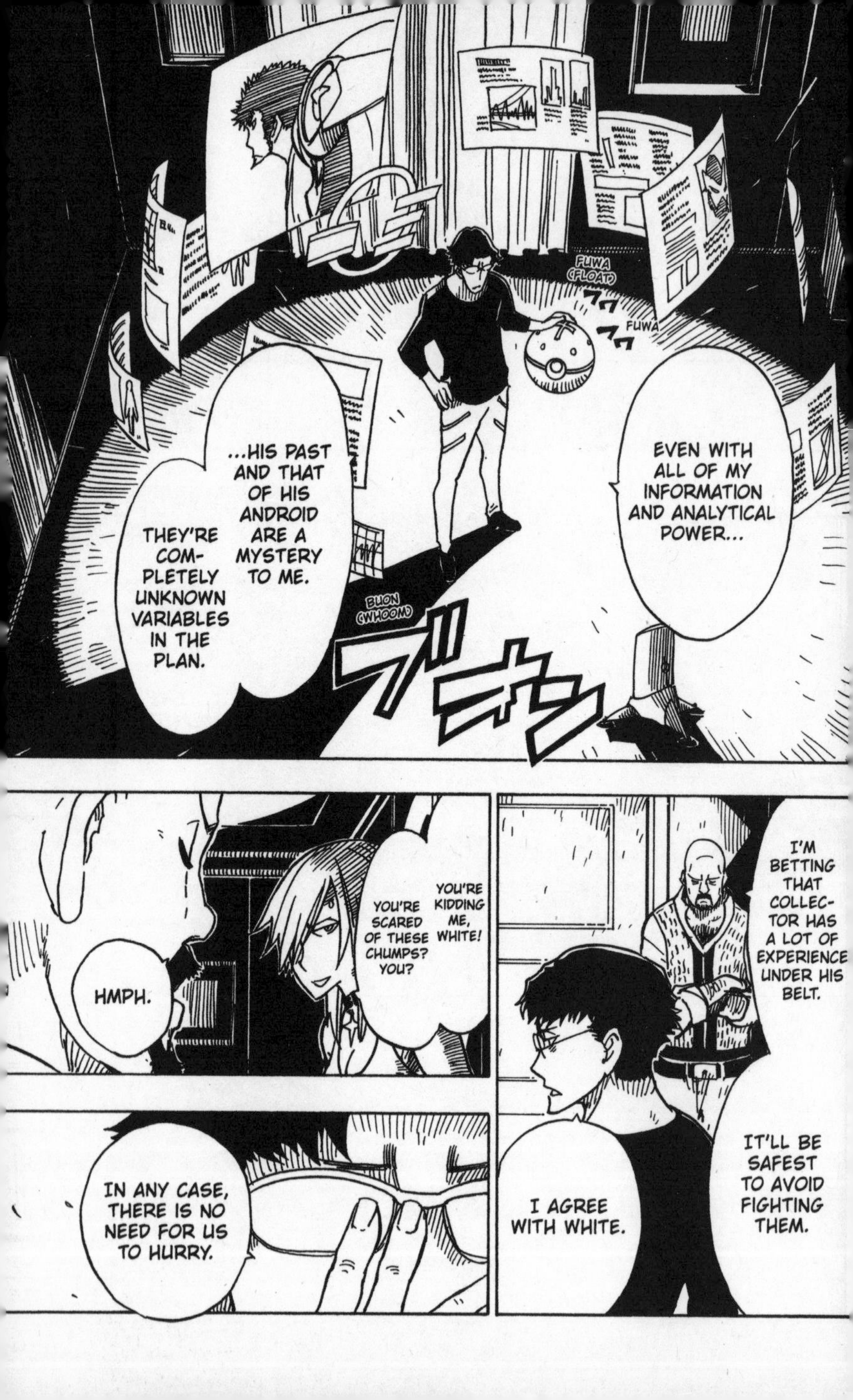
FUWA (FLOAT)
FUWA
EVEN WITH ALL OF MY INFORMATION AND ANALYTICAL POWER...
...HIS PAST AND THAT OF HIS ANDROID ARE A MYSTERY TO ME.
THEY'RE COM-PLETELY UNKNOWN VARIABLES IN THE PLAN.
BUON (WHOOM)
I'M BETTING THAT COLLEC-TOR HAS A LOT OF EXPERIENCE UNDER HIS BELT.
IT'LL BE SAFEST TO AVOID FIGHTING THEM.
I AGREE WITH WHITE.
YOU'RE KIDDING ME, WHITE!
YOU'RE SCARED OF THESE CHUMPS? YOU?
HMPH.
IN ANY CASE, THERE IS NO NEED FOR US TO HURRY.

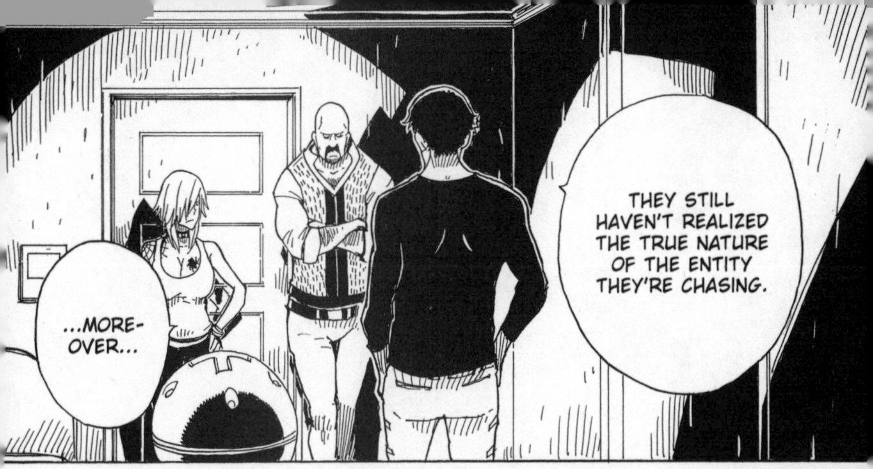
THEY STILL HAVEN'T REALIZED THE TRUE NATURE OF THE ENTITY THEY'RE CHASING.
...MORE-OVER...
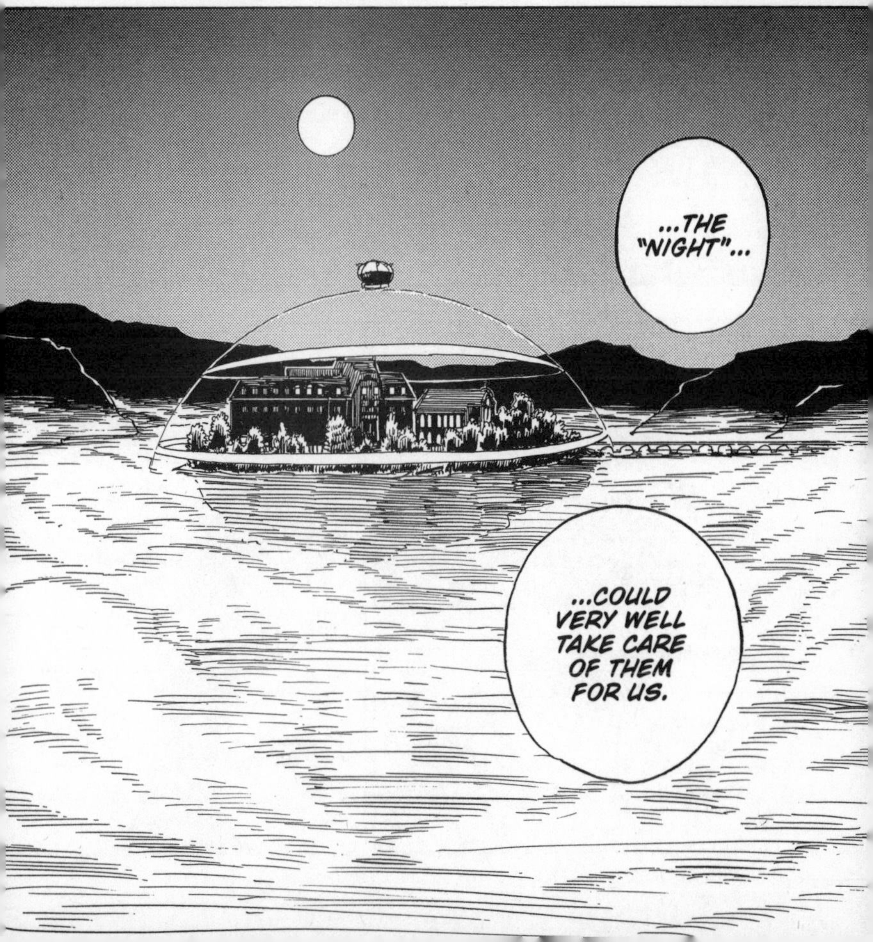
...THE "NIGHT"...
...COULD VERY WELL TAKE CARE OF THEM FOR US.

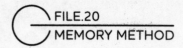

FILE.20
MEMORY METHOD

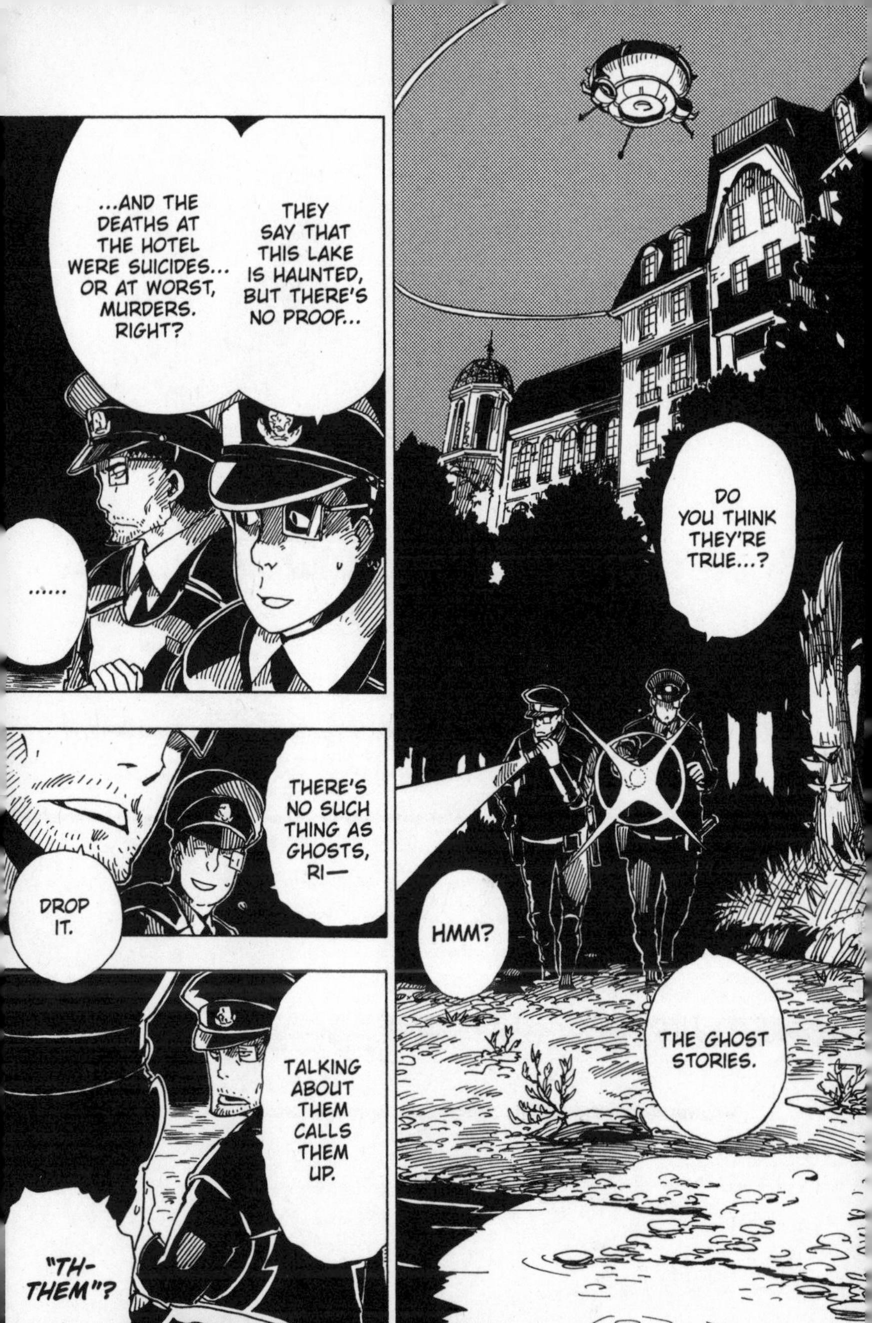
DO YOU THINK THEY'RE TRUE...?
HMM?
THE GHOST STORIES.
THEY SAY THAT THIS LAKE IS HAUNTED, BUT THERE'S NO PROOF...
...AND THE DEATHS AT THE HOTEL WERE SUICIDES... OR AT WORST, MURDERS. RIGHT?
......
THERE'S NO SUCH THING AS GHOSTS, RI—
DROP IT.
TALKING ABOUT THEM CALLS THEM UP.
"TH-THEM"?

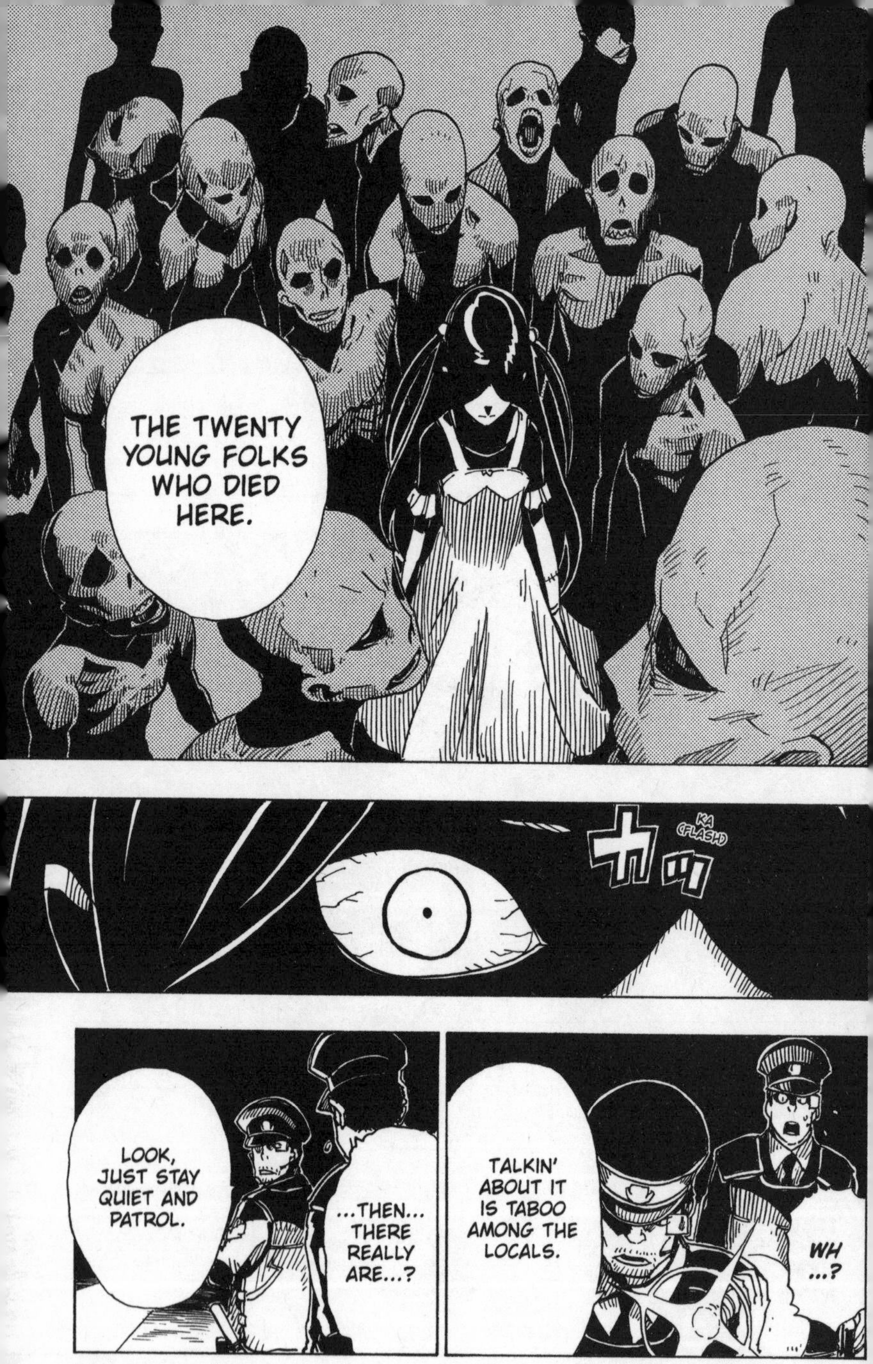
THE TWENTY YOUNG FOLKS WHO DIED HERE.
KA (FLASH)
TALKIN' ABOUT IT IS TABOO AMONG THE LOCALS.
WH ...?
...THEN... THERE REALLY ARE...?
LOOK, JUST STAY QUIET AND PATROL.

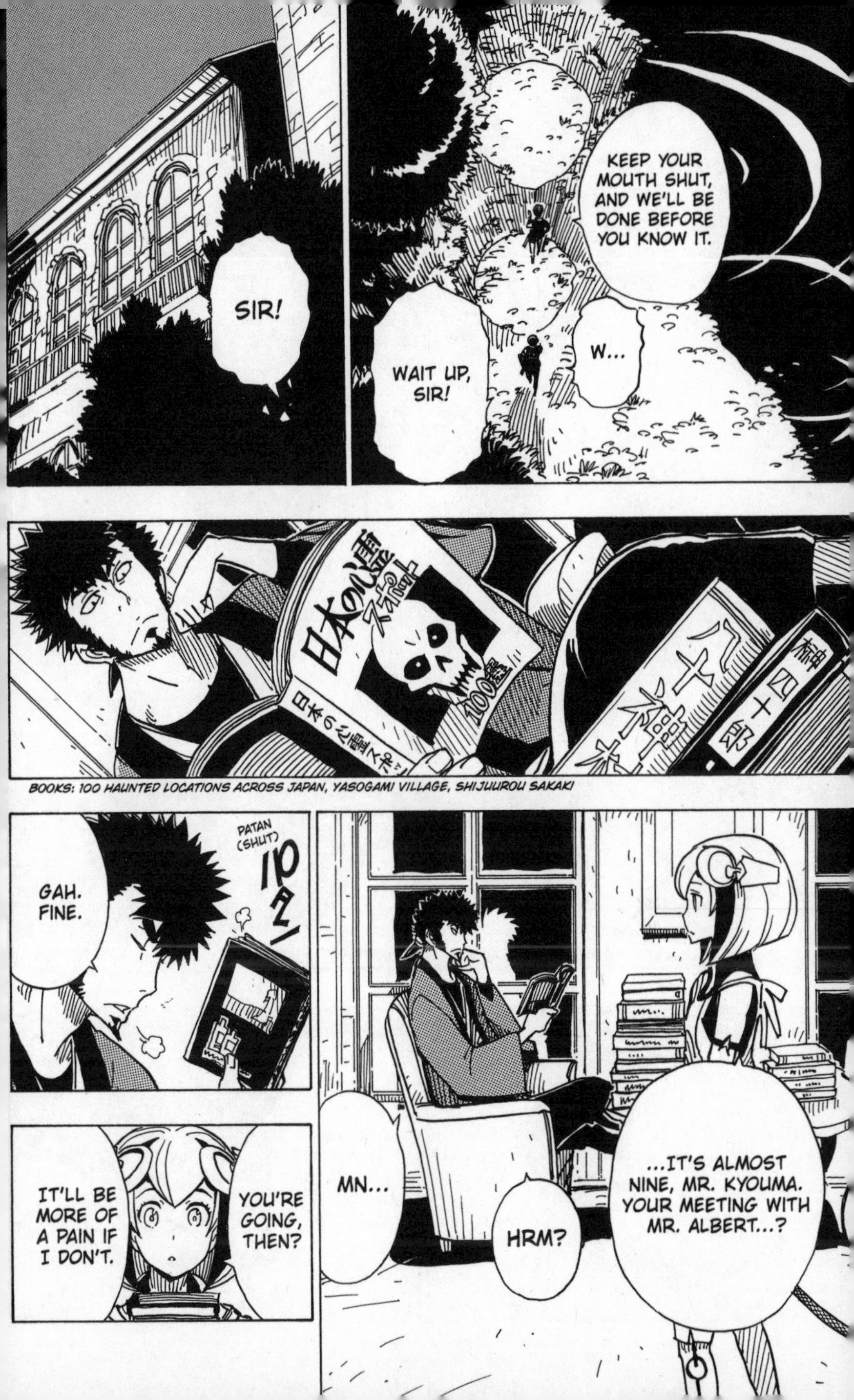
KEEP YOUR MOUTH SHUT, AND WE'LL BE DONE BEFORE YOU KNOW IT.
W...
WAIT UP, SIR!
SIR!
...IT'S ALMOST NINE, MR. KYOUMA. YOUR MEETING WITH MR. ALBERT...?
HRM?
MN...
PATAN (SHUT)
GAH. FINE.
YOU'RE GOING, THEN?
IT'LL BE MORE OF A PAIN IF I DON'T.
BOOKS: 100 HAUNTED LOCATIONS ACROSS JAPAN, YASOGAMI VILLAGE, SHIJUUROU SAKAKI

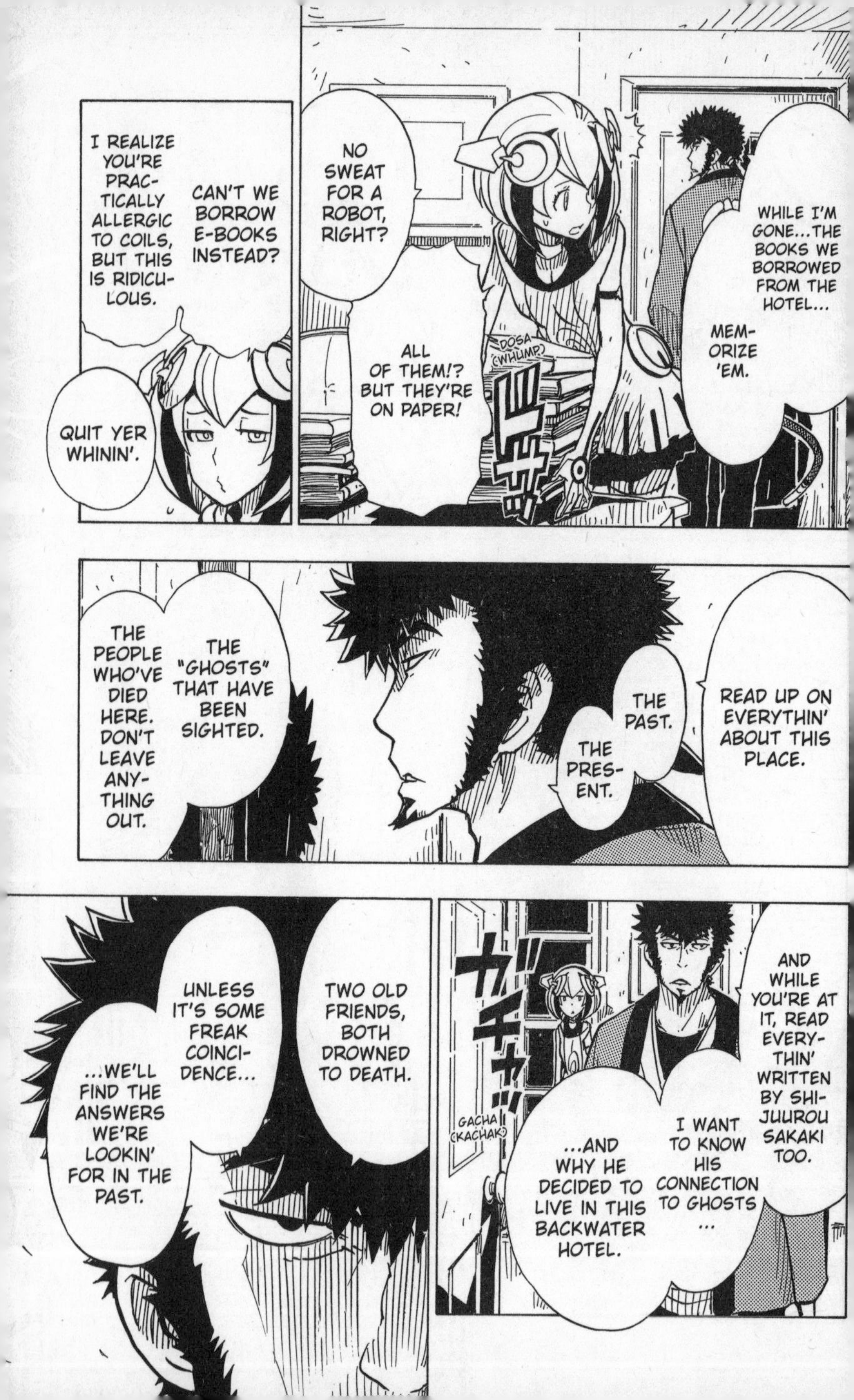
WHILE I'M GONE...THE BOOKS WE BORROWED FROM THE HOTEL...
MEMORIZE 'EM.
DOSA (WHUMP)
ALL OF THEM!? BUT THEY'RE ON PAPER!
NO SWEAT FOR A ROBOT, RIGHT?
CAN'T WE BORROW E-BOOKS INSTEAD?
I REALIZE YOU'RE PRACTICALLY ALLERGIC TO COILS, BUT THIS IS RIDICULOUS.
QUIT YER WHININ'.
READ UP ON EVERYTHIN' ABOUT THIS PLACE.
THE PAST.
THE PRESENT.
THE "GHOSTS" THAT HAVE BEEN SIGHTED.
THE PEOPLE WHO'VE DIED HERE. DON'T LEAVE ANYTHING OUT.
AND WHILE YOU'RE AT IT, READ EVERYTHIN' WRITTEN BY SHIJUUROU SAKAKI TOO.
I WANT TO KNOW HIS CONNECTION TO GHOSTS...
...AND WHY HE DECIDED TO LIVE IN THIS BACKWATER HOTEL.
GACHA (KACHAK)
TWO OLD FRIENDS, BOTH DROWNED TO DEATH.
UNLESS IT'S SOME FREAK COINCIDENCE...
...WE'LL FIND THE ANSWERS WE'RE LOOKIN' FOR IN THE PAST.

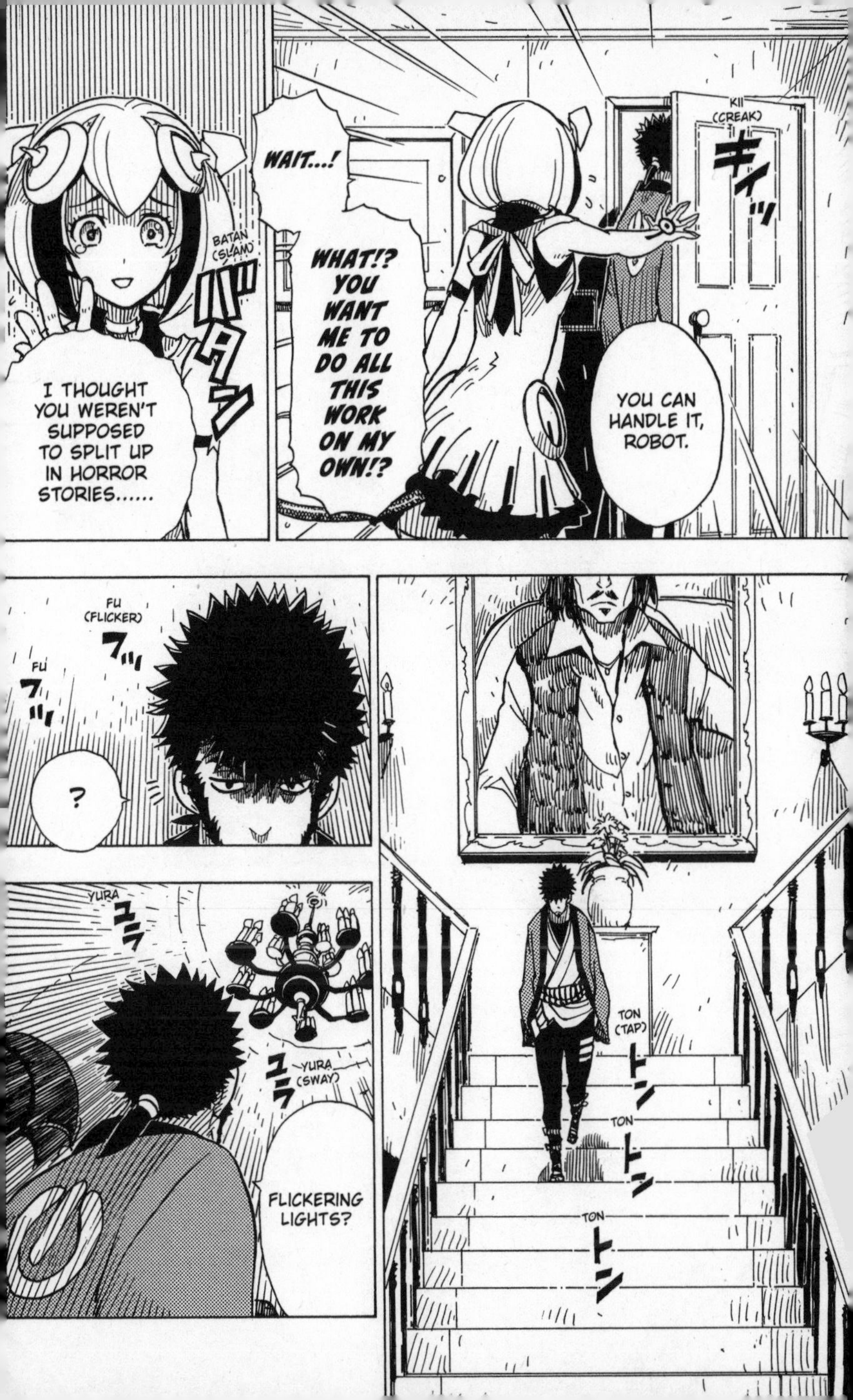
KII (CREAK)
キィッ
WAIT...!
WHAT!? YOU WANT ME TO DO ALL THIS WORK ON MY OWN!?
YOU CAN HANDLE IT, ROBOT.
BATAN (SLAM)
バタン
I THOUGHT YOU WEREN'T SUPPOSED TO SPLIT UP IN HORROR STORIES......
TON (TAP)
トン
TON
トン
TON
トン
FU (FLICKER)
フッ
FU
フッ
?
YURA
ユラ
YURA (SWAY)
ユラ
FLICKERING LIGHTS?

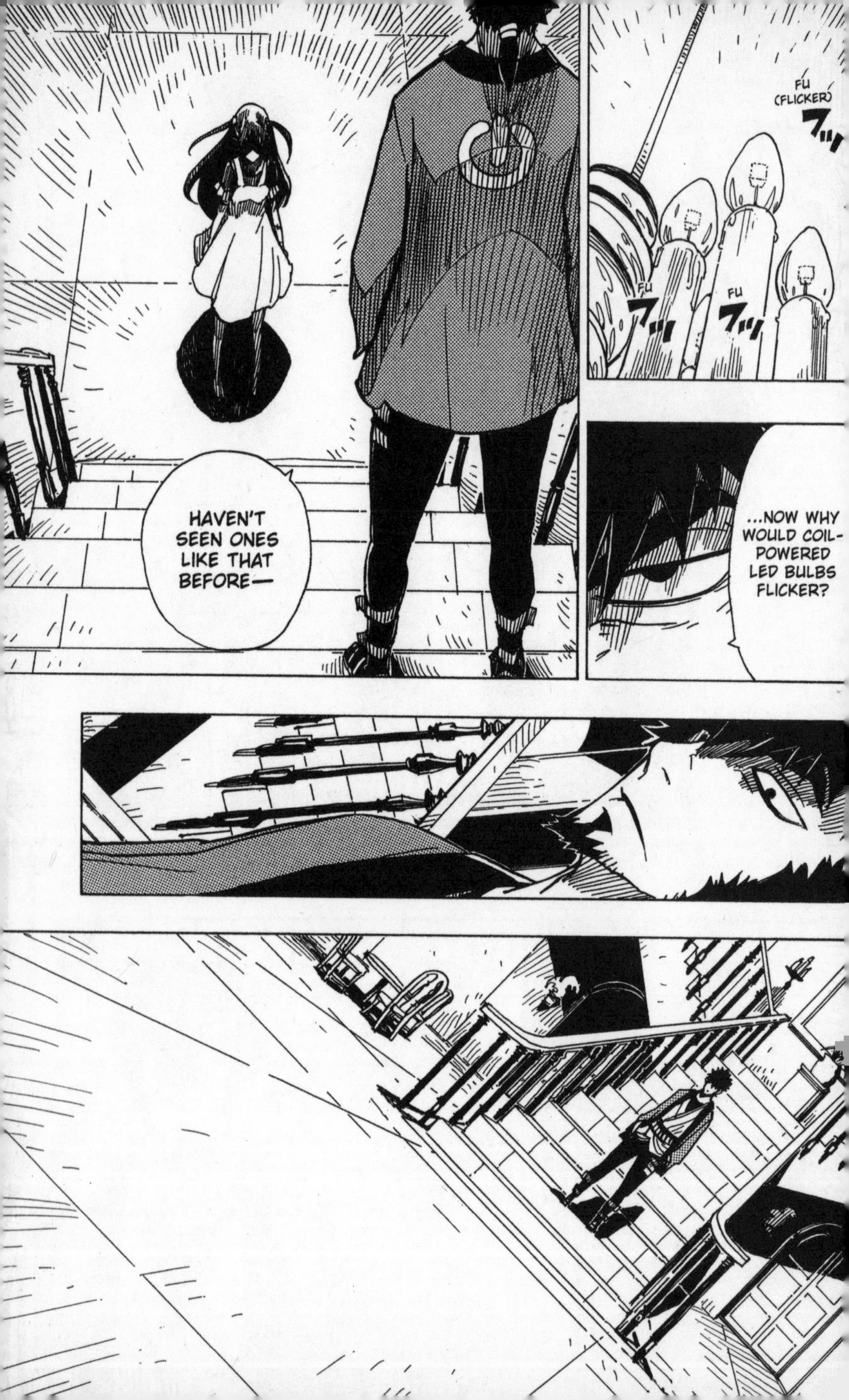
FU
(FLICKER)
フッ
FU
フッ
FU
フッ
...NOW WHY WOULD COIL-POWERED LED BULBS FLICKER?
HAVEN'T SEEN ONES LIKE THAT BEFORE—

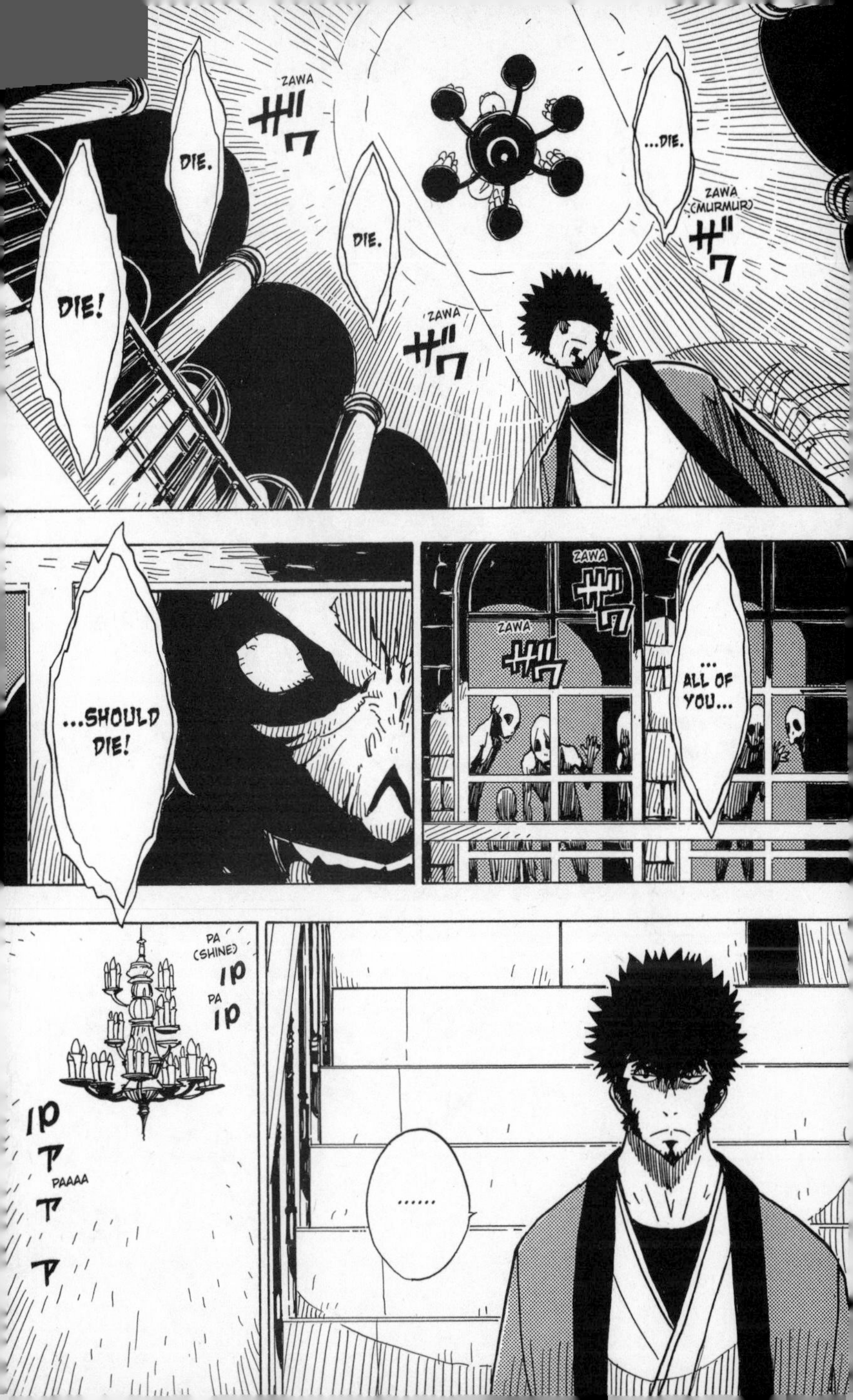
...DIE.
ZAWA (MURMUR)
ザワ
DIE.
ZAWA
ザワ
ZAWA
ザワ
DIE.
DIE!
ZAWA
ザワ
ZAWA
ザワ
... ALL OF YOU...
...SHOULD DIE!
......
PA (SHINE)
PA
PAAAA

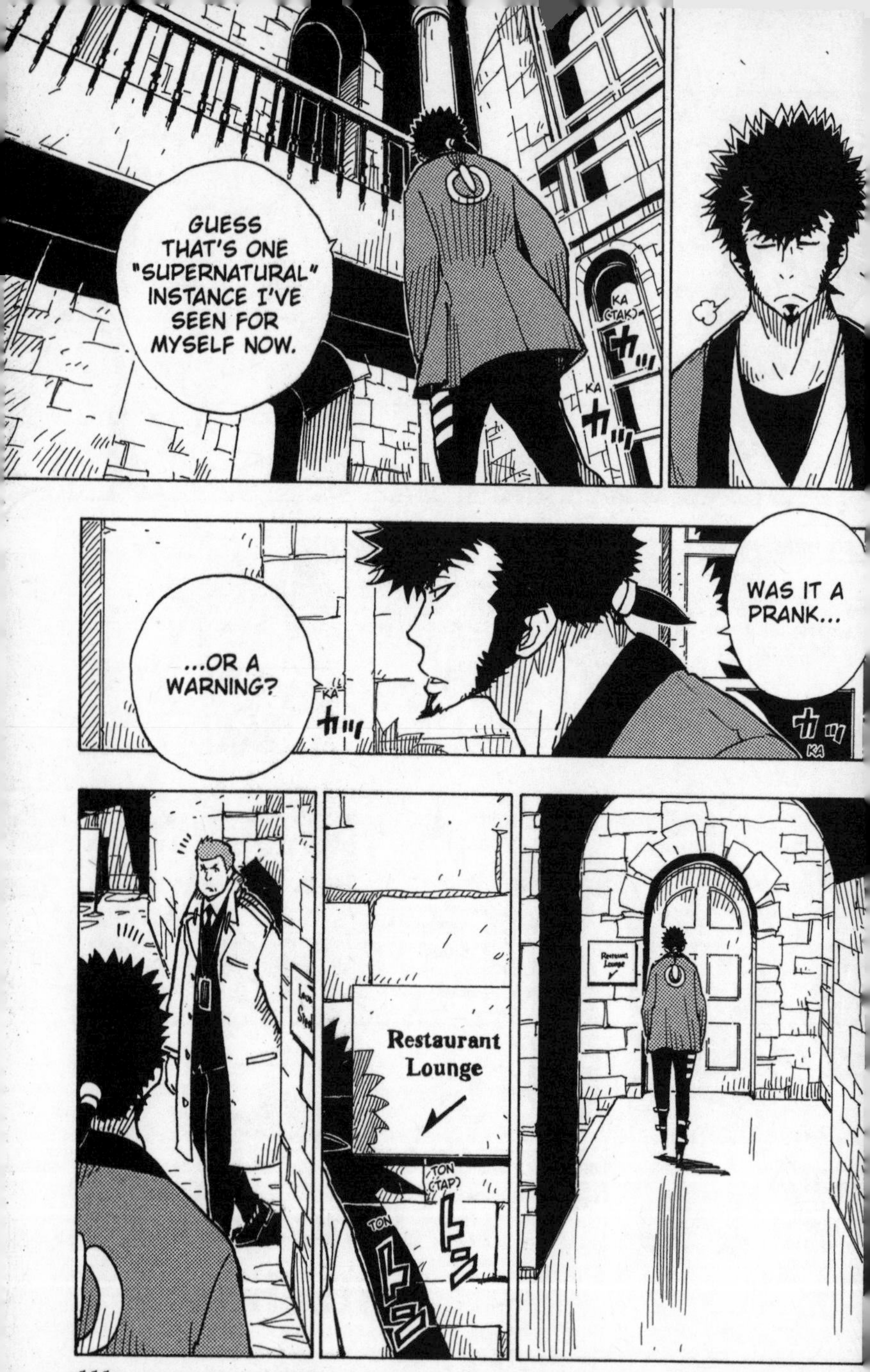
GUESS THAT'S ONE "SUPERNATURAL" INSTANCE I'VE SEEN FOR MYSELF NOW.
KA (TAK)
KA
WAS IT A PRANK...
KA
...OR A WARNING?
KA
Restaurant Lounge
TON (TAP)
TON

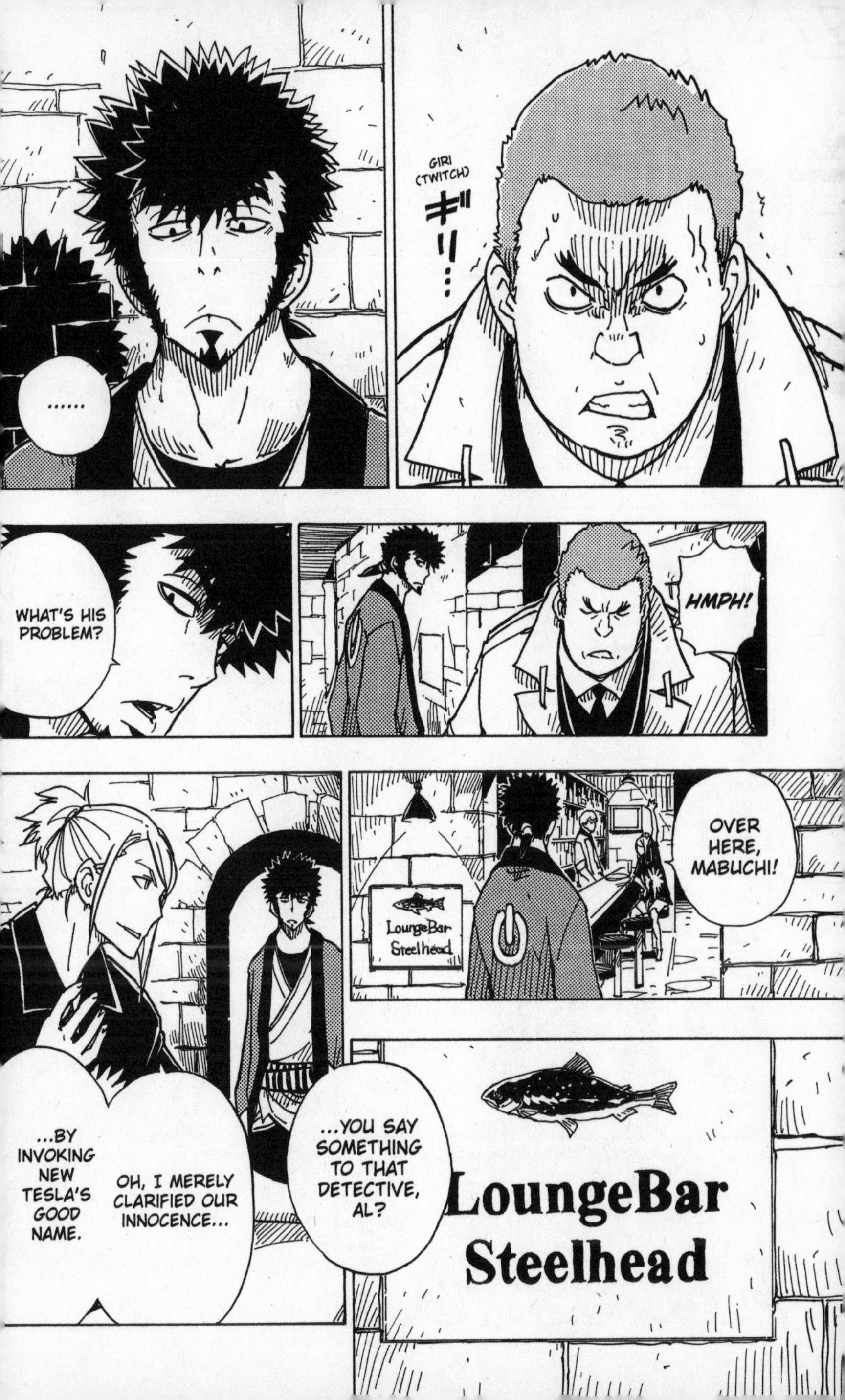
GIRI (TWITCH)
……
HMPH!
WHAT'S HIS PROBLEM?
OVER HERE, MABUCHI!
LoungeBar Steelhead
LoungeBar Steelhead
...YOU SAY SOMETHING TO THAT DETECTIVE, AL?
OH, I MERELY CLARIFIED OUR INNOCENCE...
...BY INVOKING NEW TESLA'S GOOD NAME.

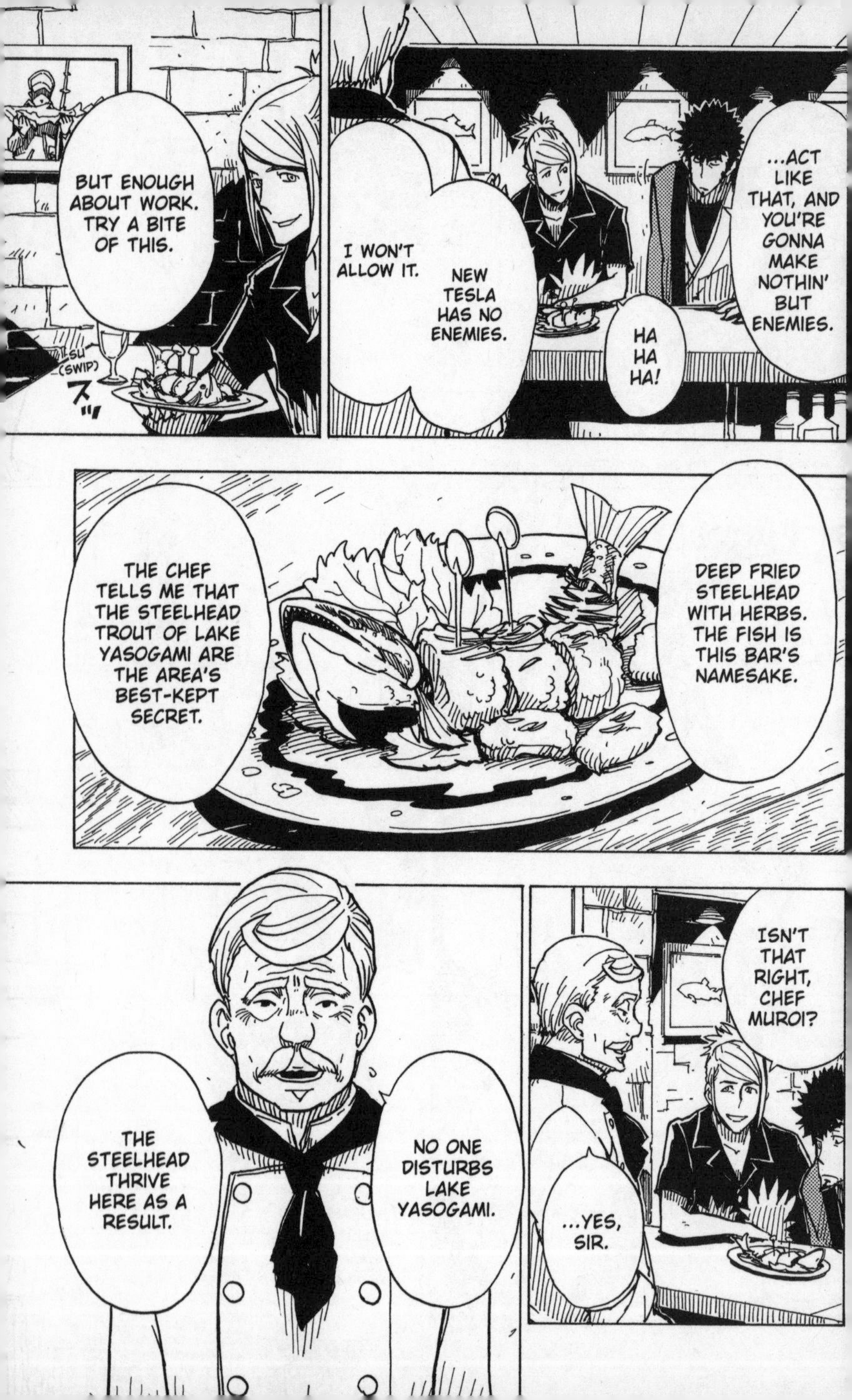
...ACT LIKE THAT, AND YOU'RE GONNA MAKE NOTHIN' BUT ENEMIES.
HA HA HA!
NEW TESLA HAS NO ENEMIES.
I WON'T ALLOW IT.
BUT ENOUGH ABOUT WORK. TRY A BITE OF THIS.
SU (SWIP)
DEEP FRIED STEELHEAD WITH HERBS. THE FISH IS THIS BAR'S NAMESAKE.
THE CHEF TELLS ME THAT THE STEELHEAD TROUT OF LAKE YASOGAMI ARE THE AREA'S BEST-KEPT SECRET.
ISN'T THAT RIGHT, CHEF MUROI?
...YES, SIR.
NO ONE DISTURBS LAKE YASOGAMI.
THE STEELHEAD THRIVE HERE AS A RESULT.

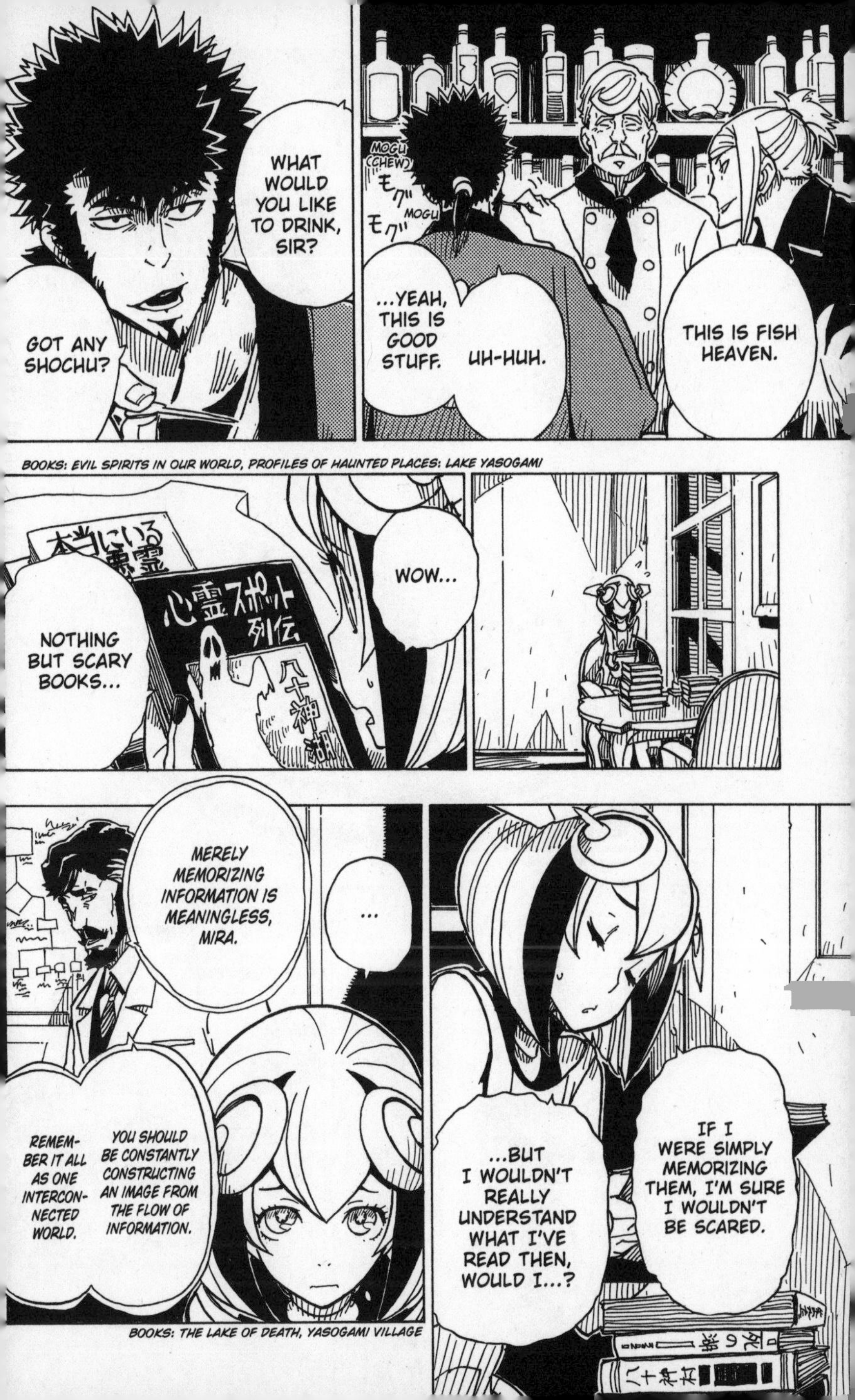
MOGU (CHEW) モグ
MOGU モグ
THIS IS FISH HEAVEN.
UH-HUH.
...YEAH, THIS IS GOOD STUFF.
WHAT WOULD YOU LIKE TO DRINK, SIR?
GOT ANY SHOCHU?
BOOKS: EVIL SPIRITS IN OUR WORLD, PROFILES OF HAUNTED PLACES: LAKE YASOGAMI
WOW...
心霊スポット列伝
八十神湖
NOTHING BUT SCARY BOOKS...
IF I WERE SIMPLY MEMORIZING THEM, I'M SURE I WOULDN'T BE SCARED.
...BUT I WOULDN'T REALLY UNDERSTAND WHAT I'VE READ THEN, WOULD I...?
死の湖
八十神村
MERELY MEMORIZING INFORMATION IS MEANINGLESS, MIRA.
...
YOU SHOULD BE CONSTANTLY CONSTRUCTING AN IMAGE FROM THE FLOW OF INFORMATION.
REMEMBER IT ALL AS ONE INTERCONNECTED WORLD.
BOOKS: THE LAKE OF DEATH, YASOGAMI VILLAGE

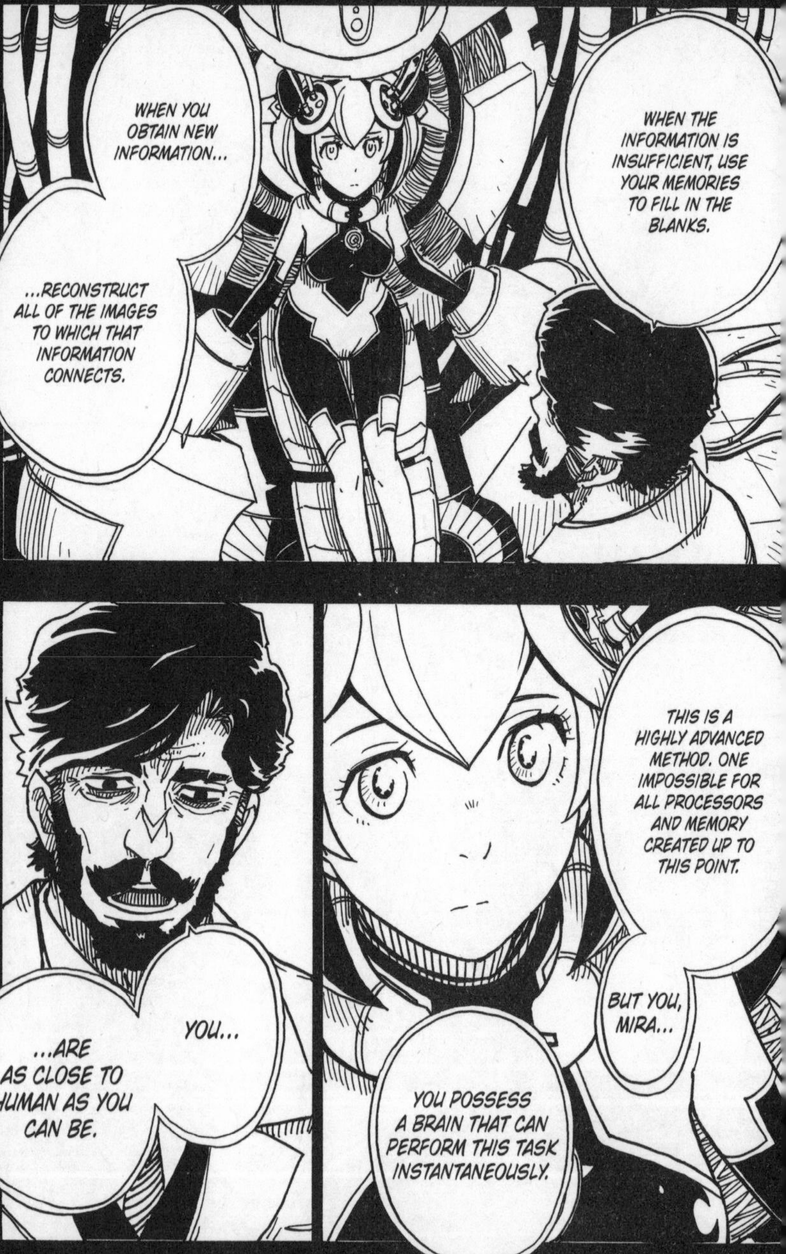
WHEN THE INFORMATION IS INSUFFICIENT, USE YOUR MEMORIES TO FILL IN THE BLANKS.
WHEN YOU OBTAIN NEW INFORMATION...
...RECONSTRUCT ALL OF THE IMAGES TO WHICH THAT INFORMATION CONNECTS.
THIS IS A HIGHLY ADVANCED METHOD. ONE IMPOSSIBLE FOR ALL PROCESSORS AND MEMORY CREATED UP TO THIS POINT.
BUT YOU, MIRA...
YOU POSSESS A BRAIN THAT CAN PERFORM THIS TASK INSTANTANEOUSLY.
YOU...
...ARE AS CLOSE TO HUMAN AS YOU CAN BE.

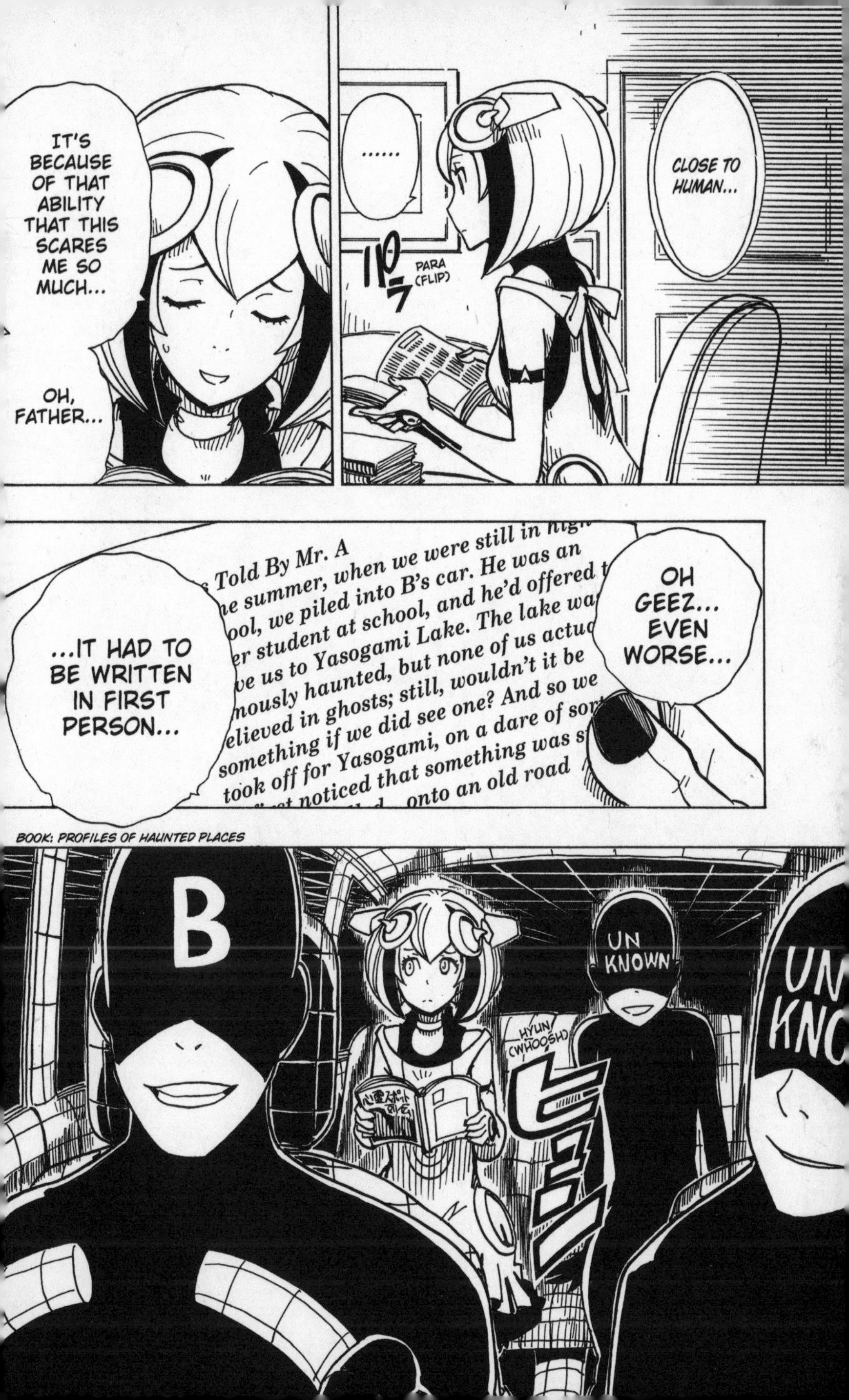
CLOSE TO HUMAN...
......
PARA (FLIP)
IT'S BECAUSE OF THAT ABILITY THAT THIS SCARES ME SO MUCH...
OH, FATHER...
OH GEEZ... EVEN WORSE...
Told By Mr. A
e summer, when we were still in hig
ool, we piled into B's car. He was an
er student at school, and he'd offered t
ve us to Yasogami Lake. The lake wa
nously haunted, but none of us actu
elieved in ghosts; still, wouldn't it be
something if we did see one? And so we
took off for Yasogami, on a dare of sor
noticed that something was s
onto an old road
...IT HAD TO BE WRITTEN IN FIRST PERSON...
BOOK: PROFILES OF HAUNTED PLACES
B
UN KNOWN
HYUN (WHOOSH)
UN KNO

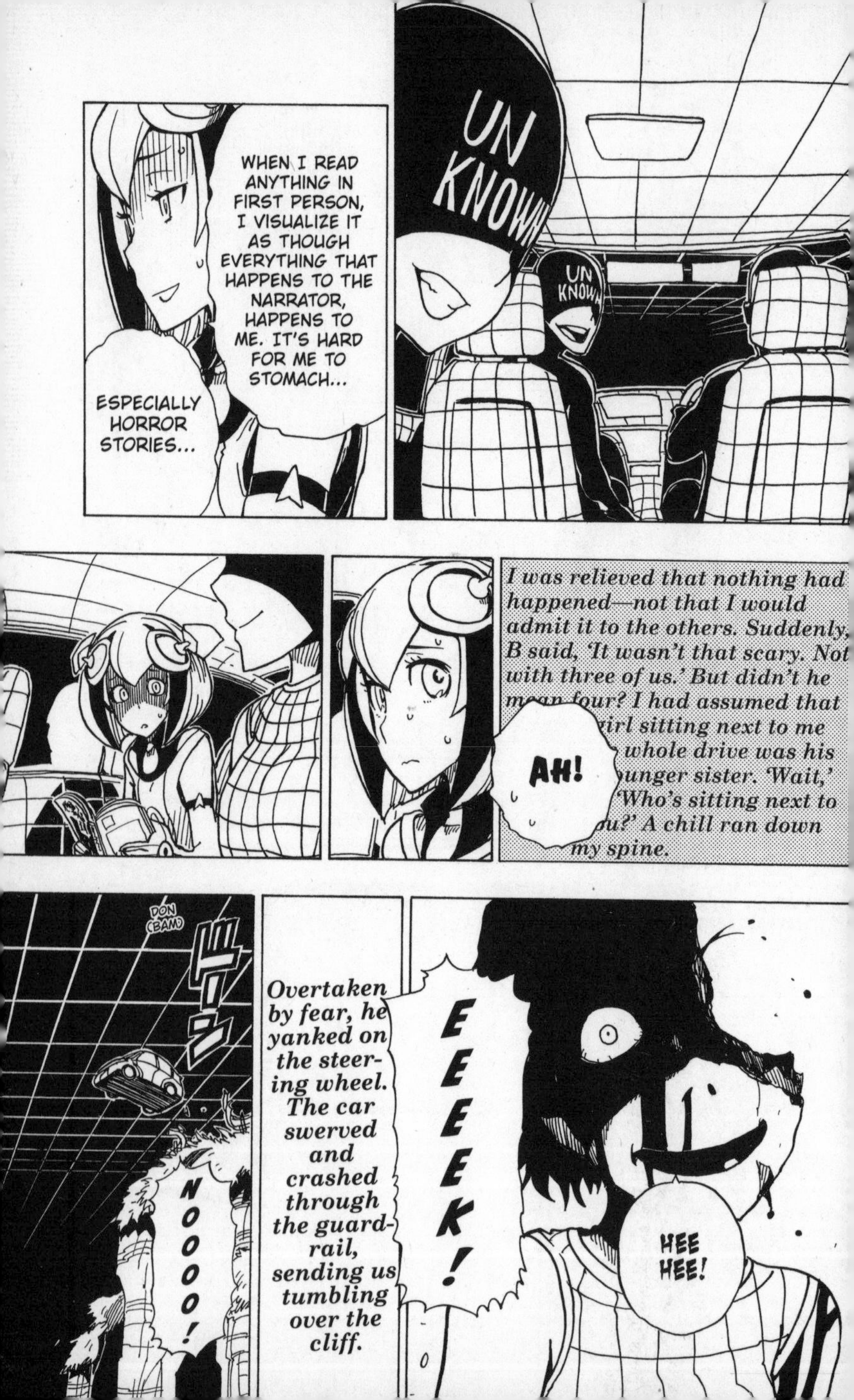
UN KNOWN
UN KNOWN
WHEN I READ ANYTHING IN FIRST PERSON, I VISUALIZE IT AS THOUGH EVERYTHING THAT HAPPENS TO THE NARRATOR, HAPPENS TO ME. IT'S HARD FOR ME TO STOMACH...
ESPECIALLY HORROR STORIES...
I was relieved that nothing had happened—not that I would admit it to the others. Suddenly, B said, 'It wasn't that scary. Not with three of us.' But didn't he four? I had assumed that girl sitting next to me whole drive was his ounger sister. 'Wait,' 'Who's sitting next to ou?' A chill ran down my spine.
AH!
EEEEK!
HEE HEE!
Overtaken by fear, he yanked on the steering wheel. The car swerved and crashed through the guardrail, sending us tumbling over the cliff.
DON (BAM)
NOOOO!

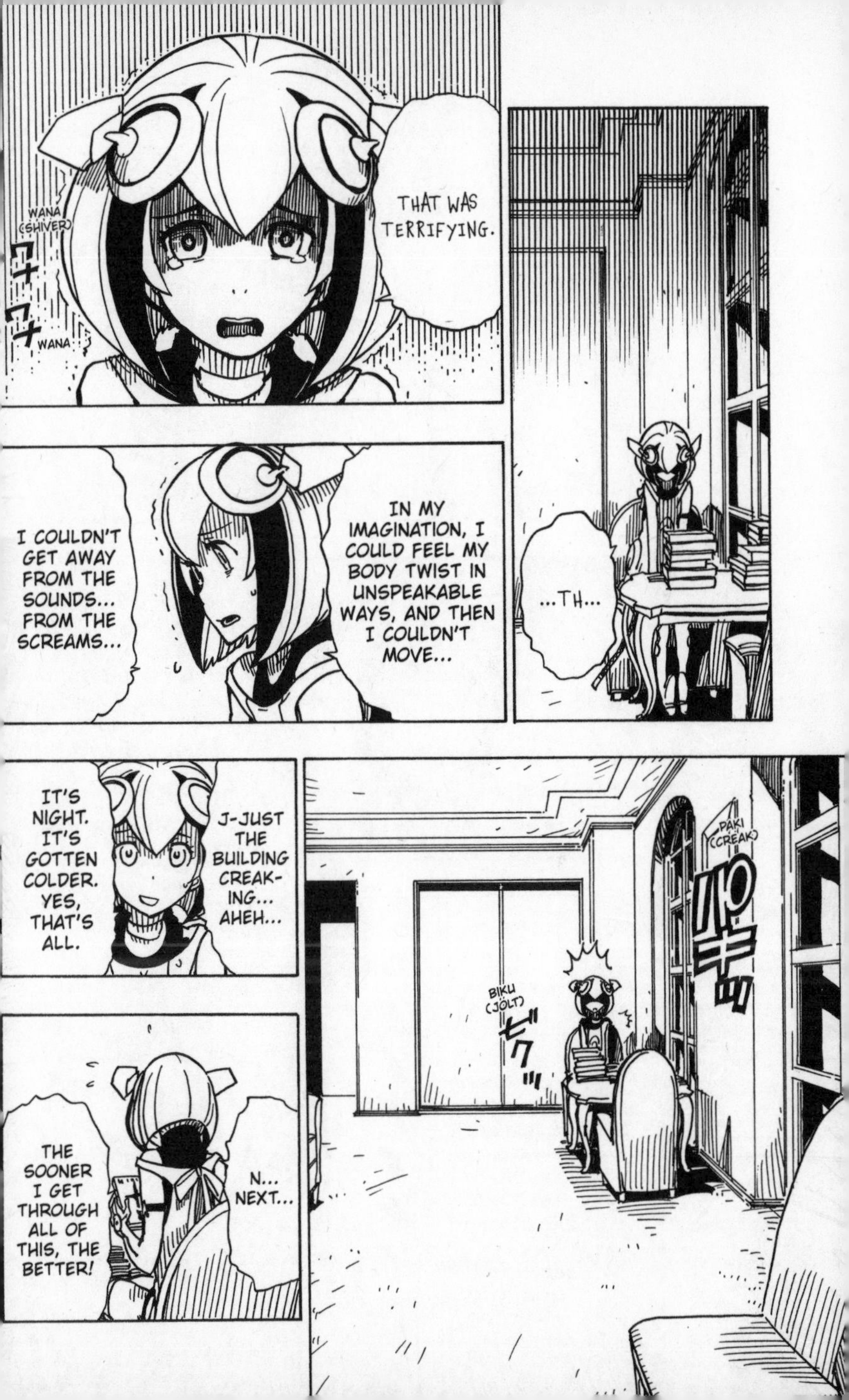
...TH...
WANA (SHIVER)
WANA
THAT WAS TERRIFYING.
IN MY IMAGINATION, I COULD FEEL MY BODY TWIST IN UNSPEAKABLE WAYS, AND THEN I COULDN'T MOVE...
I COULDN'T GET AWAY FROM THE SOUNDS... FROM THE SCREAMS...
PAKI (CREAK)
BIKU (JÖLT)
J-JUST THE BUILDING CREAK-ING... AHEH...
IT'S NIGHT. IT'S GOTTEN COLDER. YES, THAT'S ALL.
N... NEXT...
THE SOONER I GET THROUGH ALL OF THIS, THE BETTER!

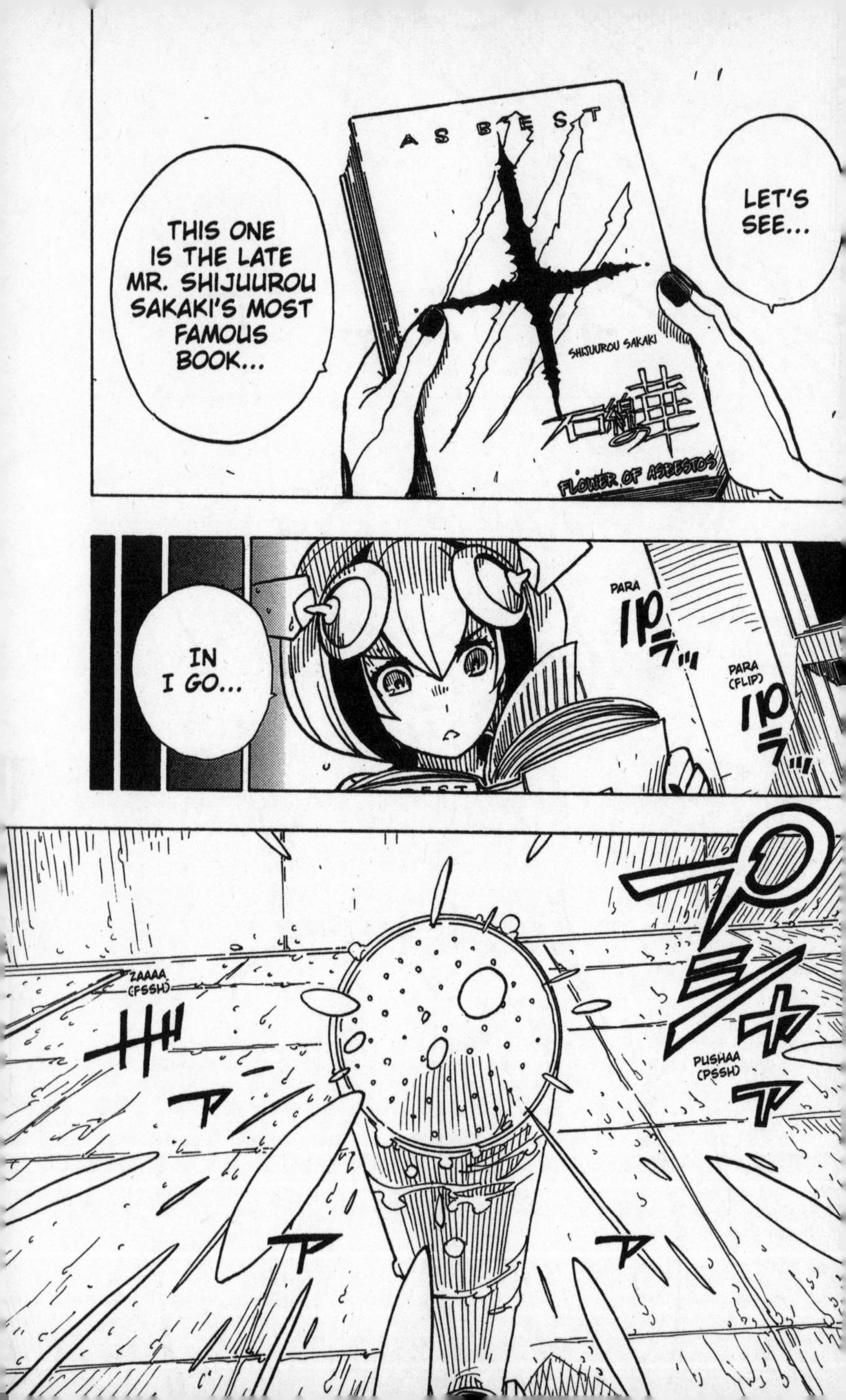
LET'S SEE...
AS BEST
THIS ONE IS THE LATE MR. SHIJUUROU SAKAKI'S MOST FAMOUS BOOK...
SHIJUUROU SAKAKI
FLOWER OF ASBESTOS
PARA
PARA (FLIP)
IN I GO...
PUSHAA (PSSH)
ZAAAA (FSSH)

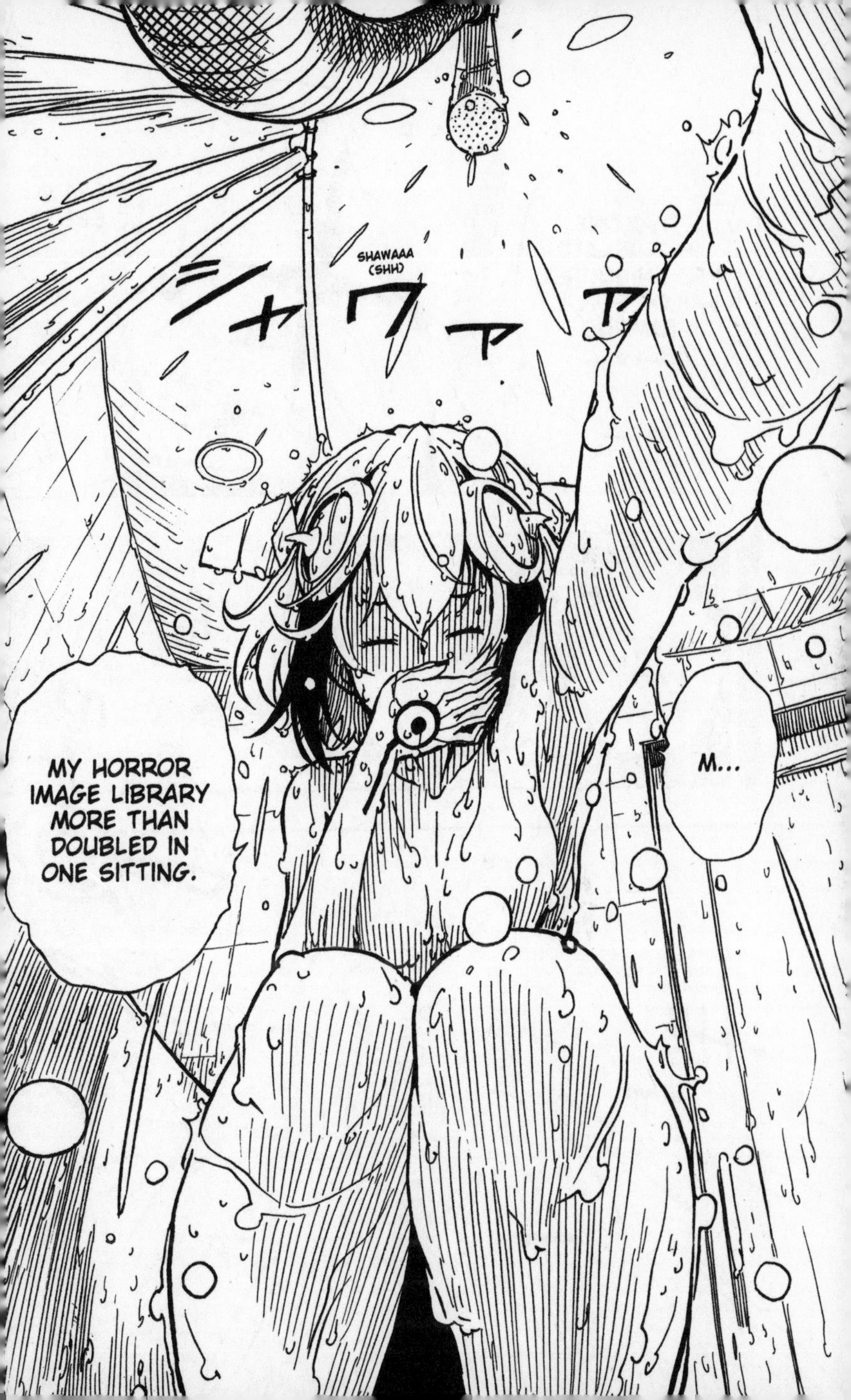

SHAWAAA (SHH)
シャワァァ
M...
MY HORROR IMAGE LIBRARY MORE THAN DOUBLED IN ONE SITTING.

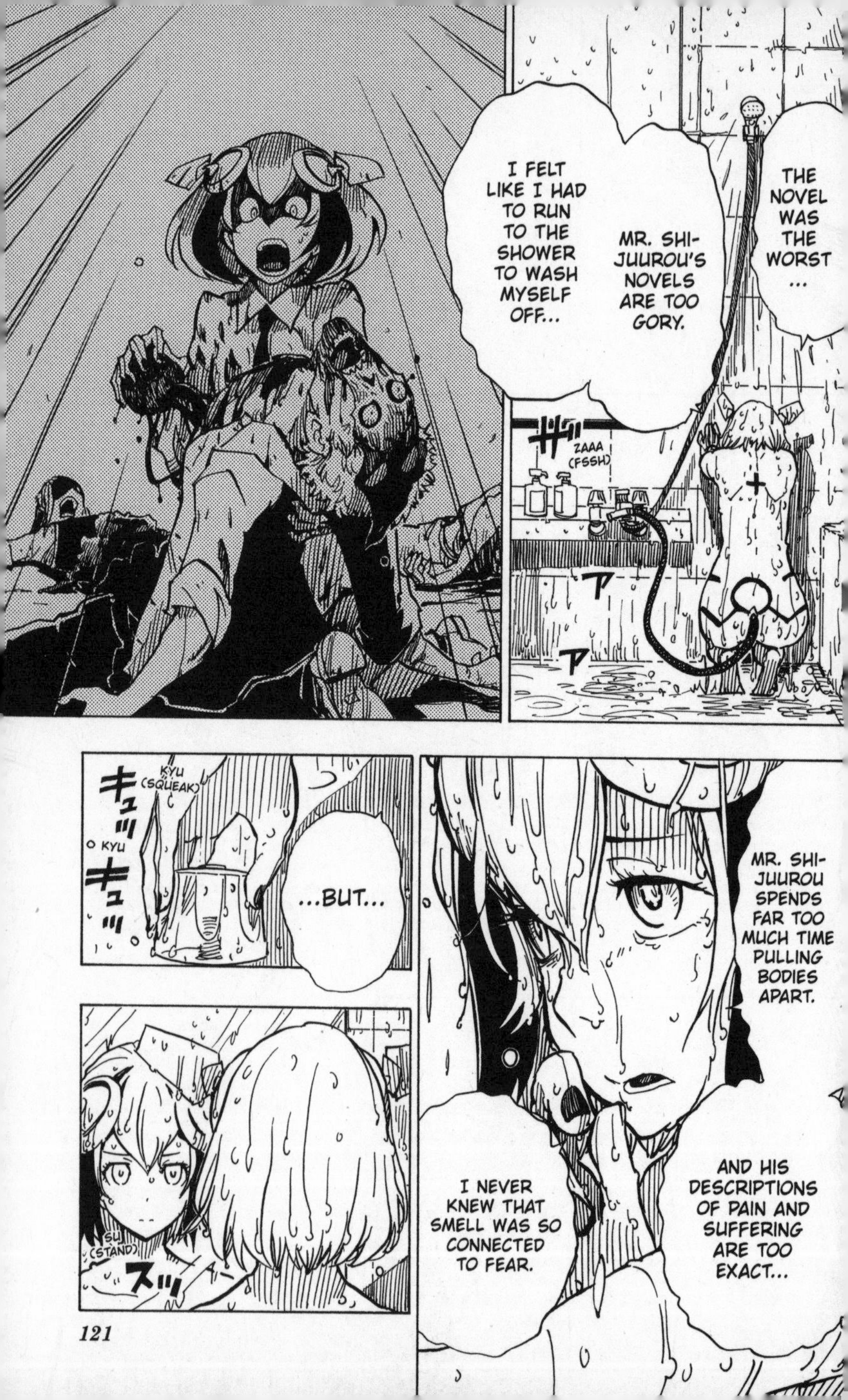
THE NOVEL WAS THE WORST ...
MR. SHI-JUUROU'S NOVELS ARE TOO GORY.
I FELT LIKE I HAD TO RUN TO THE SHOWER TO WASH MYSELF OFF...
ZAAA (FSSH)
MR. SHI-JUUROU SPENDS FAR TOO MUCH TIME PULLING BODIES APART.
AND HIS DESCRIPTIONS OF PAIN AND SUFFERING ARE TOO EXACT...
I NEVER KNEW THAT SMELL WAS SO CONNECTED TO FEAR.
KYU (SQUEAK)
KYU
...BUT...
SU (STAND)

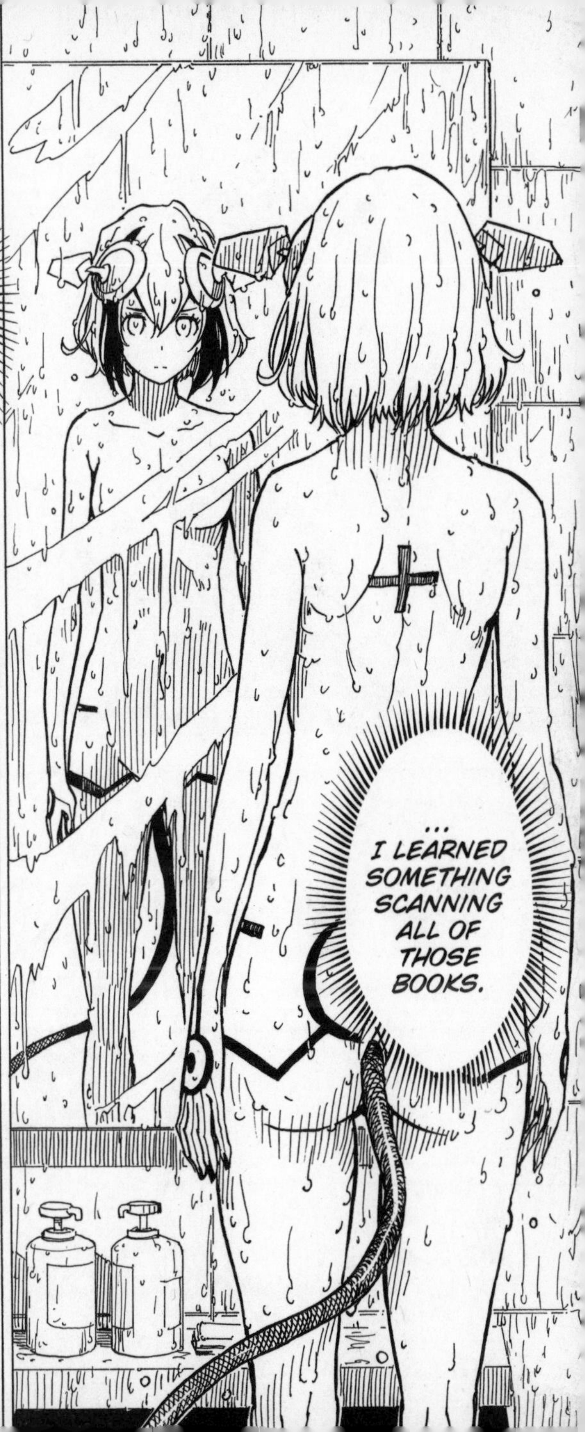
... I LEARNED SOMETHING SCANNING ALL OF THOSE BOOKS.
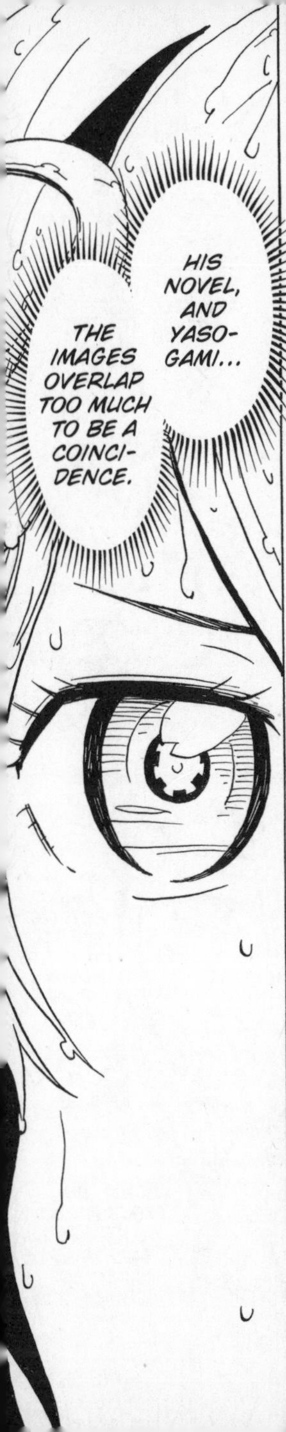
HIS NOVEL, AND YASO-GAMI...
THE IMAGES OVERLAP TOO MUCH TO BE A COINCI-DENCE.

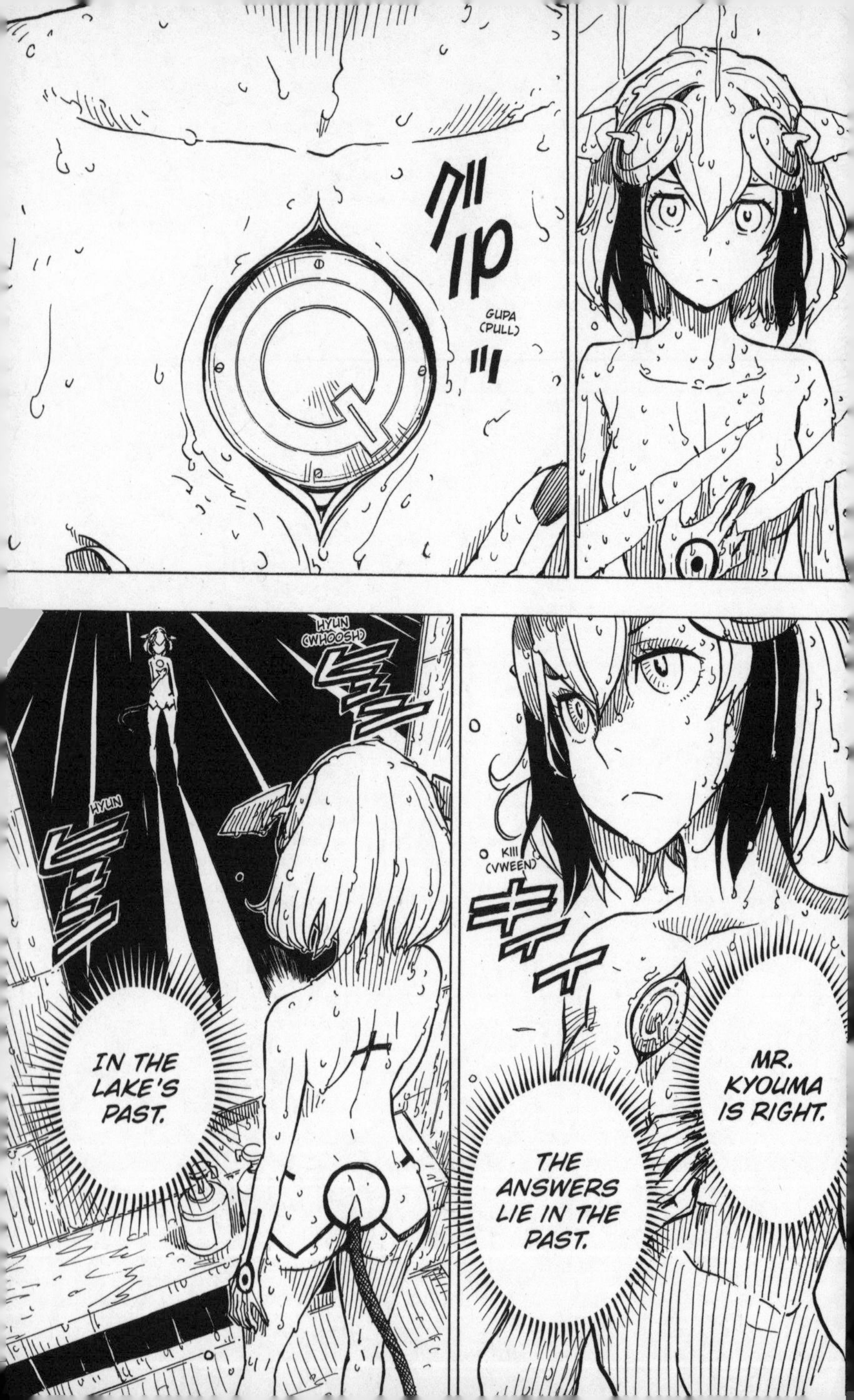
GUPA (PULL)
KIII (VWEEN)
MR. KYOUMA IS RIGHT.
THE ANSWERS LIE IN THE PAST.
HYUN (WHOOSH)
HYUN
IN THE LAKE'S PAST.

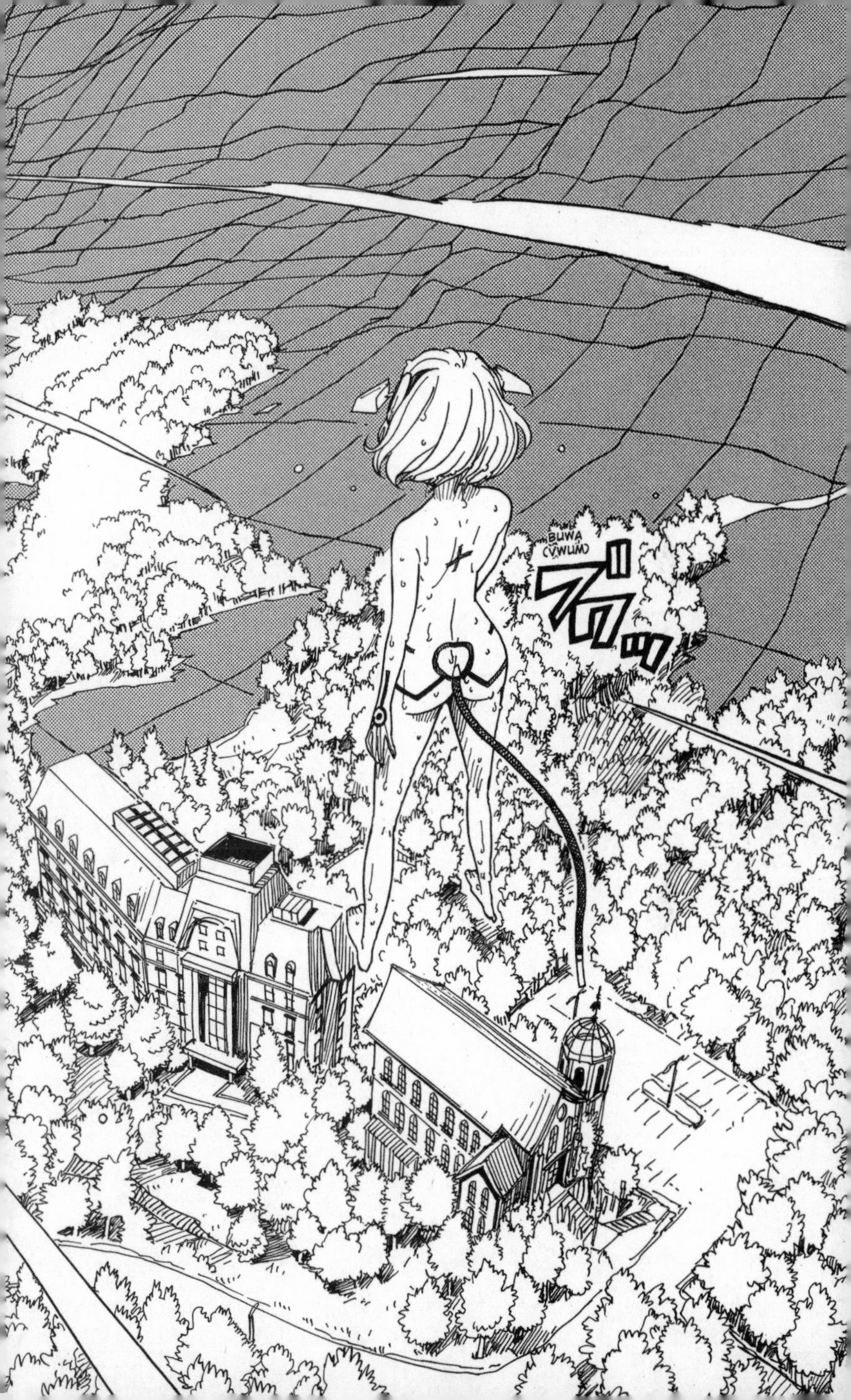
ブワッ
BUWA
(VWUM)

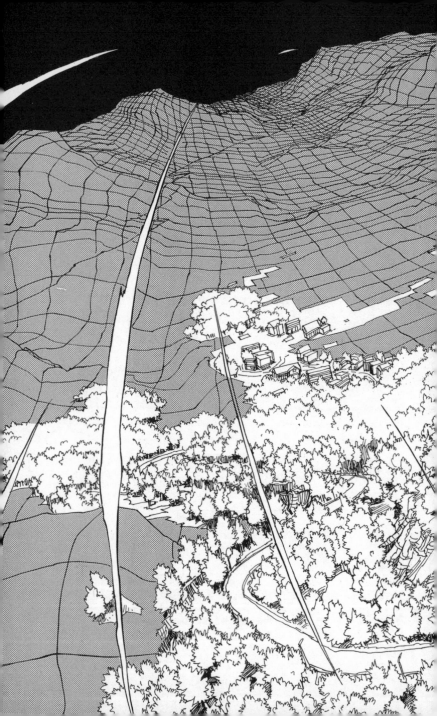

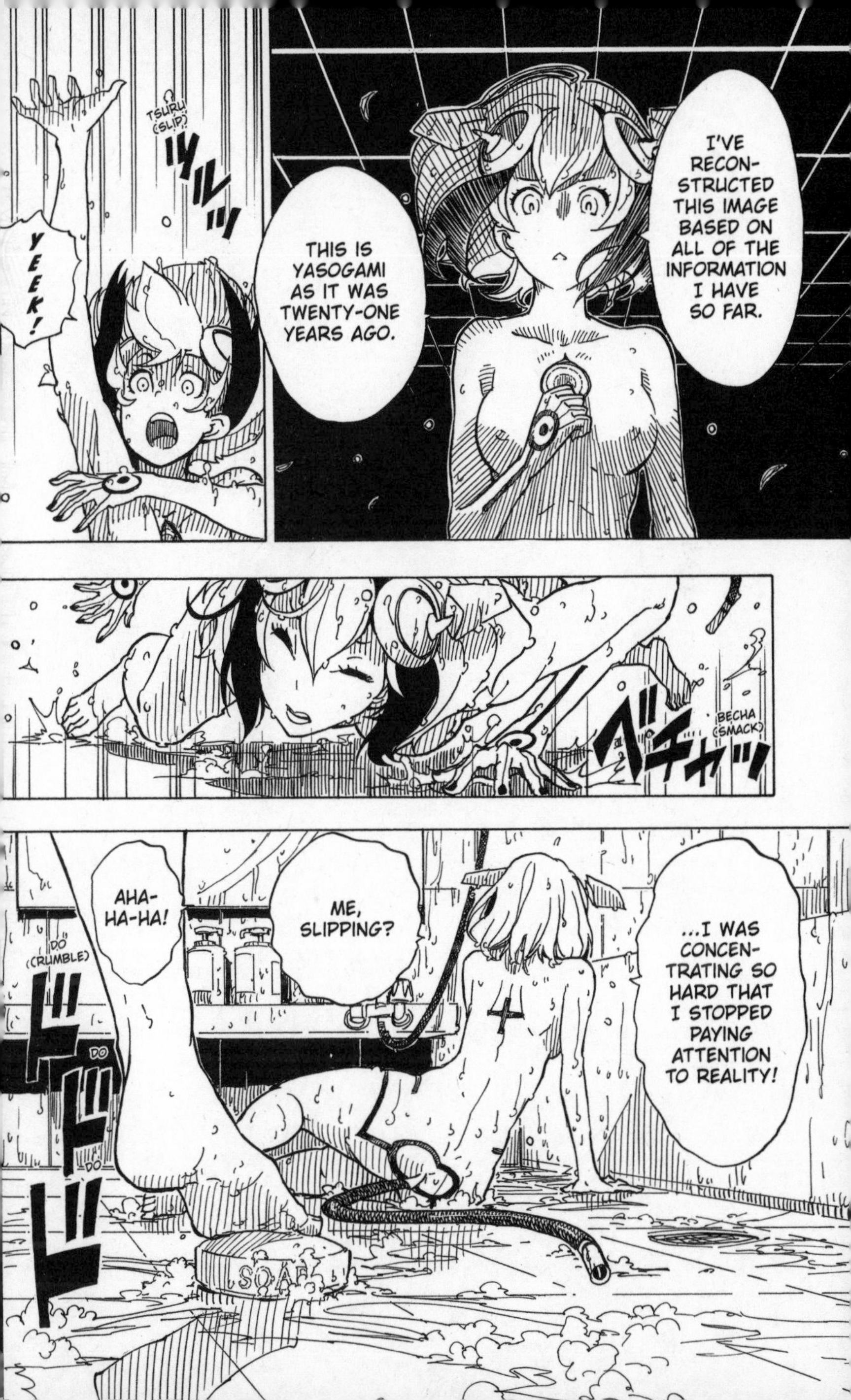
I'VE RECONSTRUCTED THIS IMAGE BASED ON ALL OF THE INFORMATION I HAVE SO FAR.
THIS IS YASOGAMI AS IT WAS TWENTY-ONE YEARS AGO.
TSURU (SLIP)
YEEK!
BECHA (SMACK)
...I WAS CONCENTRATING SO HARD THAT I STOPPED PAYING ATTENTION TO REALITY!
ME, SLIPPING?
AHA-HA-HA!
DO (RUMBLE)
DO
DO
SOAP

FILE.21
HISTORY

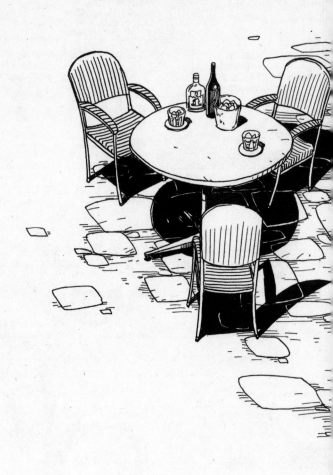

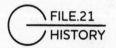

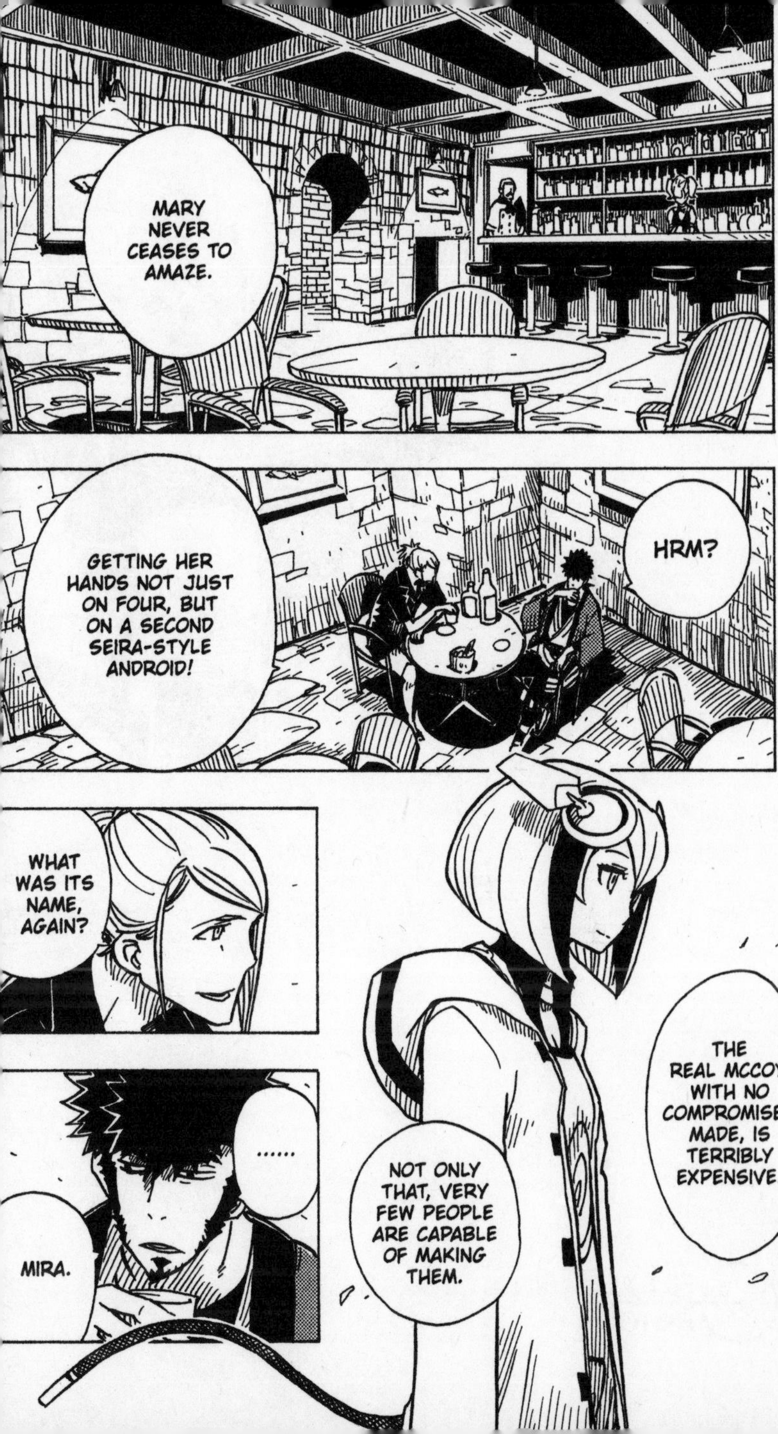
MARY NEVER CEASES TO AMAZE.
HRM?
GETTING HER HANDS NOT JUST ON FOUR, BUT ON A SECOND SEIRA-STYLE ANDROID!
THE REAL MCCOY, WITH NO COMPROMISES MADE, IS TERRIBLY EXPENSIVE.
NOT ONLY THAT, VERY FEW PEOPLE ARE CAPABLE OF MAKING THEM.
WHAT WAS ITS NAME, AGAIN?
......
MIRA.

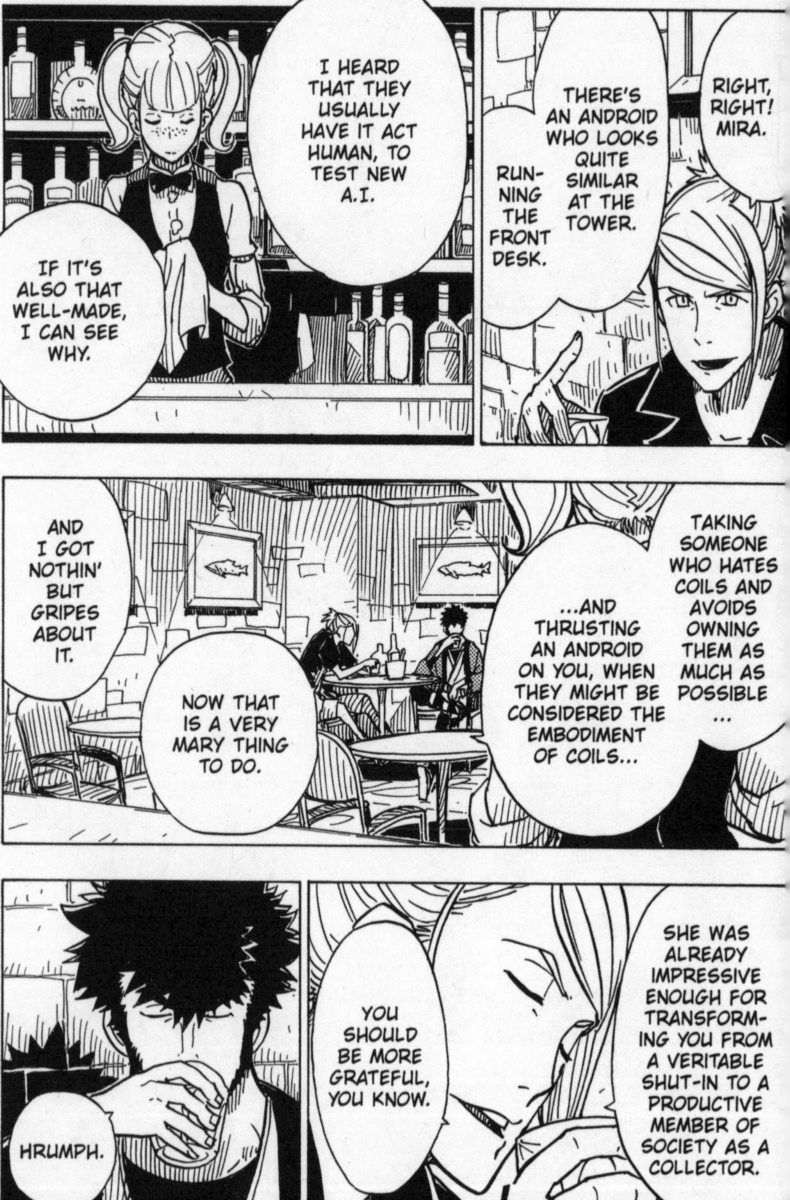
RIGHT, RIGHT! MIRA.
THERE'S AN ANDROID WHO LOOKS QUITE SIMILAR AT THE TOWER.
RUNNING THE FRONT DESK.
I HEARD THAT THEY USUALLY HAVE IT ACT HUMAN, TO TEST NEW A.I.
IF IT'S ALSO THAT WELL-MADE, I CAN SEE WHY.
TAKING SOMEONE WHO HATES COILS AND AVOIDS OWNING THEM AS MUCH AS POSSIBLE ...
...AND THRUSTING AN ANDROID ON YOU, WHEN THEY MIGHT BE CONSIDERED THE EMBODIMENT OF COILS...
NOW THAT IS A VERY MARY THING TO DO.
AND I GOT NOTHIN' BUT GRIPES ABOUT IT.
SHE WAS ALREADY IMPRESSIVE ENOUGH FOR TRANSFORMING YOU FROM A VERITABLE SHUT-IN TO A PRODUCTIVE MEMBER OF SOCIETY AS A COLLECTOR.
YOU SHOULD BE MORE GRATEFUL, YOU KNOW.
KARAN (CLINK) カラン
HRUMPH.

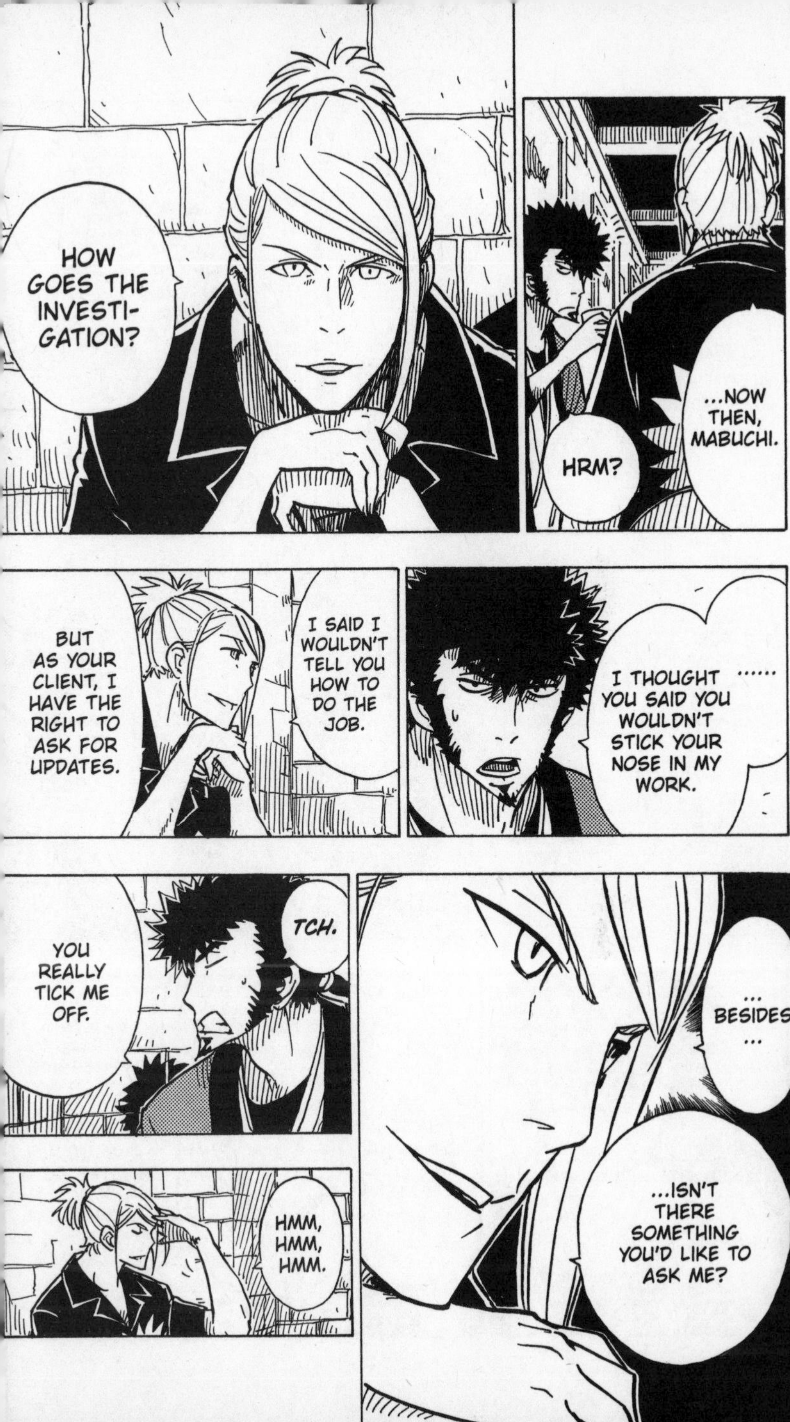
...NOW THEN, MABUCHI.
HRM?
HOW GOES THE INVESTI-GATION?
......
I THOUGHT YOU SAID YOU WOULDN'T STICK YOUR NOSE IN MY WORK.
I SAID I WOULDN'T TELL YOU HOW TO DO THE JOB.
BUT AS YOUR CLIENT, I HAVE THE RIGHT TO ASK FOR UPDATES.
...BESIDES...
...ISN'T THERE SOMETHING YOU'D LIKE TO ASK ME?
TCH.
YOU REALLY TICK ME OFF.
HMM, HMM, HMM.

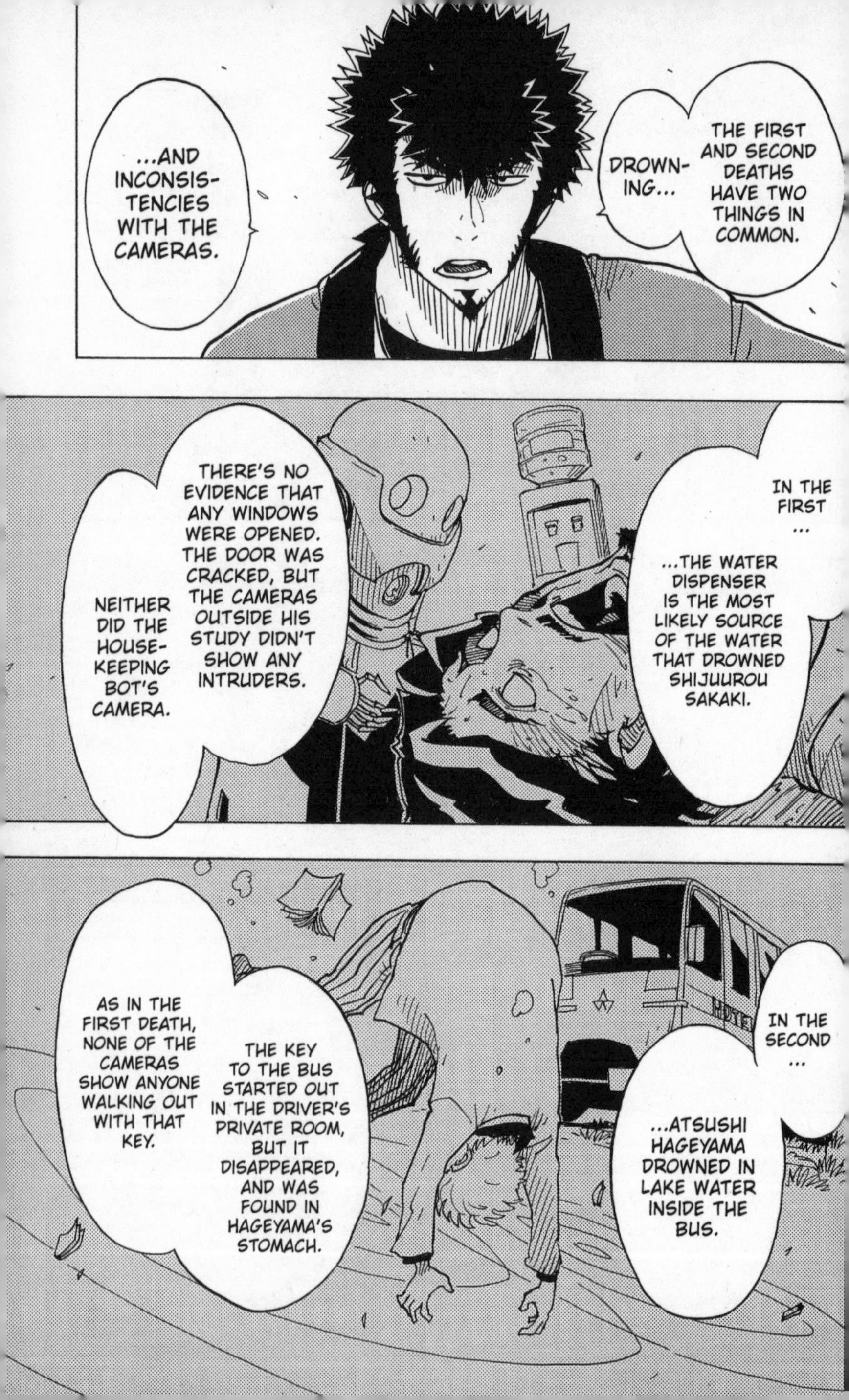
THE FIRST AND SECOND DEATHS HAVE TWO THINGS IN COMMON.
DROWNING...
...AND INCONSISTENCIES WITH THE CAMERAS.
IN THE FIRST...
...THE WATER DISPENSER IS THE MOST LIKELY SOURCE OF THE WATER THAT DROWNED SHIJUUROU SAKAKI.
THERE'S NO EVIDENCE THAT ANY WINDOWS WERE OPENED. THE DOOR WAS CRACKED, BUT THE CAMERAS OUTSIDE HIS STUDY DIDN'T SHOW ANY INTRUDERS.
NEITHER DID THE HOUSEKEEPING BOT'S CAMERA.
IN THE SECOND...
...ATSUSHI HAGEYAMA DROWNED IN LAKE WATER INSIDE THE BUS.
THE KEY TO THE BUS STARTED OUT IN THE DRIVER'S PRIVATE ROOM, BUT IT DISAPPEARED, AND WAS FOUND IN HAGEYAMA'S STOMACH.
AS IN THE FIRST DEATH, NONE OF THE CAMERAS SHOW ANYONE WALKING OUT WITH THAT KEY.

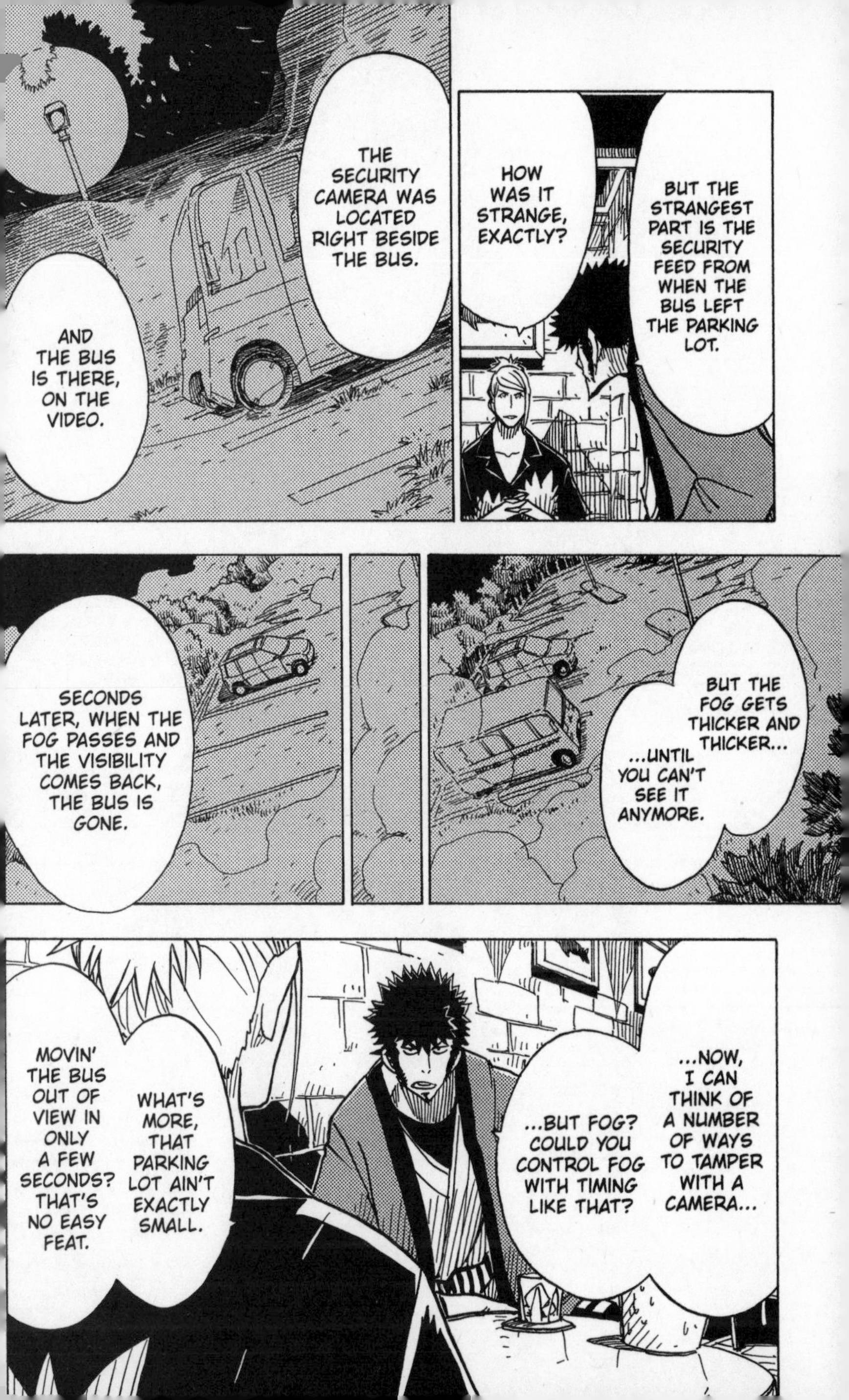
BUT THE STRANGEST PART IS THE SECURITY FEED FROM WHEN THE BUS LEFT THE PARKING LOT.
HOW WAS IT STRANGE, EXACTLY?
THE SECURITY CAMERA WAS LOCATED RIGHT BESIDE THE BUS.
AND THE BUS IS THERE, ON THE VIDEO.
BUT THE FOG GETS THICKER AND THICKER...
...UNTIL YOU CAN'T SEE IT ANYMORE.
SECONDS LATER, WHEN THE FOG PASSES AND THE VISIBILITY COMES BACK, THE BUS IS GONE.
...NOW, I CAN THINK OF A NUMBER OF WAYS TO TAMPER WITH A CAMERA...
...BUT FOG? COULD YOU CONTROL FOG WITH TIMING LIKE THAT?
MOVIN' THE BUS OUT OF VIEW IN ONLY A FEW SECONDS? THAT'S NO EASY FEAT.
WHAT'S MORE, THAT PARKING LOT AIN'T EXACTLY SMALL.

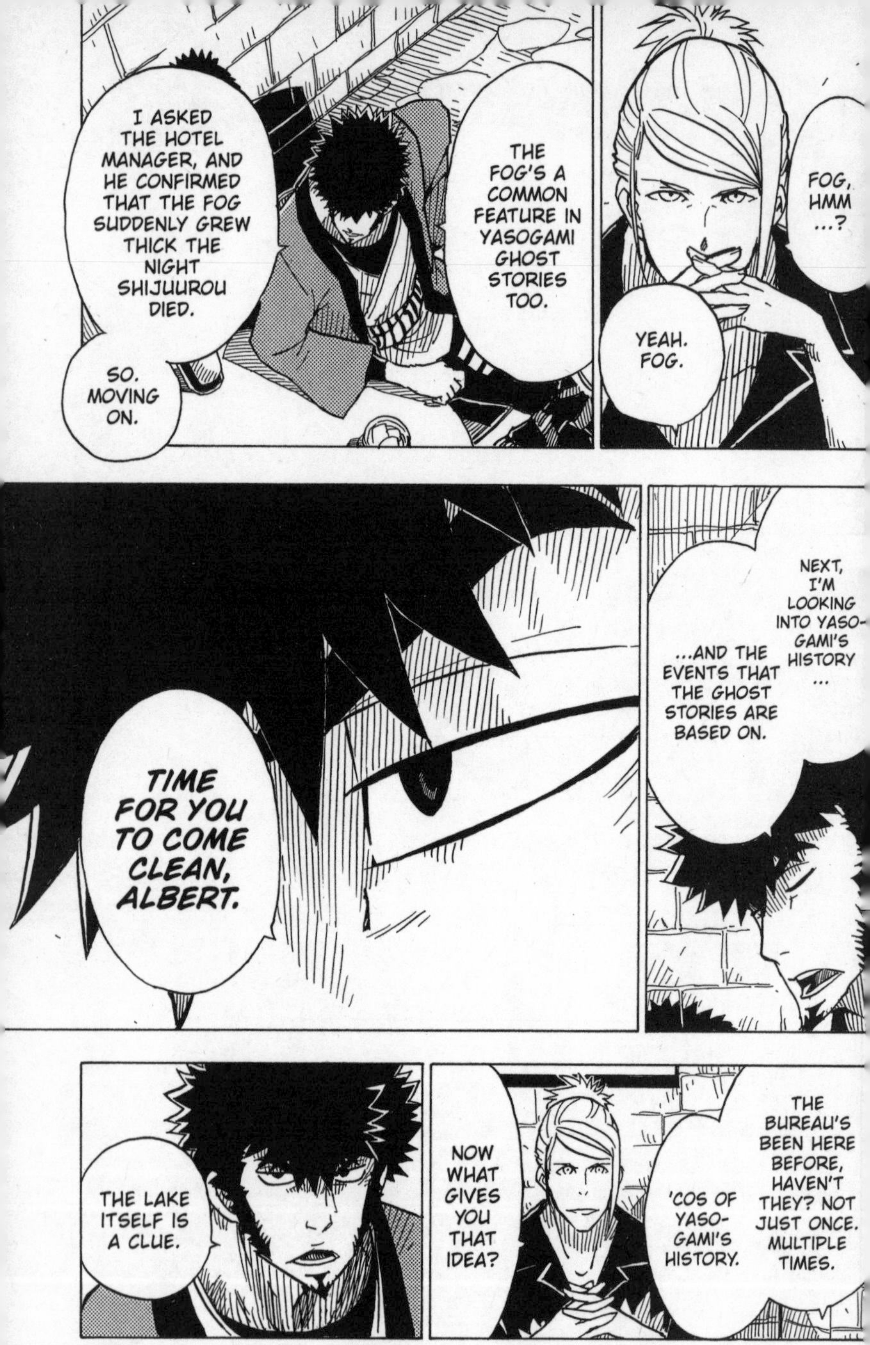
FOG, HMM ...?
YEAH. FOG.
THE FOG'S A COMMON FEATURE IN YASOGAMI GHOST STORIES TOO.
I ASKED THE HOTEL MANAGER, AND HE CONFIRMED THAT THE FOG SUDDENLY GREW THICK THE NIGHT SHIJUUROU DIED.
SO. MOVING ON.
NEXT, I'M LOOKING INTO YASOGAMI'S HISTORY ...
...AND THE EVENTS THAT THE GHOST STORIES ARE BASED ON.
TIME FOR YOU TO COME CLEAN, ALBERT.
THE BUREAU'S BEEN HERE BEFORE, HAVEN'T THEY? NOT JUST ONCE. MULTIPLE TIMES.
'COS OF YASOGAMI'S HISTORY.
NOW WHAT GIVES YOU THAT IDEA?
THE LAKE ITSELF IS A CLUE.

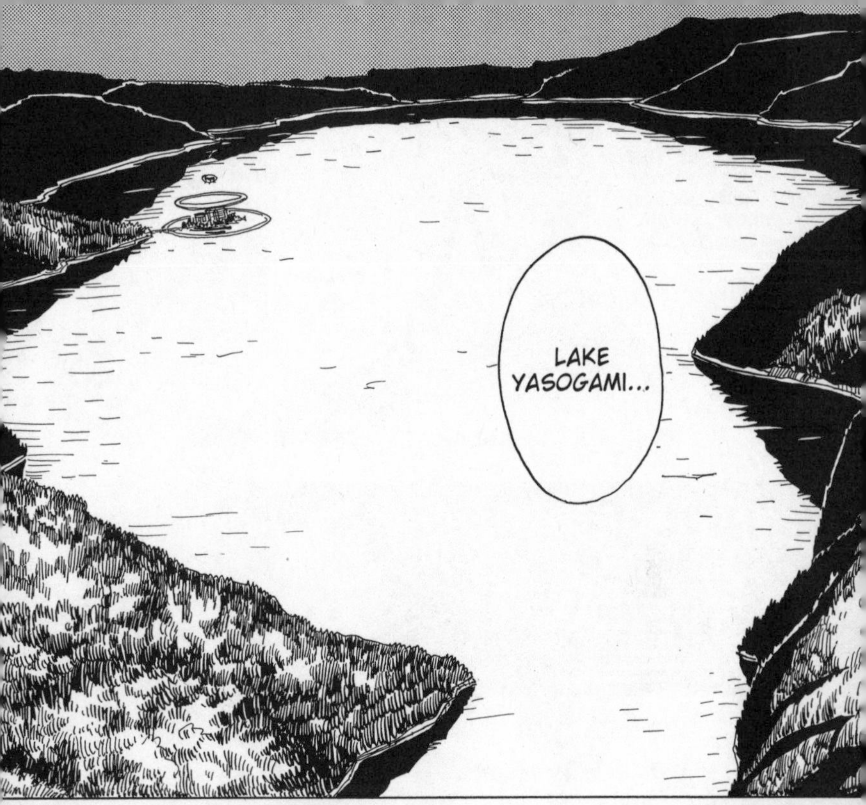
LAKE YASOGAMI...

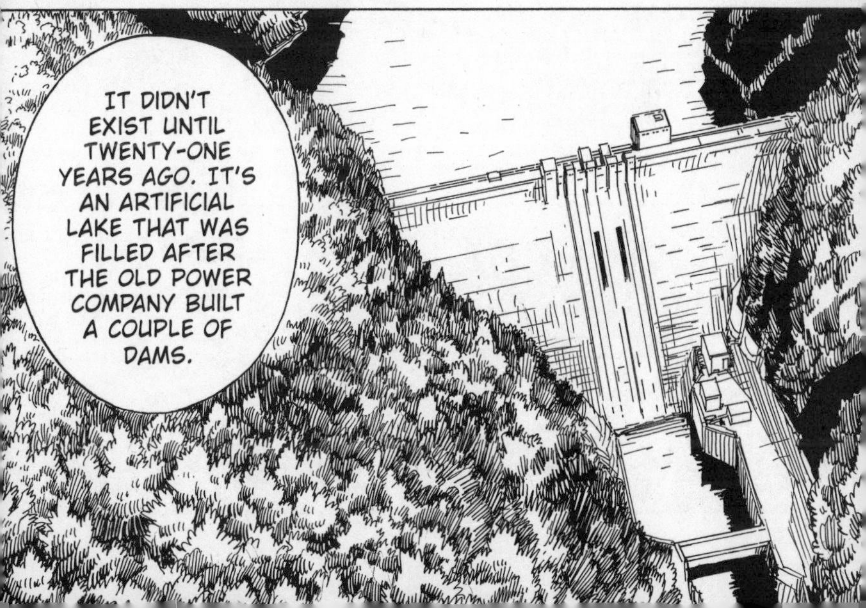
IT DIDN'T EXIST UNTIL TWENTY-ONE YEARS AGO. IT'S AN ARTIFICIAL LAKE THAT WAS FILLED AFTER THE OLD POWER COMPANY BUILT A COUPLE OF DAMS.

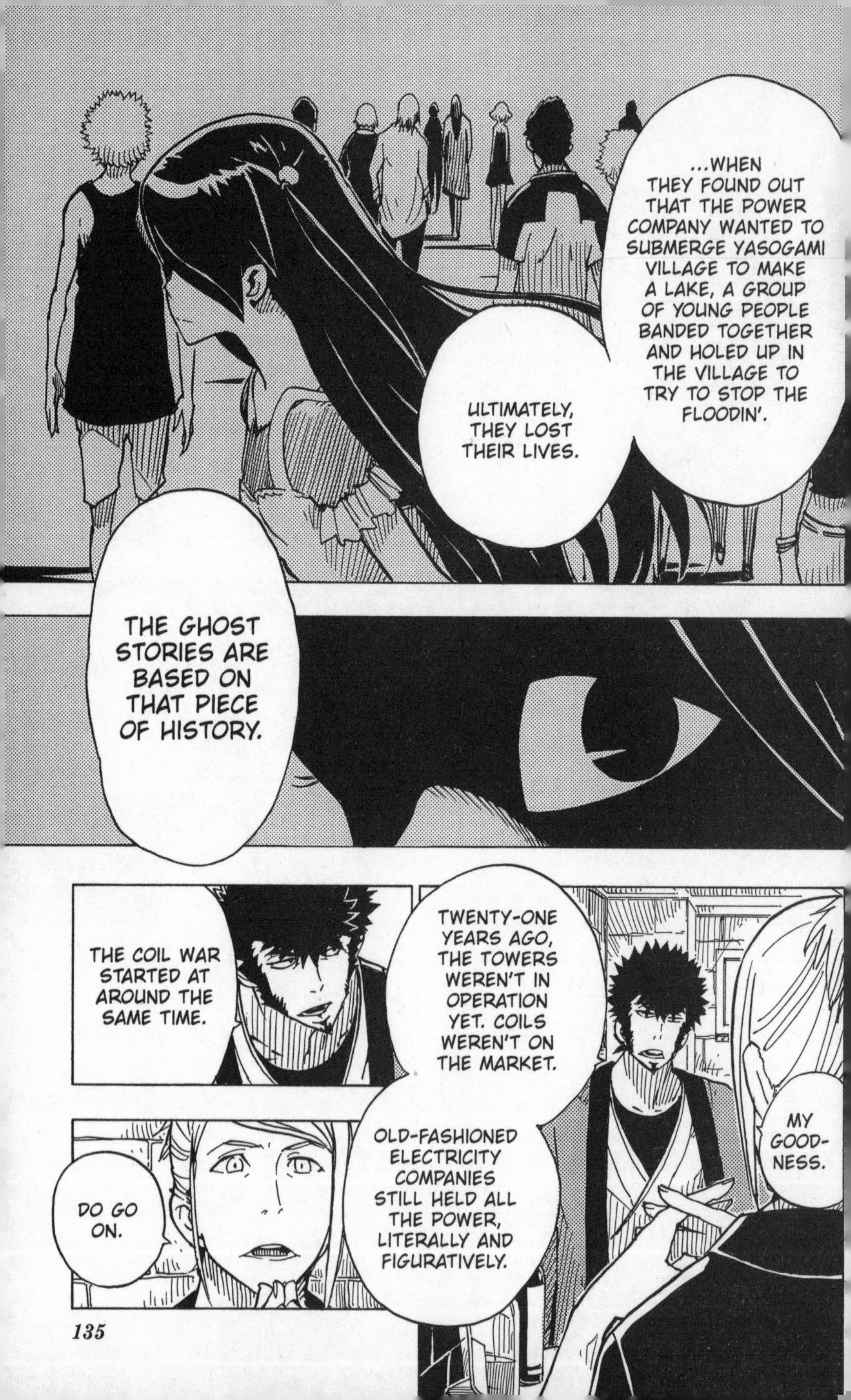
...WHEN THEY FOUND OUT THAT THE POWER COMPANY WANTED TO SUBMERGE YASOGAMI VILLAGE TO MAKE A LAKE, A GROUP OF YOUNG PEOPLE BANDED TOGETHER AND HOLED UP IN THE VILLAGE TO TRY TO STOP THE FLOODIN'.
ULTIMATELY, THEY LOST THEIR LIVES.
THE GHOST STORIES ARE BASED ON THAT PIECE OF HISTORY.
THE COIL WAR STARTED AT AROUND THE SAME TIME.
TWENTY-ONE YEARS AGO, THE TOWERS WEREN'T IN OPERATION YET. COILS WEREN'T ON THE MARKET.
OLD-FASHIONED ELECTRICITY COMPANIES STILL HELD ALL THE POWER, LITERALLY AND FIGURATIVELY.
MY GOODNESS.
DO GO ON.

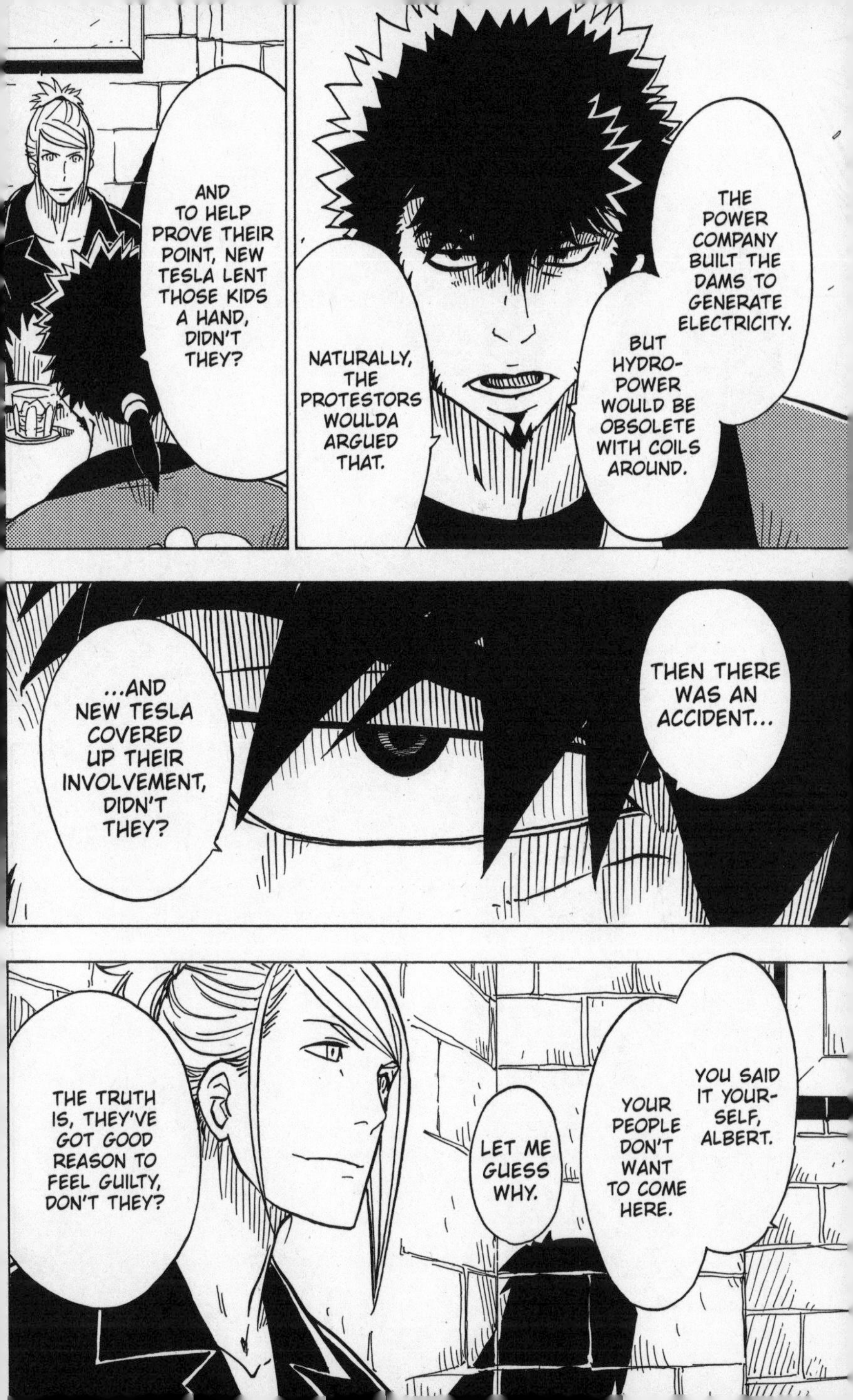
THE POWER COMPANY BUILT THE DAMS TO GENERATE ELECTRICITY.
BUT HYDRO-POWER WOULD BE OBSOLETE WITH COILS AROUND.
NATURALLY, THE PROTESTORS WOULDA ARGUED THAT.
AND TO HELP PROVE THEIR POINT, NEW TESLA LENT THOSE KIDS A HAND, DIDN'T THEY?
THEN THERE WAS AN ACCIDENT...
...AND NEW TESLA COVERED UP THEIR INVOLVEMENT, DIDN'T THEY?
YOU SAID IT YOURSELF, ALBERT.
YOUR PEOPLE DON'T WANT TO COME HERE.
LET ME GUESS WHY.
THE TRUTH IS, THEY'VE GOT GOOD REASON TO FEEL GUILTY, DON'T THEY?

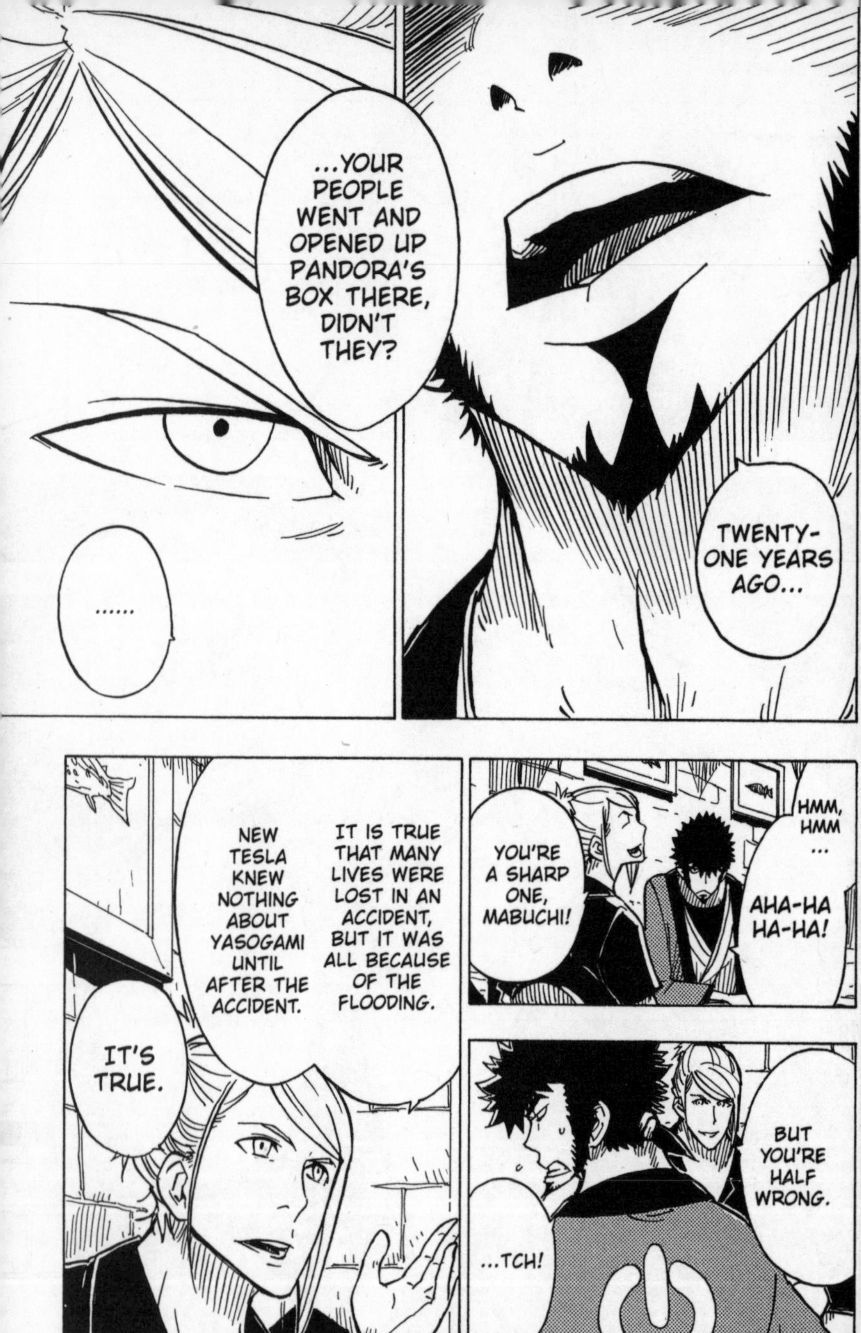
TWENTY-ONE YEARS AGO...
...YOUR PEOPLE WENT AND OPENED UP PANDORA'S BOX THERE, DIDN'T THEY?
......
HMM, HMM...
AHA-HA HA-HA!
YOU'RE A SHARP ONE, MABUCHI!
BUT YOU'RE HALF WRONG.
...TCH!
IT IS TRUE THAT MANY LIVES WERE LOST IN AN ACCIDENT, BUT IT WAS ALL BECAUSE OF THE FLOODING.
NEW TESLA KNEW NOTHING ABOUT YASOGAMI UNTIL AFTER THE ACCIDENT.
IT'S TRUE.

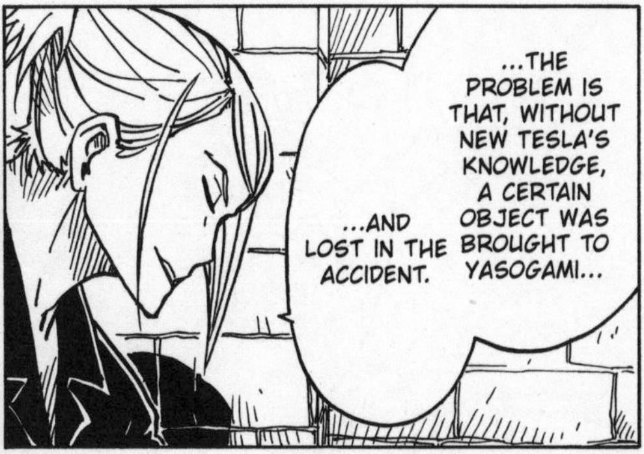
...THE PROBLEM IS THAT, WITHOUT NEW TESLA'S KNOWLEDGE, A CERTAIN OBJECT WAS BROUGHT TO YASOGAMI...
...AND LOST IN THE ACCIDENT.

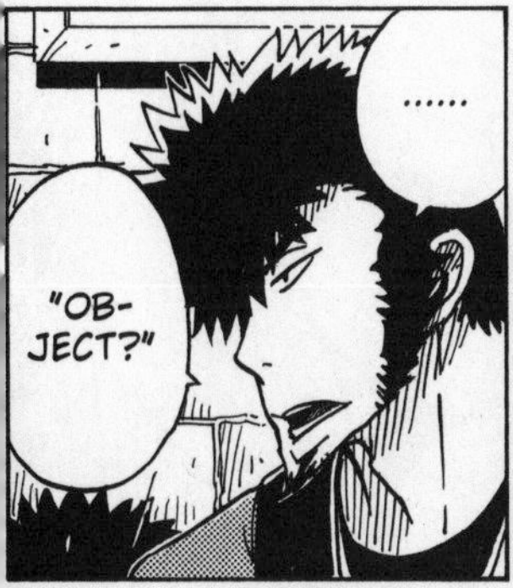
......
"OB-JECT?"

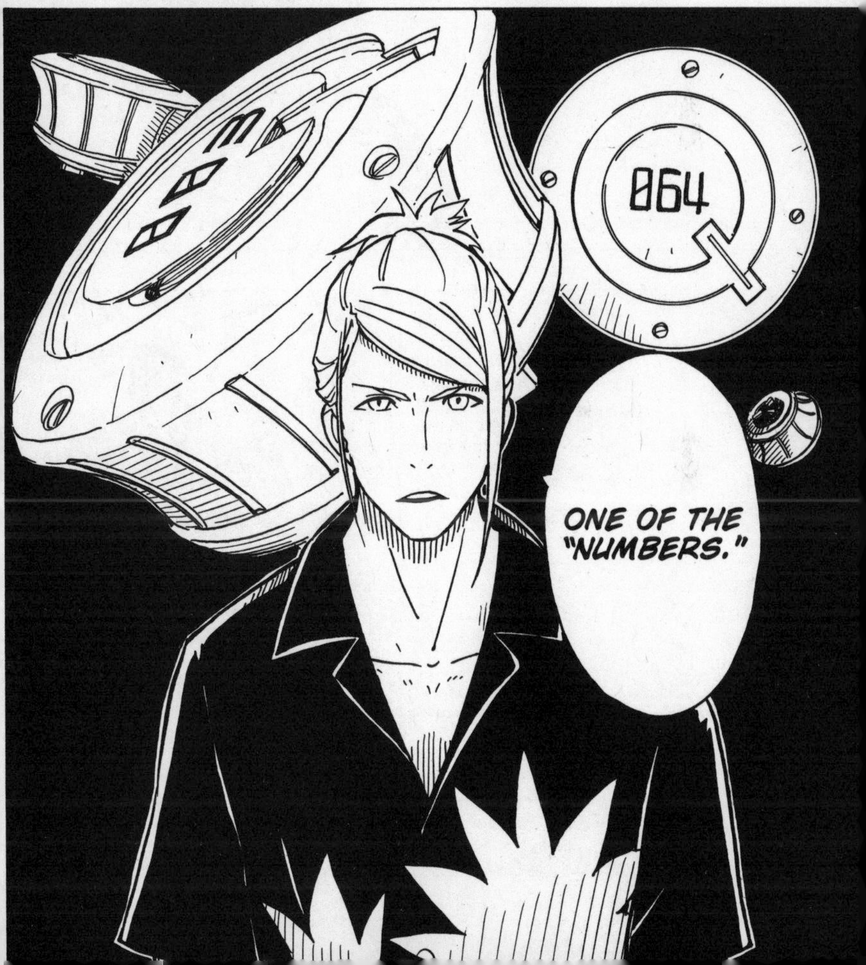
064
ONE OF THE "NUMBERS."

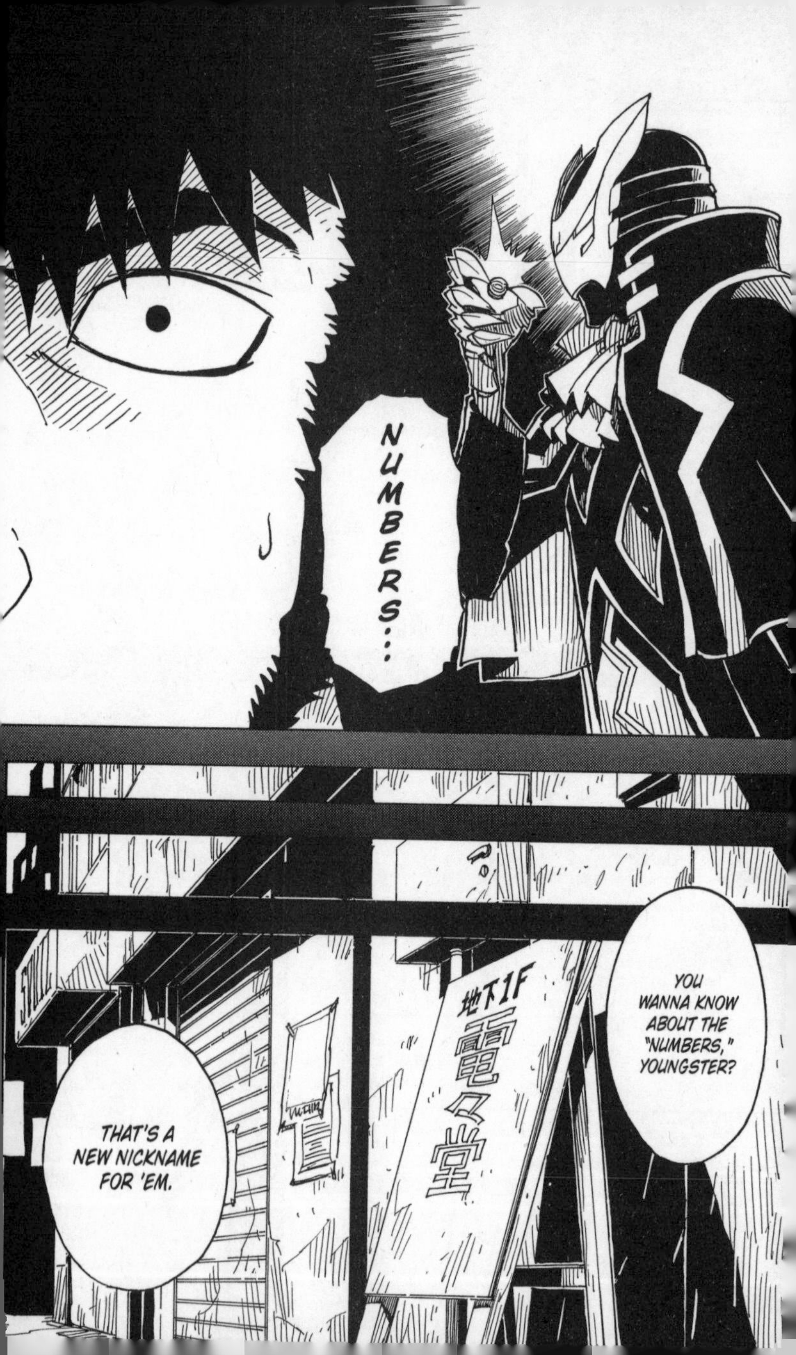
NUMBERS...
YOU WANNA KNOW ABOUT THE "NUMBERS," YOUNGSTER?
地下1F
電々堂
THAT'S A NEW NICKNAME FOR 'EM.

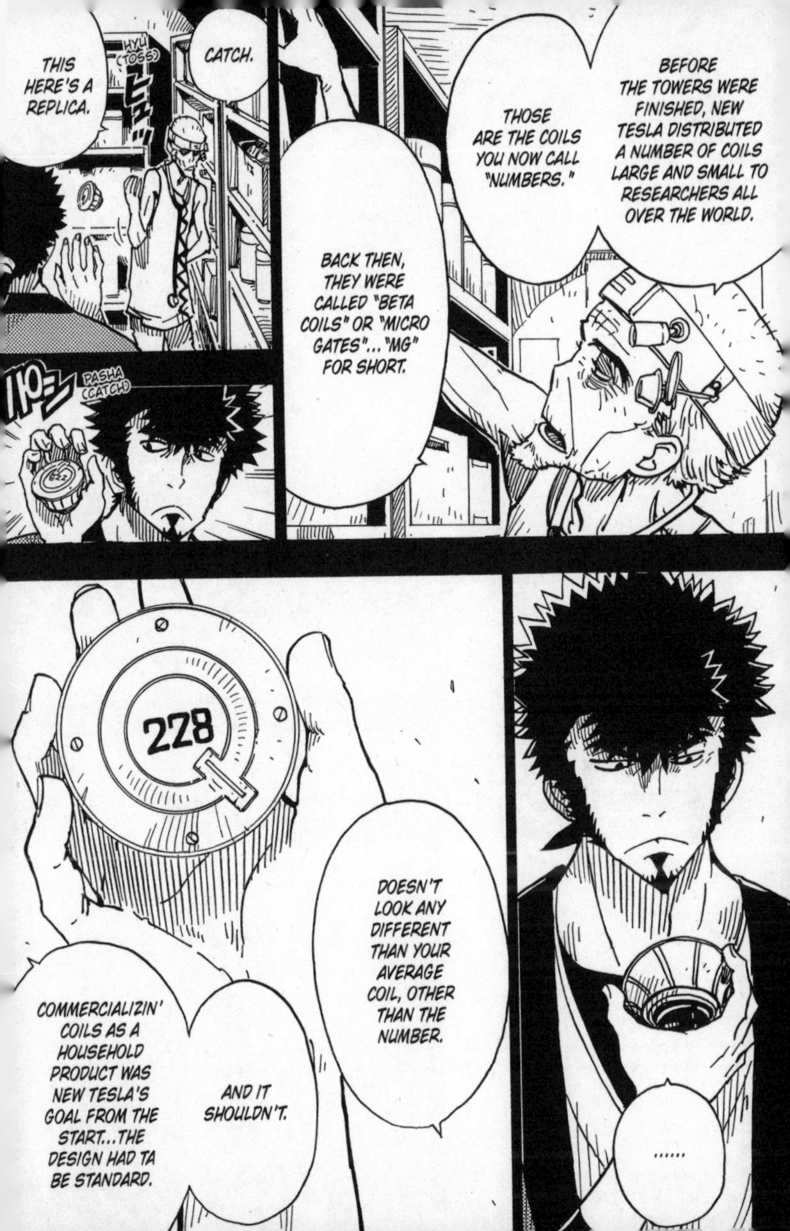
BEFORE THE TOWERS WERE FINISHED, NEW TESLA DISTRIBUTED A NUMBER OF COILS LARGE AND SMALL TO RESEARCHERS ALL OVER THE WORLD.
THOSE ARE THE COILS YOU NOW CALL "NUMBERS."
BACK THEN, THEY WERE CALLED "BETA COILS" OR "MICRO GATES"... "MG" FOR SHORT.
CATCH.
HYU (TOSS)
THIS HERE'S A REPLICA.
PASHA (CATCH)
......
228
DOESN'T LOOK ANY DIFFERENT THAN YOUR AVERAGE COIL, OTHER THAN THE NUMBER.
AND IT SHOULDN'T.
COMMERCIALIZIN' COILS AS A HOUSEHOLD PRODUCT WAS NEW TESLA'S GOAL FROM THE START...THE DESIGN HAD TA BE STANDARD.

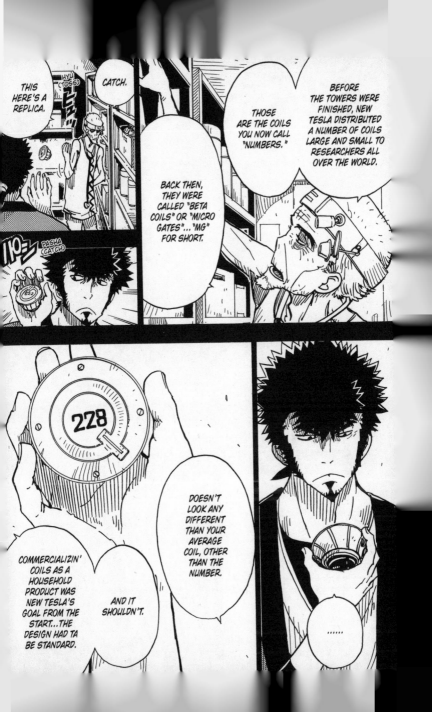

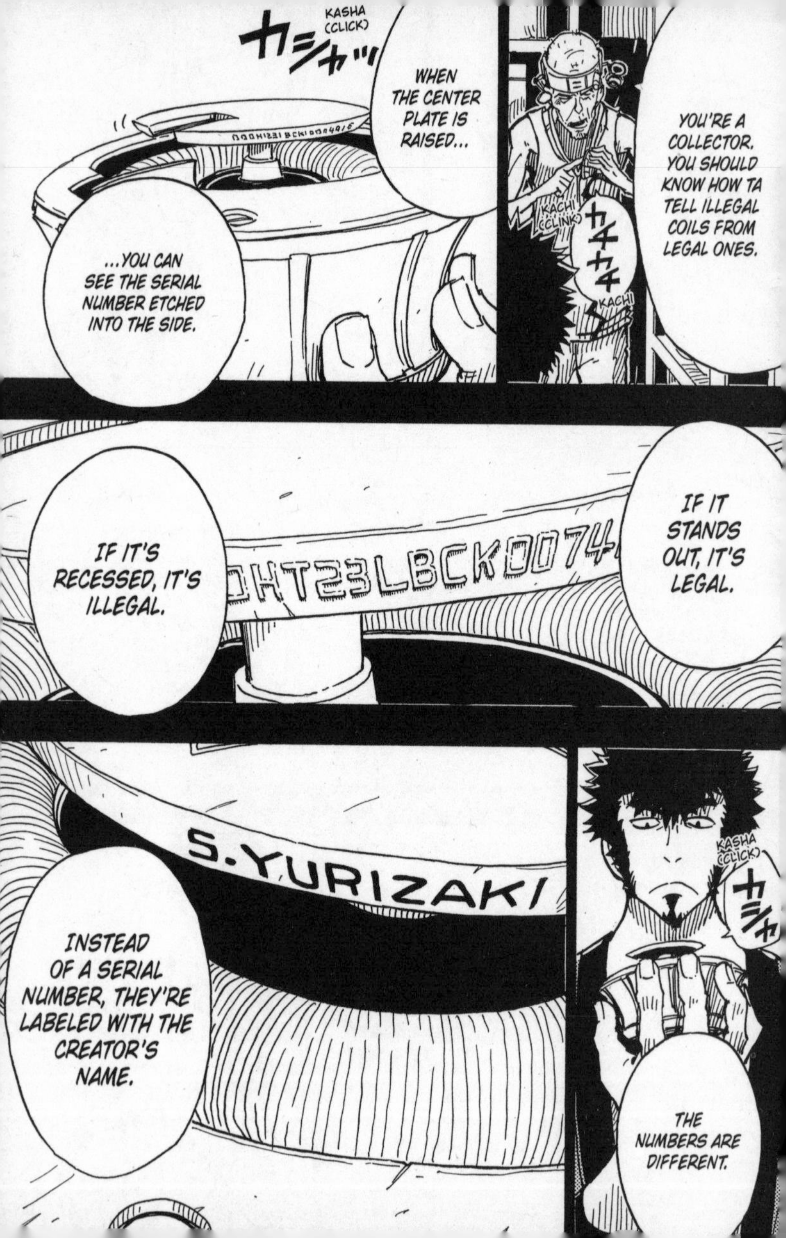
YOU'RE A COLLECTOR. YOU SHOULD KNOW HOW TA TELL ILLEGAL COILS FROM LEGAL ONES.
KACHI (CLINK)
カチカチ
KACHI
KASHA (CLICK)
カシャッ
WHEN THE CENTER PLATE IS RAISED...
...YOU CAN SEE THE SERIAL NUMBER ETCHED INTO THE SIDE.
IF IT STANDS OUT, IT'S LEGAL.
IF IT'S RECESSED, IT'S ILLEGAL.
KASHA (CLICK)
カシャ
THE NUMBERS ARE DIFFERENT.
S.YURIZAKI
INSTEAD OF A SERIAL NUMBER, THEY'RE LABELED WITH THE CREATOR'S NAME.

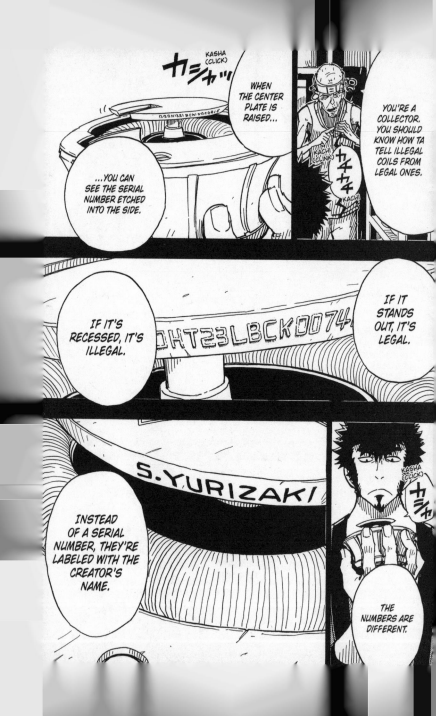

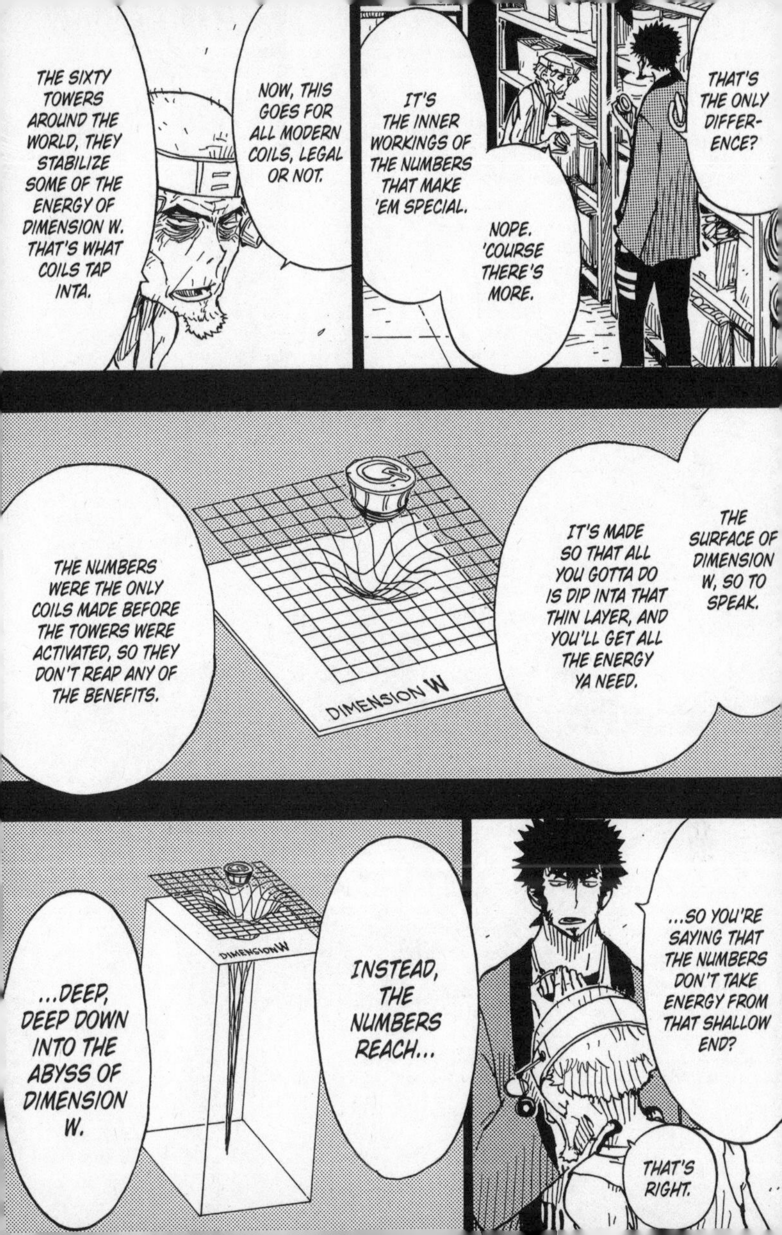
THAT'S THE ONLY DIFFERENCE?
NOPE. 'COURSE THERE'S MORE.
IT'S THE INNER WORKINGS OF THE NUMBERS THAT MAKE 'EM SPECIAL.
NOW, THIS GOES FOR ALL MODERN COILS, LEGAL OR NOT.
THE SIXTY TOWERS AROUND THE WORLD, THEY STABILIZE SOME OF THE ENERGY OF DIMENSION W. THAT'S WHAT COILS TAP INTA.
THE SURFACE OF DIMENSION W, SO TO SPEAK.
IT'S MADE SO THAT ALL YOU GOTTA DO IS DIP INTA THAT THIN LAYER, AND YOU'LL GET ALL THE ENERGY YA NEED.
DIMENSION W
THE NUMBERS WERE THE ONLY COILS MADE BEFORE THE TOWERS WERE ACTIVATED, SO THEY DON'T REAP ANY OF THE BENEFITS.
...SO YOU'RE SAYING THAT THE NUMBERS DON'T TAKE ENERGY FROM THAT SHALLOW END?
THAT'S RIGHT.
INSTEAD, THE NUMBERS REACH...
DIMENSION W
...DEEP, DEEP DOWN INTO THE ABYSS OF DIMENSION W.

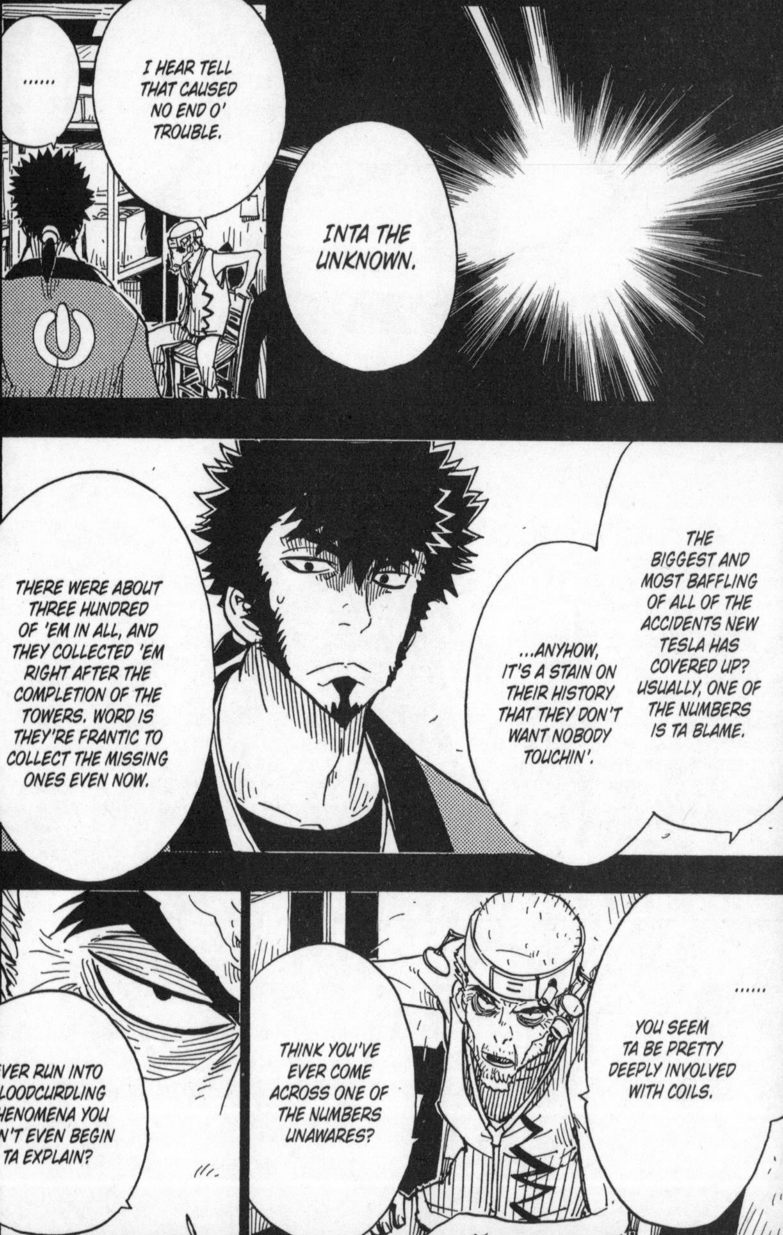
INTA THE UNKNOWN.
I HEAR TELL THAT CAUSED NO END O' TROUBLE.
......
THE BIGGEST AND MOST BAFFLING OF ALL OF THE ACCIDENTS NEW TESLA HAS COVERED UP? USUALLY, ONE OF THE NUMBERS IS TA BLAME.
...ANYHOW, IT'S A STAIN ON THEIR HISTORY THAT THEY DON'T WANT NOBODY TOUCHIN'.
THERE WERE ABOUT THREE HUNDRED OF 'EM IN ALL, AND THEY COLLECTED 'EM RIGHT AFTER THE COMPLETION OF THE TOWERS. WORD IS THEY'RE FRANTIC TO COLLECT THE MISSING ONES EVEN NOW.
......
YOU SEEM TA BE PRETTY DEEPLY INVOLVED WITH COILS.
THINK YOU'VE EVER COME ACROSS ONE OF THE NUMBERS UNAWARES?
EVER RUN INTO BLOODCURDLING PHENOMENA YOU CAN'T EVEN BEGIN TA EXPLAIN?

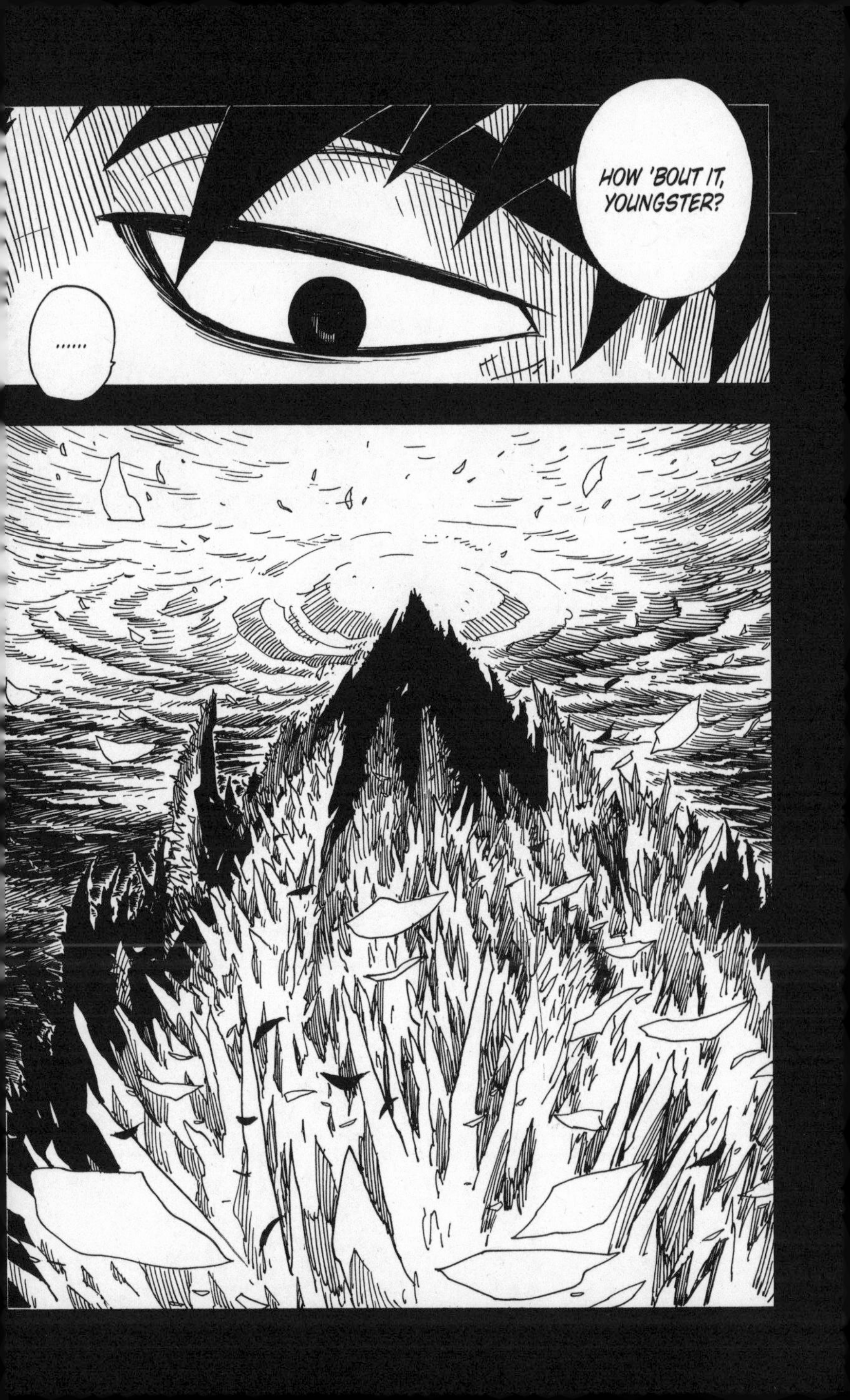
HOW 'BOUT IT, YOUNGSTER?
......

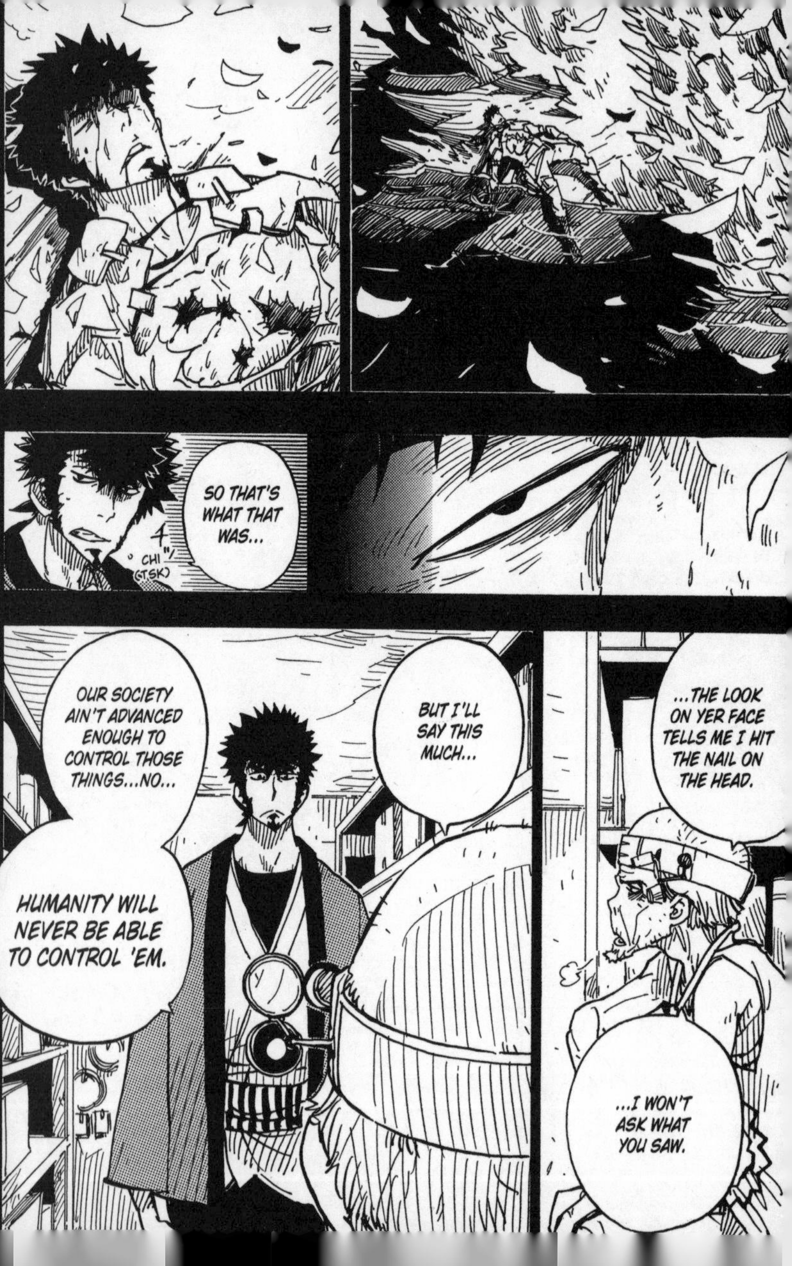
SO THAT'S WHAT THAT WAS...
CHI (TSK)
...THE LOOK ON YER FACE TELLS ME I HIT THE NAIL ON THE HEAD.
...I WON'T ASK WHAT YOU SAW.
BUT I'LL SAY THIS MUCH...
OUR SOCIETY AIN'T ADVANCED ENOUGH TO CONTROL THOSE THINGS...NO...
HUMANITY WILL NEVER BE ABLE TO CONTROL 'EM.

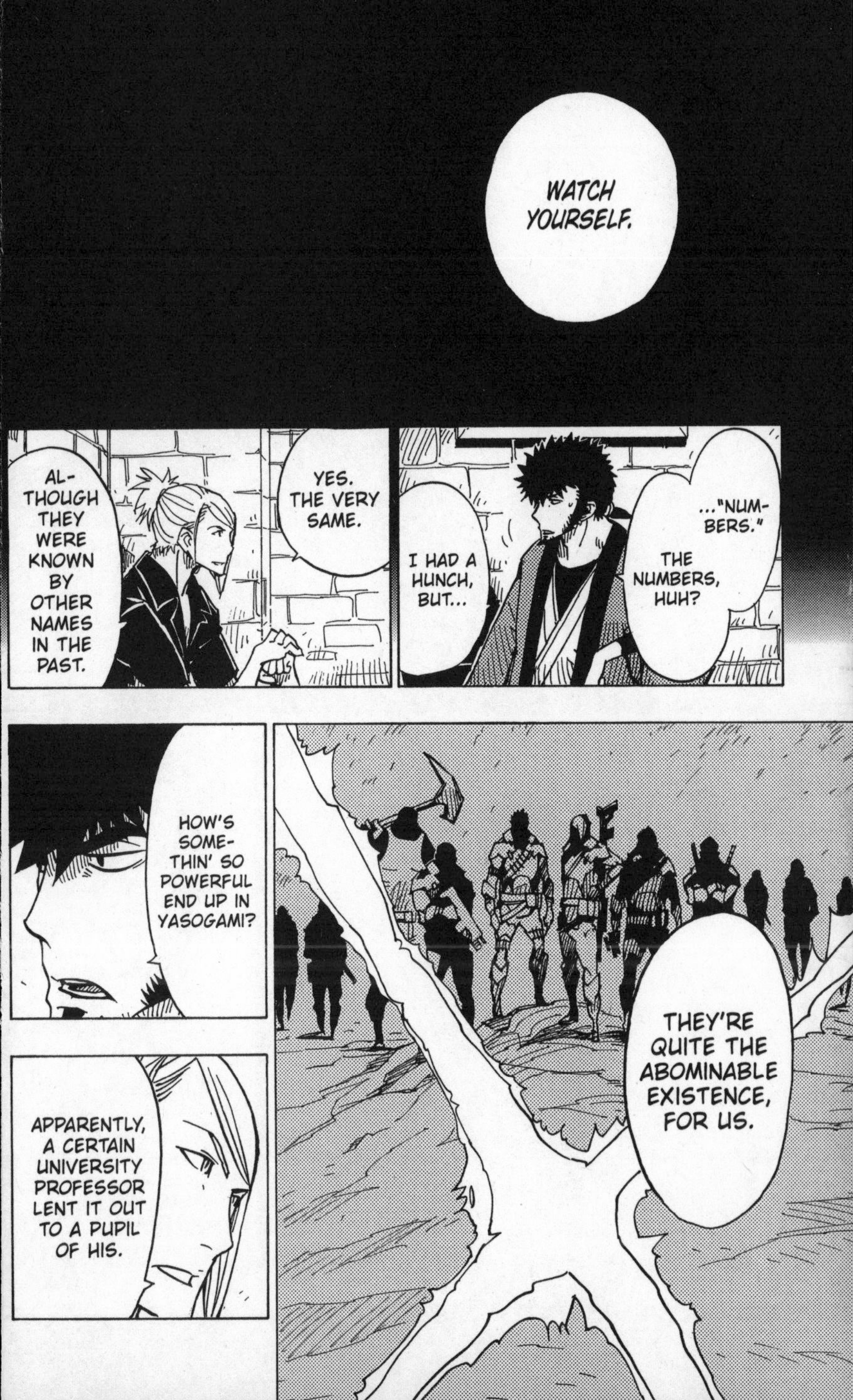
WATCH YOURSELF.
..."NUMBERS."
THE NUMBERS, HUH?
I HAD A HUNCH, BUT...
YES. THE VERY SAME.
ALTHOUGH THEY WERE KNOWN BY OTHER NAMES IN THE PAST.
THEY'RE QUITE THE ABOMINABLE EXISTENCE, FOR US.
HOW'S SOMETHIN' SO POWERFUL END UP IN YASOGAMI?
APPARENTLY, A CERTAIN UNIVERSITY PROFESSOR LENT IT OUT TO A PUPIL OF HIS.

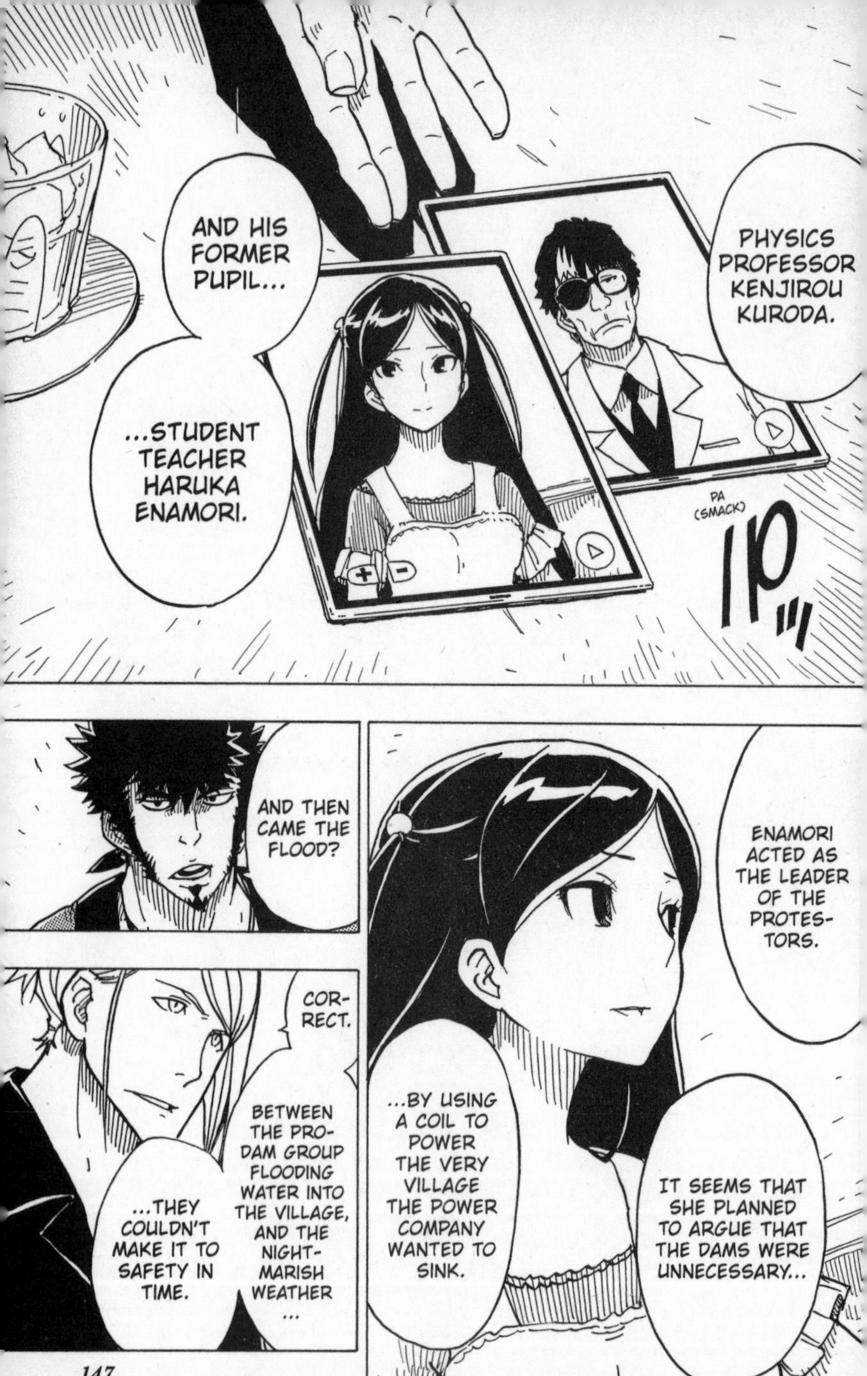
PHYSICS PROFESSOR KENJIROU KURODA.
AND HIS FORMER PUPIL...
...STUDENT TEACHER HARUKA ENAMORI.
PA (SMACK)
ENAMORI ACTED AS THE LEADER OF THE PROTES-TORS.
IT SEEMS THAT SHE PLANNED TO ARGUE THAT THE DAMS WERE UNNECESSARY...
...BY USING A COIL TO POWER THE VERY VILLAGE THE POWER COMPANY WANTED TO SINK.
AND THEN CAME THE FLOOD?
COR-RECT.
BETWEEN THE PRO-DAM GROUP FLOODING WATER INTO THE VILLAGE, AND THE NIGHT-MARISH WEATHER...
...THEY COULDN'T MAKE IT TO SAFETY IN TIME.

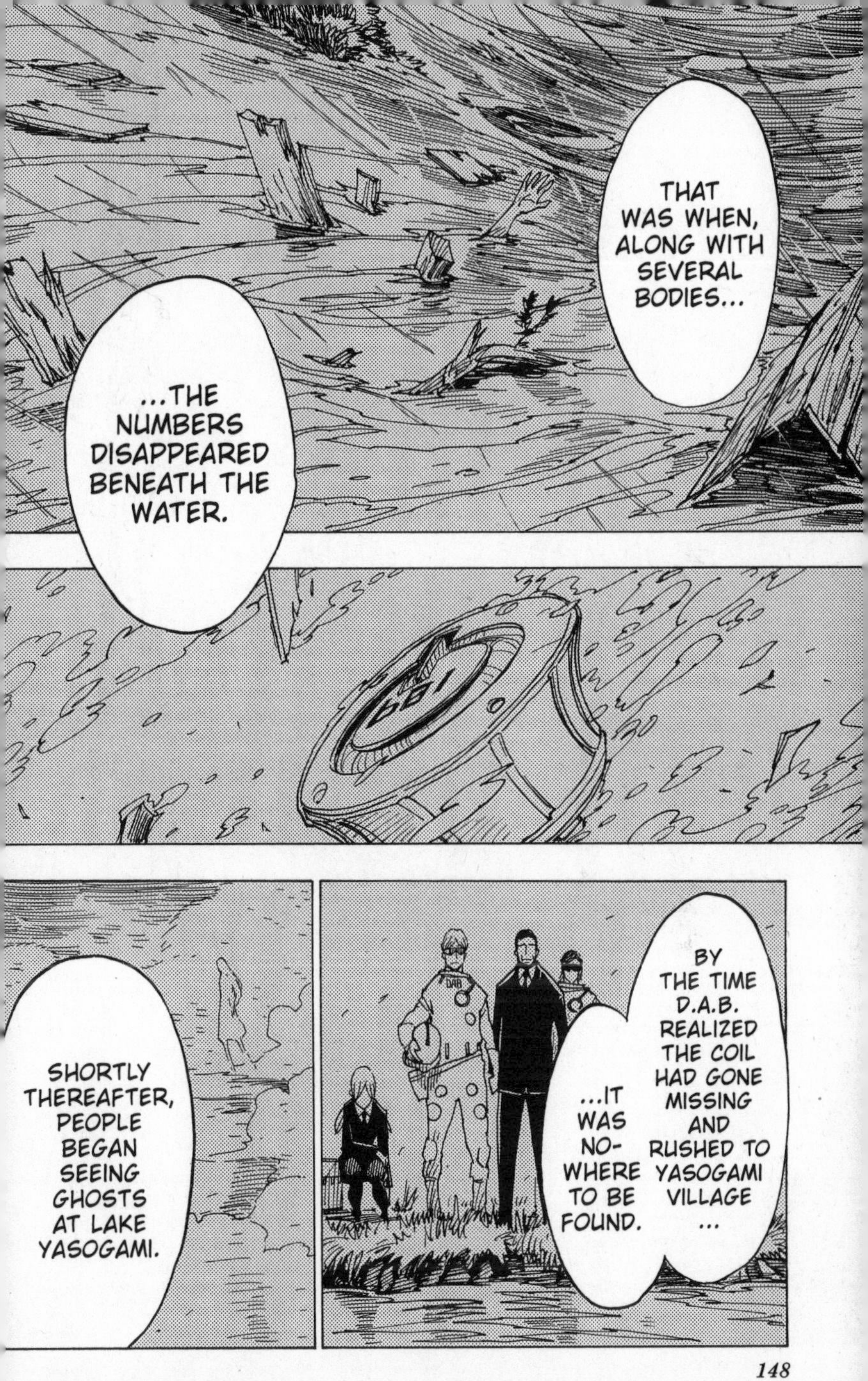

THAT WAS WHEN, ALONG WITH SEVERAL BODIES...
...THE NUMBERS DISAPPEARED BENEATH THE WATER.
BY THE TIME D.A.B. REALIZED THE COIL HAD GONE MISSING AND RUSHED TO YASOGAMI VILLAGE ...
...IT WAS NO-WHERE TO BE FOUND.
SHORTLY THEREAFTER, PEOPLE BEGAN SEEING GHOSTS AT LAKE YASOGAMI.

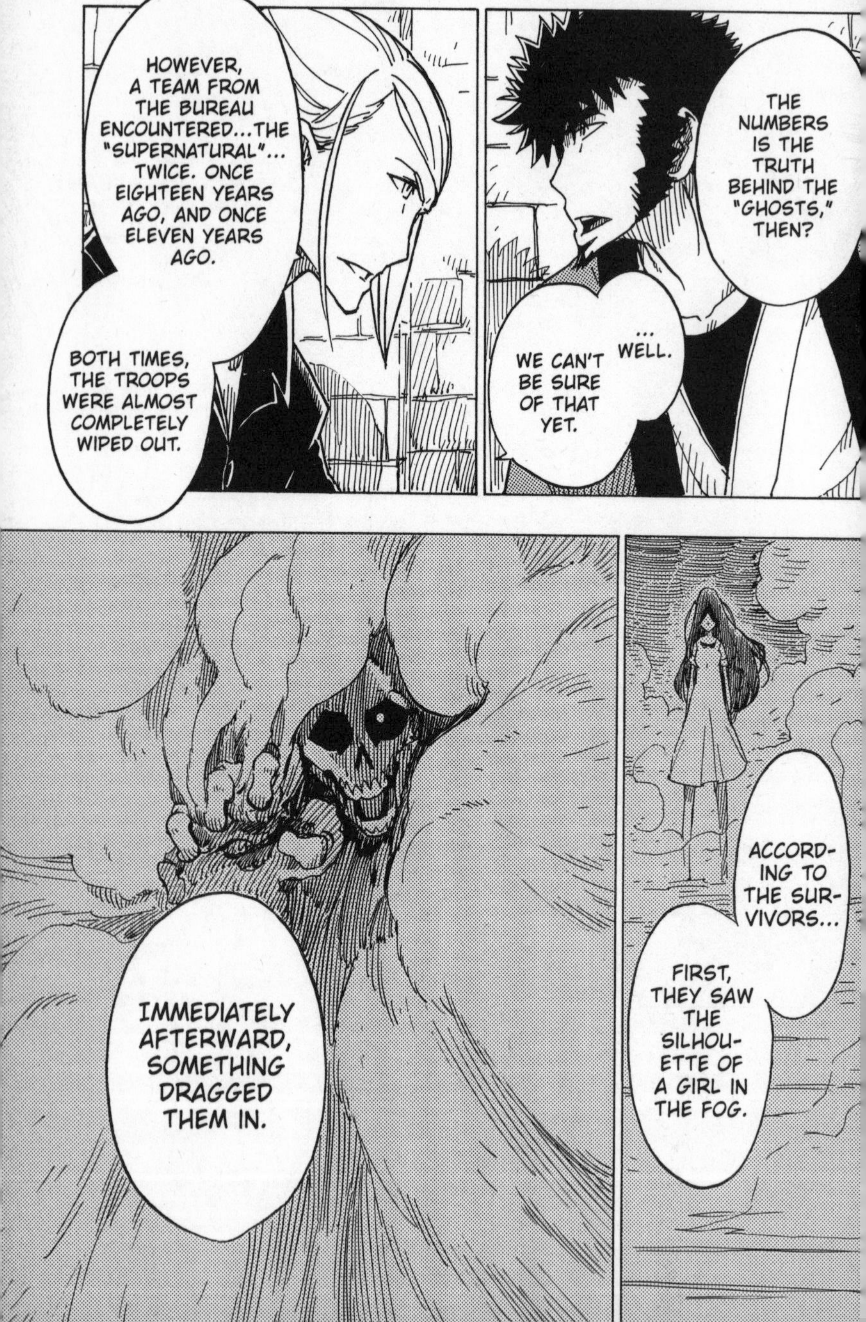
THE NUMBERS IS THE TRUTH BEHIND THE "GHOSTS," THEN?
...WELL.
WE CAN'T BE SURE OF THAT YET.
HOWEVER, A TEAM FROM THE BUREAU ENCOUNTERED...THE "SUPERNATURAL"... TWICE. ONCE EIGHTEEN YEARS AGO, AND ONCE ELEVEN YEARS AGO.
BOTH TIMES, THE TROOPS WERE ALMOST COMPLETELY WIPED OUT.
ACCORD-ING TO THE SUR-VIVORS...
FIRST, THEY SAW THE SILHOU-ETTE OF A GIRL IN THE FOG.
IMMEDIATELY AFTERWARD, SOMETHING DRAGGED THEM IN.

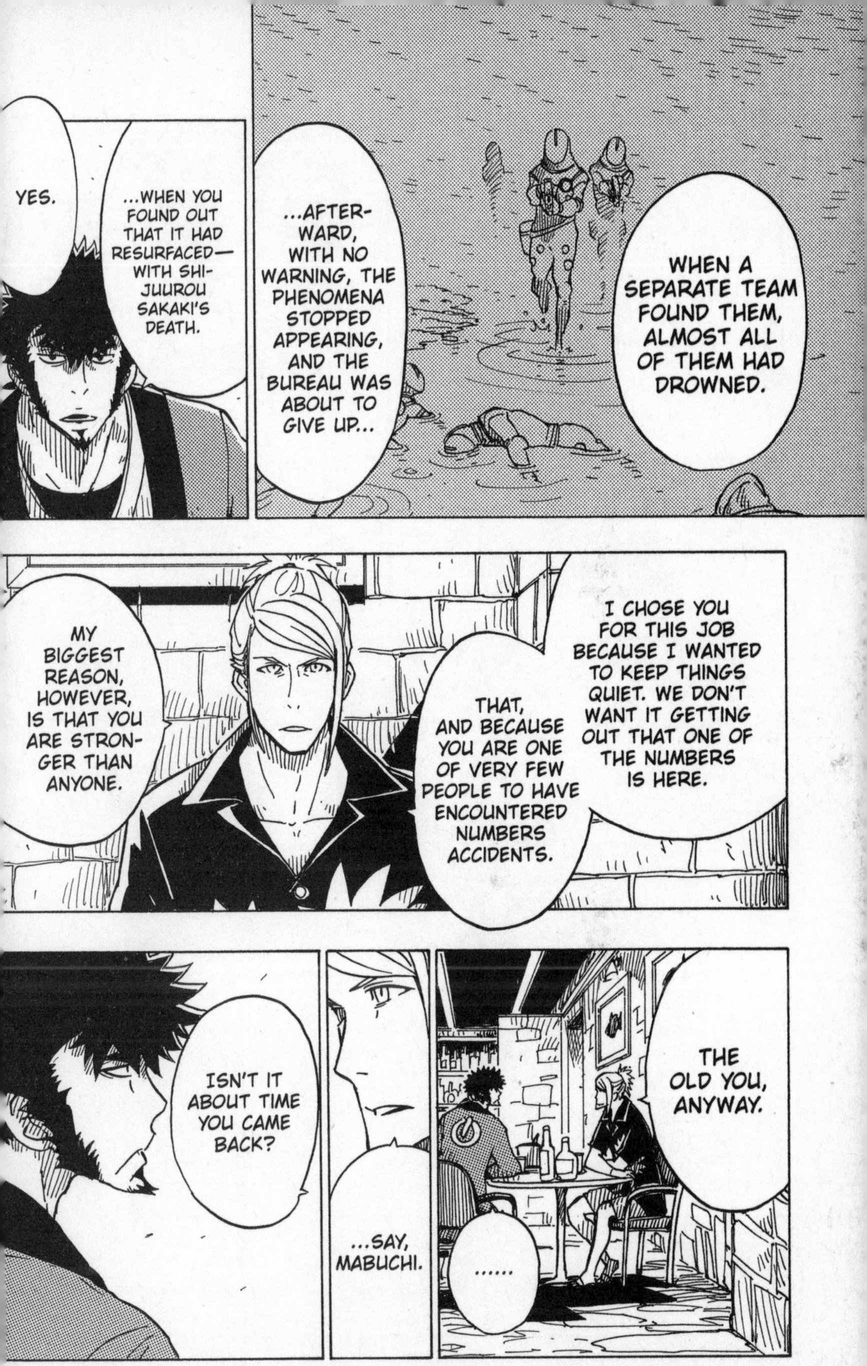
WHEN A SEPARATE TEAM FOUND THEM, ALMOST ALL OF THEM HAD DROWNED.
...AFTER-WARD, WITH NO WARNING, THE PHENOMENA STOPPED APPEARING, AND THE BUREAU WAS ABOUT TO GIVE UP...
...WHEN YOU FOUND OUT THAT IT HAD RESURFACED—WITH SHIJUUROU SAKAKI'S DEATH.
YES.
I CHOSE YOU FOR THIS JOB BECAUSE I WANTED TO KEEP THINGS QUIET. WE DON'T WANT IT GETTING OUT THAT ONE OF THE NUMBERS IS HERE.
THAT, AND BECAUSE YOU ARE ONE OF VERY FEW PEOPLE TO HAVE ENCOUNTERED NUMBERS ACCIDENTS.
MY BIGGEST REASON, HOWEVER, IS THAT YOU ARE STRONGER THAN ANYONE.
THE OLD YOU, ANYWAY.
......
...SAY, MABUCHI.
ISN'T IT ABOUT TIME YOU CAME BACK?

Dimension W

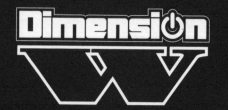

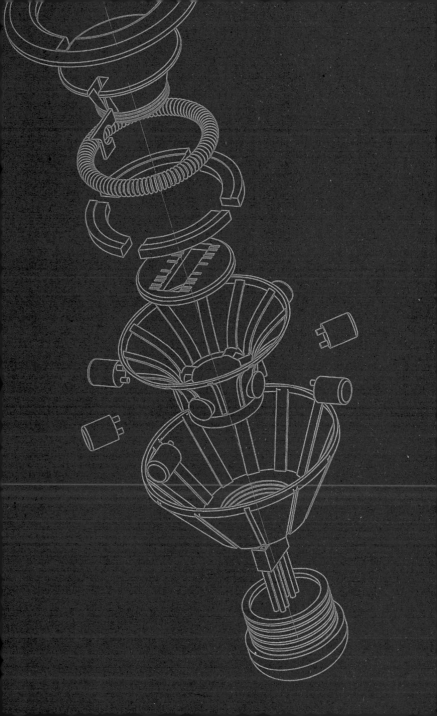

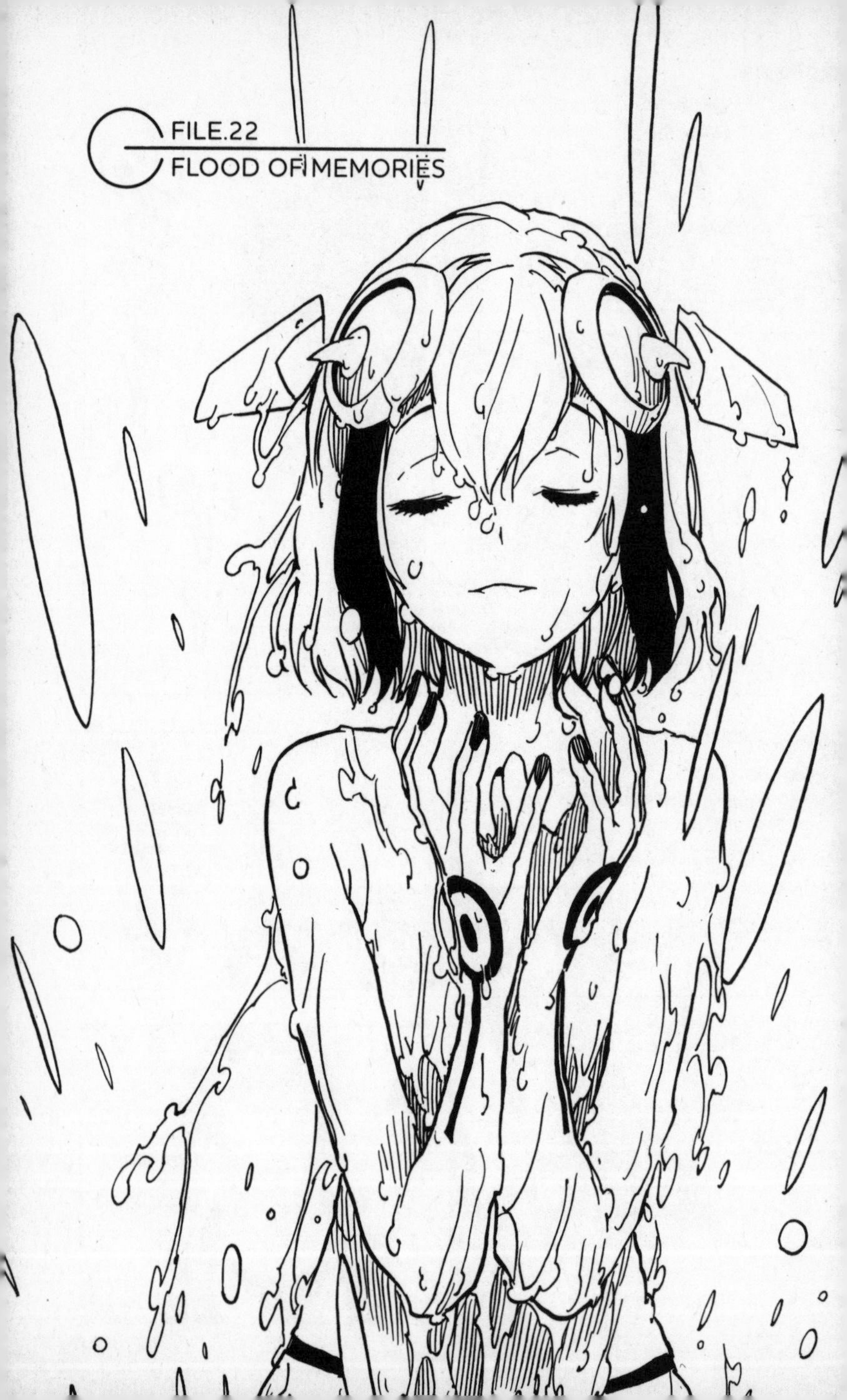
FILE.22
FLOOD OF MEMORIES

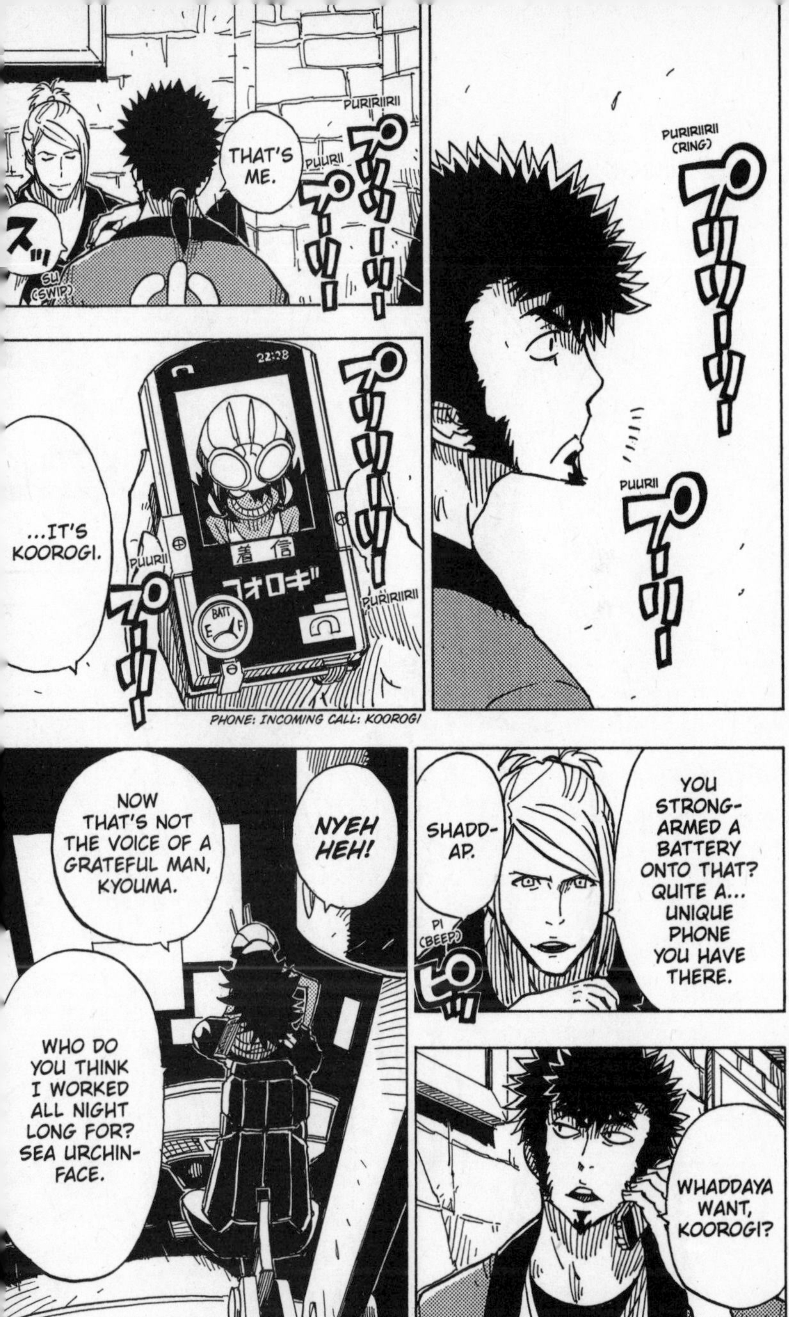
PURIRIIRII (RING)
PUURII
PURIRIIRII
THAT'S ME.
PUURII
SU (SWIP)
PURIRIIRII
...IT'S KOOROGI.
PUURII
PHONE: INCOMING CALL: KOOROGI
YOU STRONG-ARMED A BATTERY ONTO THAT? QUITE A... UNIQUE PHONE YOU HAVE THERE.
SHADD-AP.
PI (BEEP)
WHADDAYA WANT, KOOROGI?
NYEH HEH!
NOW THAT'S NOT THE VOICE OF A GRATEFUL MAN, KYOUMA.
WHO DO YOU THINK I WORKED ALL NIGHT LONG FOR? SEA URCHIN-FACE.

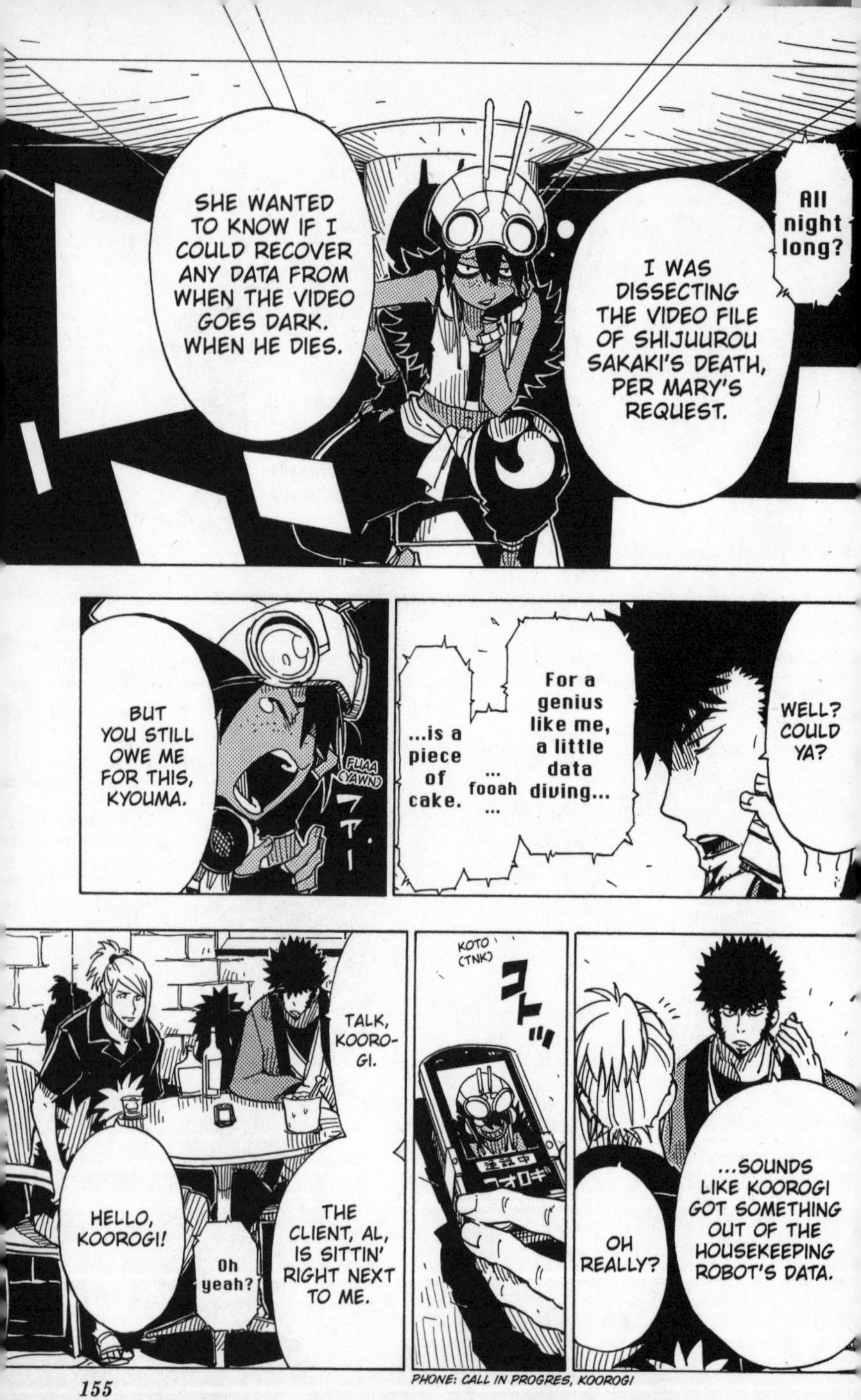
All night long?
I WAS DISSECTING THE VIDEO FILE OF SHIJUUROU SAKAKI'S DEATH, PER MARY'S REQUEST.
SHE WANTED TO KNOW IF I COULD RECOVER ANY DATA FROM WHEN THE VIDEO GOES DARK. WHEN HE DIES.
WELL? COULD YA?
For a genius like me, a little data diving...
... fooah ...
...is a piece of cake.
BUT YOU STILL OWE ME FOR THIS, KYOUMA.
FUAA (YAWN)
...SOUNDS LIKE KOOROGI GOT SOMETHING OUT OF THE HOUSEKEEPING ROBOT'S DATA.
OH REALLY?
KOTO (TNK)
TALK, KOORO-GI.
THE CLIENT, AL, IS SITTIN' RIGHT NEXT TO ME.
Oh yeah?
HELLO, KOOROGI!

PHONE: CALL IN PROGRES, KOOROGI

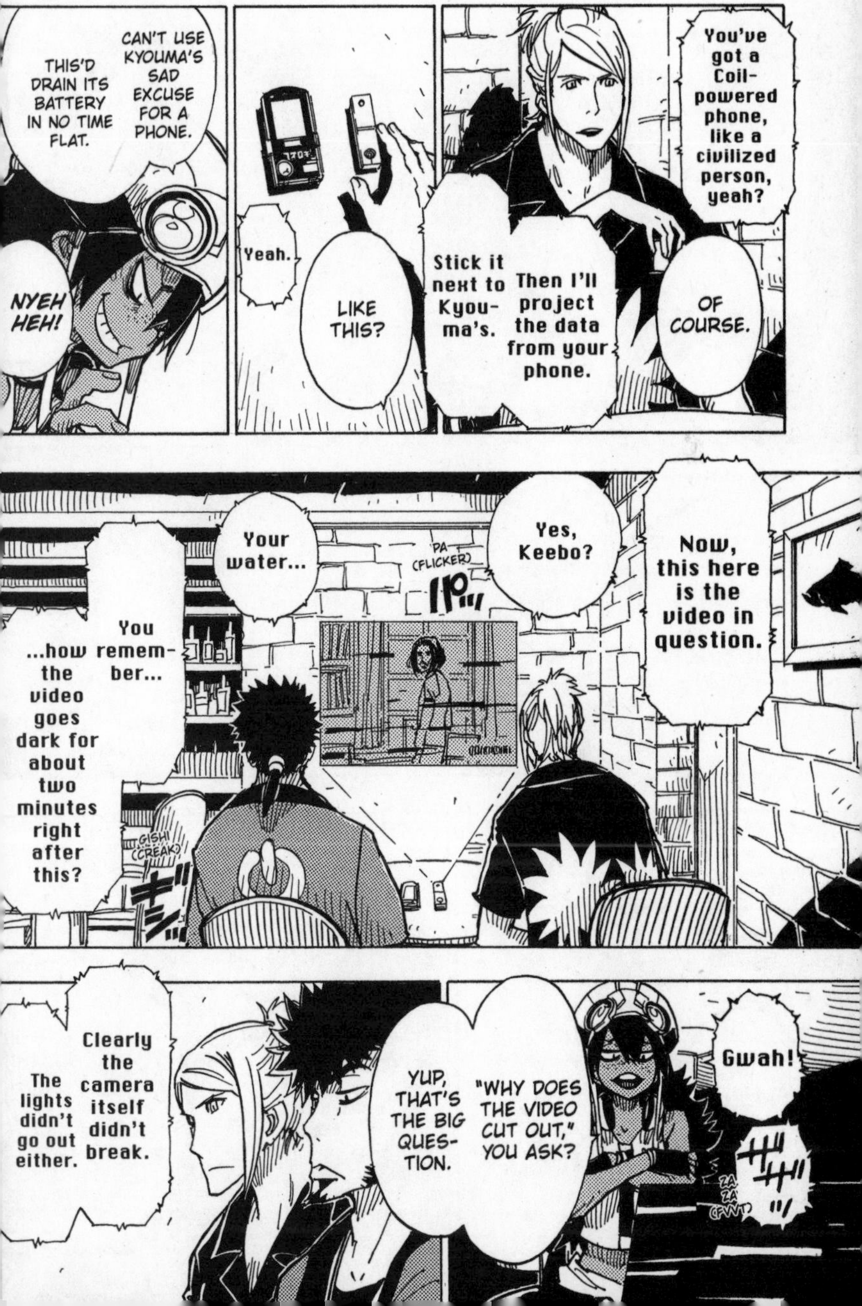

You've got a Coil-powered phone, like a civilized person, yeah?
OF COURSE.
Then I'll project the data from your phone.
Stick it next to Kyouma's.
LIKE THIS?
Yeah.
CAN'T USE KYOUMA'S SAD EXCUSE FOR A PHONE.
THIS'D DRAIN ITS BATTERY IN NO TIME FLAT.
NYEH HEH!
Now, this here is the video in question.
Yes, Keebo?
PA (FLICKER)
Your water...
You remember...
...how the video goes dark for about two minutes right after this?
GISHI (CREAK)
Gwah!
ZA ZA (FVVT)
"WHY DOES THE VIDEO CUT OUT," YOU ASK?
YUP, THAT'S THE BIG QUESTION.
Clearly the camera itself didn't break.
The lights didn't go out either.

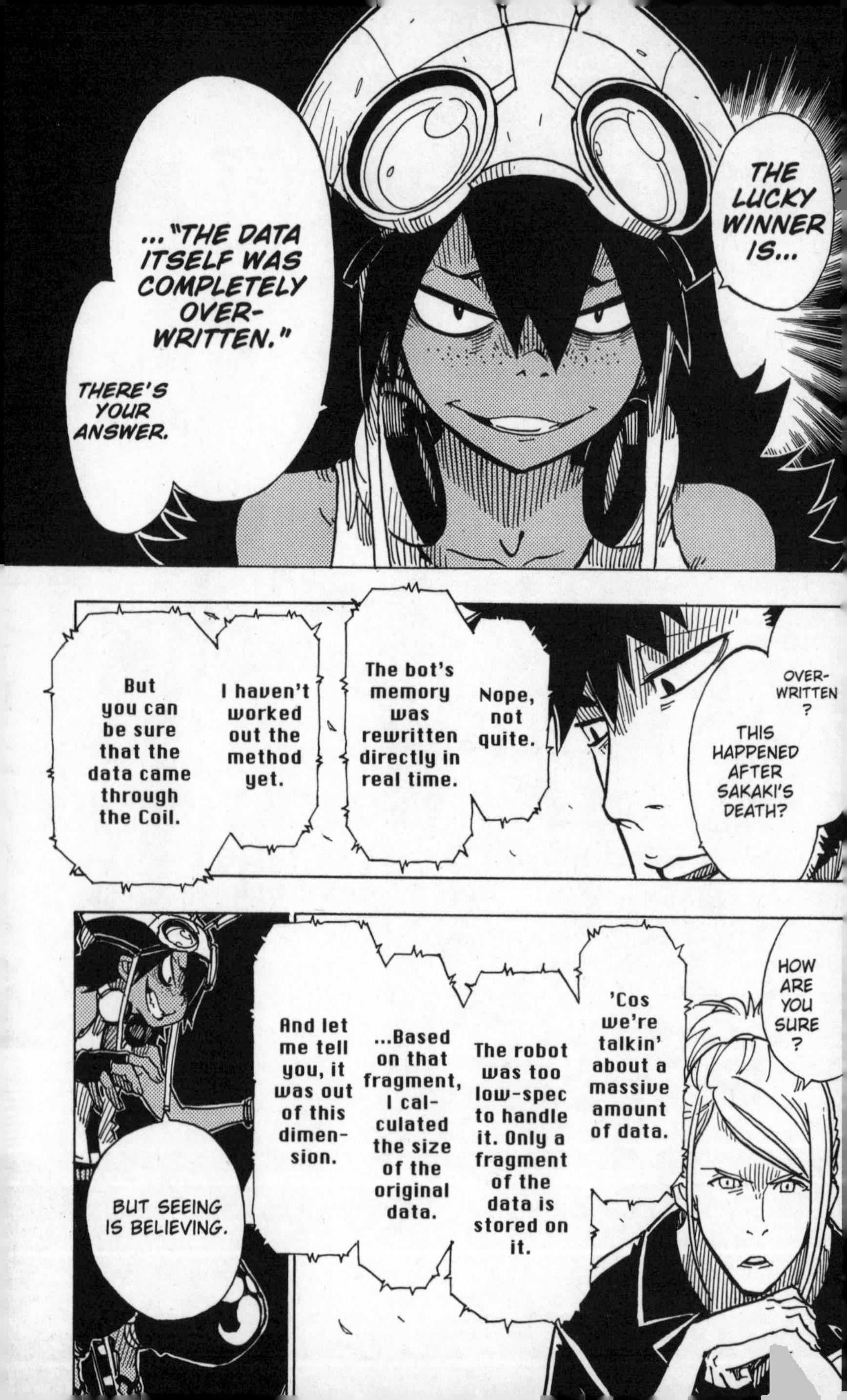
THE LUCKY WINNER IS...
..."THE DATA ITSELF WAS COMPLETELY OVER-WRITTEN."
THERE'S YOUR ANSWER.
OVER-WRITTEN? THIS HAPPENED AFTER SAKAKI'S DEATH?
Nope, not quite.
The bot's memory was rewritten directly in real time.
I haven't worked out the method yet.
But you can be sure that the data came through the Coil.
HOW ARE YOU SURE?
'Cos we're talkin' about a massive amount of data.
The robot was too low-spec to handle it. Only a fragment of the data is stored on it.
...Based on that fragment, I cal-culated the size of the original data.
And let me tell you, it was out of this dimen-sion.
BUT SEEING IS BELIEVING.

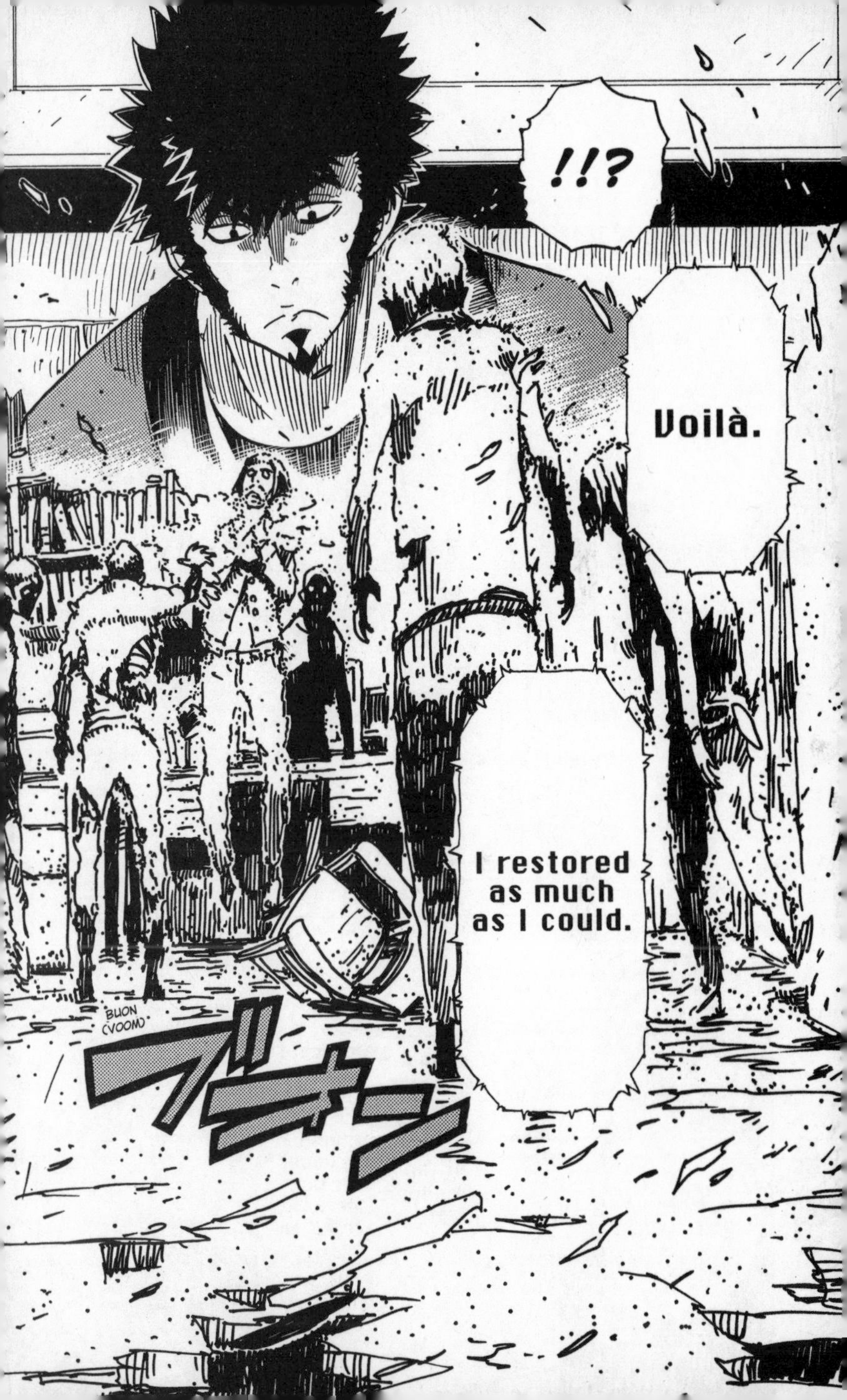
!!?
Voilà.
I restored as much as I could.
BUON (VOOM)

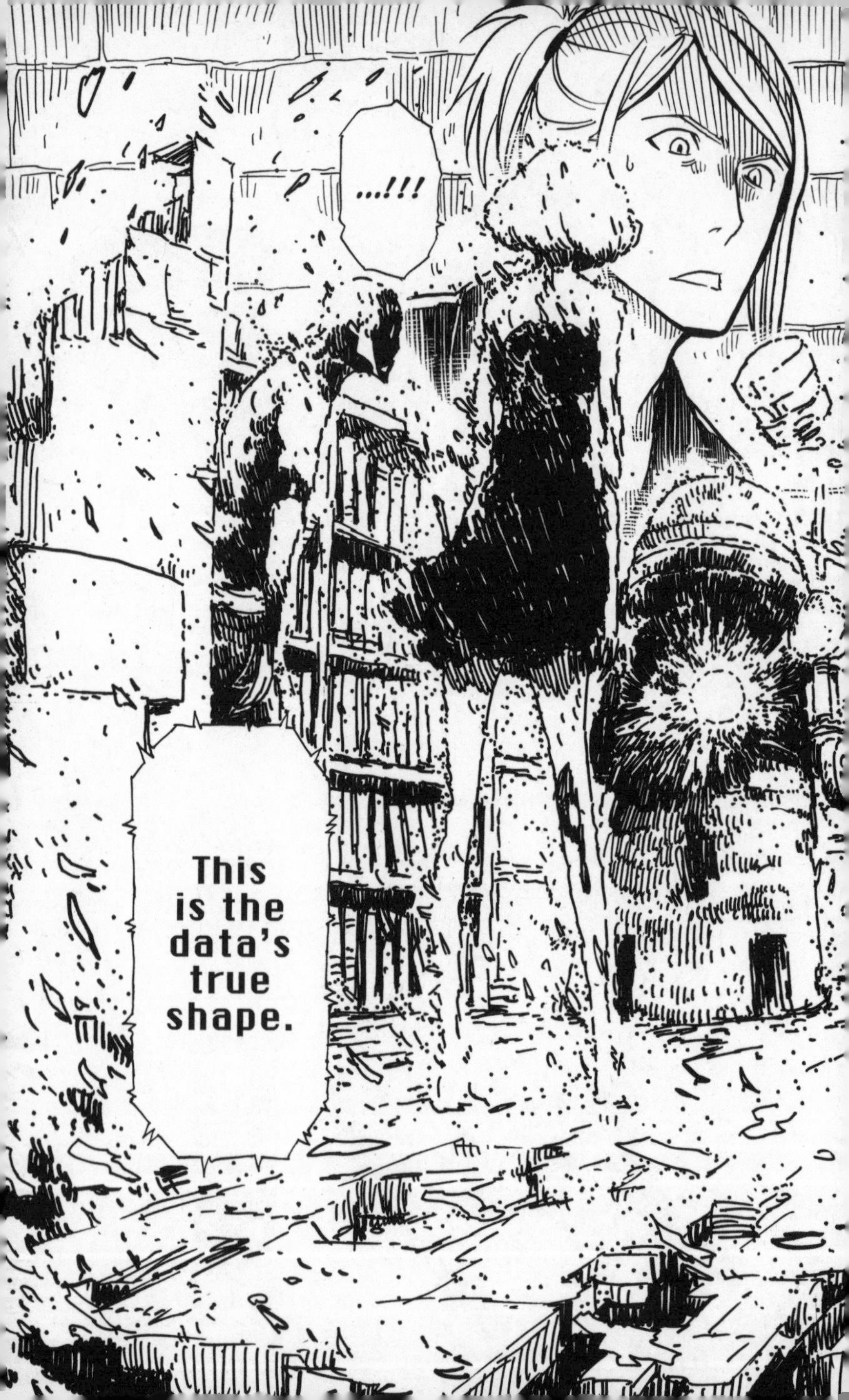
...!!!
This is the data's true shape.

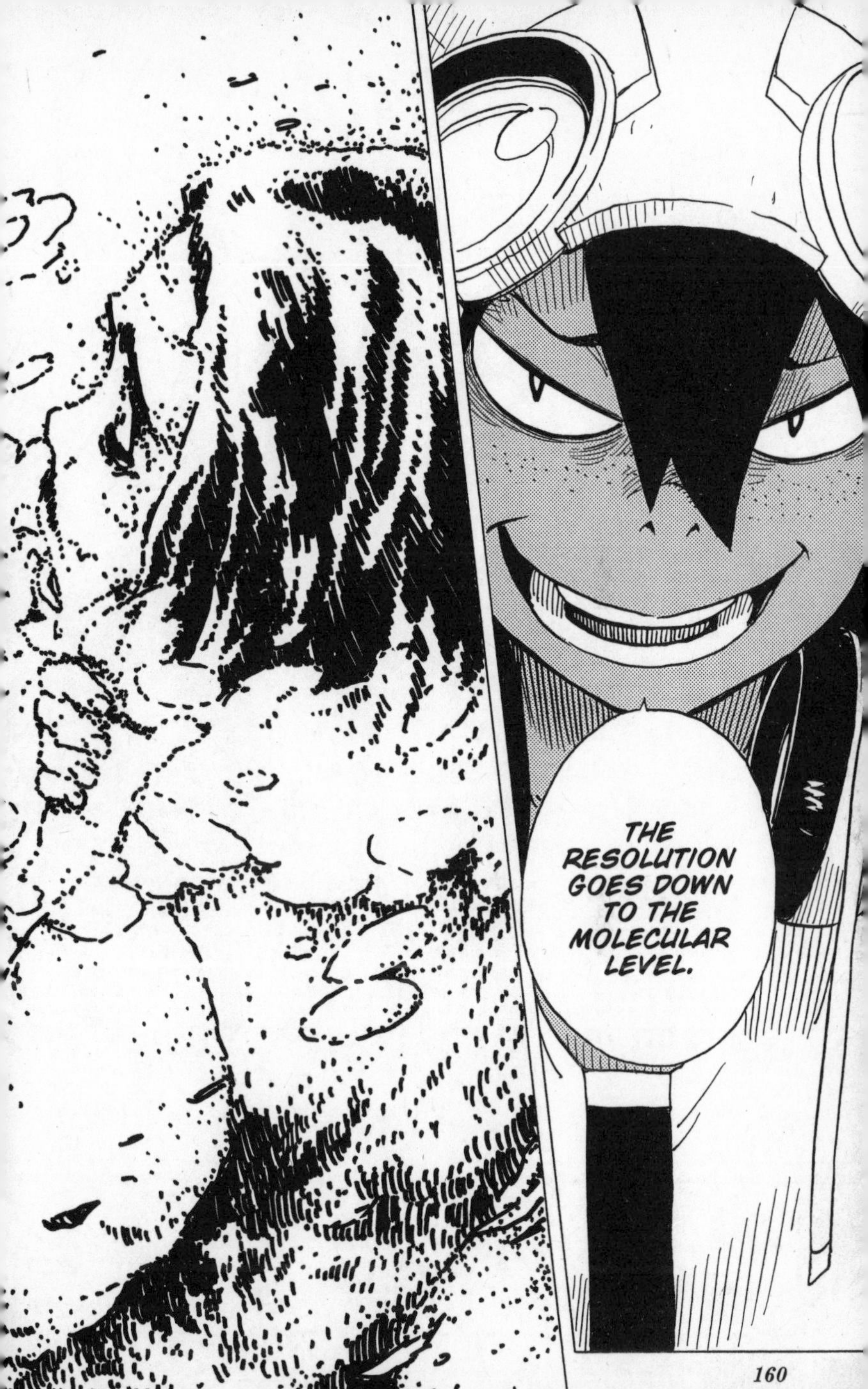
THE RESOLUTION GOES DOWN TO THE MOLECULAR LEVEL.

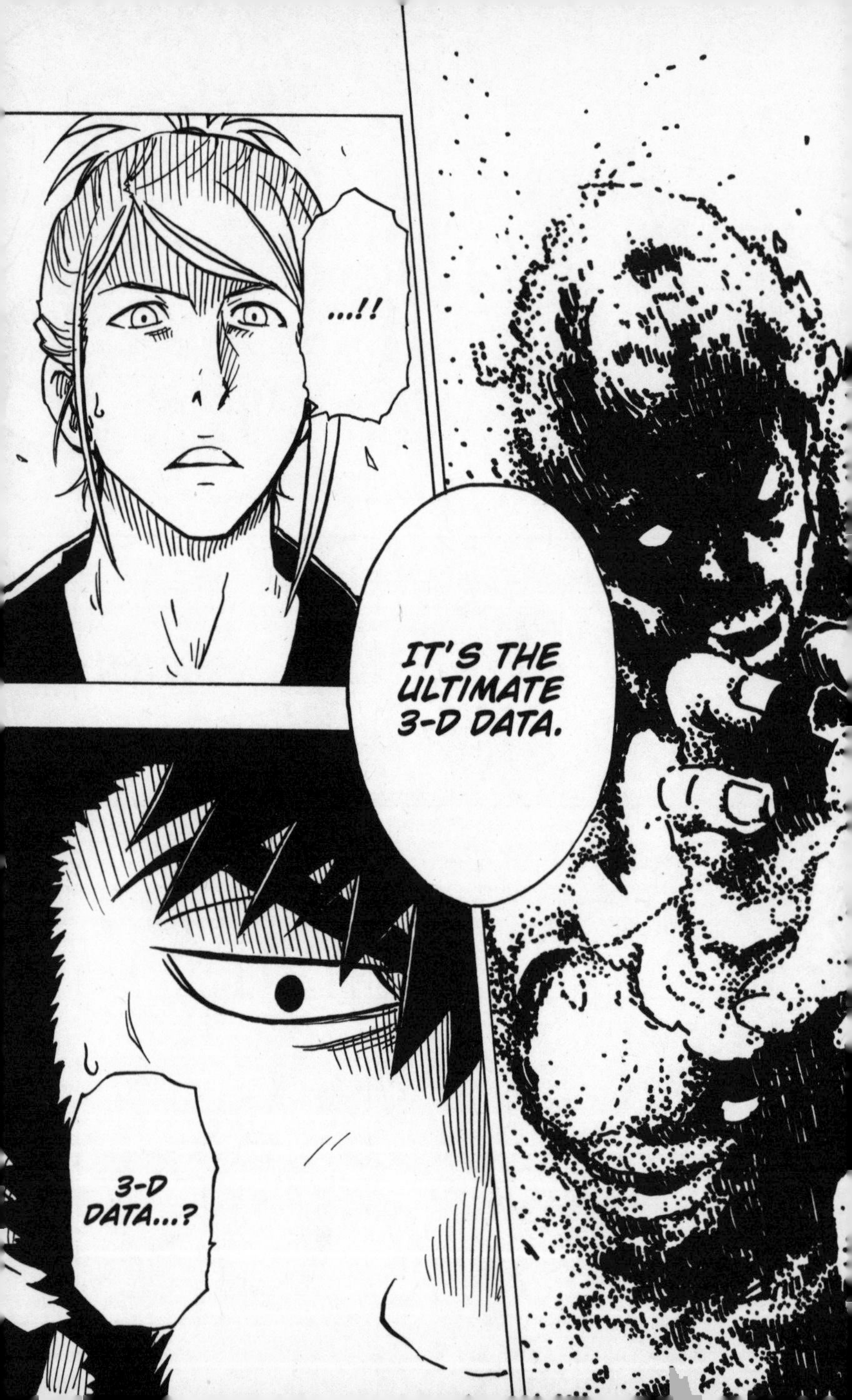
IT'S THE ULTIMATE 3-D DATA.
...!!
3-D DATA...?

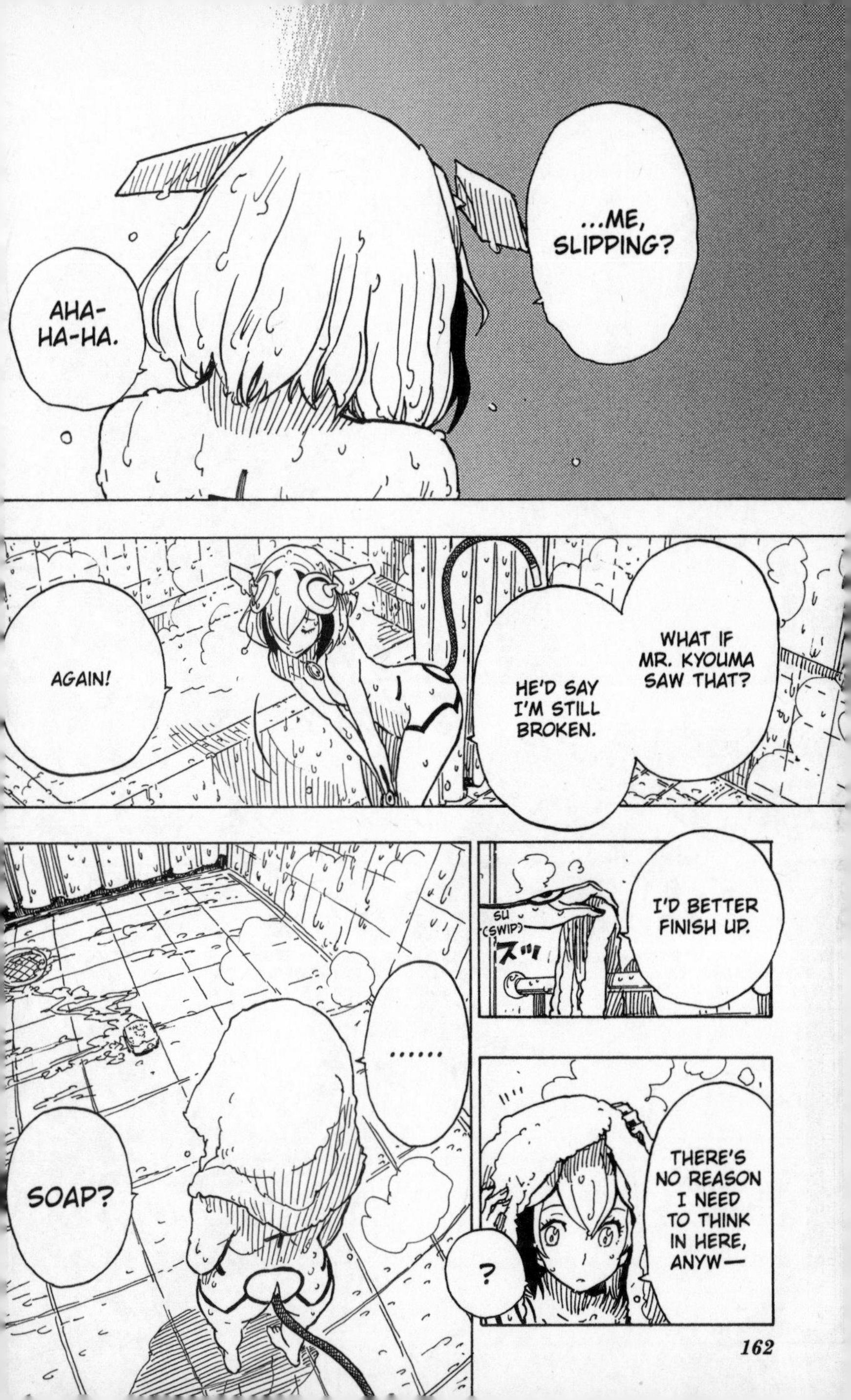
...ME, SLIPPING?
AHA-HA-HA.
WHAT IF MR. KYOUMA SAW THAT?
HE'D SAY I'M STILL BROKEN.
AGAIN!
I'D BETTER FINISH UP.
SU (SWIP)
ズッ
THERE'S NO REASON I NEED TO THINK IN HERE, ANYW—
?
......
SOAP?

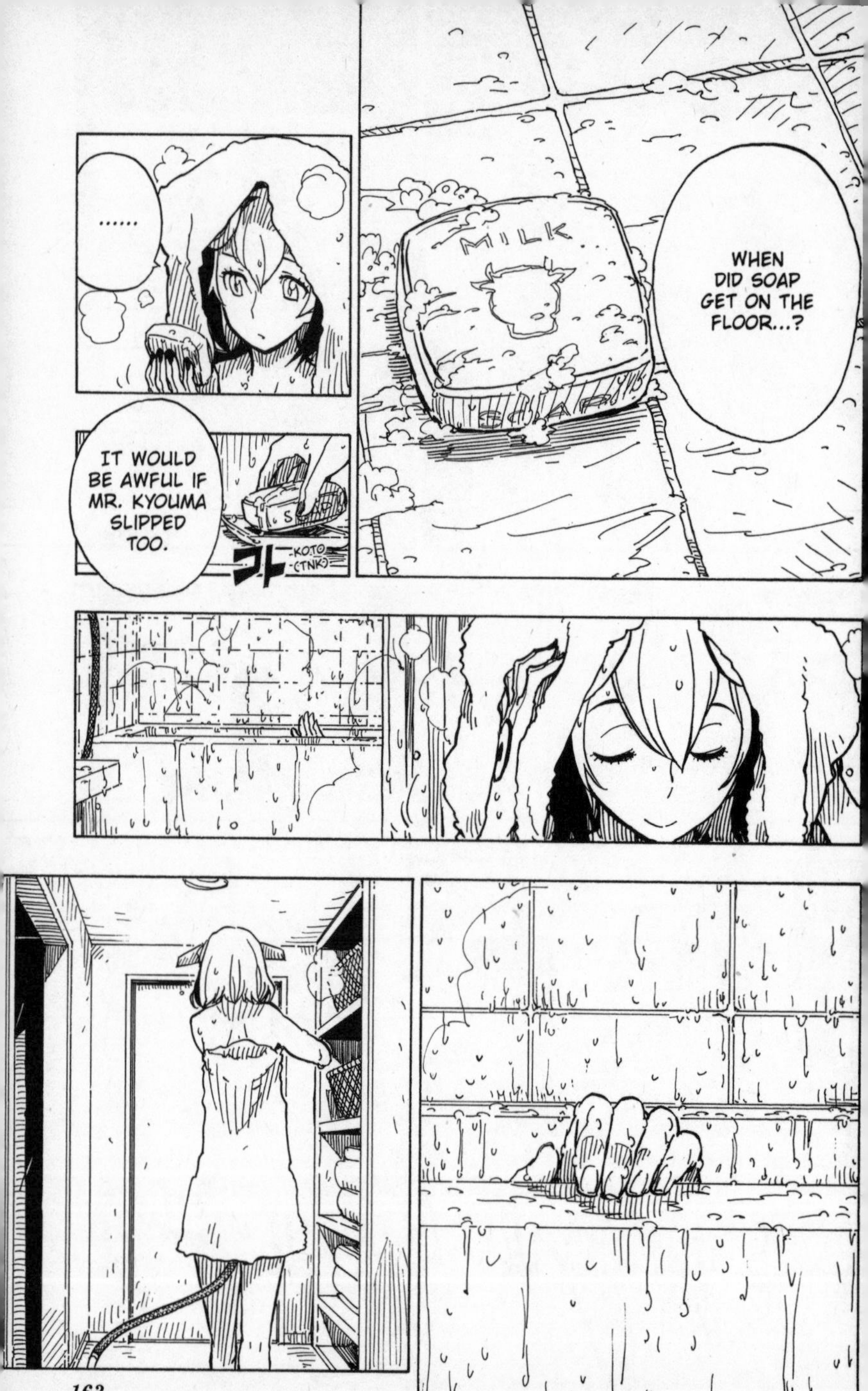
MILK
WHEN DID SOAP GET ON THE FLOOR...?
......
IT WOULD BE AWFUL IF MR. KYOUMA SLIPPED TOO.
コト
KOTO
(TNK)

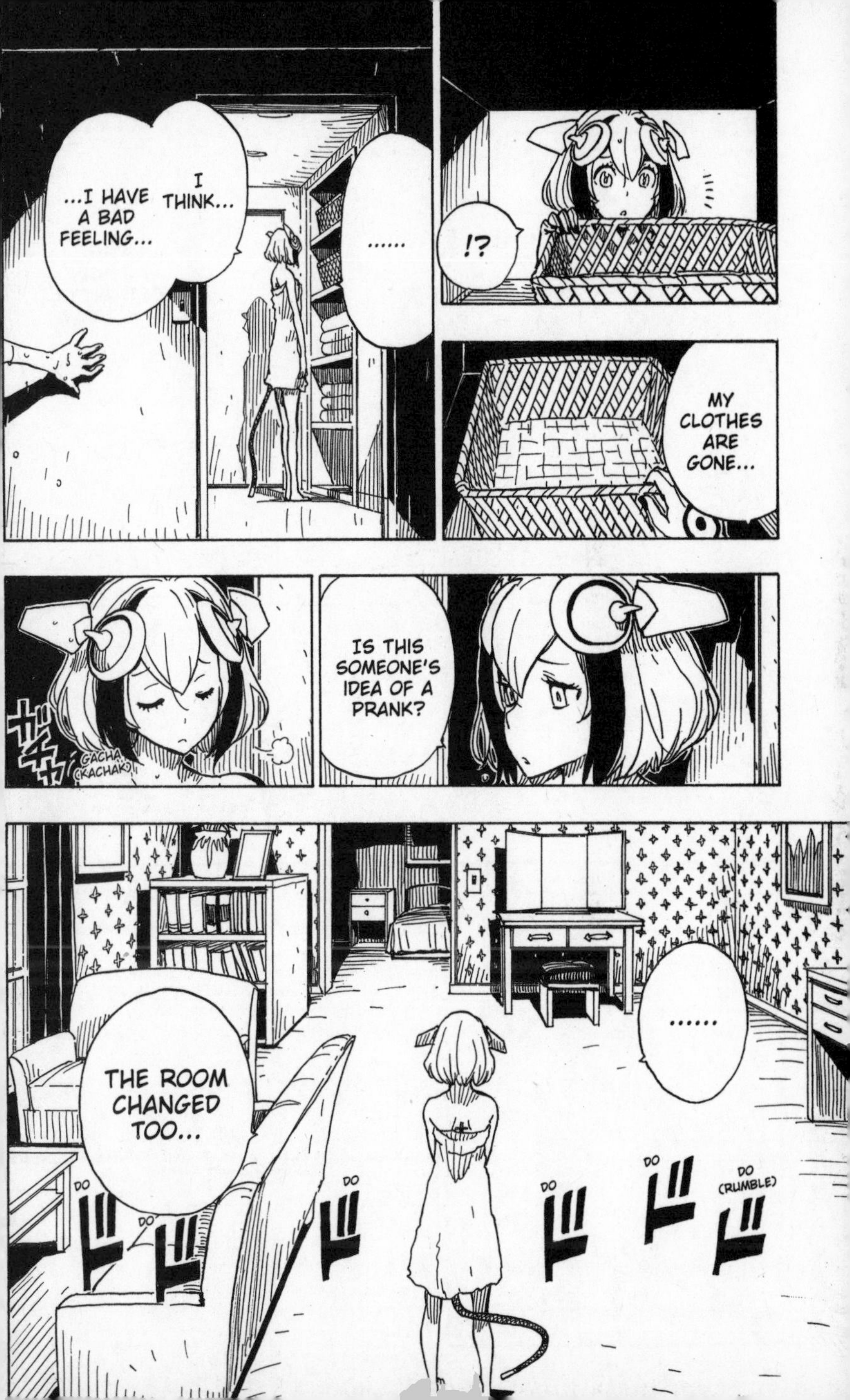
!?
MY CLOTHES ARE GONE...
......
I THINK...
...I HAVE A BAD FEELING...
IS THIS SOMEONE'S IDEA OF A PRANK?
GACHA (KACHAK)
......
DO (RUMBLE)
DO
DO
DO
DO
DO
THE ROOM CHANGED TOO...

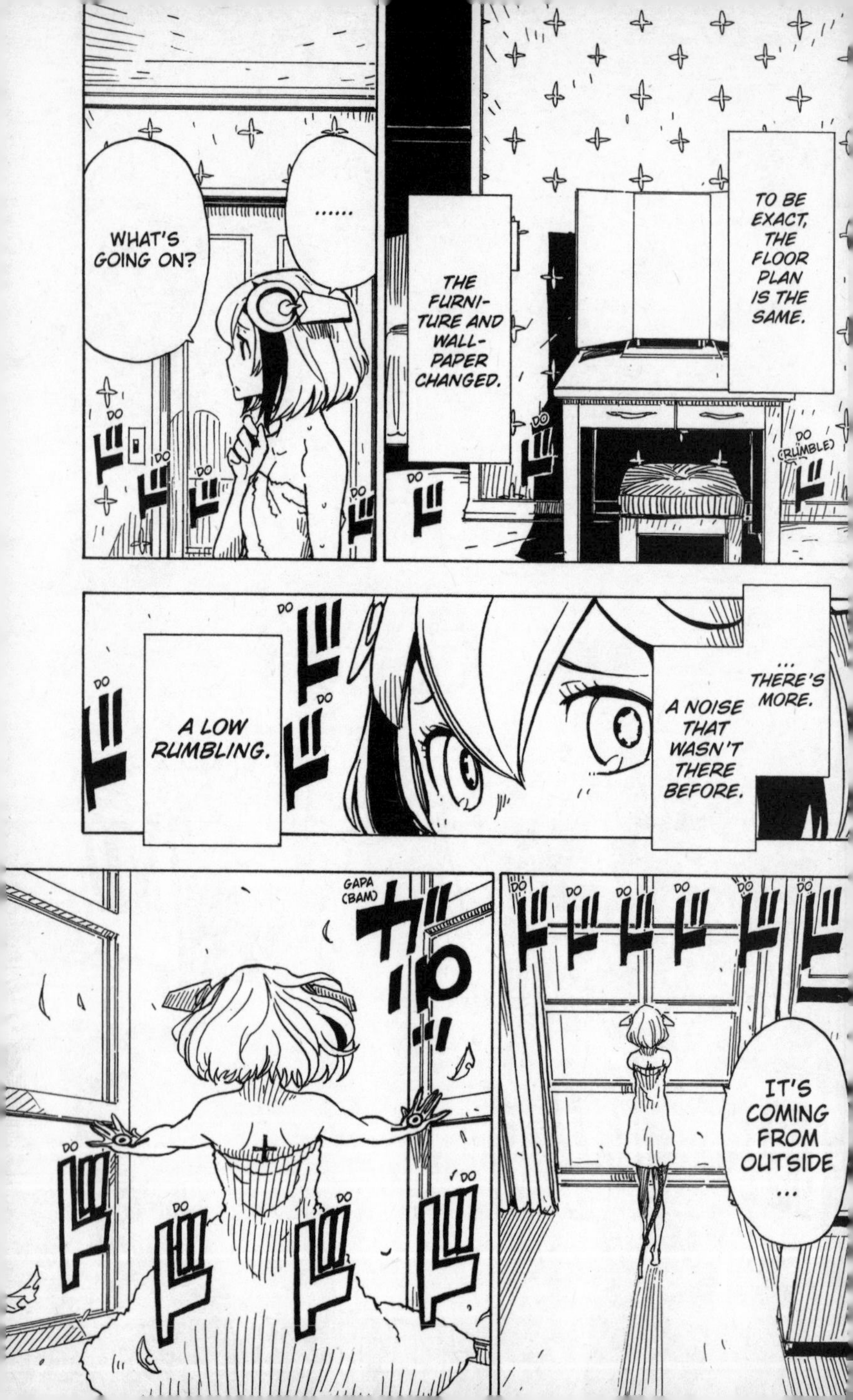
TO BE EXACT, THE FLOOR PLAN IS THE SAME.
THE FURNITURE AND WALLPAPER CHANGED.
DO (RUMBLE)
DO
DO
......
WHAT'S GOING ON?
DO
DO
DO
DO
... THERE'S MORE.
A NOISE THAT WASN'T THERE BEFORE.
DO
DO
A LOW RUMBLING.
DO
DO DO DO DO DO DO
IT'S COMING FROM OUTSIDE ...
GAPA (BAM)
DO
DO
DO
DO

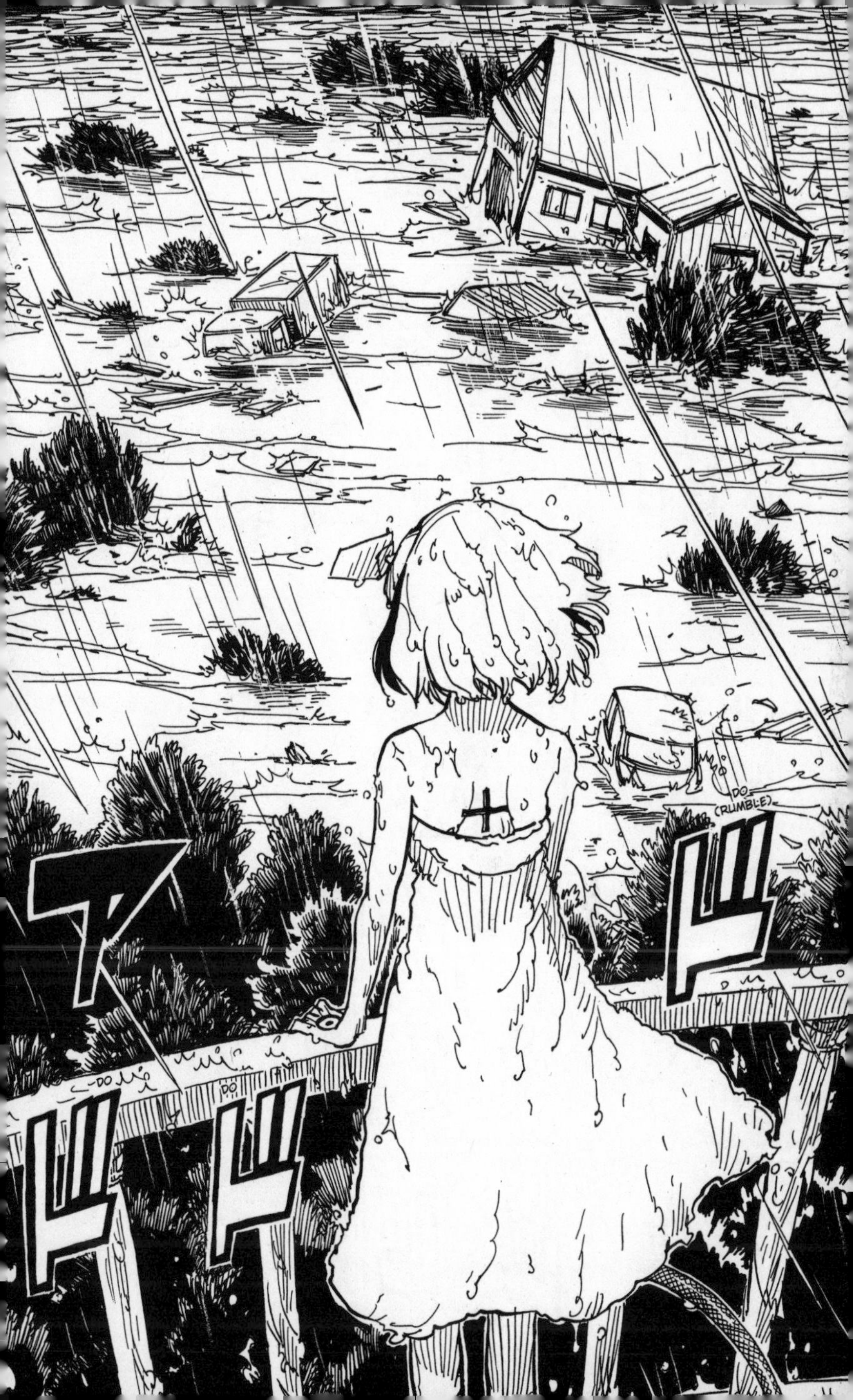
DO (RUMBLE)
DO
DO

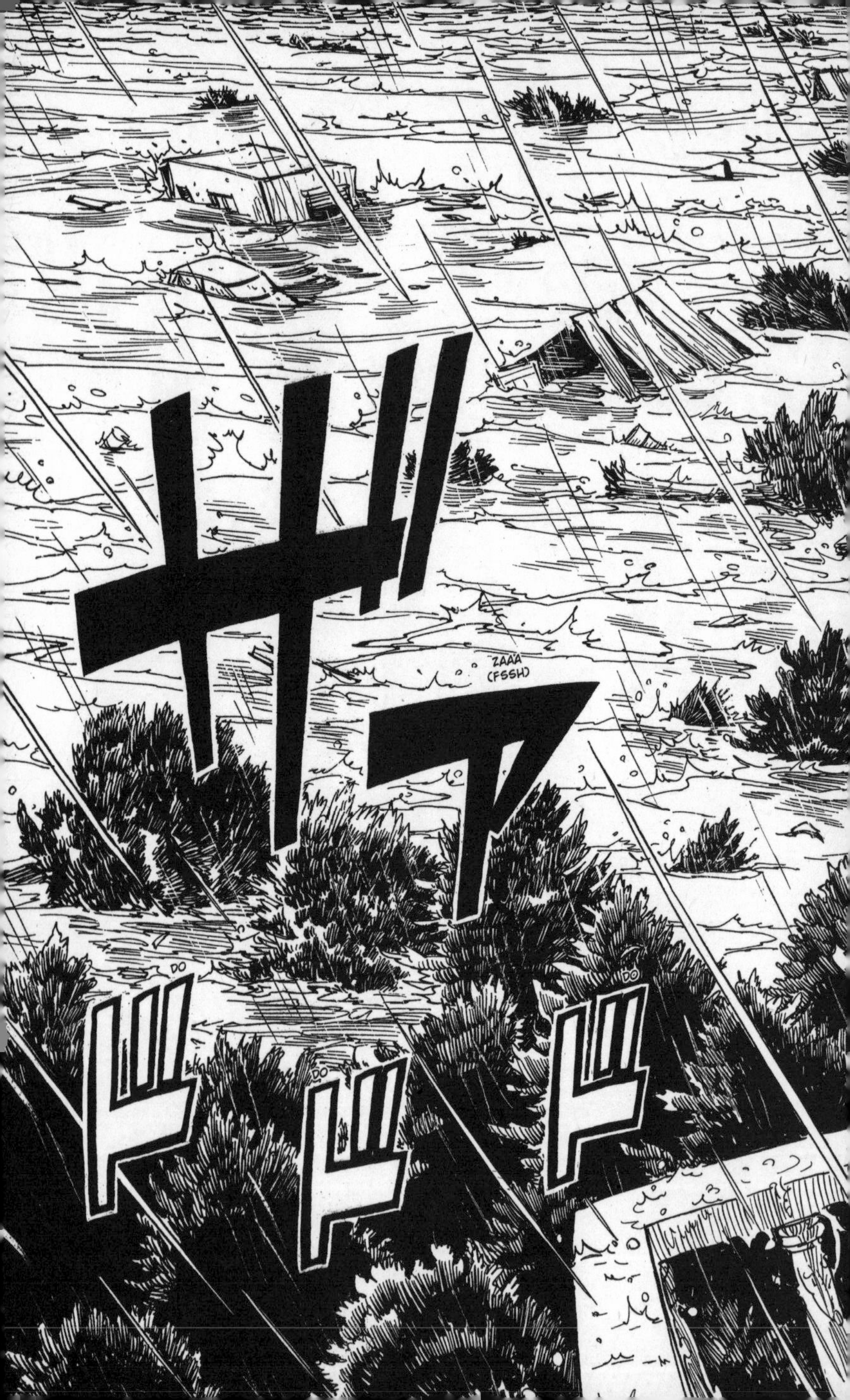
ザァ
ZAAA
(FSSH)
ドドド
DO
DO
DO

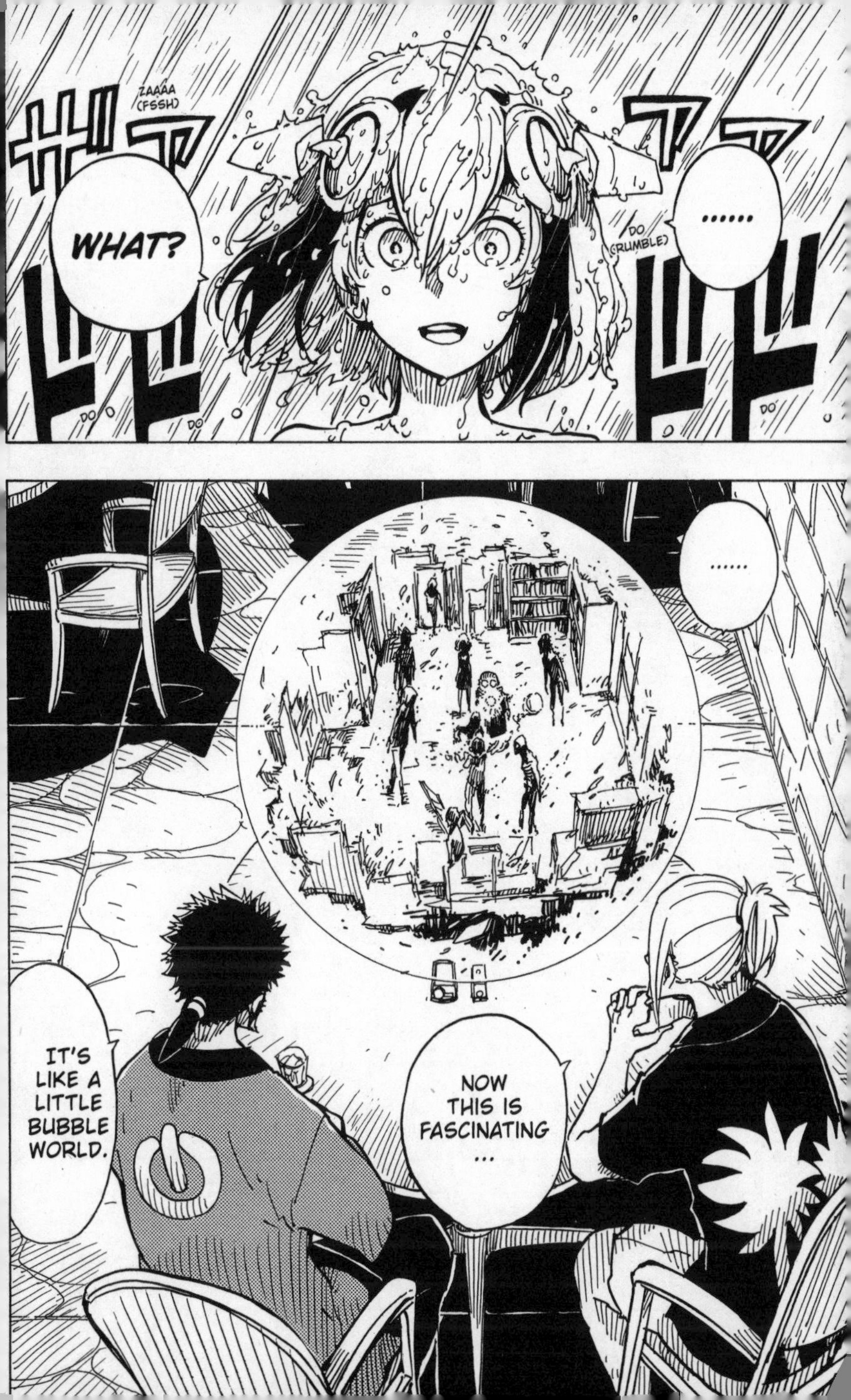
......
DO (RUMBLE)
DO
ZAAAA (FSSH)
WHAT?
DO
DO
......
NOW THIS IS FASCINATING ...
IT'S LIKE A LITTLE BUBBLE WORLD.

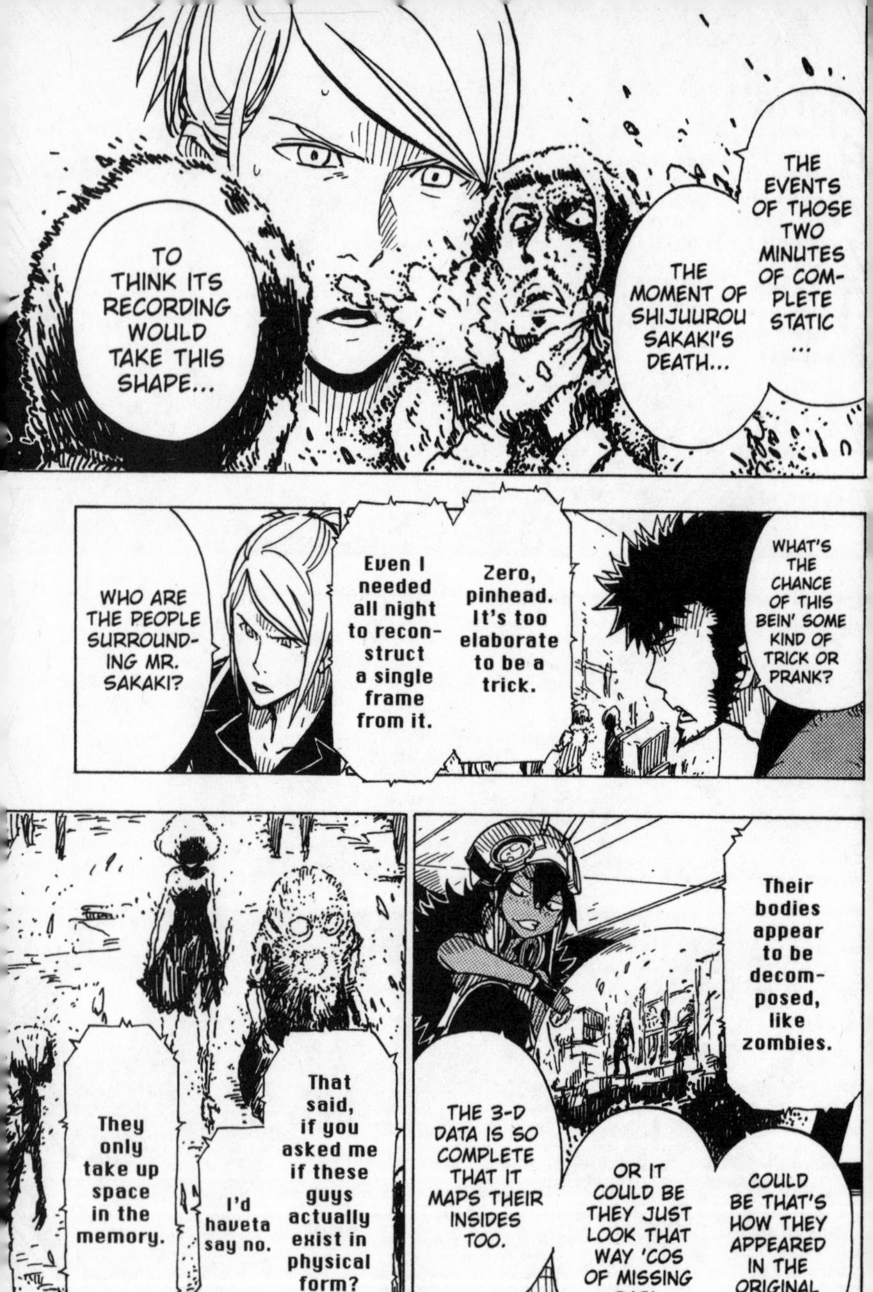
THE EVENTS OF THOSE TWO MINUTES OF COMPLETE STATIC...
THE MOMENT OF SHIJUUROU SAKAKI'S DEATH...
TO THINK ITS RECORDING WOULD TAKE THIS SHAPE...
WHAT'S THE CHANCE OF THIS BEIN' SOME KIND OF TRICK OR PRANK?
Zero, pinhead. It's too elaborate to be a trick.
Even I needed all night to reconstruct a single frame from it.
WHO ARE THE PEOPLE SURROUNDING MR. SAKAKI?
Their bodies appear to be decomposed, like zombies.
COULD BE THAT'S HOW THEY APPEARED IN THE ORIGINAL DATA.
OR IT COULD BE THEY JUST LOOK THAT WAY 'COS OF MISSING DATA.
THE 3-D DATA IS SO COMPLETE THAT IT MAPS THEIR INSIDES TOO.
That said, if you asked me if these guys actually exist in physical form?
I'd haveta say no.
They only take up space in the memory.

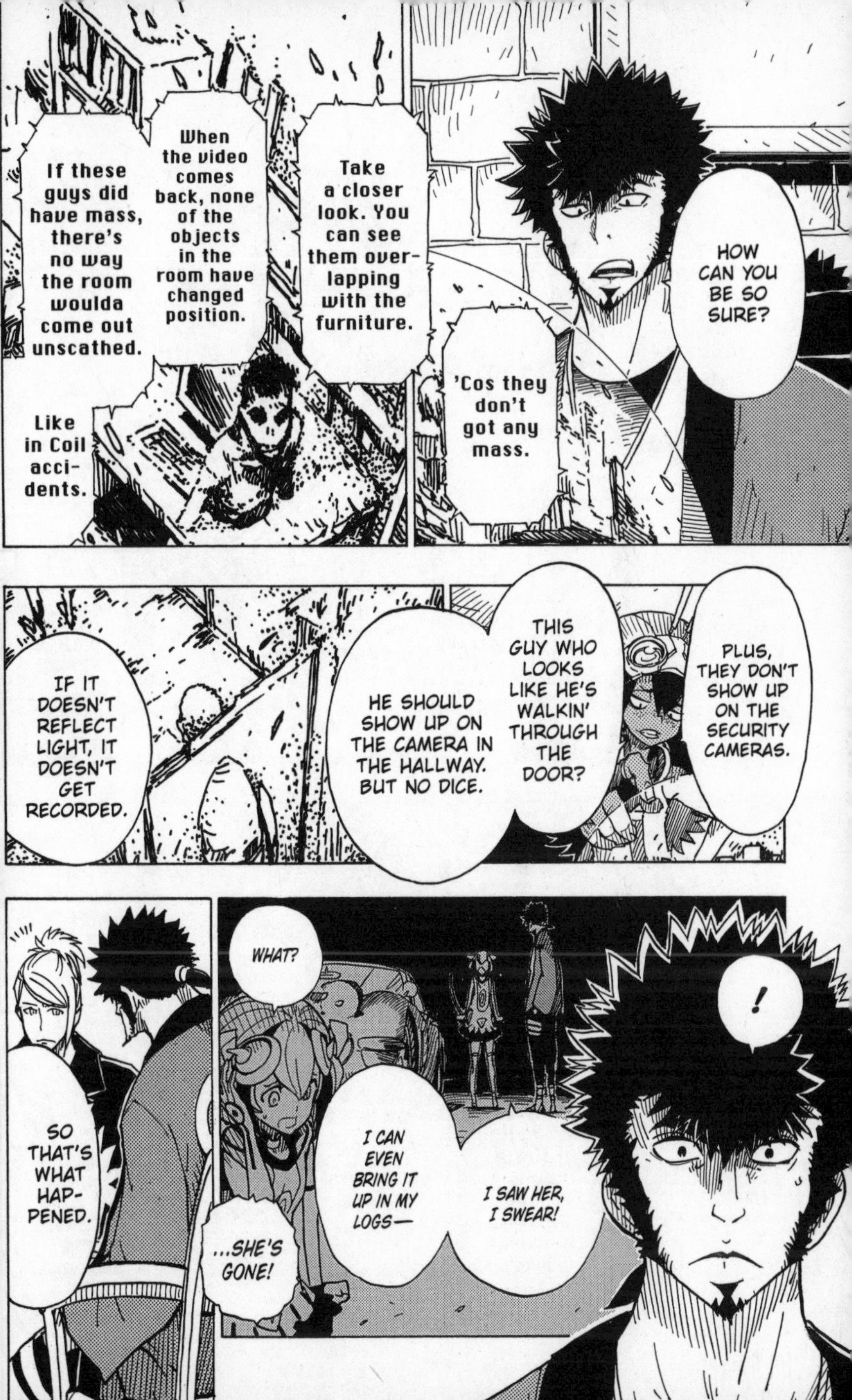
HOW CAN YOU BE SO SURE?
'Cos they don't got any mass.
Take a closer look. You can see them over-lapping with the furniture.
When the video comes back, none of the objects in the room have changed position.
If these guys did have mass, there's no way the room woulda come out unscathed.
Like in Coil acci-dents.
PLUS, THEY DON'T SHOW UP ON THE SECURITY CAMERAS.
THIS GUY WHO LOOKS LIKE HE'S WALKIN' THROUGH THE DOOR?
HE SHOULD SHOW UP ON THE CAMERA IN THE HALLWAY. BUT NO DICE.
IF IT DOESN'T REFLECT LIGHT, IT DOESN'T GET RECORDED.
!
WHAT?
I SAW HER, I SWEAR!
I CAN EVEN BRING IT UP IN MY LOGS—
...SHE'S GONE!
SO THAT'S WHAT HAP-PENED.

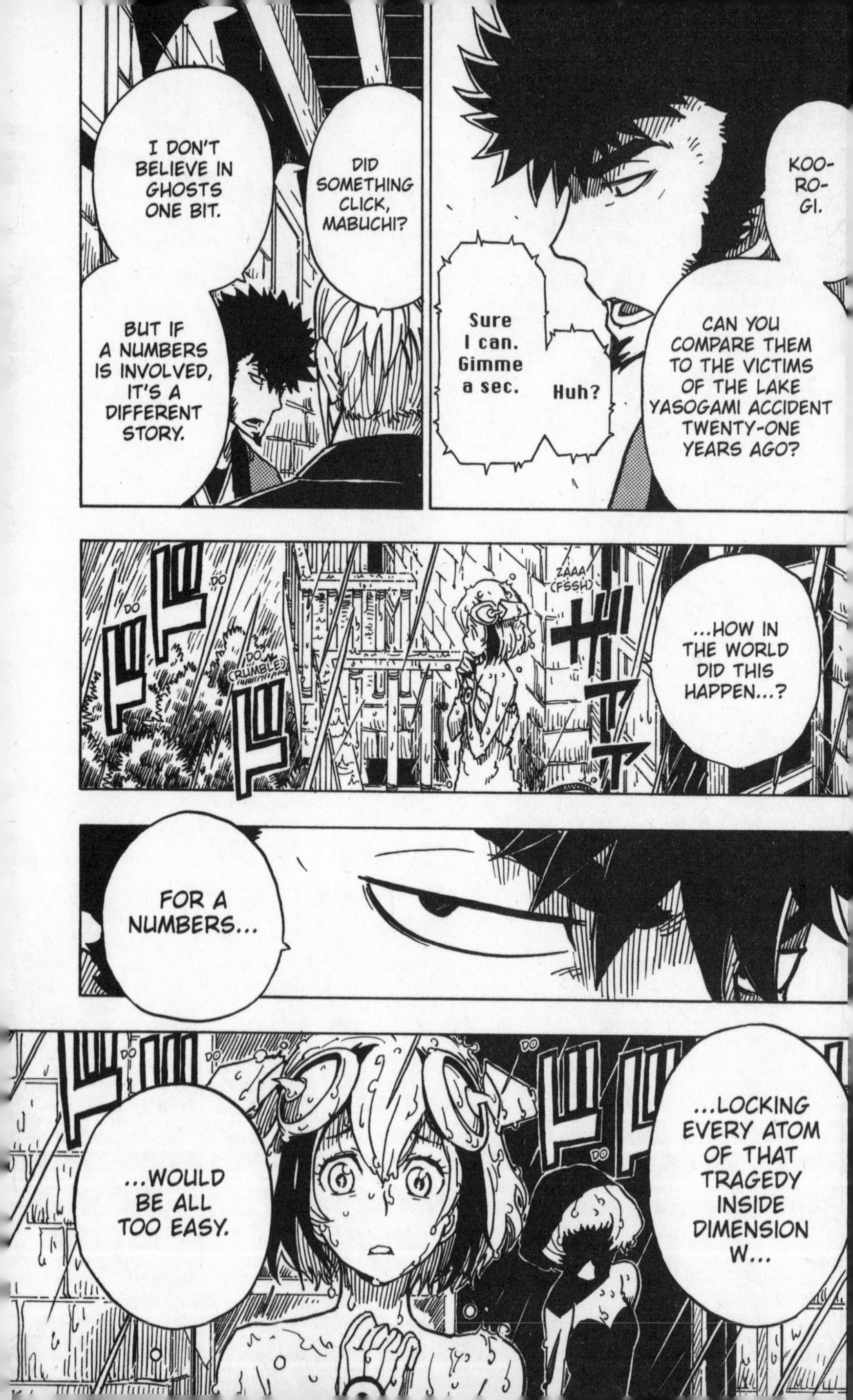
KOO-RO-GI.
CAN YOU COMPARE THEM TO THE VICTIMS OF THE LAKE YASOGAMI ACCIDENT TWENTY-ONE YEARS AGO?
Huh?
Sure I can. Gimme a sec.
DID SOMETHING CLICK, MABUCHI?
I DON'T BELIEVE IN GHOSTS ONE BIT.
BUT IF A NUMBERS IS INVOLVED, IT'S A DIFFERENT STORY.
...HOW IN THE WORLD DID THIS HAPPEN...?
ZAAA (FSSH)
DO (RUMBLE)
DO
DO
FOR A NUMBERS...
...LOCKING EVERY ATOM OF THAT TRAGEDY INSIDE DIMENSION W...
DO
DO
DO
DO
...WOULD BE ALL TOO EASY.

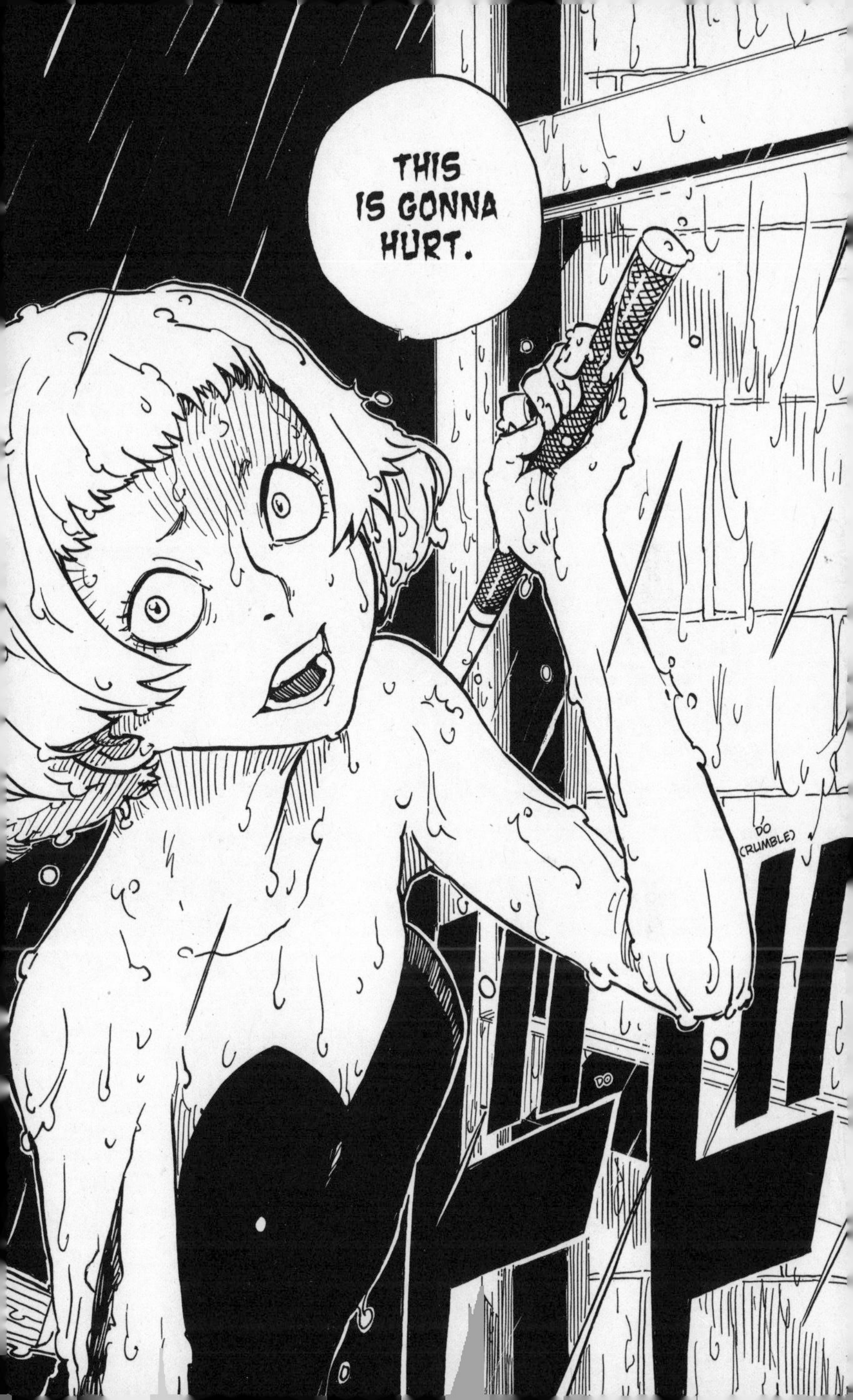
THIS IS GONNA HURT.
DO (RUMBLE)
DO

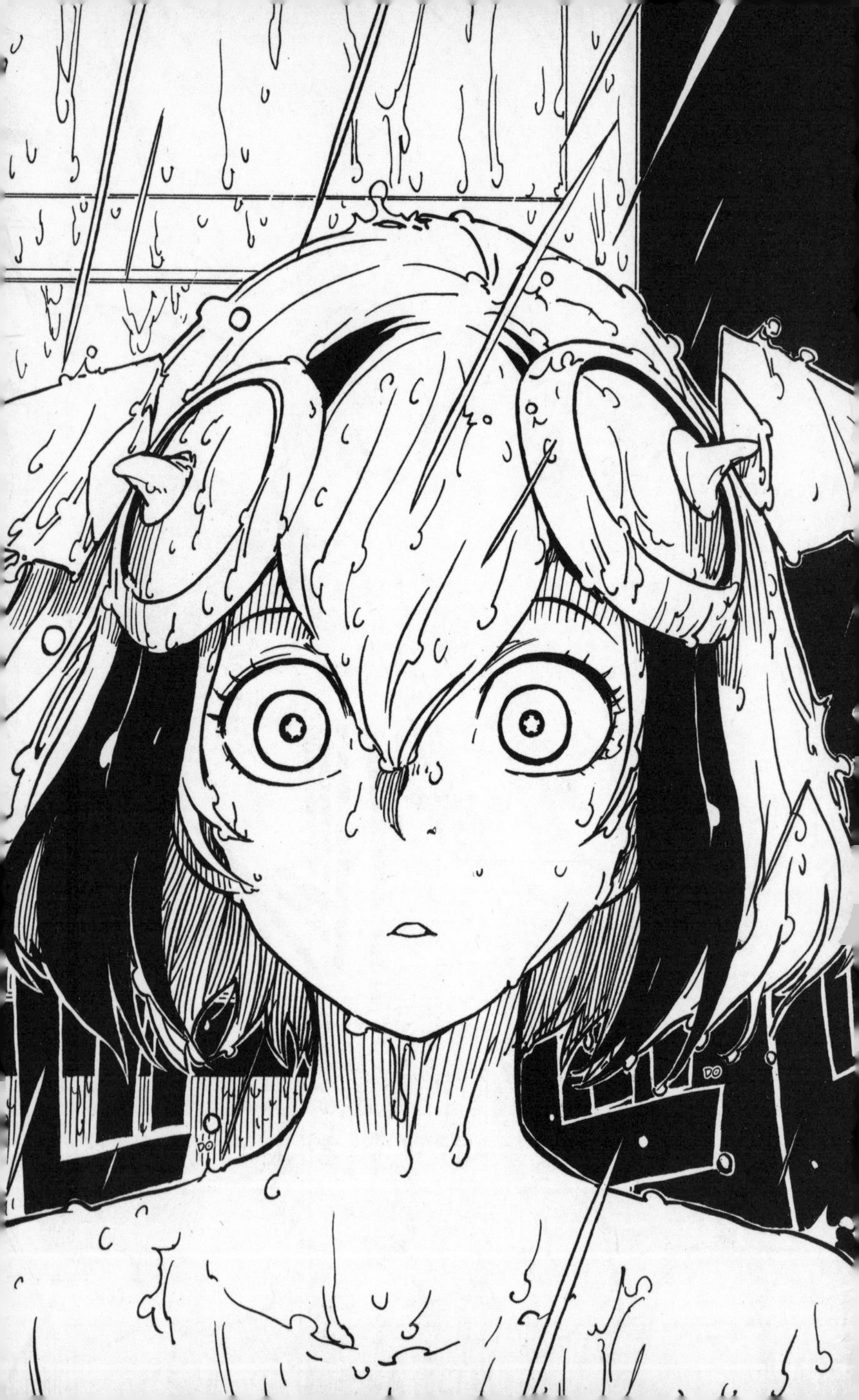
DO
DO

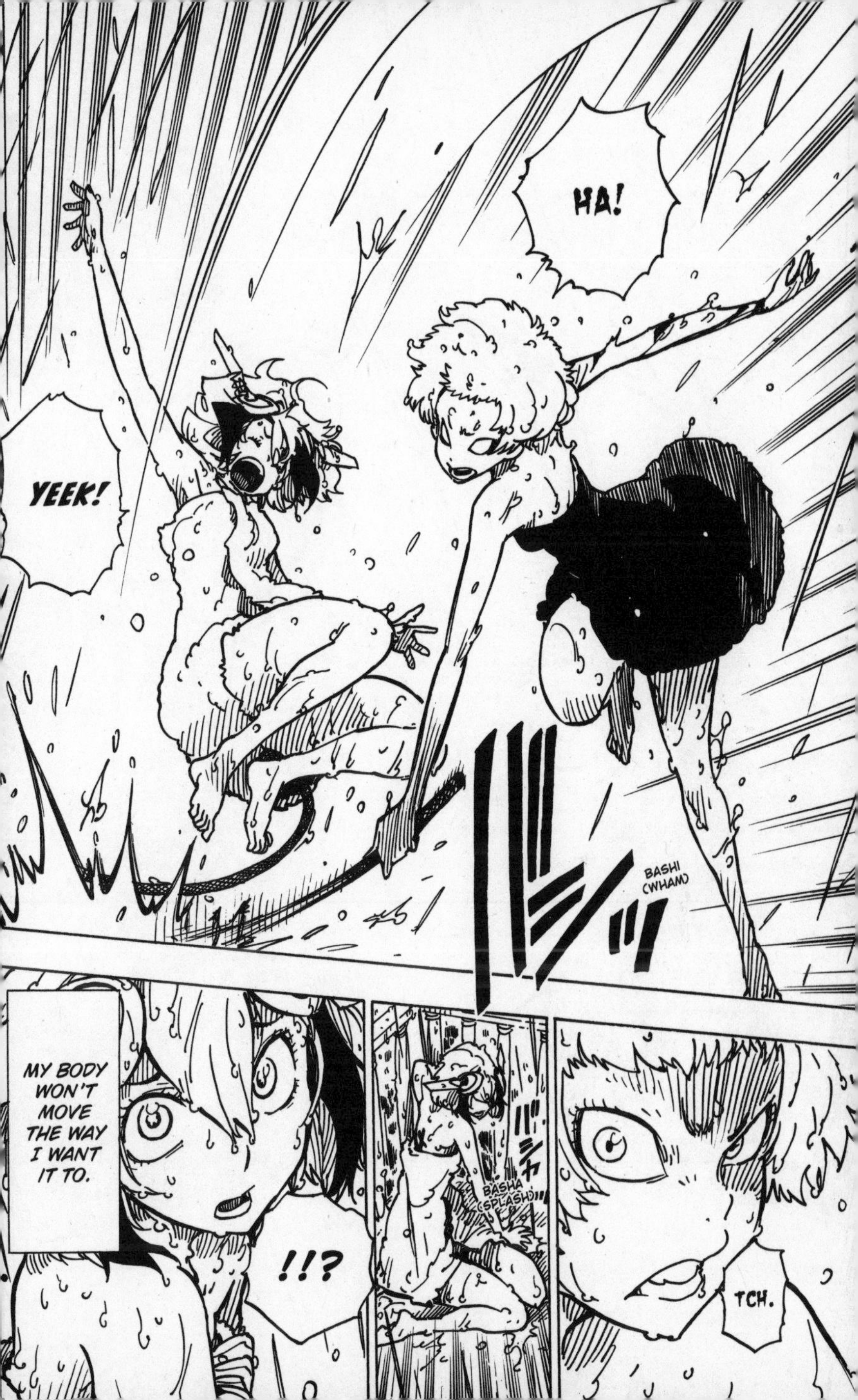
HA!
YEEK!
BASHI (WHAM)
TCH.
BASHA (SPLASH)
MY BODY WON'T MOVE THE WAY I WANT IT TO.
!!?

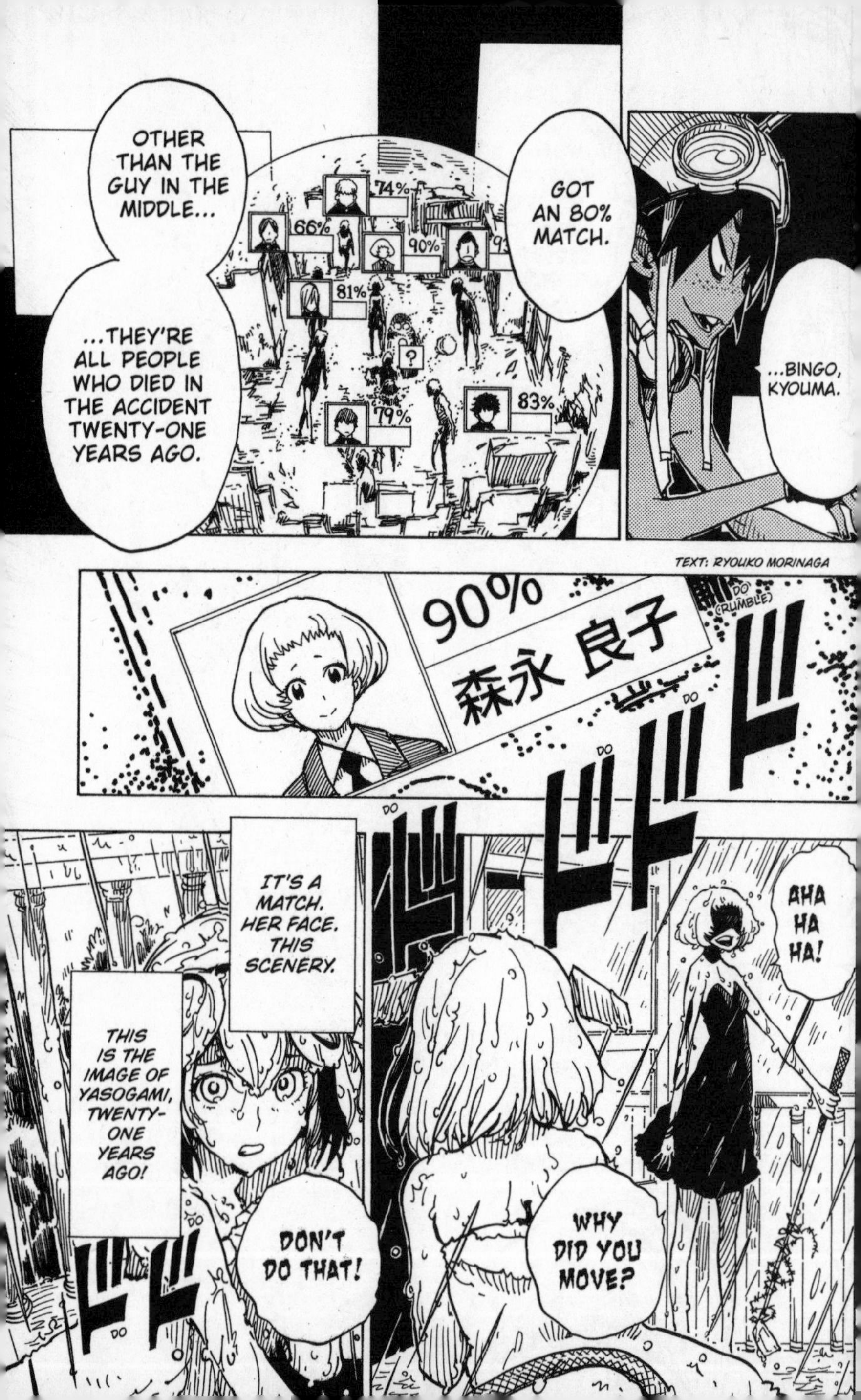
...BINGO, KYOUMA.
GOT AN 80% MATCH.
OTHER THAN THE GUY IN THE MIDDLE...
...THEY'RE ALL PEOPLE WHO DIED IN THE ACCIDENT TWENTY-ONE YEARS AGO.
74%
66%
90%
81%
?
79%
83%
TEXT: RYOUKO MORINAGA
90%
森永 良子
DO (RUMBLE)
DO
DO
DO
AHA HA HA!
IT'S A MATCH. HER FACE. THIS SCENERY.
WHY DID YOU MOVE?
THIS IS THE IMAGE OF YASOGAMI, TWENTY-ONE YEARS AGO!
DON'T DO THAT!
DO
DO

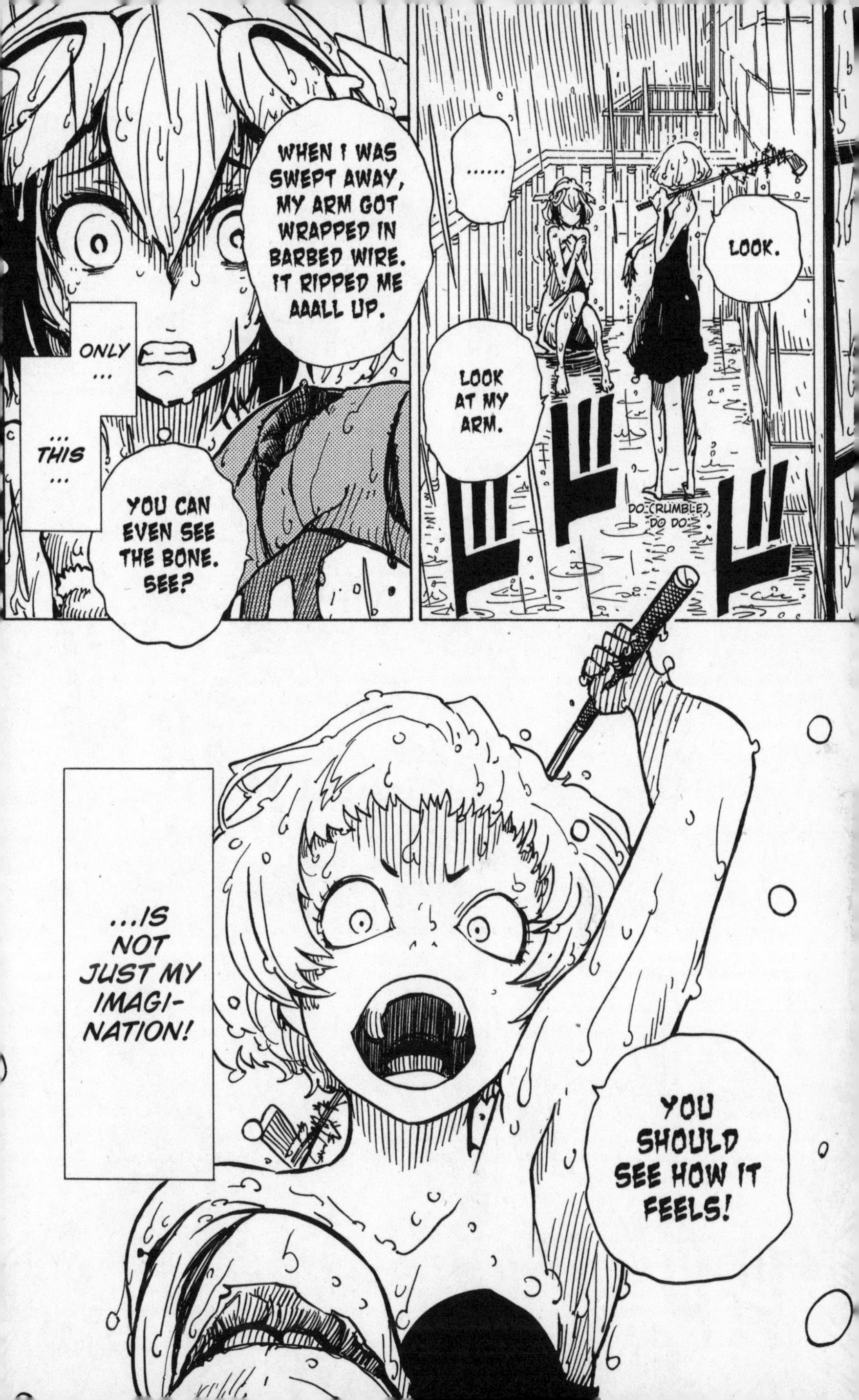
......
LOOK.
LOOK AT MY ARM.
DO (RUMBLE) DO DO
WHEN I WAS SWEPT AWAY, MY ARM GOT WRAPPED IN BARBED WIRE. IT RIPPED ME AAALL UP.
ONLY...
...THIS...
YOU CAN EVEN SEE THE BONE. SEE?
...IS NOT JUST MY IMAGINATION!
YOU SHOULD SEE HOW IT FEELS!

FILE.23
TWO WORLDS

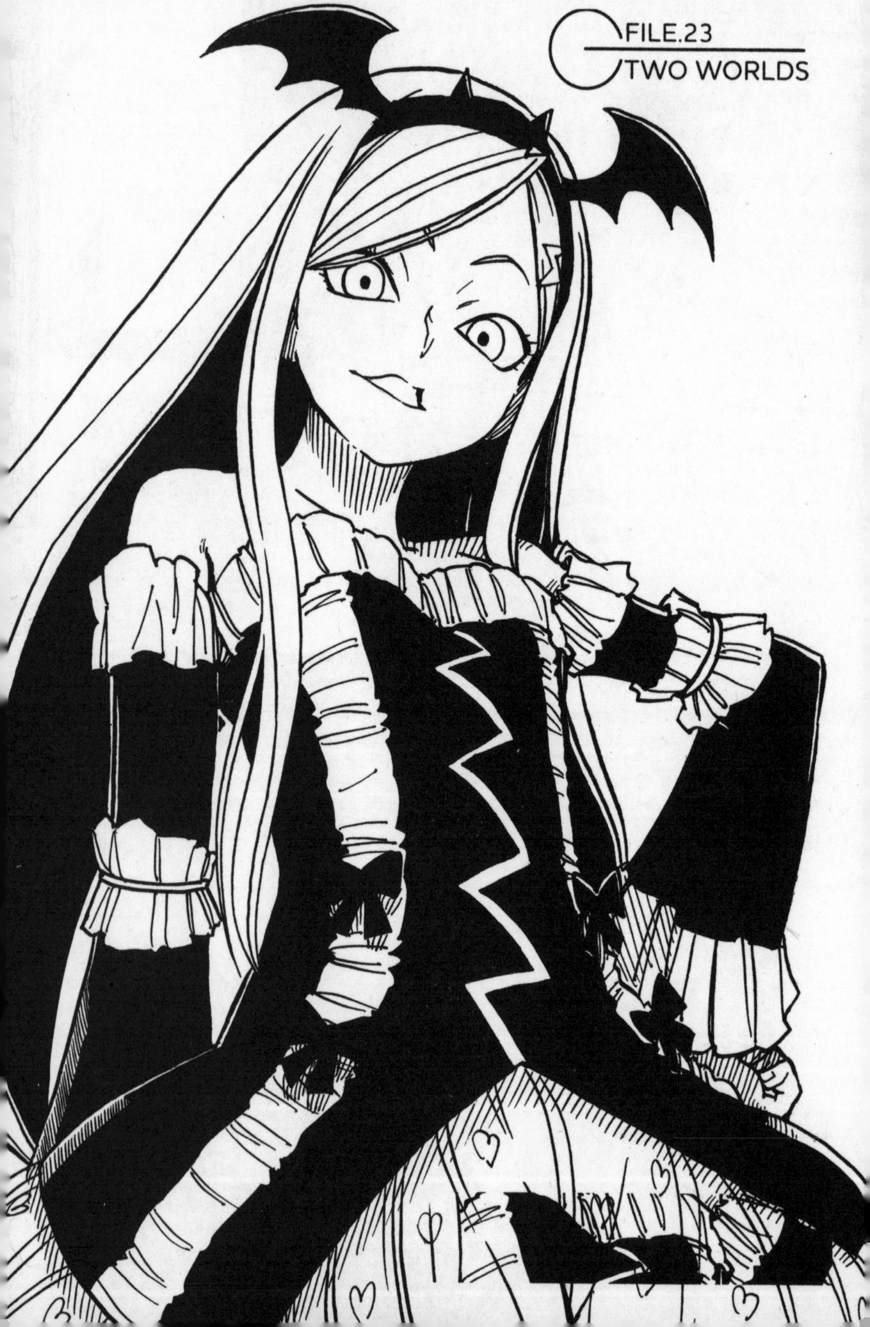

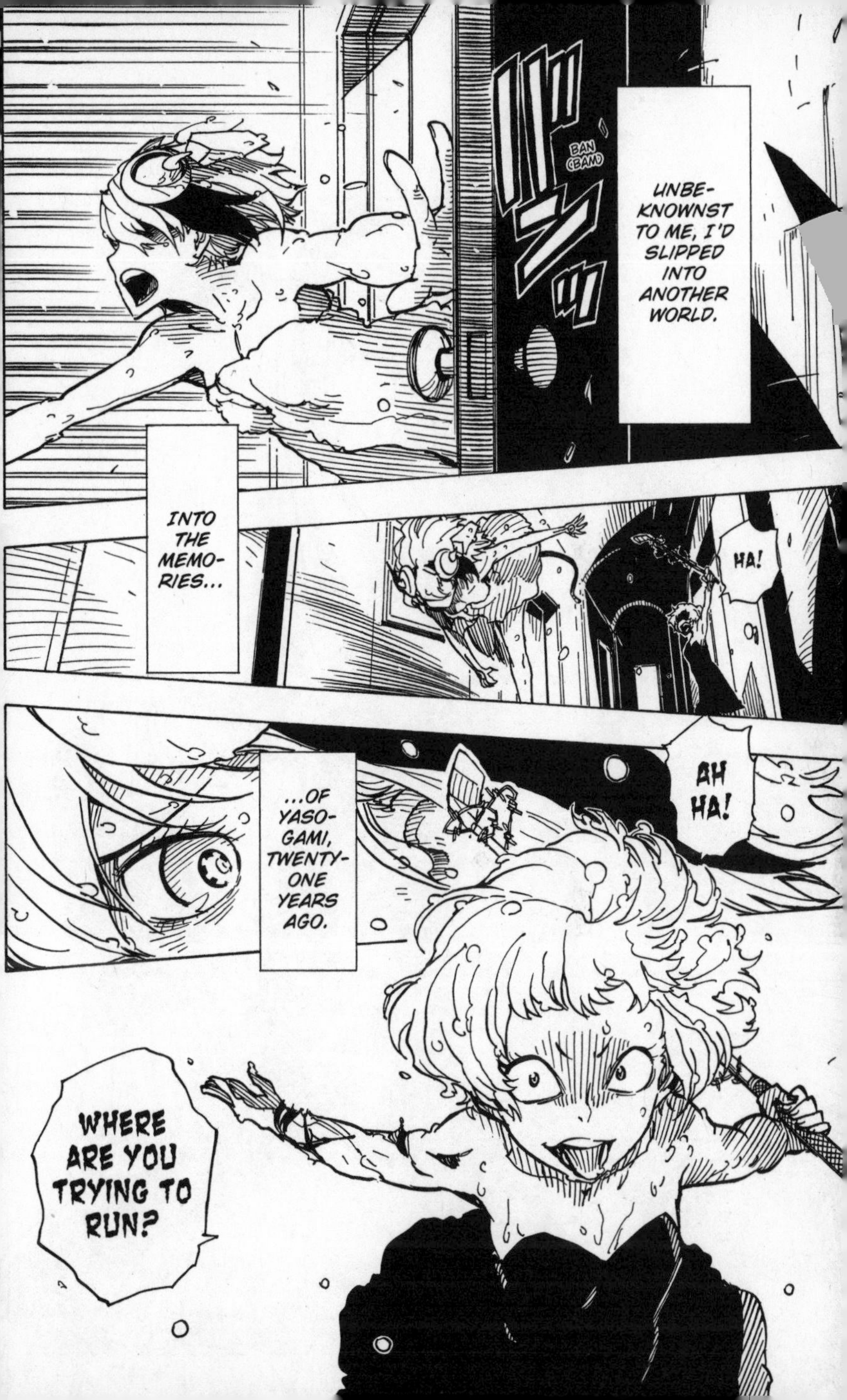
UNBE-KNOWNST TO ME, I'D SLIPPED INTO ANOTHER WORLD.
BAN (BAM)
INTO THE MEMO-RIES...
HA!
AH HA!
...OF YASO-GAMI, TWENTY-ONE YEARS AGO.
WHERE ARE YOU TRYING TO RUN?

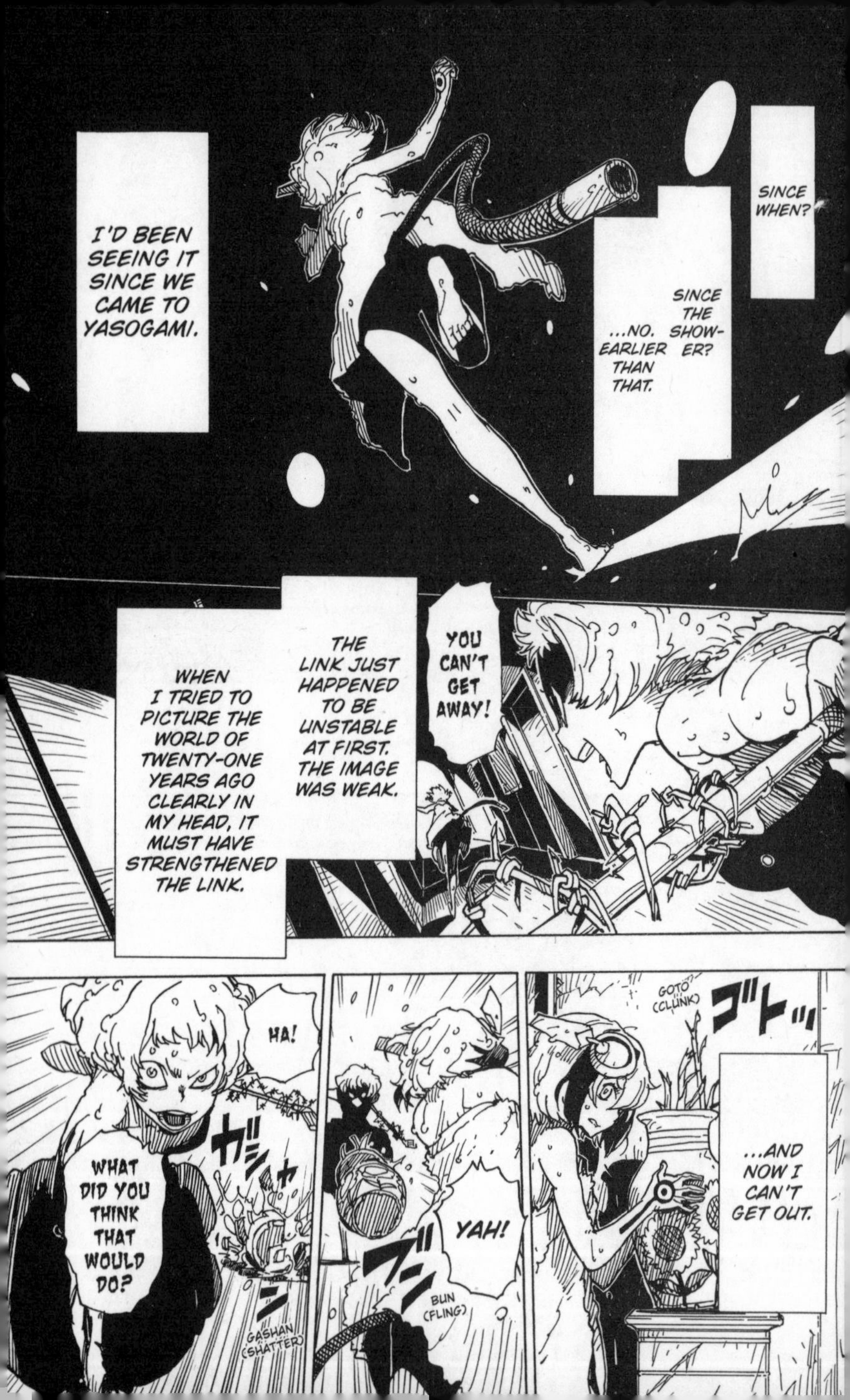
SINCE WHEN?
SINCE THE SHOWER?
...NO. EARLIER THAN THAT.
I'D BEEN SEEING IT SINCE WE CAME TO YASOGAMI.
YOU CAN'T GET AWAY!
THE LINK JUST HAPPENED TO BE UNSTABLE AT FIRST. THE IMAGE WAS WEAK.
WHEN I TRIED TO PICTURE THE WORLD OF TWENTY-ONE YEARS AGO CLEARLY IN MY HEAD, IT MUST HAVE STRENGTHENED THE LINK.
GOTO (CLUNK)
...AND NOW I CAN'T GET OUT.
YAH!
BUN (FLING)
HA!
WHAT DID YOU THINK THAT WOULD DO?
GASHAN (SHATTER)

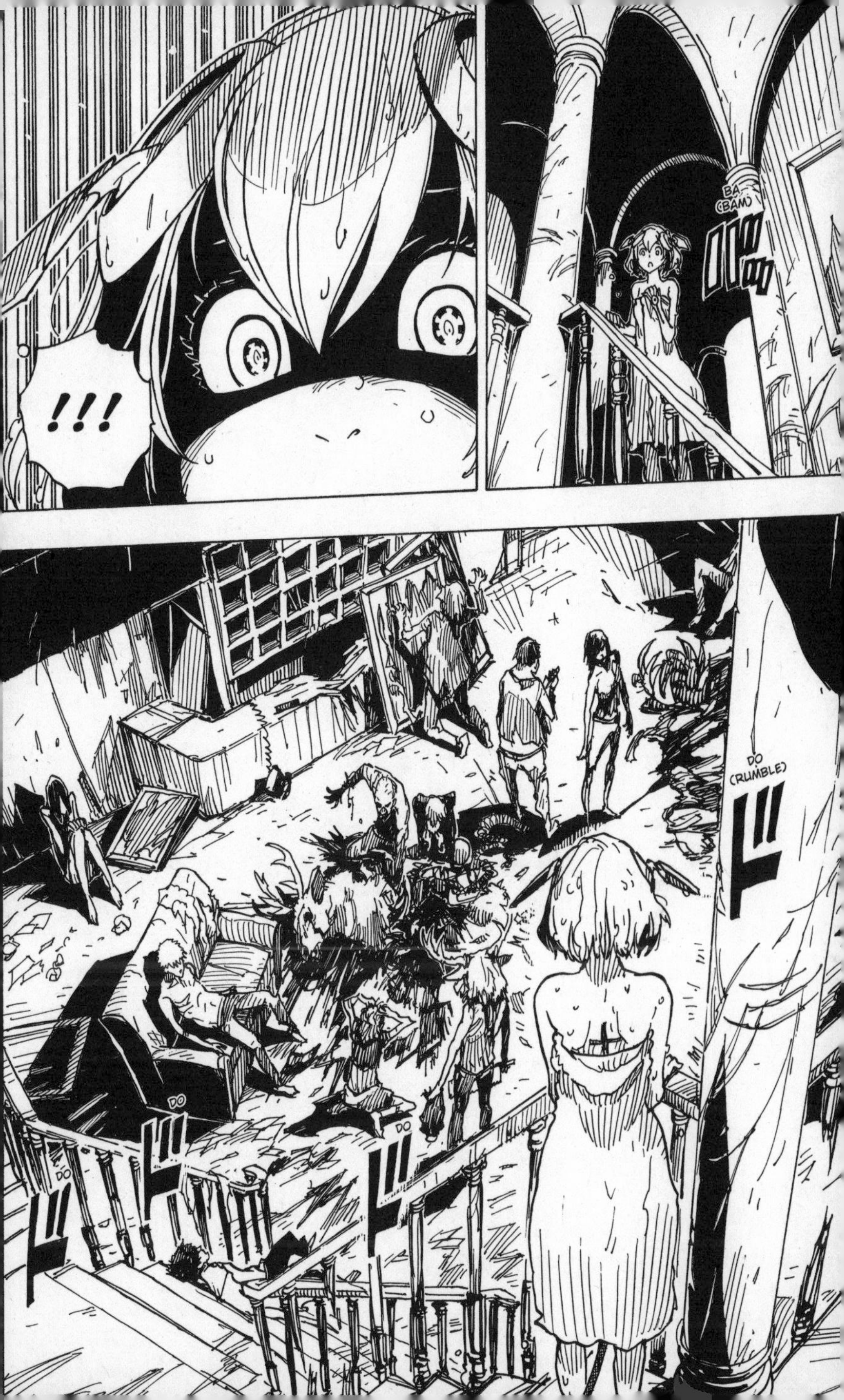
BA (BAM)
!!!
DO (RUMBLE)
DO
DO
DO

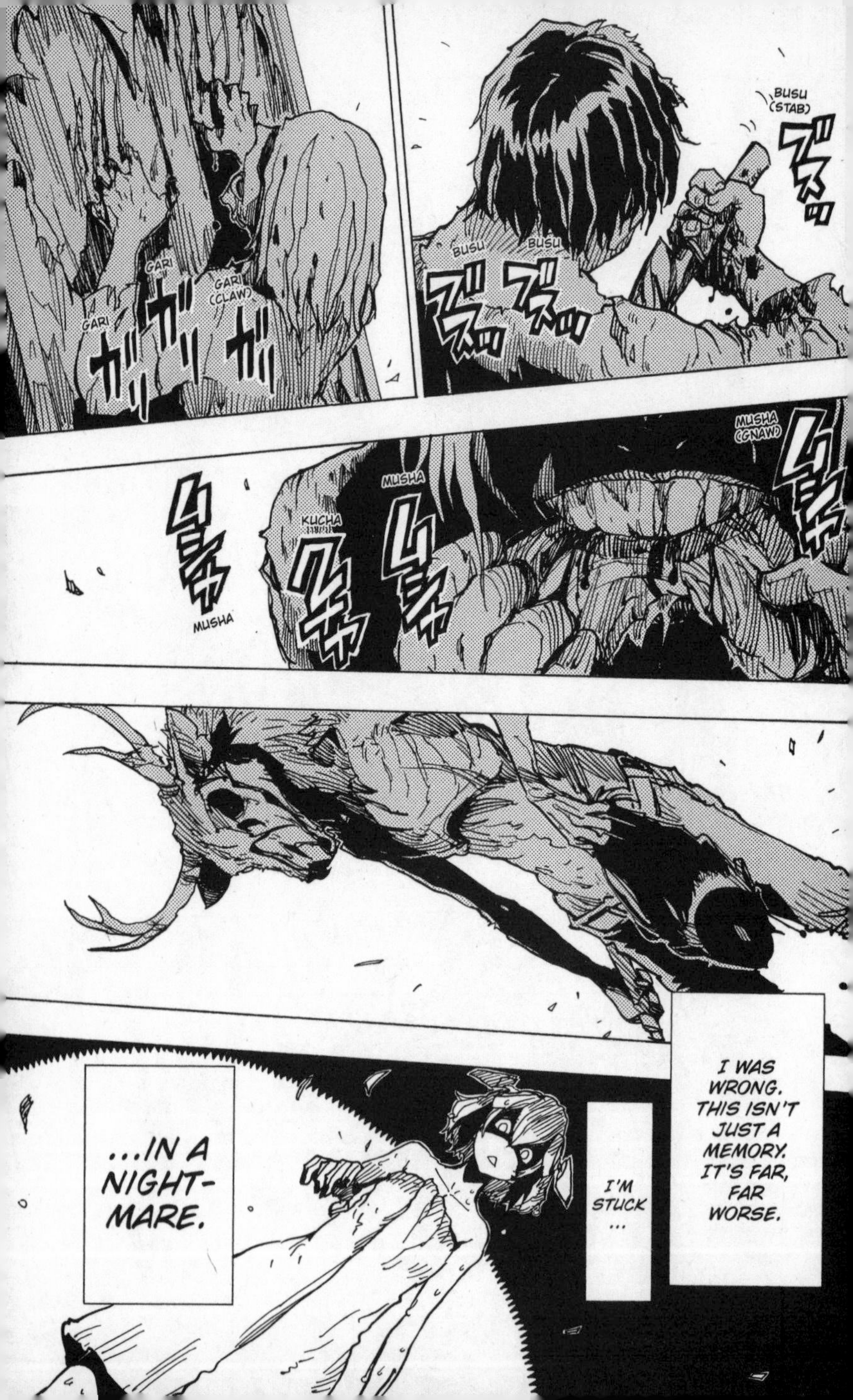
BUSU (STAB)
BUSU
BUSU
GARI
GARI (CLAW)
GARI
MUSHA (GNAW)
MUSHA
KUCHA
MUSHA
I WAS WRONG. THIS ISN'T JUST A MEMORY. IT'S FAR, FAR WORSE.
I'M STUCK ...
...IN A NIGHT-MARE.

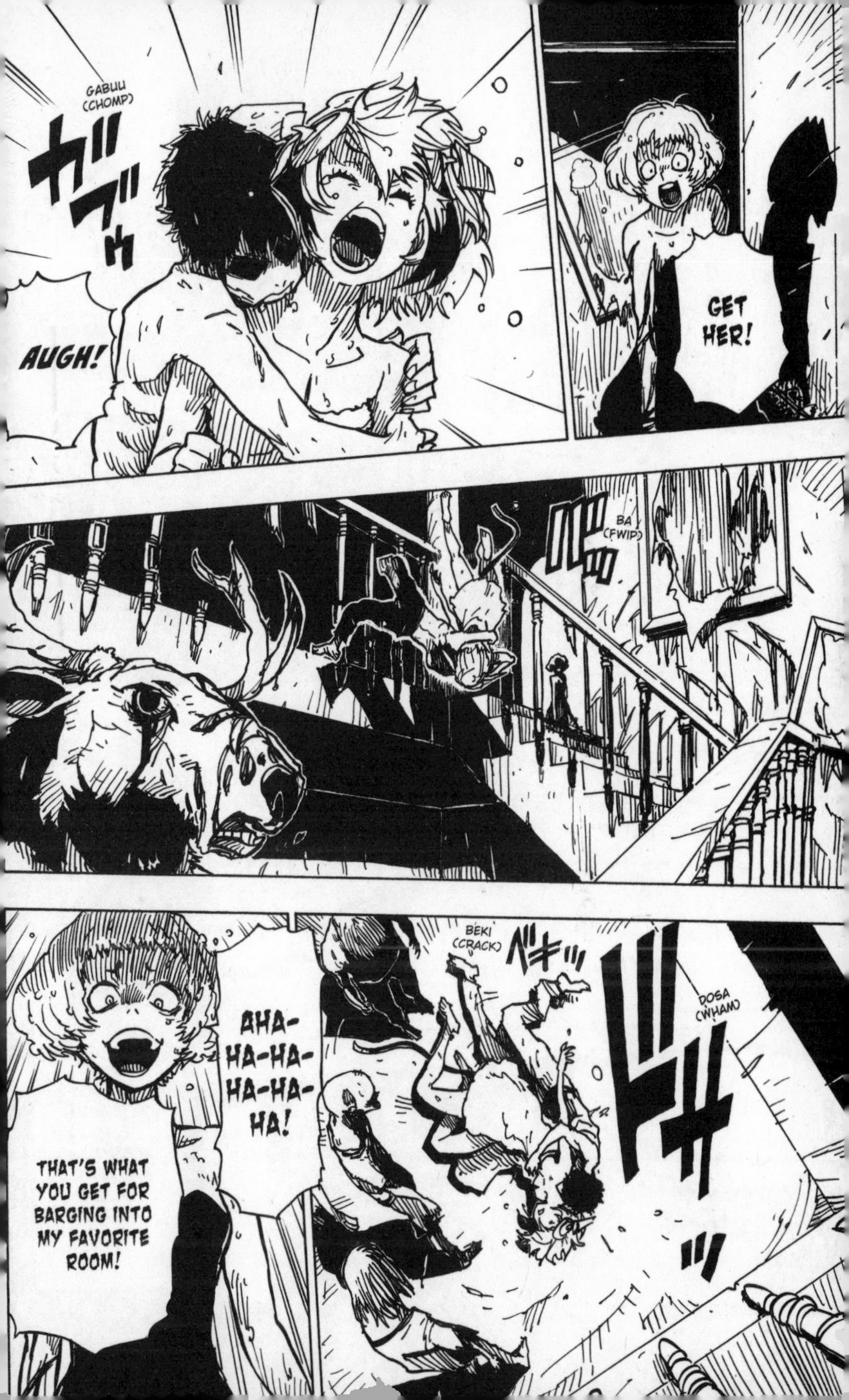
GET HER!
GABUU (CHOMP)
AUGH!
BA (FWIP)
DOSA (WHAM)
BEKI (CRACK)
AHA-HA-HA-HA-HA-HA!
THAT'S WHAT YOU GET FOR BARGING INTO MY FAVORITE ROOM!

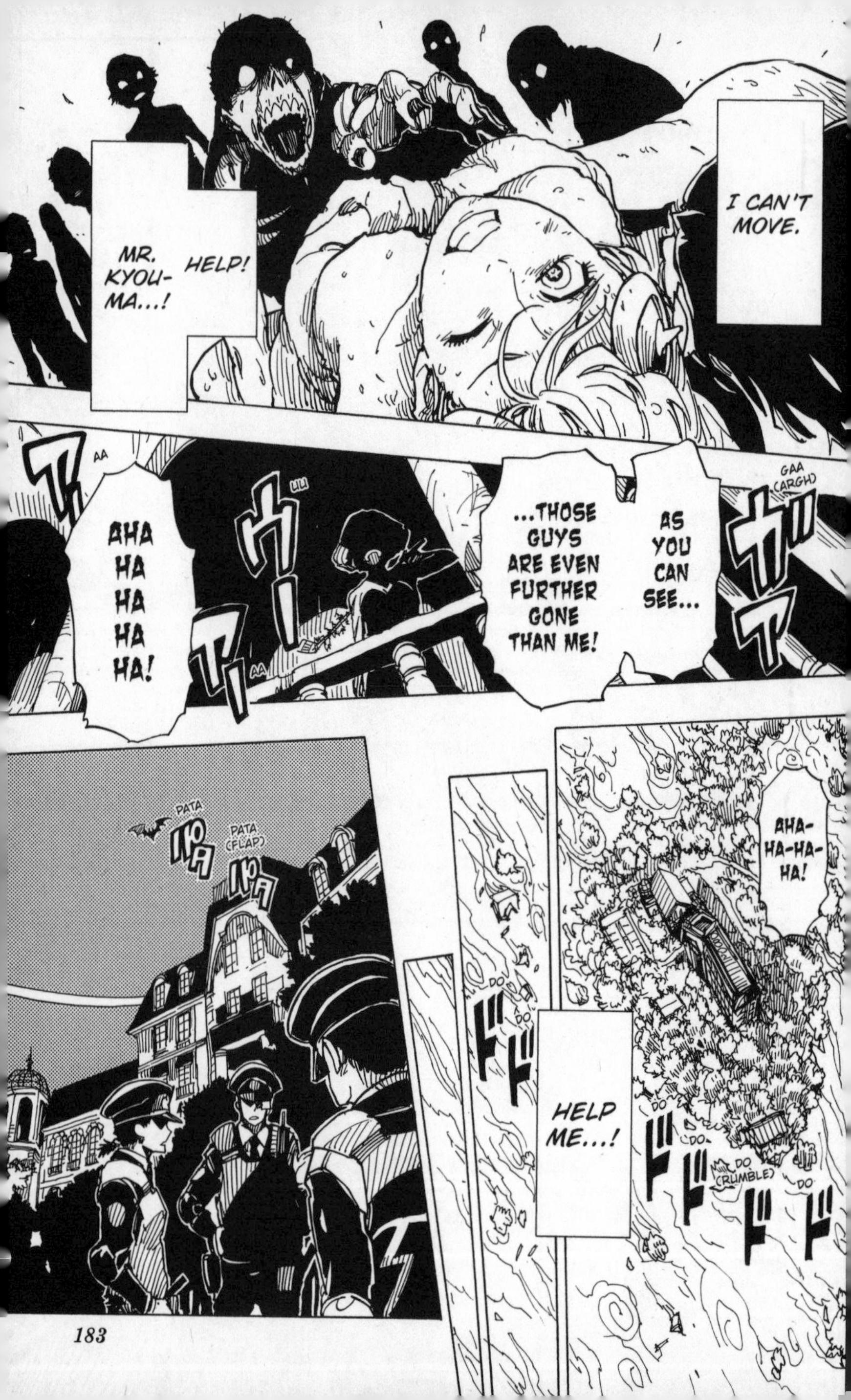
I CAN'T MOVE.
HELP!
MR. KYOUMA...!
GAA (ARGH)
AS YOU CAN SEE...
...THOSE GUYS ARE EVEN FURTHER GONE THAN ME!
UU
AA
AA
AHA HA HA HA HA!
AHA-HA-HA-HA!
DO
DO
DO (RUMBLE)
DO
HELP ME...!
DO
DO
PATA
PATA (FLAP)

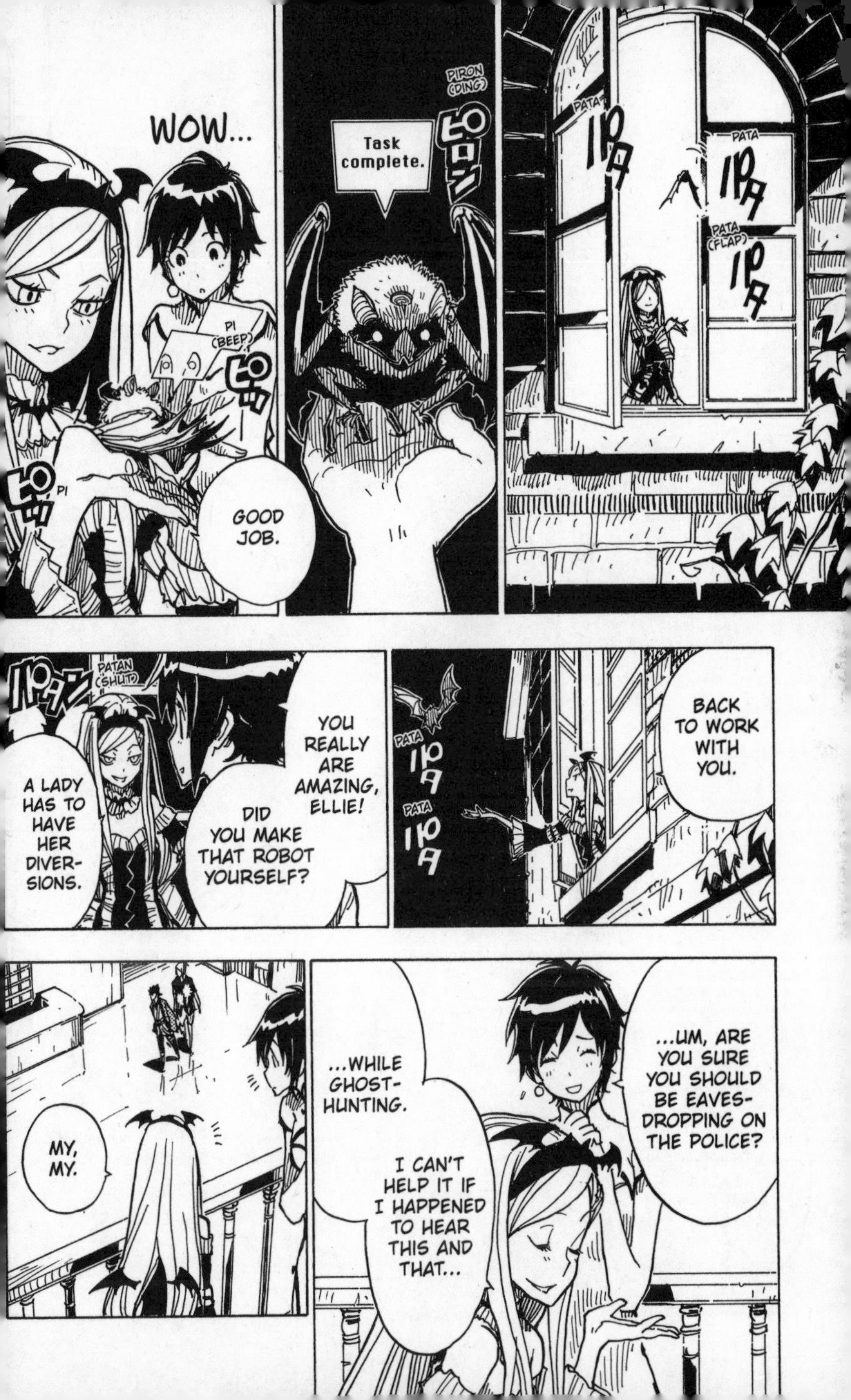
PATA
PATA
PATA (FLAP)
PIRON (DING)
Task complete.
WOW...
PI (BEEP)
PI
GOOD JOB.
PATA
PATA
BACK TO WORK WITH YOU.
PATAN (SHUT)
YOU REALLY ARE AMAZING, ELLIE!
DID YOU MAKE THAT ROBOT YOURSELF?
A LADY HAS TO HAVE HER DIVERSIONS.
...UM, ARE YOU SURE YOU SHOULD BE EAVES-DROPPING ON THE POLICE?
I CAN'T HELP IT IF I HAPPENED TO HEAR THIS AND THAT...
...WHILE GHOST-HUNTING.
MY, MY.

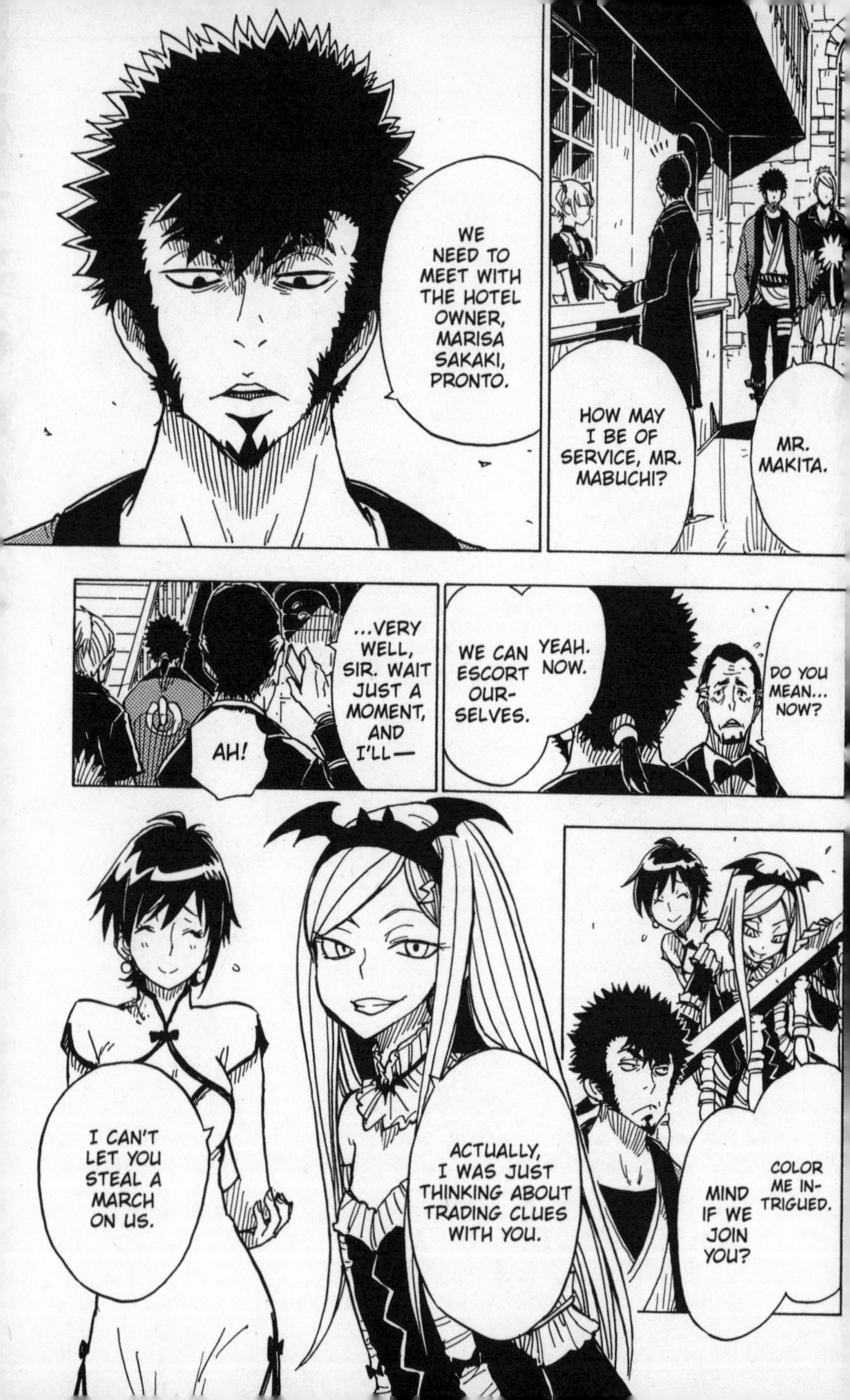
MR. MAKITA.
HOW MAY I BE OF SERVICE, MR. MABUCHI?
WE NEED TO MEET WITH THE HOTEL OWNER, MARISA SAKAKI, PRONTO.
DO YOU MEAN... NOW?
YEAH. NOW.
WE CAN ESCORT OURSELVES.
...VERY WELL, SIR. WAIT JUST A MOMENT, AND I'LL—
AH!
COLOR ME INTRIGUED.
MIND IF WE JOIN YOU?
ACTUALLY, I WAS JUST THINKING ABOUT TRADING CLUES WITH YOU.
I CAN'T LET YOU STEAL A MARCH ON US.

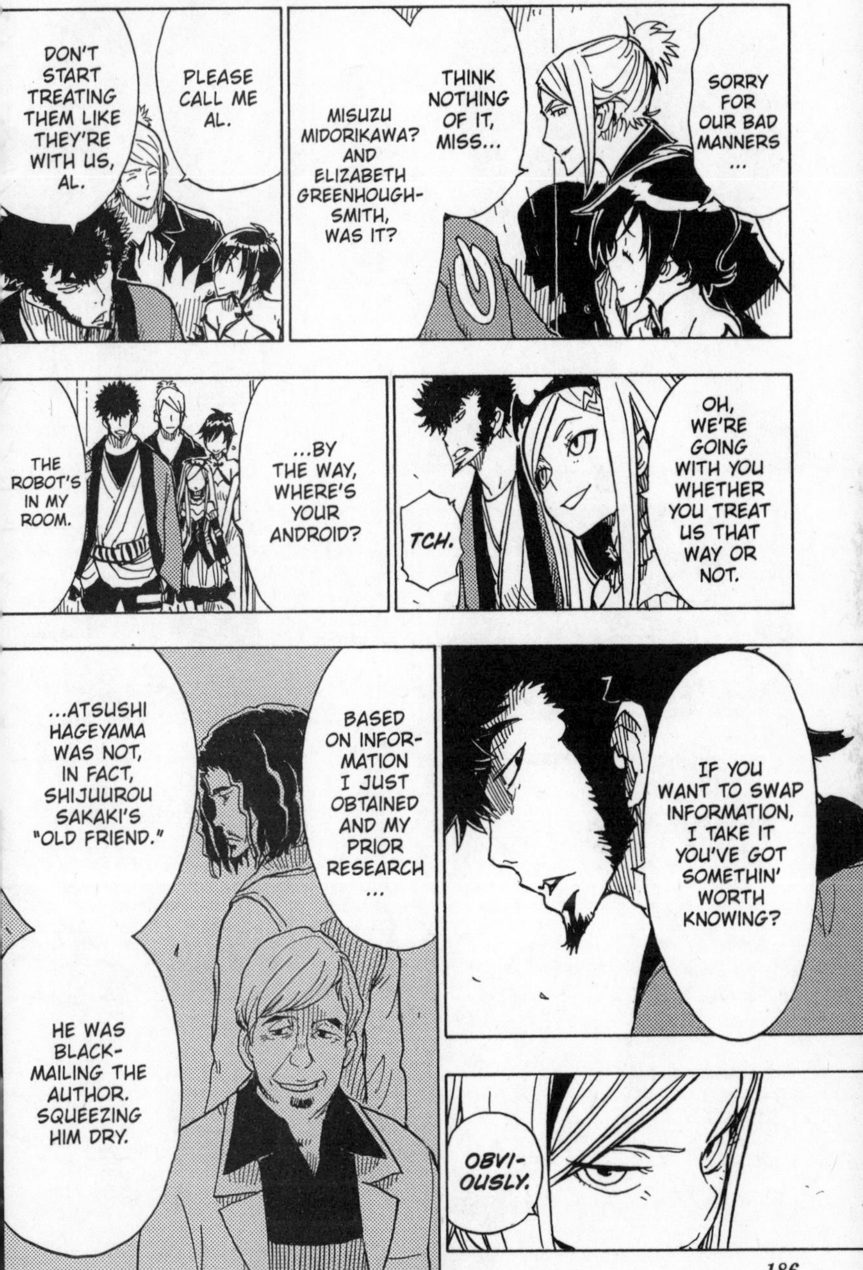
SORRY FOR OUR BAD MANNERS ...
THINK NOTHING OF IT, MISS...
MISUZU MIDORIKAWA? AND ELIZABETH GREENHOUGH-SMITH, WAS IT?
PLEASE CALL ME AL.
DON'T START TREATING THEM LIKE THEY'RE WITH US, AL.
OH, WE'RE GOING WITH YOU WHETHER YOU TREAT US THAT WAY OR NOT.
TCH.
...BY THE WAY, WHERE'S YOUR ANDROID?
THE ROBOT'S IN MY ROOM.
IF YOU WANT TO SWAP INFORMATION, I TAKE IT YOU'VE GOT SOMETHIN' WORTH KNOWING?
OBVI-OUSLY.
BASED ON INFOR-MATION I JUST OBTAINED AND MY PRIOR RESEARCH ...
...ATSUSHI HAGEYAMA WAS NOT, IN FACT, SHIJUUROU SAKAKI'S "OLD FRIEND."
HE WAS BLACK-MAILING THE AUTHOR. SQUEEZING HIM DRY.

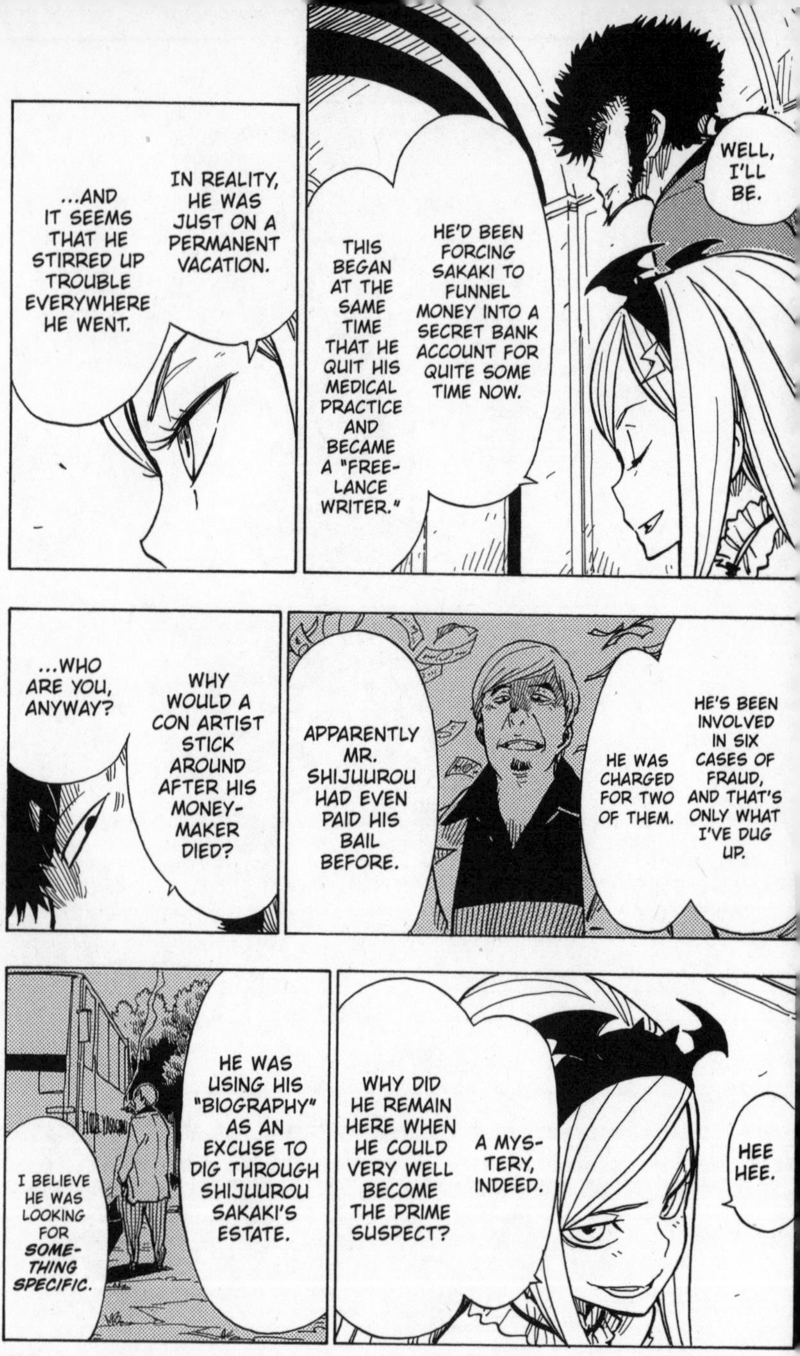
WELL, I'LL BE.
HE'D BEEN FORCING SAKAKI TO FUNNEL MONEY INTO A SECRET BANK ACCOUNT FOR QUITE SOME TIME NOW.
THIS BEGAN AT THE SAME TIME THAT HE QUIT HIS MEDICAL PRACTICE AND BECAME A "FREE-LANCE WRITER."
IN REALITY, HE WAS JUST ON A PERMANENT VACATION.
...AND IT SEEMS THAT HE STIRRED UP TROUBLE EVERYWHERE HE WENT.
HE'S BEEN INVOLVED IN SIX CASES OF FRAUD, AND THAT'S ONLY WHAT I'VE DUG UP.
HE WAS CHARGED FOR TWO OF THEM.
APPARENTLY MR. SHIJUUROU HAD EVEN PAID HIS BAIL BEFORE.
WHY WOULD A CON ARTIST STICK AROUND AFTER HIS MONEY-MAKER DIED?
...WHO ARE YOU, ANYWAY?
HEE HEE.
A MYS-TERY, INDEED.
WHY DID HE REMAIN HERE WHEN HE COULD VERY WELL BECOME THE PRIME SUSPECT?
HE WAS USING HIS "BIOGRAPHY" AS AN EXCUSE TO DIG THROUGH SHIJUUROU SAKAKI'S ESTATE.
I BELIEVE HE WAS LOOKING FOR *SOME-THING SPECIFIC*.

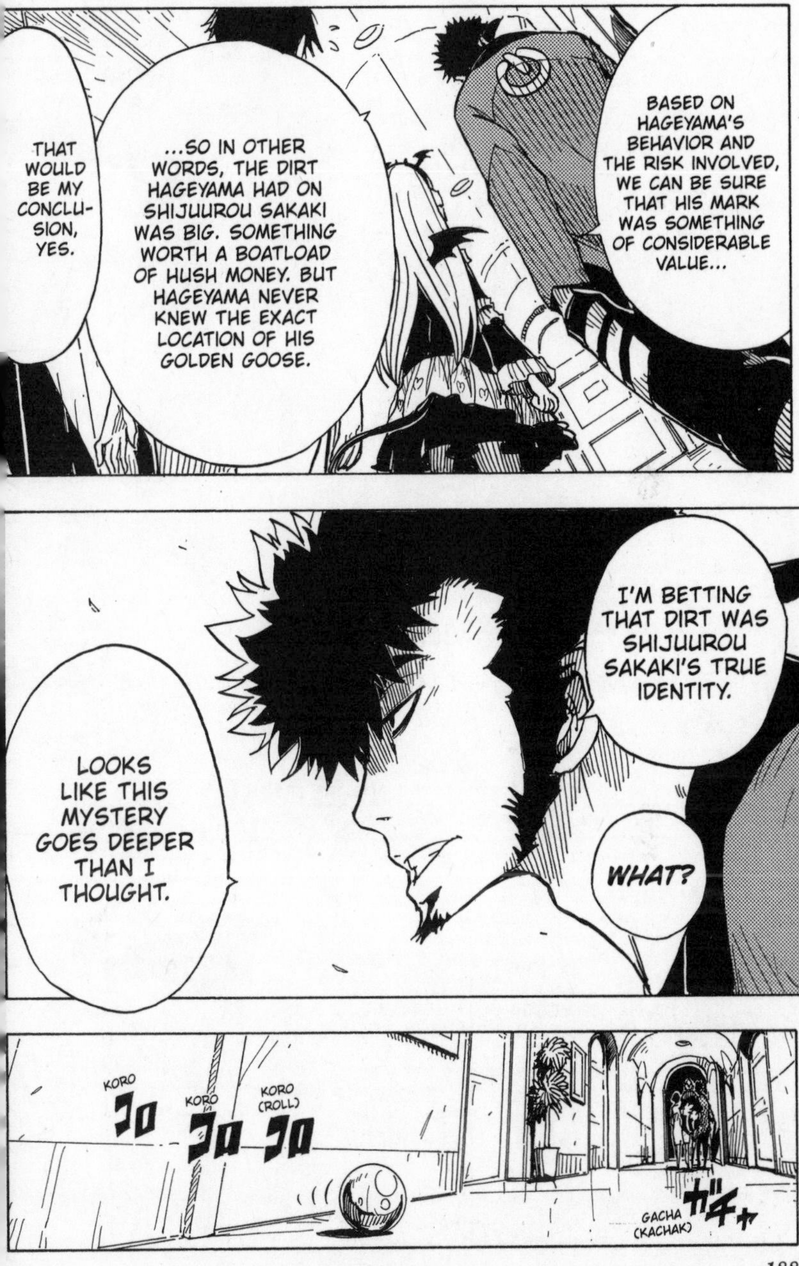
BASED ON HAGEYAMA'S BEHAVIOR AND THE RISK INVOLVED, WE CAN BE SURE THAT HIS MARK WAS SOMETHING OF CONSIDERABLE VALUE...
...SO IN OTHER WORDS, THE DIRT HAGEYAMA HAD ON SHIJUUROU SAKAKI WAS BIG. SOMETHING WORTH A BOATLOAD OF HUSH MONEY. BUT HAGEYAMA NEVER KNEW THE EXACT LOCATION OF HIS GOLDEN GOOSE.
THAT WOULD BE MY CONCLUSION, YES.
I'M BETTING THAT DIRT WAS SHIJUUROU SAKAKI'S TRUE IDENTITY.
WHAT?
LOOKS LIKE THIS MYSTERY GOES DEEPER THAN I THOUGHT.
ガチャ GACHA (KACHAK)
コロ KORO (ROLL)
コロ KORO
コロ KORO

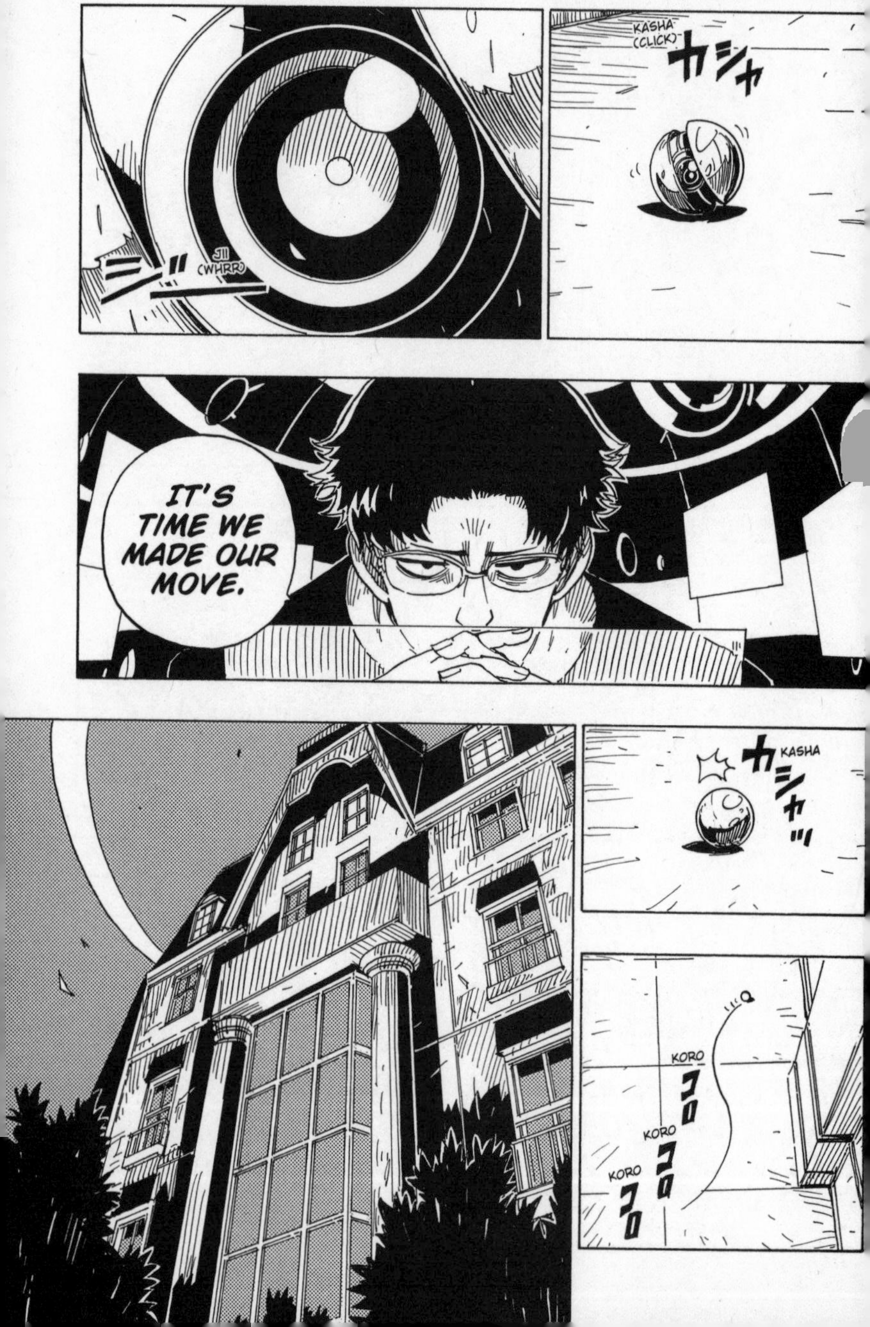
KASHA (CLICK)
カシャ
JII (WHRR)
ジーッ
IT'S TIME WE MADE OUR MOVE.
KASHA
カシャッ
KORO
コロ
KORO
コロ
KORO
コロ

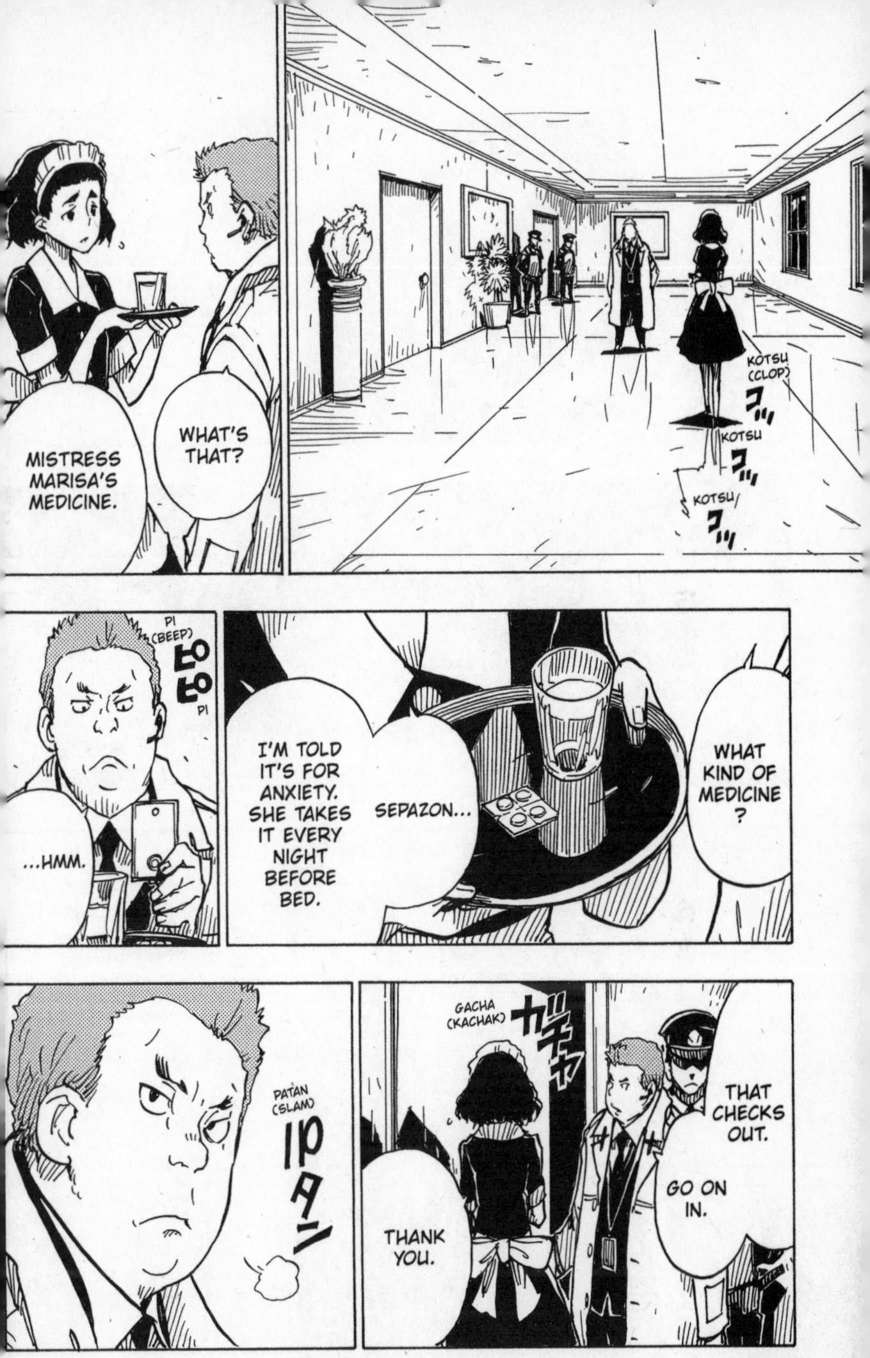
KOTSU (CLOP)
KOTSU
KOTSU
WHAT'S THAT?
MISTRESS MARISA'S MEDICINE.
WHAT KIND OF MEDICINE?
SEPAZON...
I'M TOLD IT'S FOR ANXIETY. SHE TAKES IT EVERY NIGHT BEFORE BED.
PI (BEEP)
PI
...HMM.
GACHA (KACHAK)
THAT CHECKS OUT.
GO ON IN.
THANK YOU.
PATAN (SLAM)

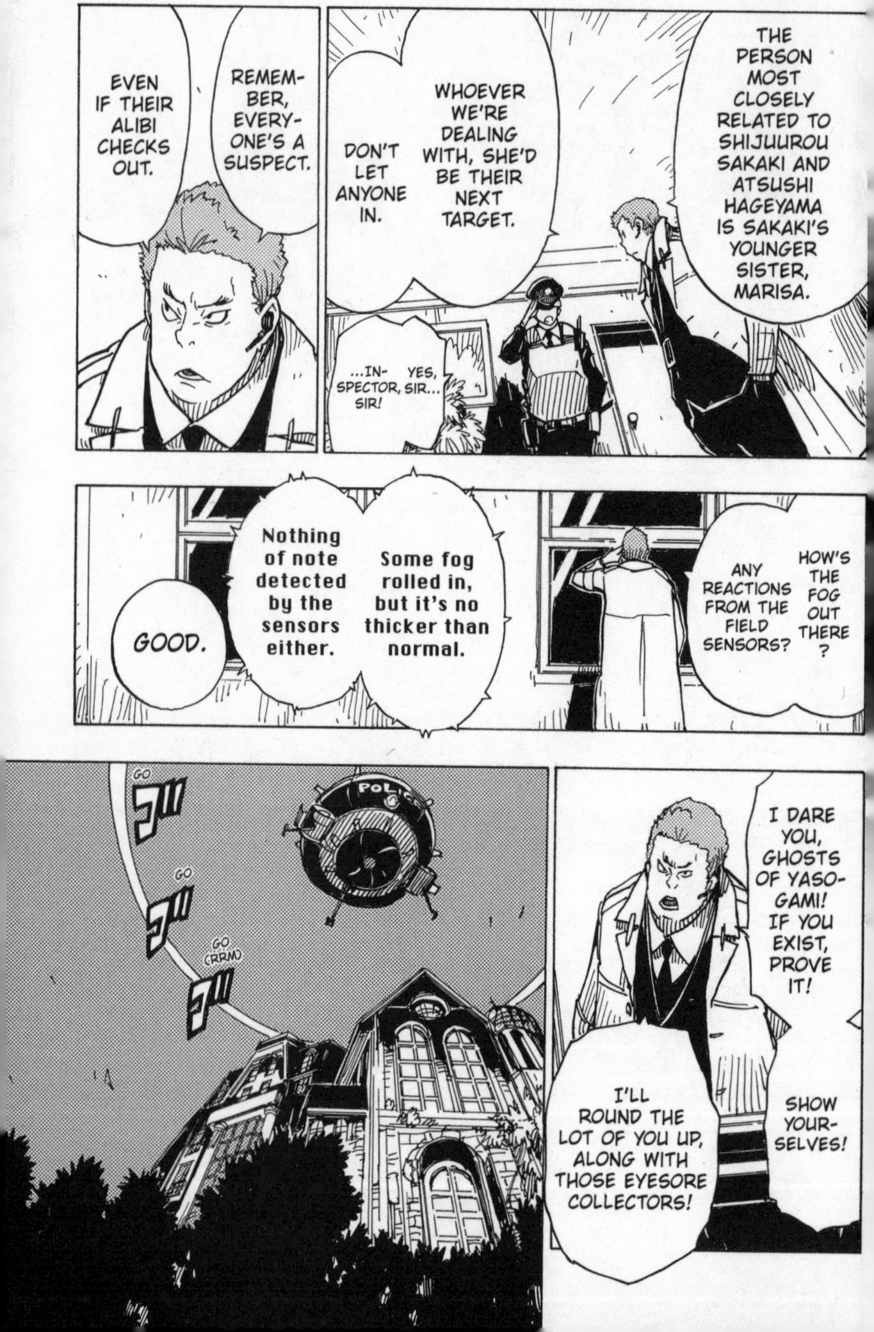
THE PERSON MOST CLOSELY RELATED TO SHIJUUROU SAKAKI AND ATSUSHI HAGEYAMA IS SAKAKI'S YOUNGER SISTER, MARISA.
WHOEVER WE'RE DEALING WITH, SHE'D BE THEIR NEXT TARGET.
DON'T LET ANYONE IN.
YES, SIR...
...INSPECTOR, SIR!
REMEMBER, EVERYONE'S A SUSPECT.
EVEN IF THEIR ALIBI CHECKS OUT.
HOW'S THE FOG OUT THERE?
ANY REACTIONS FROM THE FIELD SENSORS?
Some fog rolled in, but it's no thicker than normal.
Nothing of note detected by the sensors either.
GOOD.
I DARE YOU, GHOSTS OF YASOGAMI! IF YOU EXIST, PROVE IT!
SHOW YOURSELVES!
I'LL ROUND THE LOT OF YOU UP, ALONG WITH THOSE EYESORE COLLECTORS!
POLICE
GO
GO
GO (RRM)

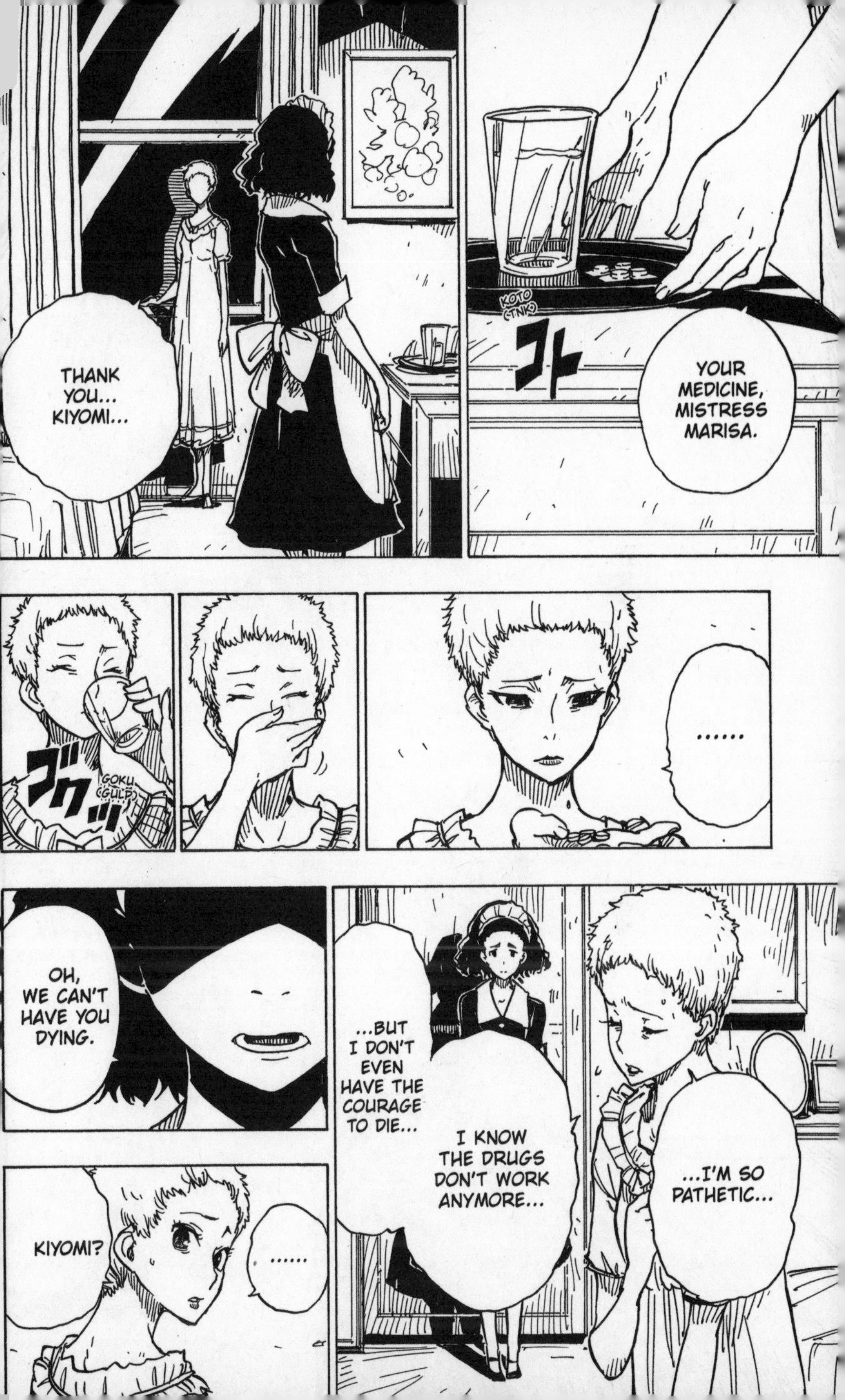
YOUR MEDICINE, MISTRESS MARISA.
KOTO (TNK)
THANK YOU... KIYOMI...
......
GOKU (GULP)
...I'M SO PATHETIC...
I KNOW THE DRUGS DON'T WORK ANYMORE...
...BUT I DON'T EVEN HAVE THE COURAGE TO DIE...
OH, WE CAN'T HAVE YOU DYING.
......
KIYOMI?

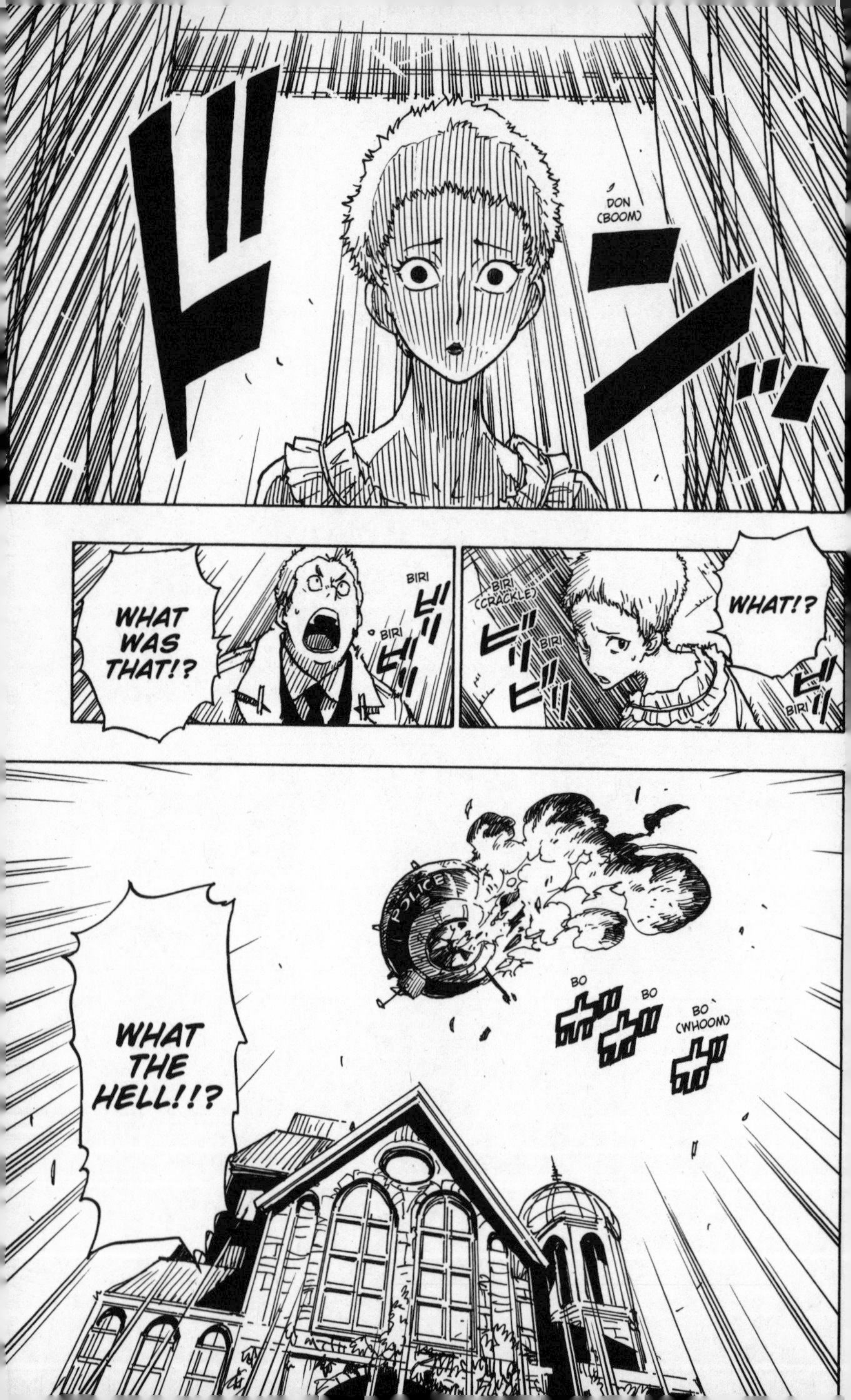
DON (BOOM)
WHAT!?
BIRI (CRACKLE)
BIRI
BIRI
BIRI
BIRI
WHAT WAS THAT!?
POLICE
BO
BO
BO (WHOOM)
WHAT THE HELL!!?

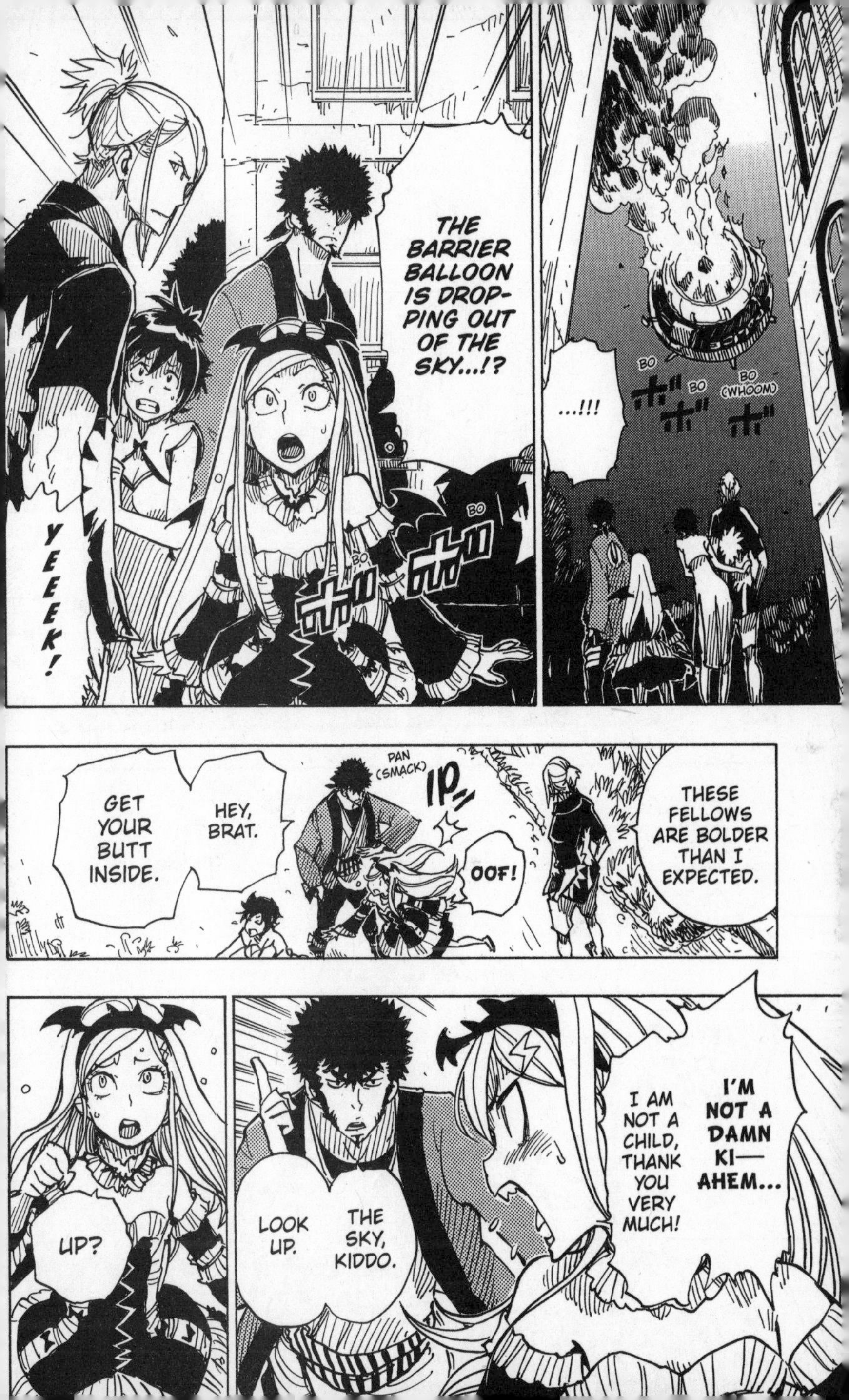
BO
BO
BO (WHOOM)
...!!!
THE BARRIER BALLOON IS DROPPING OUT OF THE SKY...!?
BO
BO
YEEEEK!
THESE FELLOWS ARE BOLDER THAN I EXPECTED.
PAN (SMACK)
OOF!
HEY, BRAT.
GET YOUR BUTT INSIDE.
I'M NOT A DAMN KI— AHEM...
I AM NOT A CHILD, THANK YOU VERY MUCH!
THE SKY, KIDDO.
LOOK UP.
UP?

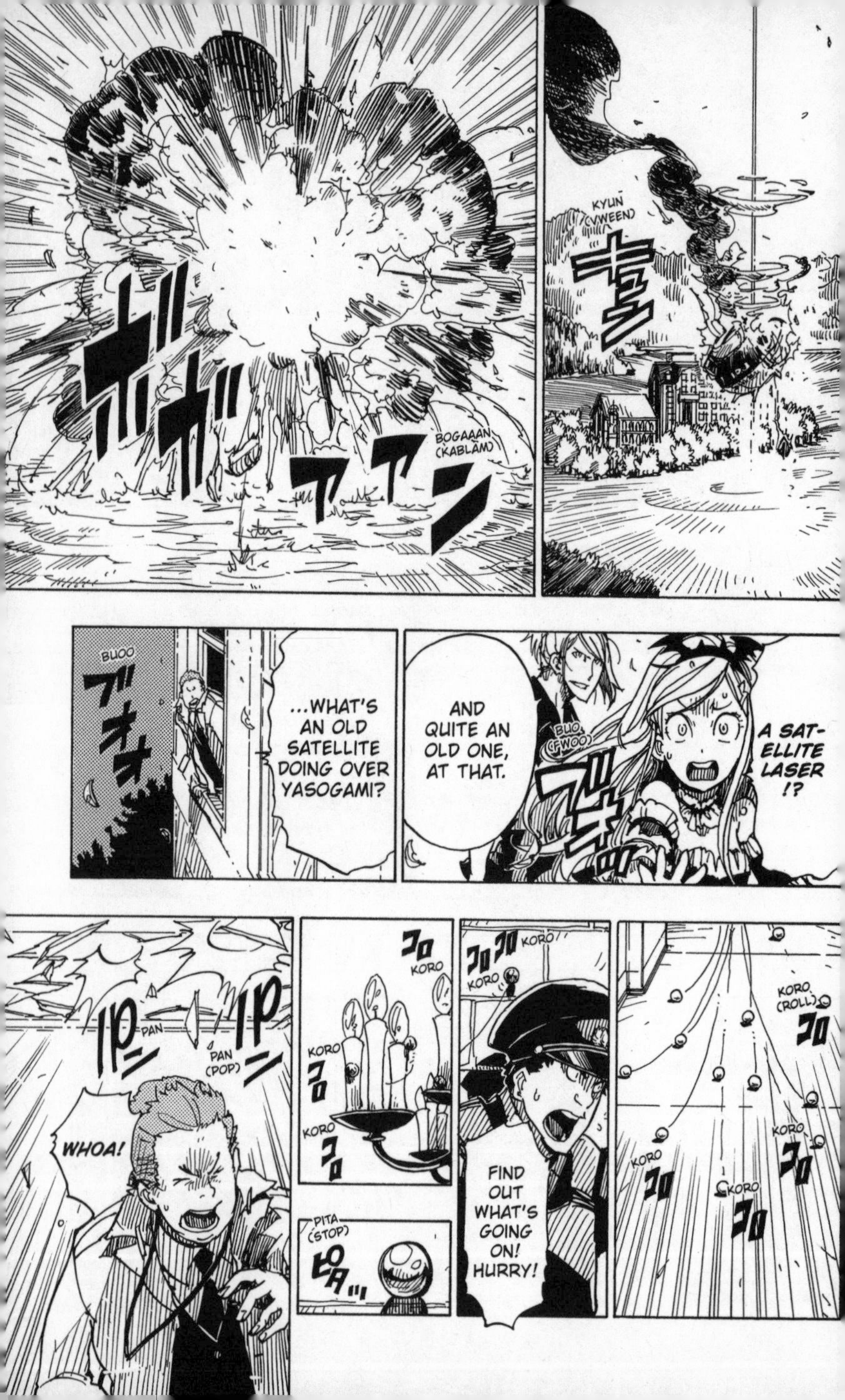

KYUN (VWEEN)
BOGAAAN (KABLAM)
A SATELLITE LASER!?
BUO (FWOO)
AND QUITE AN OLD ONE, AT THAT.
...WHAT'S AN OLD SATELLITE DOING OVER YASOGAMI?
BUOO
KORO (ROLL)
KORO
KORO
KORO
KORO
KORO
FIND OUT WHAT'S GOING ON! HURRY!
KORO
KORO
KORO
PITA (STOP)
PAN
PAN (POP)
WHOA!

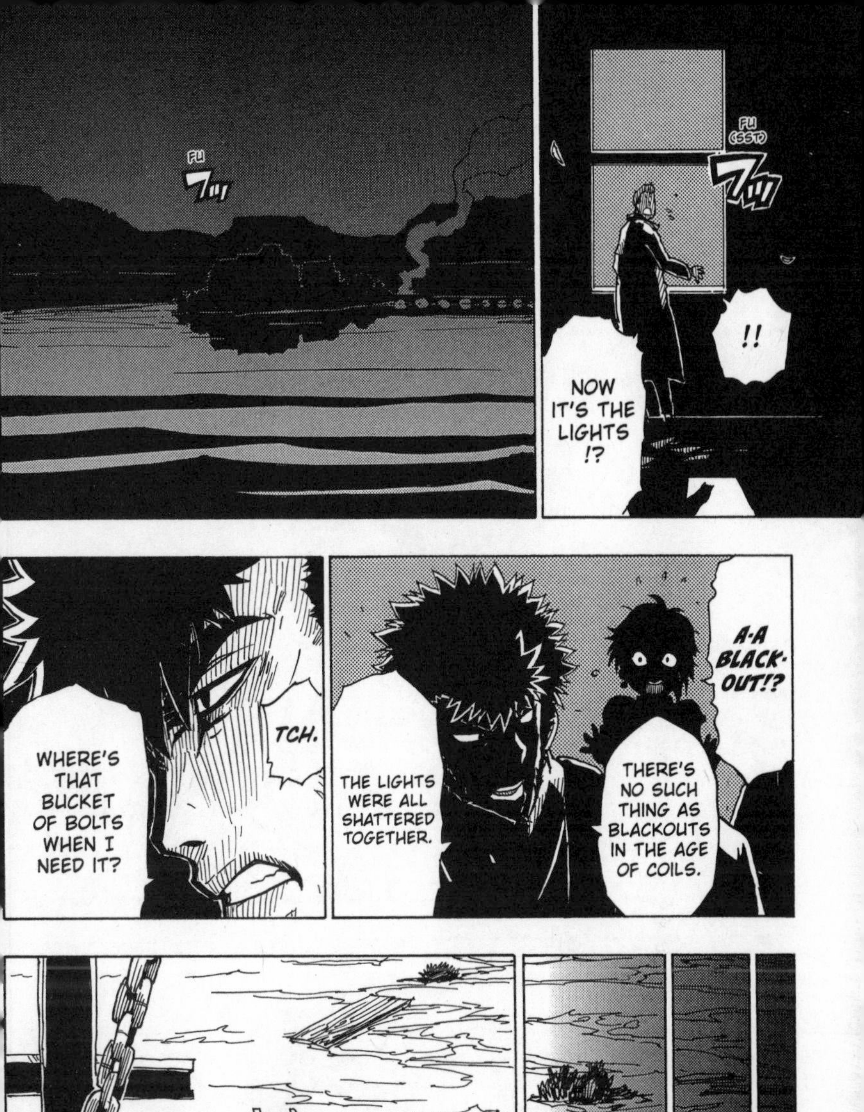
FU (SST)
!!
NOW IT'S THE LIGHTS !?
FU
A-A BLACK-OUT!?
THERE'S NO SUCH THING AS BLACKOUTS IN THE AGE OF COILS.
THE LIGHTS WERE ALL SHATTERED TOGETHER.
TCH.
WHERE'S THAT BUCKET OF BOLTS WHEN I NEED IT?
ZAAAAA (FSSH)

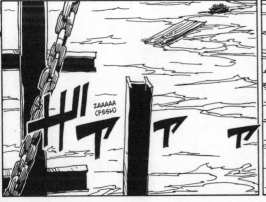

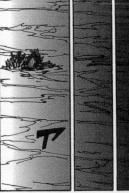

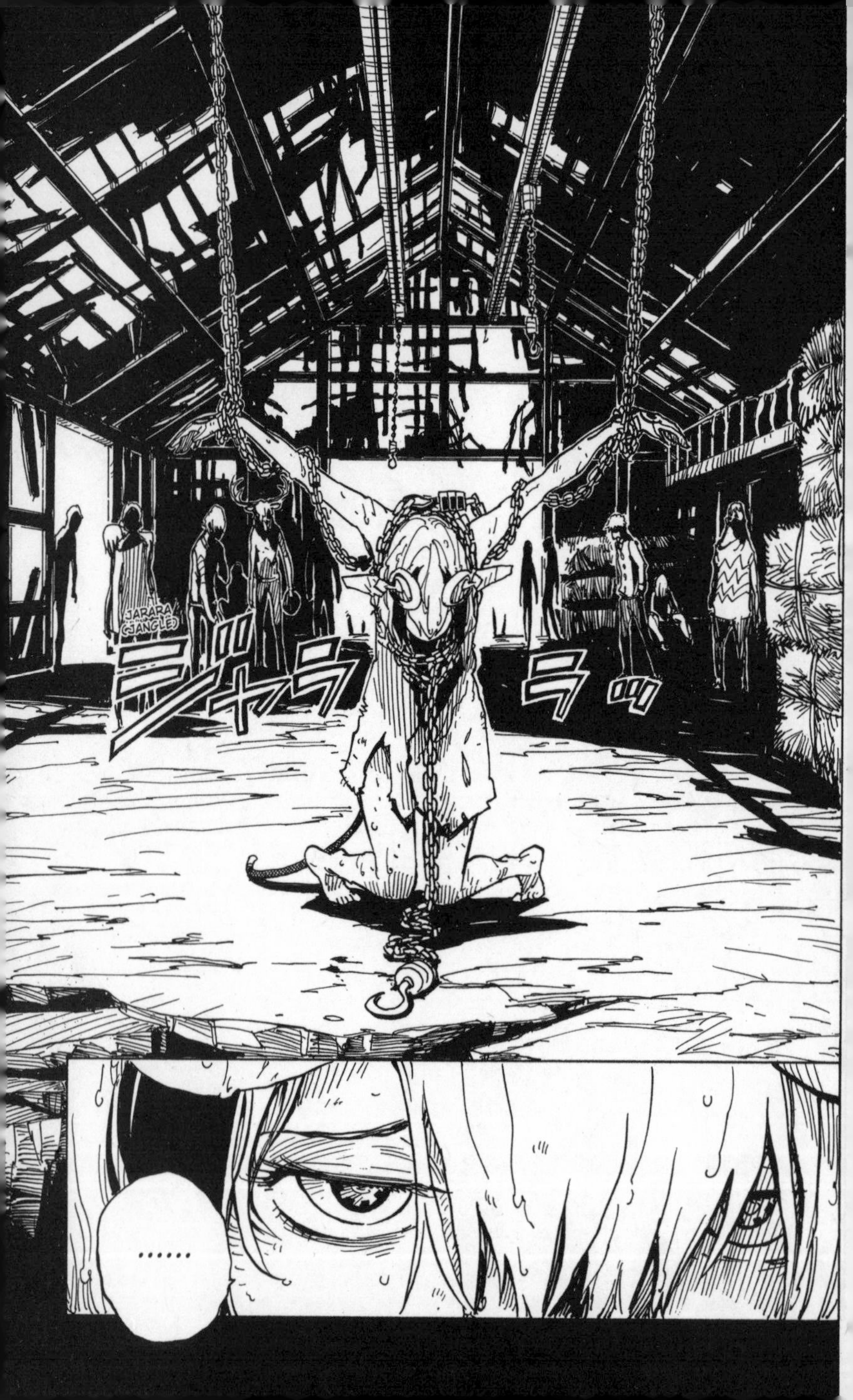
JARARA (JANGLE)
ジャラ
ラ
......

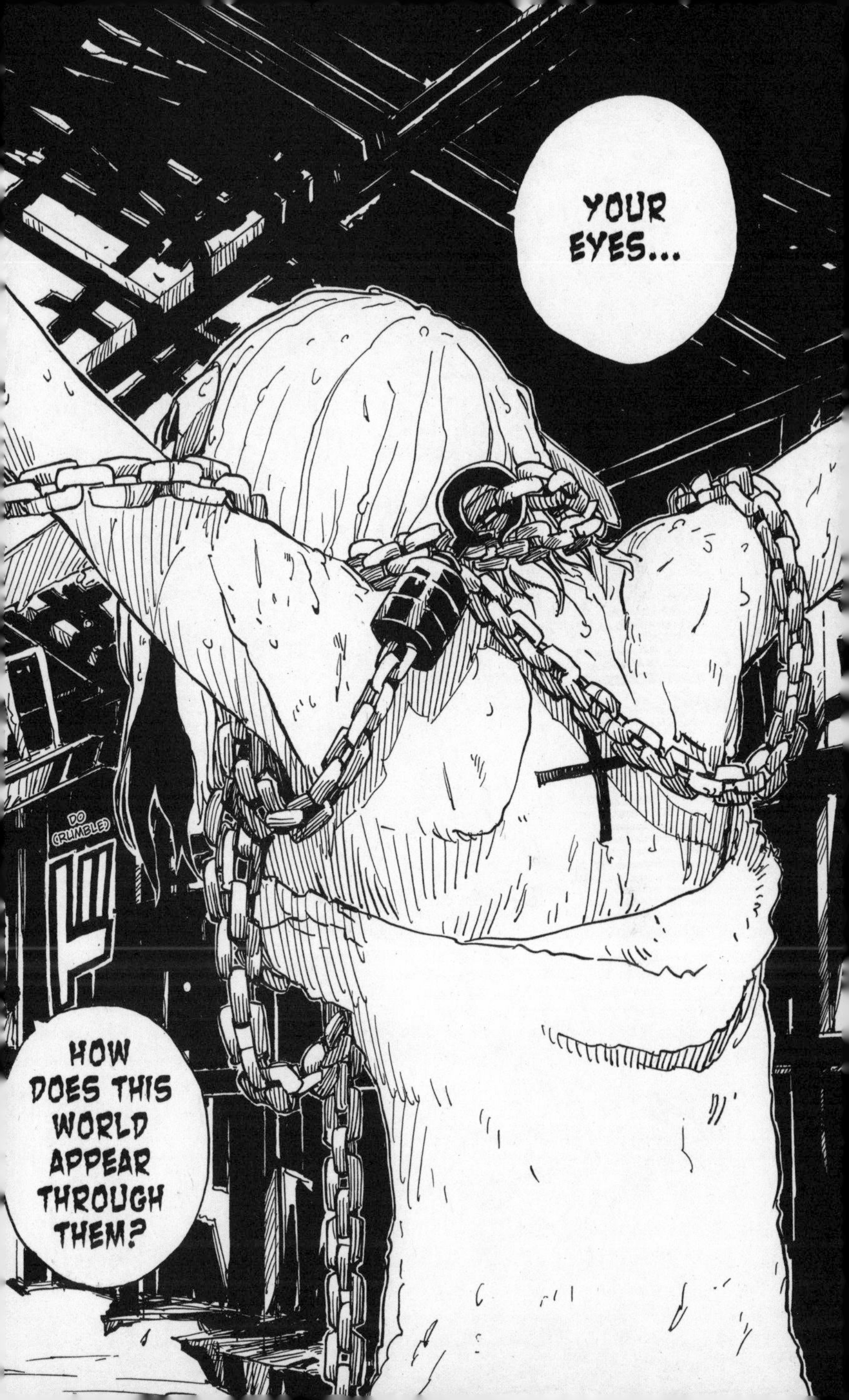
YOUR EYES...
DO (CRUMBLE)
HOW DOES THIS WORLD APPEAR THROUGH THEM?

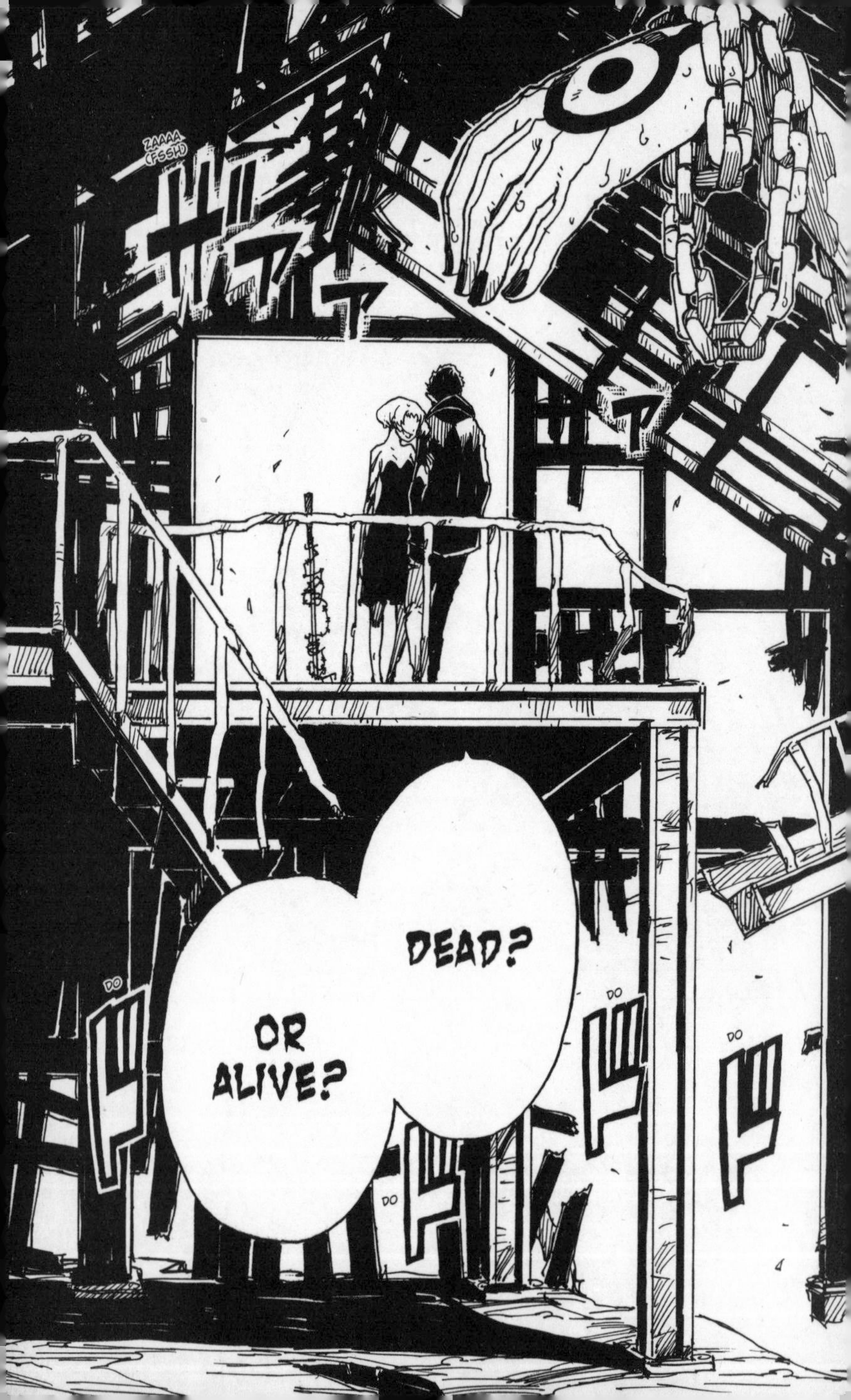
ZAAAA
(FSSH)
DEAD?
OR
ALIVE?
DO
DO
DO
DO

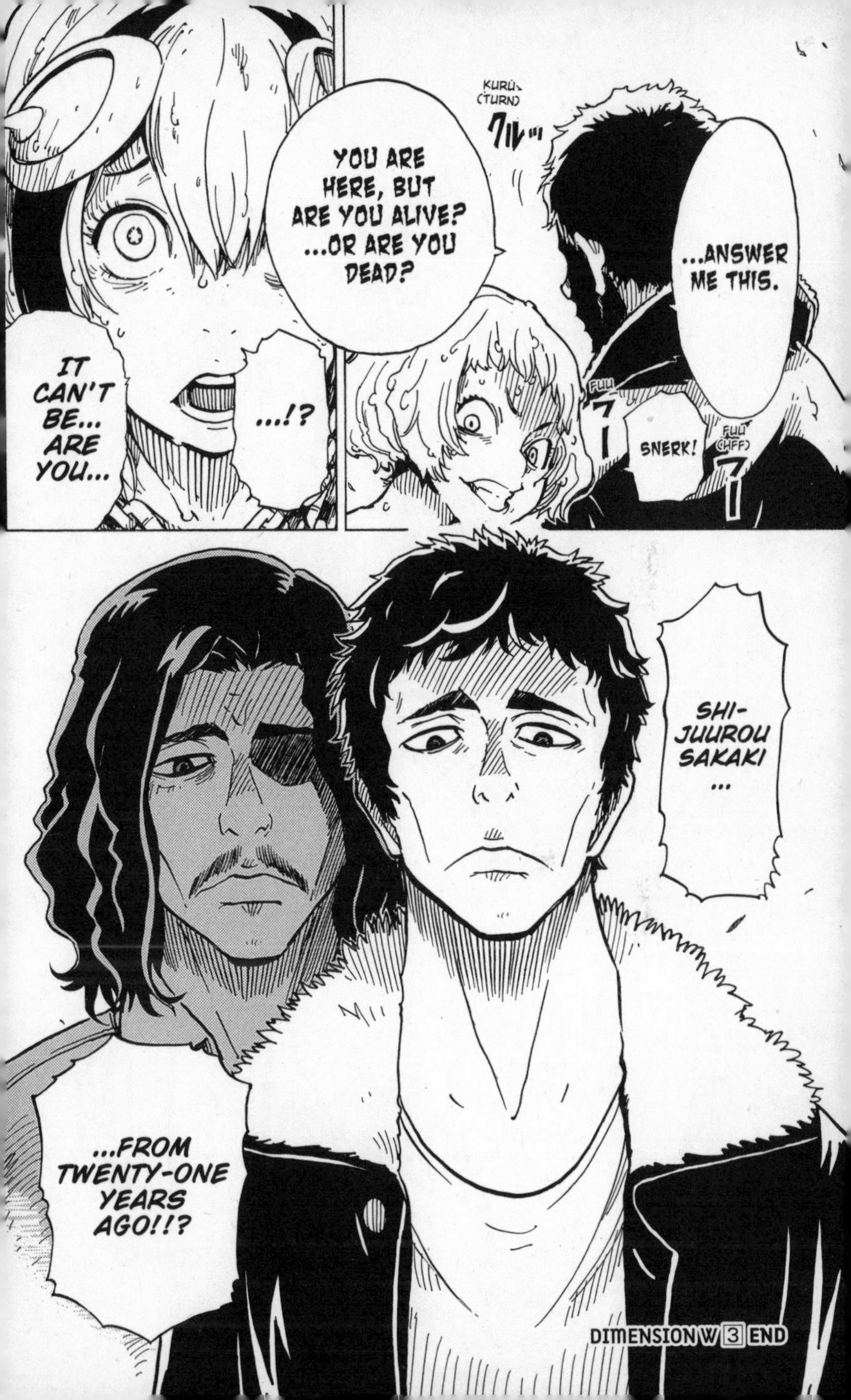
KURU (TURN)
クルッ
...ANSWER ME THIS.
YOU ARE HERE, BUT ARE YOU ALIVE? ...OR ARE YOU DEAD?
FUU
SNERK!
FUU (HFF)
...!?
IT CAN'T BE... ARE YOU...
SHI-JUUROU SAKAKI ...
...FROM TWENTY-ONE YEARS AGO!!?
DIMENSION W 3 END

Dimension W

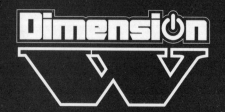

MINI CORNER

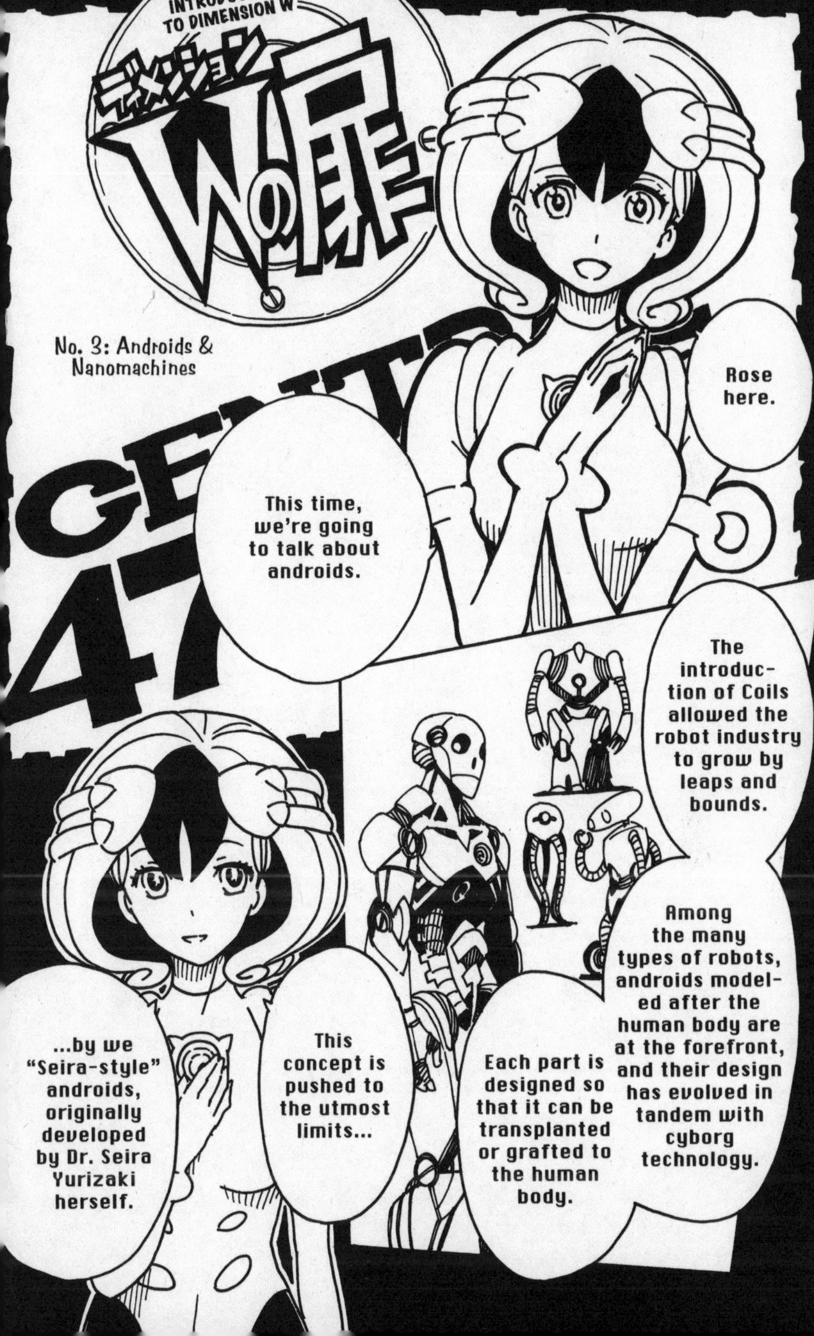
INTRODUCTION TO DIMENSION W
ディメンションWの扉
No. 3: Androids & Nanomachines
Rose here.
This time, we're going to talk about androids.
The introduction of Coils allowed the robot industry to grow by leaps and bounds.
Among the many types of robots, androids modeled after the human body are at the forefront, and their design has evolved in tandem with cyborg technology.
Each part is designed so that it can be transplanted or grafted to the human body.
This concept is pushed to the utmost limits...
...by we "Seira-style" androids, originally developed by Dr. Seira Yurizaki herself.

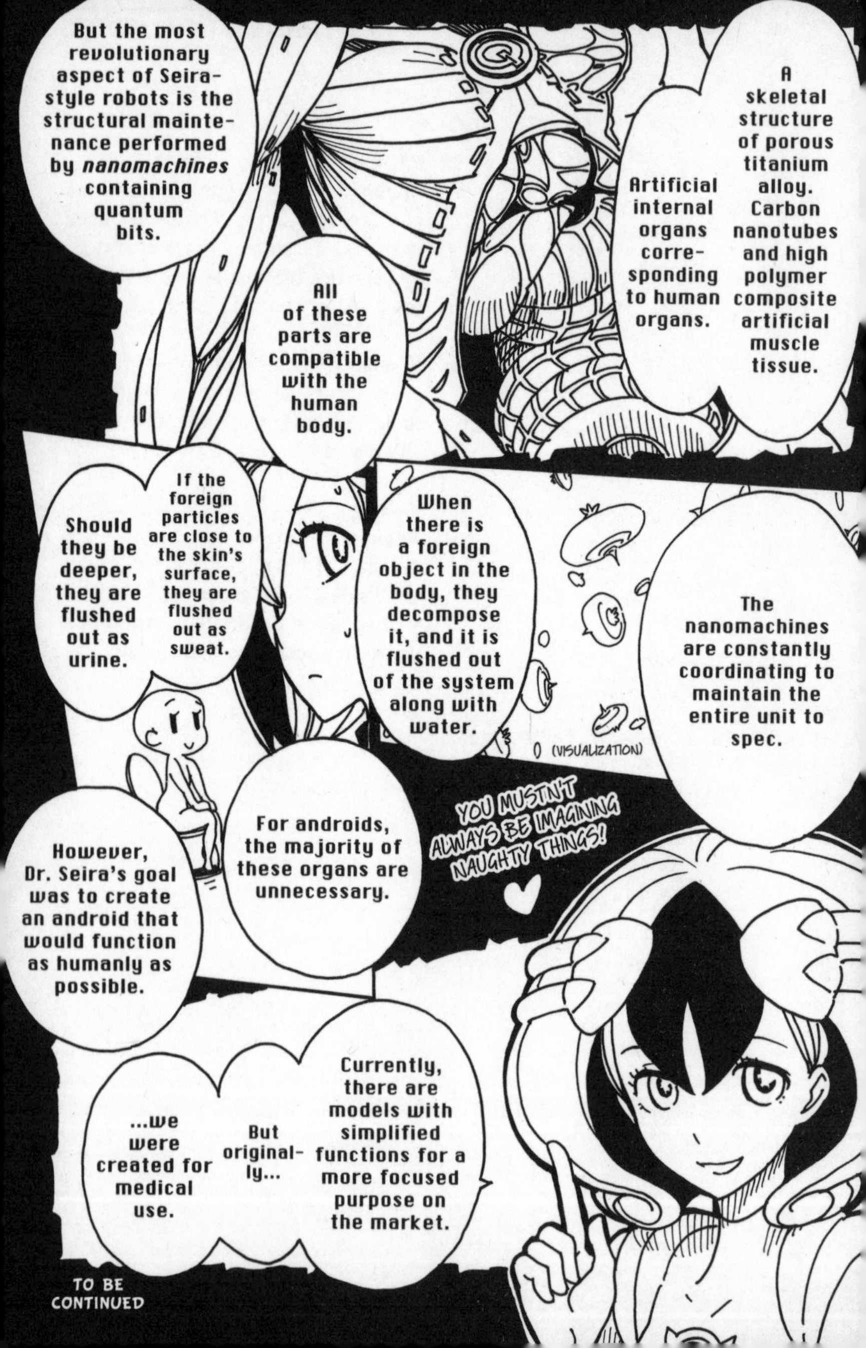
A skeletal structure of porous titanium alloy. Carbon nanotubes and high polymer composite artificial muscle tissue.
Artificial internal organs corre-sponding to human organs.
All of these parts are compatible with the human body.
But the most revolutionary aspect of Seira-style robots is the structural mainte-nance performed by *nanomachines* containing quantum bits.
The nanomachines are constantly coordinating to maintain the entire unit to spec.
When there is a foreign object in the body, they decompose it, and it is flushed out of the system along with water.
(VISUALIZATION)
If the foreign particles are close to the skin's surface, they are flushed out as sweat.
Should they be deeper, they are flushed out as urine.
YOU MUSTN'T ALWAYS BE IMAGINING NAUGHTY THINGS!
For androids, the majority of these organs are unnecessary.
However, Dr. Seira's goal was to create an android that would function as humanly as possible.
Currently, there are models with simplified functions for a more focused purpose on the market.
But original-ly...
...we were created for medical use.
TO BE CONTINUED

APPENDIX.01
TRANSLATION NOTES

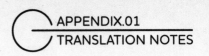

PAGE 9

Matcha: Finely-ground green tea powder. This is the kind of tea used in the tea ceremony; the preparation of both the tea plants and later the tea itself is relatively laborious.

Mama: In Japan, it's common for the proprietress of a bar or nightclub to be addressed as the "Mama" or "Mama-san."

PAGE 33

Beginner driver's decal: It's mandatory for new drivers in Japan to display this green and yellow V-shaped symbol on their car for one year after obtaining their license.

Dimension W

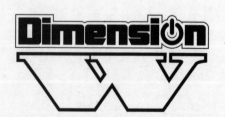

To become the ultimate weapon, one boy must eat the souls of 99 humans...

...and one witch.

Maka is a scythe meister, working to perfect her demon scythe until it is good enough to become Death's Weapon—the weapon used by Shinigami-sama, the spirit of Death himself. And if that isn't strange enough, her scythe also has the power to change form—into a human-looking boy!

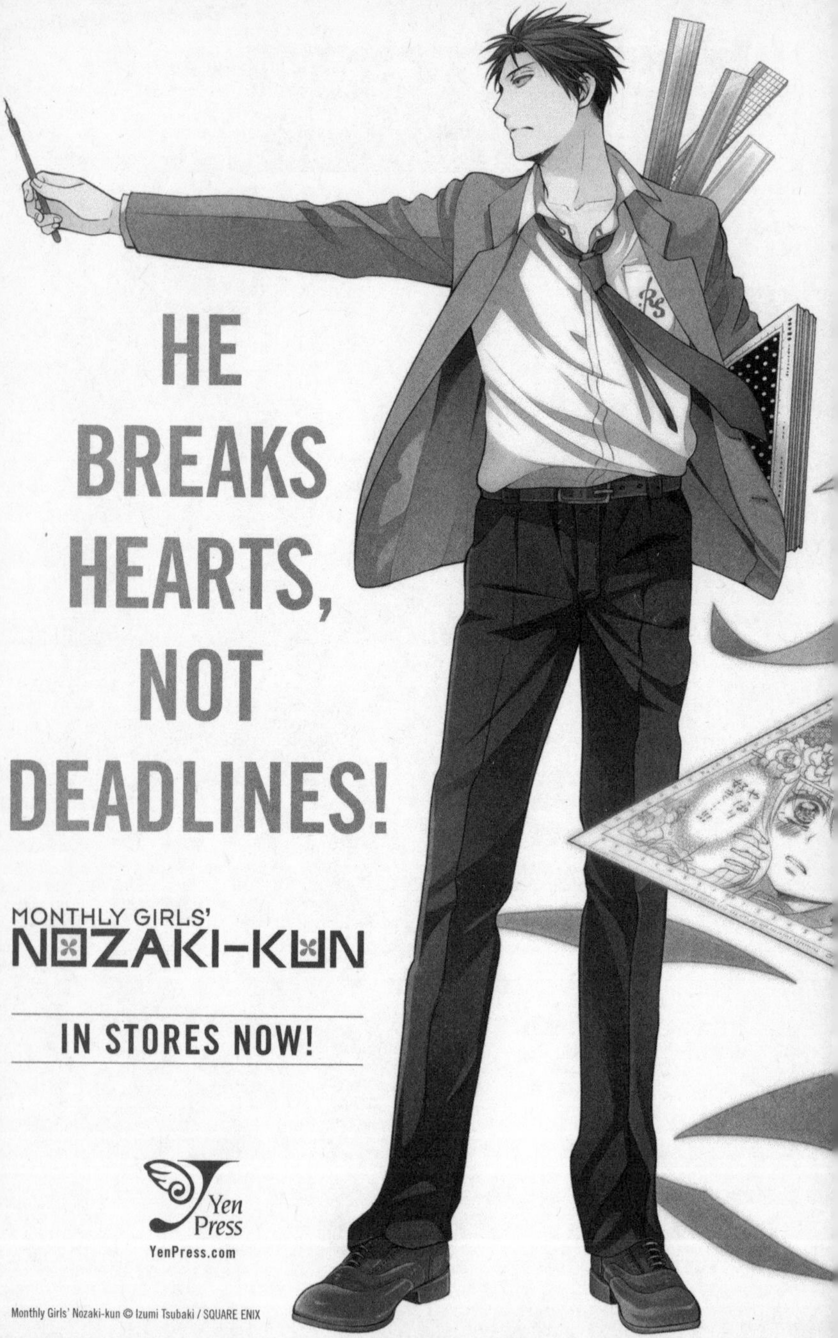
HE BREAKS HEARTS, NOT DEADLINES!
MONTHLY GIRLS'
NOZAKI-KUN
IN STORES NOW!
Yen Press
YenPress.com

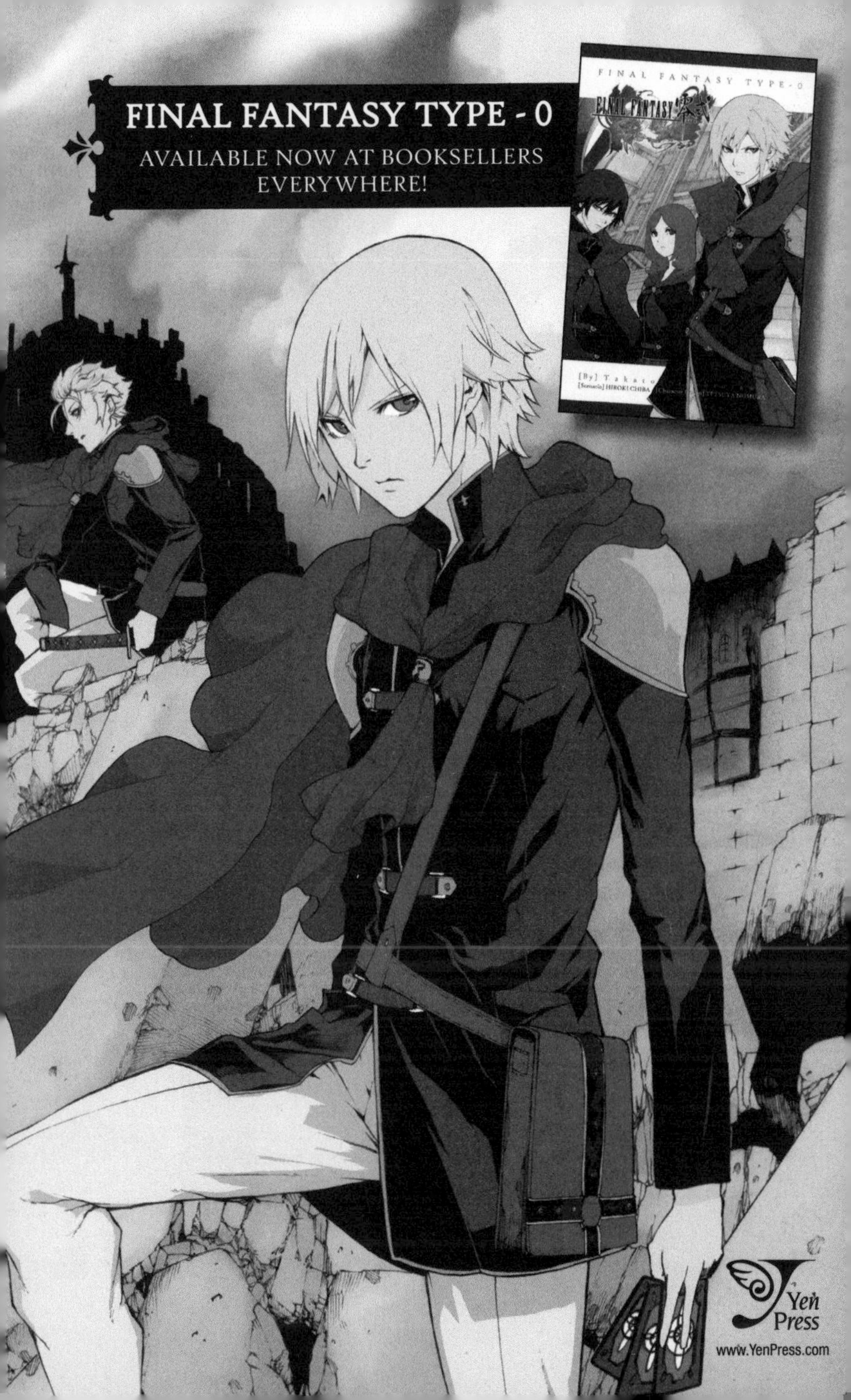
FINAL FANTASY TYPE - 0
AVAILABLE NOW AT BOOKSELLERS EVERYWHERE!
FINAL FANTASY TYPE-0
[Scenario] HIROKI CHIBA
Yen Press
www.YenPress.com

FINAL FANTASY 零式 TYPE-0™

Art: TAKATOSHI SHIOZAWA
Character Design: TETSUYA NOMURA
Scenario: HIROKI CHIBA

The cadets of Akademeia's Class Zero are legends, with strength and magic unrivaled, and crimson capes symbolizing the great Vermilion Bird of the Dominion. But will their elite training be enough to keep them alive when a war breaks out and the Class Zero cadets find themselves at the front and center of a bloody political battlefield?!

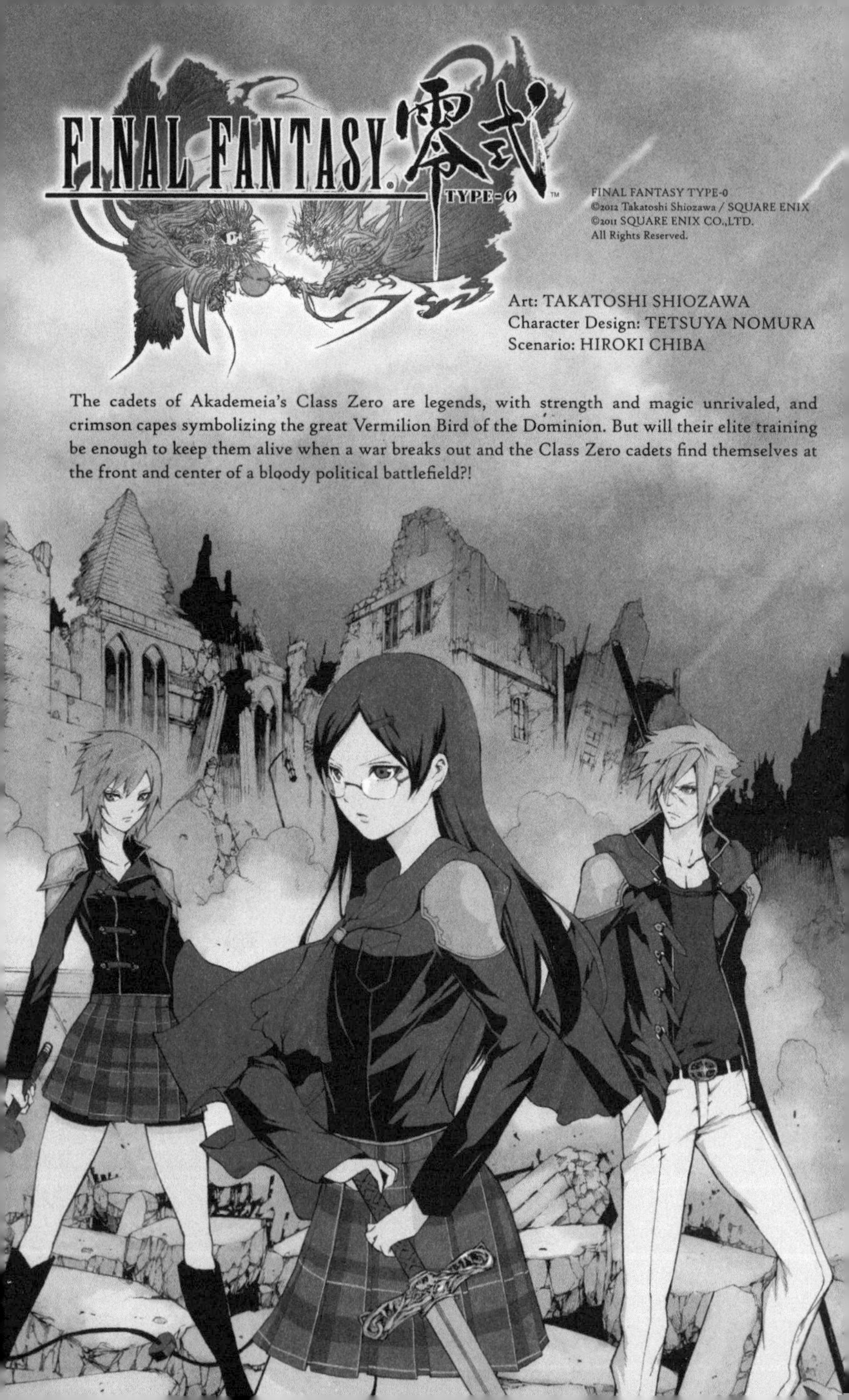

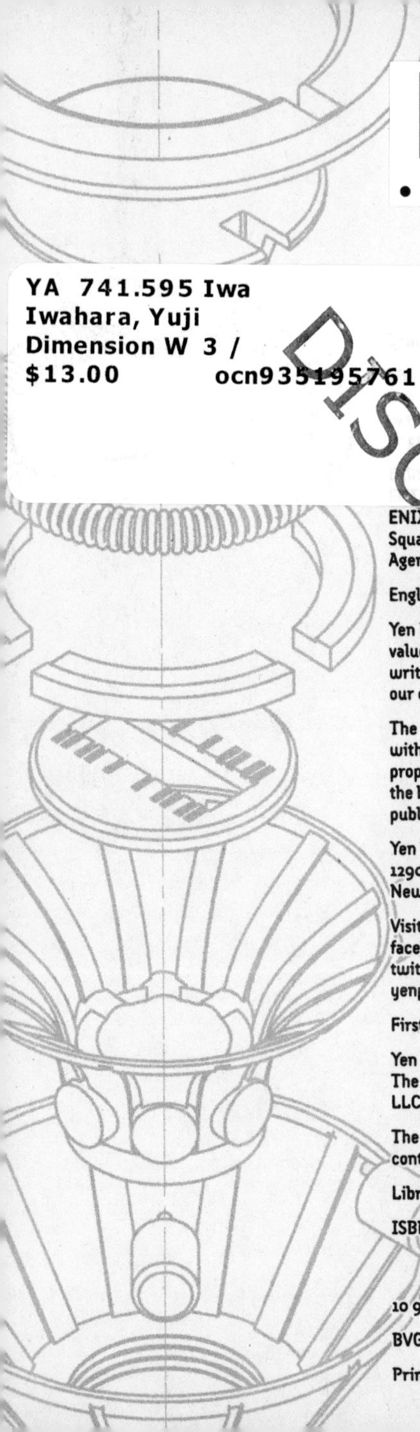

by **YUJI IWAHARA**

Amanda Haley • Lettering: Phil Christie

...W Volume 3 ©2013 Yuji Iwahara/SQUARE
...D. First published in Japan in 2013 by SQUARE
ENIX CO., LTD. English translation rights arranged with
Square Enix Co., Ltd. and Yen Press, LLC through Tuttle-Mori
Agency, Inc.

English translation © 2016 by SQUARE ENIX CO., LTD.

Yen Press
1290 Avenue of the Americas
New York, NY 10104

Visit us at yenpress.com
facebook.com/yenpress
twitter.com/yenpress
yenpress.tumblr.com

First Yen Press Edition: August 2016

Yen Press is an imprint of Yen Press, LLC.
The Yen Press name and logo are trademarks of Yen Press,
LLC.

The publisher is not responsible for websites (or their
content) that are not owned by the publisher.

Library of Congress Control Number: 2015956889

ISBN: 978-0-316-27613-9 (paperback)
 978-0-316-27679-5 (ebook)
 978-0-316-27681-8 (app)

10 9 8 7 6 5 4 3 2 1

BVG

Printed in the United States of America